Dancing in the Flames

Dancing in the Flames

Spiritual Journey in the Novels of Lee Smith

LINDA BYRD COOK

McFarland & Company, Inc., Publishers
Jefferson, North Carolina, and London

Frontispiece: Lee Smith

LIBRARY OF CONGRESS CATALOGUING-IN-PUBLICATION DATA

Cook, Linda Byrd, 1954–
    Dancing in the flames : spiritual journey in the novels of Lee Smith / Linda Byrd Cook.
        p.   cm.
    Includes bibliographical references and index.

    ISBN 978-0-7864-4110-5
    softcover : 50# alkaline paper ∞

    1. Smith, Lee, 1944– —Criticism and interpretation. I. Title.
PS3569.M5376Z64   2009
813'.54—dc22   2009004649

British Library cataloguing data are available

©2009 Linda Byrd Cook. All rights reserved

No part of this book may be reproduced or transmitted in any form or by any means, electronic or mechanical, including photocopying or recording, or by any information storage and retrieval system, without permission in writing from the publisher.

Cover photograph ©2009 Alloy Photography

Manufactured in the United States of America

McFarland & Company, Inc., Publishers
  Box 611, Jefferson, North Carolina 28640
    www.mcfarlandpub.com

For my sons, Clint and Chad, two of the most amazing
people in my life and the ones who have allowed
me the most sacred experience of all,

for my husband Rich, my "divine other,"
for showing me how to truly give and
receive love and also how to have fun,

and *especially*

for my grandsons, Graham Evan and Killian Garrett.
The journey continues... .

*In memory of my own divine mother, Myrtle Hollis Roark,
who gave me life and taught me how to live it
with her unconditional love
and
in honor of my big brother, Kenneth Ray Roark,
who made me believe I was a princess.*

ACKNOWLEDGMENTS

This project has reached completion because of the guidance and support of many people. My deepest gratitude goes to Lee Smith for her generosity, kindness, interest, and support over the past several years. My relationship with Lee, both professional and personal, has been a beacon for me throughout the long, arduous process of writing this book. I would also like to thank Dr. Pamela Matthews, who many years ago introduced me to Lee Smith's writing and also recognized the value of my work. Dr. Bill Bridges, chair of the English Department at Sam Houston State University, has, over the years, offered the most supportive environment imaginable for a teacher and scholar trying to balance all her duties. Representing my interests to the administration and rooting for me all the way, Bill has been an integral part of my academic journey. In addition, I would like to thank Dr. John de Castro, dean of the College of Humanities & Social Sciences at SHSU, for his continued support of this project.

Members of both my biological family and my acquired family have generously given of themselves when I most needed them. I am especially grateful for my daddy, Perlon Roark, and my brother, Danny Roark, for maintaining a steadfast faith that I could complete this project and for their abiding love and reassurance; Toni Bobruk and Kathy Laughlin, my sisters and soulmates, for rescuing me from what Ivy Rowe calls that "great soft darkness" and for laughing and crying with me as we make this life journey together; Rhiannon Byrd, my daughter-in-law and mother of my twin grandsons Killian Garrett Byrd and Graham Evan Byrd, for being my cheerleader and also my sounding board, but mostly for giving me herself as a daughter; Misty Schwartz, my surrogate daughter, for her understanding, patience, generosity, and love and also for joining our family; and Barbara Tyson, my surrogate mother, for nurturing me as a fledging scholar and for her persistent faith in me and my abilities.

Another group of people I would like to thank are those closest to me, outside my family, that have been my backbone, my heart, and my soul throughout this entire process. I am grateful for Brenda (Marie) Guillory, the red-headed goddess, my companion and biggest fan during this entire journey, who always reminds me of, and returns me to, my real self; Tracy (Marie) Bilsing, the brunette goddess, who for twenty years has shared with me everything that matters in my life and has touched each part with tenderness and respect; Renée Landry, the blonde goddess, for the gift of her abiding friendship and for reading and discussing Lee Smith's novels with me; and Paul Child, for his support of and interest in my work and for the richness he has added to my journey.

In the world of one's career, it is rare to find a group like the Sappho Society. The presence and power of these amazing women, linked together by common ideas, interests, and aspirations, has surrounded, supported, and sustained me throughout the entire process of re-envisioning and revising my manuscript. I am indebted to each for her unique contribution to the successful completion of this book. I especially want to thank Carroll Nardone for her expert advice on my conclusion, Kim Bell and April Shemak for their constant gift of "Sappho Power," and Tracy Bilsing, once more, for always standing beside me.

And above all, I am grateful to the three men in my life who have given me the world: my sons, Clint Byrd and Chad Byrd, and my husband, Rich Cook.

Table of Contents

Acknowledgments	vii
Preface	1
Lee Smith Chronology	3
Introduction	5

I.	"Nothing left to say": Silenced by the Dichotomy in *The Last Day the Dogbushes Bloomed* and *Something in the Wind*	15
II.	"Visions of rape": Patriarchal Assault in *Fancy Strut* and *Black Mountain Breakdown*	37
III.	"Enclosed ... in God's womb": The Chance for Rebirth in *Oral History*	61
IV.	"Upended among these roses": Damage and Hope for Healing in *Family Linen*	86
V.	"I walked in my body like a Queen": The Honey-Imbued Goddess in *Fair and Tender Ladies*	106
VI.	"Figures a-dancing ... in the flames": Toward Healing the Wound in *The Devil's Dream*	141
VII.	"Swimming free ... in and out of undersea caverns": Reconciliation with the Feminine Divine in *Saving Grace*	161
VIII.	"Praying straight into the wind": The Sacred Circular Journey in *The Last Girls*	178

IX.	"Part of the earth and the sky, the living and the dead": The Divine Cycle of Life in *On Agate Hill*	198

Conclusion	223
Works Cited	227
Index	231

Preface

In my twenty-year relationship with Lee Smith's fiction, I have become acutely aware of the centrality of women's spiritual journeys in her work. When I first read *Fair and Tender Ladies* as a Ph.D. student in an independent studies course on contemporary Southern women writers at Texas A&M University, Lee's words not only stimulated my mind with the questions she raised, but also reached into my heart and began massaging back to life my own spirituality, reminding me of my passion for literature *and* for life. Until that time, I had not experienced the kind of writing, fiction or nonfiction, that spoke so directly to me as a female struggling for a sense of validation and spiritual reconciliation in a world inundated with and governed by patriarchal religion. After this first taste of Lee's fiction, I immediately devoured every piece of her writing I could get my hands on, and it's been the same ever since. In Lee's stories, her characters often express their love and need for language and stories, and for them, storytelling is as necessary as food, water, and air. Lee's writing has filled the same need for me, in both my personal life and professional endeavors. Recently Lee, with a big grin, said to me, "You're so crazy—just like one of my characters!" After thinking about her comment for a few minutes, I realized the truth of her statement, and since I know how much Lee loves her characters, I took her words as a compliment.

When I began my study of Lee Smith's writing that eventually developed into my doctoral dissertation, I didn't know that I would continue to focus on Lee's writing for my entire academic career. But, when a writer is as talented and prolific as Lee Smith, this undertaking can keep a scholar busy for many years. The scope of this study disallows an examination of Lee's entire oeuvre. *Dancing in the Flames* explores only Smith's eleven novel-length works. Although Lee's short fiction shares similar themes with the novels, the short fiction lacks the demonstrable progression of the protagonist's spiritual search and eventual recognition and integration of the feminine divine that the novels illustrate.

My two personal interviews with Lee and our continued contact and friendship through the years have not only highlighted my academic career, but also proven pivotal in informing my work while allowing me the rare advantage of firsthand information for my book. Most recently, I traveled to Hillsborough, North Carolina, to visit Lee at her home, and together we journeyed to her cabin nestled in the Appalachian Mountains. Sitting out on the front porch, in this breathtaking setting that transported me to Lee's fictional world, Lee and I talked extensively about her writing and her spiritual vision. My argument throughout this current study relies heavily on Lee's comments during this (as yet unpublished) interview. When we left to drive back down the winding, steep roads, Lee looked over at me and said, "See why I had to take you up here?" And I certainly did.

Most critics writing on Smith focus on the popular woman's theme—the search for identity—that characterizes so many of her protagonists. At present no other work attempts to do what this study does. Only two books totally devoted to the study of Lee Smith's fiction exist. Dorothy Combs Hill's *Lee Smith*, published in 1992 by Twayne, offers an insightful mythological analysis of Smith's novels up through *Fair and Tender Ladies*. One of the first to point out the mythic roles of female characters, Hill's analysis provided crucial groundwork for later studies. In 1997, International Scholars Press published *Gender Dynamics in the Fiction of Lee Smith: Examining Language and Narrative Strategies* by Rebecca Smith, a study that analyzes Smith's writing from a feminist perspective and provides helpful insight into the author's critique of gender roles and her characters' struggle to achieve wholeness. Paula Gallant Eckard's 2002 publication, *Maternal Body and Voice in Toni Morrison, Bobbie Ann Mason, and Lee Smith*, acknowledges the mythic elements in Smith's fiction and notes the contradiction for Smith's characters between Christianity and their instinctual female natures. Although this study of Smith is limited since it only devotes a third of the book to Smith's writing, Eckard offers astute observations in regard to three of Smith's most critically acclaimed novels (*Oral History, Fair and Tender Ladies,* and *Saving Grace*).

In addition to the above, Smith scholars to whom I am indebted for their early work on Smith in article-length studies include: Tanya Long Bennett, Elizabeth Pell Broadwell, Harriette C. Buchanan, Corinne Dale, Anne Goodwyn Jones, Suzanne Jones, Katherine Kearns, Susan Ketchin, Lucinda MacKethan, and Rosalind B. Reilly. Additionally, Lee Smith has been extraordinarily generous with interviews; thus, the current study has been greatly enriched by the benefit of a number of these, in the use of not only Lee's words, but also those of her interviewers.

I have also relied on the scholarship of French feminists such as Hélène Cixous, Luce Irigaray, and Julia Kristeva; feminist theologians such as René Girard, Rita M. Gross, Gerda Lerner, Carol Ochs, and Rosemary Radford Ruether; and experts on goddess mythology such as Carol P. Christ, Paul Friedrich, Nor Hall, Kathryn Allen Rabuzzi, and Barbara G. Walker. For archaeological details, I have referred to the work of Marija Gimbutas, noted Lithuanian archaeomythologist.

LEE SMITH CHRONOLOGY

1944—Born in Grundy, Virginia
1968—*The Last Day the Dogbushes Bloomed*
1971—*Something in the Wind*
1973—*Fancy Strut*
1981—*Black Mountain Breakdown*
       Cakewalk (stories)
1983—*Oral History*
1985—*Family Linen*
1988—*Fair and Tender Ladies*
1990—*Me and My Baby View the Eclipse* (stories)
1992—*The Devil's Dream*
1995—*Saving Grace*
1996—*The Christmas Letters* (novella)
1997—*News of the Spirit* (stories)
2002—*The Last Girls*
2006—*On Agate Hill*

Awards, Honors, and Grants (most recent first)

Southern Book Critics Circle Award, 2002
Academy Award in Fiction from American Academy of Arts & Letters, 1999
Lila Wallace/Readers Digest Award, 1995–1997
Robert Penn Warren Prize for Fiction, 1991
Lyndhurst Grant, 1990–1992
Weatherford Award for Appalachian Literature, 1988
North Carolina Award for Literature, 1984
Sir Walter Raleigh Award for *Fair and Tender Ladies*, 1989, and *Oral History*, 1983
O. Henry Awards, 1979 and 1981

INTRODUCTION

> *"In a way my writing is a lifelong search for belief. I have always been particularly interested in expressions of religious ecstasy, and in those moments when we are most truly 'out of ourselves' and experience the Spirit directly"* (Lee Smith, notes at the end of *Saving Grace*).

Lee Smith has been open and articulate about her lifelong spiritual journey, admitting that she has always struggled with the confinement of traditional Christianity in its denial of the feminine divine and acceptance of a solely male-imaged God. She identifies her writing as a "search for authenticity, for the real self, the true self" (Per),* and in her own heroic quest, she has sought and journeyed toward an understanding of her spiritual self. Smith said as a child, she was very religious, always desiring that ecstatic moment, that feeling of being "on fire." Institutional religion, with the deadening rituals and constraints of females, "knocked out" all her passion. In her 1994 interview with Susan Ketchin, Smith discussed her need to find a religion that doesn't "put down women." At this point in Smith's life and writing career, she admitted that she might "just die struggling with it and never get it reconciled" (qtd. in Ketchin 47–50).

Now in 2008, having made an arduous journey, Lee Smith has come a long way and sits poised to continue on her life path. Now she doesn't fear she will die without having recognized and embraced a sense of the divine that elevates and honors females and feminine experience, "things that [she] believe[s] are basically good" (qtd. in Ketchin 50). Smith recently shared with me her belief that "writing is born ... out of great unresolved conflict." For Smith, that conflict has been a spiritual one. Admitting she had been "at odds" with traditional patriarchal religion her entire life, Smith explained her sense of the sacred as encompassing not only those "transcendent moments," but also moments within our everyday feminine experiences. Smith said that through her writing, she feels she has come to articulate her questions and concerns

---

*Smith's comments during my personal interview with the writer on May 19 and 22, 2008, are parenthetically cited throughout this study as (Per).

5

about her spiritual search. She continued, "I think the very act of writing causes us to focus upon what we are feeling and to put our own experiences and thoughts and feelings into a certain context" (Per). In Smith's fiction, the writer's spiritual search becomes that of her protagonists, and in both the life and the writing, the journey leads to recognition, acceptance, and integration of the feminine divine.

Smith acknowledged that her writing does, and always has, transgressed boundaries since she has consistently expressed "untraditional kinds of spiritual searches" and an "open sort of sexuality" (Per). Smith's openness to the multitudinous possibilities for women's lives explains the tolerance and respect for her characters she consistently demonstrates in her writing. In a collection of essays on Southern women and spirituality, Dorothy Allison posits, "In art, transgression is holy, revelation a sacrament, and pursuing one's truth the only sure validation" (25). This statement resonates with the themes in Smith's fiction. In order for Smith's characters to participate in the sacred, to experience the divine, they must first cross over the line, break through the wall of expectations and imposed definitions. Smith identifies, for many of her characters, the barrier to breaking through as the training they received when they were young that taught them they should forego bodily pleasures in favor of spiritual transcendence. However, in Smith's literary and spiritual vision, to use the writer's own words, "The way to the mind and the heart is only through the body. The way to the soul is through the body" (Per). For this reason, with Smith's protagonists, the search—the journey—dictates that they move outside their routine lives, that they "transgress" in some way, in order to experience holiness and attain a sense of the feminine divine.

Noted theologian Rita M. Gross identifies the need to get in touch with a feminine spirituality as "the longing for the Goddess" and suggests that this yearning simply expresses the need for "respect for ourselves *as we are*—female" (*Feminism* 272). For an immeasurably long time, patriarchal traditions have alienated women from any understanding of the feminine divine. In using the term "feminine divine," my intention is to elicit a composite deity of many religions, cultures, and names, not any one particular figure. Furthermore, Smith acknowledges that she neither fixates on the nature of God, nor obsesses about goddess mythology. Smith's vision of the divine encompasses what she defines as a "feminine divinity"; her sense of the sacred exists "completely outside the box" (Per).

Smith's fiction over the last forty years powerfully reflects her personal search for spiritual reconciliation, and all eleven of her novels exemplify the writer's numinous journey. The protagonists of Smith's novels feel estranged from any sense of feminine sacredness as they struggle in their individual searches for a belief system that offers them hope and validation. In the early novels (those written prior to 1983), Smith examines the limitations and resultant angst of Southern females raised to accept traditional Christianity's imposed dichotomy between mind and body, flesh and spirit, sexuality and maternity. A split identity often manifests these characters' internal conflict. The damage these females suffer cannot be healed by adherence to patriarchal religious beliefs; only the recovery of a sense of the feminine divine can assuage their anguish. Smith's novels, beginning in 1983 with *Oral History*, increasingly depict female characters who exhibit divine qualities, as Smith describes them with imagery linked to goddess mythology. At the end of the 1995 novel *Saving Grace*, Smith provides peace and reconciliation for her protagonist as Grace Shepherd completes her circular journey to personal salvation. Then, with Smith's most recent novels, the author re-mythologizes the heroic journey with female protagonists who emanate sacredness in their everyday lives.

In Lee Smith's novels written after 1980, we clearly see a new female character emerge, one apparently in conflict with patriarchal religion in its denial of the feminine divine. This woman possesses qualities tied to goddess mythology. In *Of Woman Born*, Adrienne Rich observes the disturbing lacuna that has been equally troubling to Lee Smith. Rich writes, "Patriarchal monotheism did not simply change the sex of the divine presence; it stripped the universe of female divinity" (119), a female divinity around which the earliest religions were centered. Over a period of time, however, patriarchal religion gradually obliterated the ancient matriarchies, chiefly by violence, and the mother goddess was ostensibly overthrown by her sons.* The notion that sensual pleasures were divine gifts that could lead to a state of spiritual grace became anathema to patriarchal religion. Gross stresses the relevance to feminist theology and contemporary society of "re-imaging the Goddess." In a spiritual framework that includes the feminine divine, Gross asserts, birthing and nurturing obviously are vital symbols, but areas of focus are not limited to these stereotypically feminine roles. In her thorough and thought-provoking analysis, Gross presents several basic images helpful in re-imaging the feminine divine. The goddess figure that emerges from Gross's study encompasses a vast range of qualities and activities: sexuality, maternity, androgyny, dynamic creativity, and transcendence ("Hindu" 271–74), key elements recognizable in Smith's literary iconography.

Smith's fiction works to de-limit women in their sex roles, in their spirituality, in their language. Gross argues that the greatest symbol for women's denigration in "Western religio-cultural heritage" is "the inability to say 'God-She'" ("Hindu" 276), the absence of a *female* language that speaks to *female*

---

*Barbara Walker explains that many male scholars continue to deny the existence of the original Great Mother Goddess, and if they do acknowledge her at all, usually they reduce her significance to a "cult" figure associated with "sexual promiscuity and/or fertility." Walker notes the predominant inability of male scholars to recognize that "religious feeling" for the Great Mother Goddess was "much deeper and more passionate than feelings for a divine patriarch" (Women's 692).

experience. In *Sexes and Genealogies,* French feminist Luce Irigaray insists that society must give mothers "the right to pleasure, to sexual experience, to passion, give her back the right to speak, or even to shriek and rage aloud" (18). Paula Gallant Eckard has pointed out how Smith, using "maternal body and voice," has tendered to mothers these rights in her depictions of powerful, maternal characters. In creating these characters, Smith begins healing a wound inflicted on women by patriarchal society. Through her writing, she reaches back to the ancient Celtic mythology of her native Appalachia, back to the mountains of her youth. Eckard discusses the Appalachian Mountains, with their "rounded curvatures and gentle peaks," as symbols of the female body (159), and Smith has confirmed the deep symbolic significance of her beloved mountains. Smith reclaims the ability and the right to say "God-She" as she embraces the sacredness of the female body and women's experiences.

In her essay "Women's Time," French feminist Julia Kristeva identifies one problem of contemporary culture as an abandonment of spirituality and wonders if "the sexual revolution and feminism have merely been transitions into spiritualism" (367). Kristeva argues that without this integral part of all human beings, our lives are void of meaning and fulfillment. She explains the virtual disappearance of religion with the entrance of technology and science in the seventeenth and eighteenth centuries, then the subsequent suspicion of science and technology in the nineteenth and twentieth, leaving people empty and in need of connection and meaning (364–68). Smith's imagination restores healing spirituality to its rightful place of prominence in the modern female psyche, thereby allowing for reconnection among women and rediscovery of the feminine divine. Although some of the images and symbols that relate to goddess worship also appear in many other religions worldwide, my contention is that through her fiction, Smith provides an alternative spirituality based on the feminine divine, a belief system that counters traditional male-dominated Christianity.

Smith has spoken of the necessity for women to find an alternative to the linear, "prototypical American male journey" (qtd. in Byrd 107) that is inadequate to represent what Smith sees as the circular pattern of female experience.* Feminist scholar Kathryn Rabuzzi also finds the "quest of the hero" an unsatisfactory means for a woman to achieve selfhood and offers a new path, "the way of the mother that leads to motherselfhood" (10), which draws on the ancient maternal goddess and her dual qualities of sexuality and maternity. Smith's female protagonists are likewise associated with goddess mythol-

---

The significance of circles in goddess religions is discussed at length in Peg Streep's Sanctuaries of the Goddess: The Sacred Landscapes and Objects. *According to Streep, two of the largest and most clearly symbolic sites of goddess worship are the circular stone formations located at Stenness in Scotland and on the Antrium Coast Road in Ireland. Both "sanctuaries" invoke the "Goddess' regenerative powers" and allow a glimpse of "the Goddess in all of her glory, as source of all that is" (128).*

ogy as Smith attempts to reintegrate the splintered female. Rabuzzi's paradigm provides a useful tool for understanding Smith's writing as a spiritual quest.

Smith's interest in circularity and consistent use of circle imagery have been noted previously by several scholars. Lithuanian archaeomythologist Marija Gimbutas* explains the significance of circles and cyclical time in conveying the energy of the goddess (*Language* 277). Ancient European cult objects and symbolism indicate the preponderance of prehistoric matrilineal societies, with the goddess the central focus of worship. This goddess-centered religion existed for a much longer period of time than either Indo-European or Christian religions and left an indelible imprint on the Western psyche. Goddess symbolism focuses on the mysteries of life and death with particular attention to nature. Water in its many forms (such as streams, wells, and springs), along with caves and mountains, stones, bears, ravens and hawks, bees and honey, circles, and the number three are consistently associated with the female deity in her numerous representations as goddess of sexuality, fertility, birth, maternity, and death in sculptures, carvings, and pottery dating as far back as 500,000 years. These images tied to the most ancient religion in the world permeate Smith's novels. Smith explained that as a child she associated God with nature and the life force because she experienced the sensual, the concrete, in the mountains and springs and among the flowers. In Ketchin's words, "In her [Smith's] beloved mountains God and nature were one" (45).

Smith's spiritual journey begins in her first two novels. Although the protagonists of *The Last Day the Dogbushes Bloomed* (1968) and *Something in the Wind* (1971) encounter elements linked with the feminine divine, Susan and Brooke both remain trapped in an oppressive patriarchal society. Searching for a means of validation, these Southern girls, as a matter of conditioning, turn to traditional religion but experience disappointment and disillusionment at the absence of any guidance. In these early novels, Smith dallies with the imagery she later develops fully as she begins to explore the sacredness of nature and feminine experience. At this point in her writing career, Smith, due to her own upbringing in a strict Methodist home, viewed the possibilities for female lives as extremely limited. For these characters, limitations often manifest themselves as the commonly accepted incongruity between sexuality and motherhood. The imposed split between these two facets of the original mother goddess goes back to the Christian influence when the two were severed from one another and depicted as mutually exclusive. Since the

---

Although Gimbutas's work, labeled "highly suspect" by Lawrence Osborne ("The Women Warriors," Lingua Franca [December/January 1998]: 50–57), has been considered controversial by some archaeologists, her revisionist history corresponds with the scholarly work of such giants as Robert Briffault (The Mothers, 1927) and Johann Jakob Bachofen (Mutterrecht und Urreligion, 1926). Osborne dismisses Gimbutas's theory of goddess religions as merely a popular but short-lived trend among feminists.

integration of these two complexes is necessary for any understanding of the complexity of the feminine divine, neither Susan nor Brooke achieves a sense of wholeness and validation.

In Smith's next two novels, *Fancy Strut* (1973) and *Black Mountain Breakdown* (1980), the protagonists, unlike Susan and Brooke, grow to adulthood and marry or are already grown and married when the story begins. Although Monica Neighbors of *Fancy Strut* supplies only one of several narrative voices in the novel, she is easily recognizable as another divided female psychologically split between her salient sexuality and the community-validated role of motherhood. She tries to express her sexuality within her marriage, but her husband Manly is unable to accept it. At the end of the novel, confused and unfulfilled, she tries the conventional path; she decides to have a baby. She will opt for maternity and suppress her sexuality. Similarly, Crystal Spangler of *Black Mountain Breakdown* also suffers from the inability to express her sexuality and thereby integrate the two disparate parts of herself. Like Brooke, Monica and Crystal encounter the possibility for integration in relationships that supply immediate but temporary excitement, passion, and ecstasy. However, Smith suggests that for her struggling protagonists, sex is only part of the process, and if a female fails to realize this and deceives herself by believing she has discovered the sacredness for which she has been yearning without embracing her inner sanctity, she will not achieve integration and wholeness. Crystal's inability to act on her own behalf results in physical paralysis as she becomes catatonic at the end of the novel.

Beginning with *Oral History* (1983), Smith attributes to women mythic qualities strongly linked to the feminine divine. In restoring sacredness to female characters, Smith offers a multi-generational study of women in this novel. The curse of the Cantrell family begins with Red Emmy, the red-haired goddess, and continues through two generations of Cantrell women, with Dory being the last full embodiment of the goddess (although Dory's daughters take on some of their mother's sacred qualities). Smith populates this novel with sexually expressive women, but Dory Cantrell is the key mythic female who openly exhibits both sexual passion and feminine spirituality. Although Dory's divine presence permeates the novel, society is not yet ready to accept her, and Richard Burlage's abandonment drives her to suicide. In the novel, Smith focuses on the destruction caused by an intolerant, rigid society and the denial of the feminine divine. From the first female voice in the novel to the last, Smith progresses toward the portrayal of female characters that are both mothers and sexually expressive women who bridge the cultural split maintained between maternity and sexuality and, with their sacred presence, suggest healing and integration. Not until *Fair and Tender Ladies* (1988), however, does Smith focus on an integrated, sacred female and allow her a long and fulfilling life.

Family Linen (1985) also depicts powerful female characters who struggle with society's imposed dichotomy between sexuality and motherhood, and like earlier characters, some women in the novel choose to deny their sexuality in an effort to conform or to survive. Other female characters, however, come to terms with their internal conflict and find healing in acceptance of both their sexual and maternal natures as Smith again draws on images of the feminine divine in portraying these women as sacred creatures. As in *Oral History*, the central mystery of *Family Linen* involves a family secret and its effect on the female characters in particular. In this novel, Smith traces the damage done to various females, focusing on their personal battles with sexuality, maternity, and spirituality. Of all the characters in the novel, Candy—a beautician—represents the well-integrated, divine adult female, in touch with her own sexuality and her sense of inner sacredness.

Fair and Tender Ladies' sacred-sexual-maternal figure, Ivy Rowe, evinces the deep and natural connections among sexuality, maternity, and spirituality. Although Ivy begins her long life of motherhood as a teenager, she is not permanently defined by her maternal role. Ivy refuses condemnation for her open sexuality by both polite society and the church. Her brief extramarital interlude with Honey Breeding, described in religious terms, revitalizes Ivy, enhancing both her motherliness and her sexuality within her marriage. Even though she blames herself when she returns home and finds her daughter LuIda dead, Ivy never repudiates the joy of her relationship with Honey or the newly discovered divinity within herself that he helps awaken. A personified reunification of the various attributes of the mother goddess, Ivy rises above all hardships to become a woman of legendary, mythic strength and vitality who discovers and accepts the divinity within feminine experience.

Smith's sprawling fictional history of country music, *The Devil's Dream* (1992), teems with imagery associated with the feminine divine. Katie Cocker, the famous progeny of the musical Bailey family, eventually escapes definition through others and accepts her inner sacredness. Katie serves as the novel's center and is most closely aligned with the fully integrated mythic goddess, but Smith also relies heavily on religious imagery in her portrayal of five other female characters: Kate Malone, the first goddess figure of the novel, with her golden hair blowing halo-like around her face; Nonnie Bailey, the sexual maternal goddess standing naked in the moonlight; Lucie Queen, the red-haired mother of five children who is able to openly express her sexuality in a divine union with R.C. Bailey; Tampa Rainette, the sexual matriarchal goddess with her fuzzy white halo-like hair; and Rose Annie Bailey, a damaged goddess who so yearns for the divine symbiosis she experienced with her childhood sweetheart that she eventually becomes schizophrenic and commits murder. In this novel, Smith interrogates the conflicts among music, religion, sexuality, and maternity, exploring one family's struggle for survival and painful journey to fame and fortune where reconciliation and healing are offered in the reclamation of the feminine divine.

In *Saving Grace* (1995), Smith goes a step further in her portrayal of a female protagonist's integration of sexuality, motherhood, and spirituality. Florida Grace's sensuality is revealed in an early incident; then, when at age fourteen she first experiences her own sexuality, like Ivy Rowe, she does not feel guilty although her father is a preacher. After years of a marriage that has produced two daughters, Grace also engages in an extramarital affair. Smith's description of Grace's ardent sexual relationship is reminiscent of the brief affair between Ivy and Honey; each encounter is rendered in religious terms. Other characters call both Ivy and Grace "whores of Babylon" for their presumed sexual promiscuity, but Smith clearly depicts these women as equally sexual and maternal beings, aligned with nature and sacred feminine experience. While Ivy leaves her children only temporarily to spend time with Honey, Grace abandons her two daughters permanently to reside with her lover. Smith neither condemns nor justifies these desertions. After decades of searching for the salvation that has continuously evaded her, Grace eventually completes her circular journey toward integration and self-knowledge at Scrabble Creek, ending where she began, finally discovering and embodying the feminine divine.

Circularity in women's lives resonates in Smith's 2002 novel, *The Last Girls*. Based on Smith's real-life experience of rafting down the Mississippi River with a group of college classmates, this story explores the sacred possibilities and realities of five women's lives over a thirty-five-year time period. The seemingly linear river journey actually turns out to be a study in the complexity, the inexplicability, the sanctity of women's lives. Smith centers the novel on the "absent presence" of Baby Ballou, who serves as the impetus for the group's reunion. Endowed with qualities of the feminine divine, Baby defies definition and classification. As the five friends make their river journey to sprinkle the ashes of their beloved Baby, they succeed in reconnecting not only with each other and their memories of Baby, but also with their inner divine selves. Smith rewrites the myth of the American heroic journey as she bestows hero status on five middle-aged women.

Smith returns to the mountains in the circular journey of Molly Petree, the protagonist of Smith's 2006 novel, *On Agate Hill*. All the motifs and themes seen in Smith's earlier works are here tweaked to perfection as Molly experiences the pain, suffering, joy and exhilaration of a fully integrated and completely *lived* existence. Alienated from a sense of her own sacredness, Molly, a "refugee girl," a ghost, as she calls herself, struggles to survive a harsh environment. Her fairytale world, the realm of her imagination, provides her only solace for many difficult years. The primary action of the novel is in the post Civil War era, and through Molly's experiences that she writes about in her diary, we learn of the displacement and disillusionment of a whole generation of Americans. Both Molly's life journey and Smith's two-year journey of writing the book are spiritual quests, and at the end of the novel, both Molly and her creator find acceptance and reconciliation in the feminine divine.

One of few contemporary Southern women writers who treats motherhood, creativity, sexuality, and spirituality as equal and important facets of female selfhood, Smith overcomes the destructive dualisms that have long plagued Western consciousness. In Smith's spiritual vision, women experience and embody the feminine divine in their day-to-day lives. Smith has retrieved in her fiction a source of transformative power—the power of the sexual, maternal, feminine divine—in hopes of creating a new image of the total, sacred female whose sexuality, creativity, spirituality, and maternity can reside comfortably in the bodies of everyday heroines.

Chapter I

"NOTHING LEFT TO SAY"

Silenced by the Dichotomy in
The Last Day the Dogbushes Bloomed
and *Something in the Wind*

Lee Smith's first two novels, *The Last Day the Dogbushes Bloomed* (1968) and *Something in the Wind* (1971), portray female protagonists who suffer from the imposed dichotomy between sexuality and maternity that has persistently plagued women in Western civilization, preventing them from understanding the innate sacredness of feminine experience. In these first two novels, Smith primarily explores daughters raised to focus on the body and define themselves through others, and mothers are not allowed a voice since the stories are told, respectively, from the first person point of view of nine-year-old Susan and seventeen-year-old Brooke. Although these protagonists search for a divine presence, they both experience disappointment with traditional Christianity, which insists on the split between mind and body. Just as Brooke, at the end of her relationship with Bentley (*Wind*), has "nothing left to say" (231), Susan (*Dogbushes*) is equally silent in the absence of the feminine divine.

Both Susan and Brooke feel disconnected from their mothers, and, deprived of a female role model and finding a patriarchal God insufficient to meet their spiritual needs, they desperately search for something in which to believe. Both Susan Tobey and Brooke Kincaid come from conventional Southern families in which keeping up appearances is paramount; however, each girl struggles with internal conflicts concerning sexuality, violence, maternity, and religion. In the course of the novels, neither of Smith's protagonists fully matures, but the author dallies with the integration of sexuality and maternity in her portraitures of Susan's mother, "the Queen," and Brooke's mother, Carolyn. While placing Susan and Brooke in symbolic settings and attributing to them scant mythic qualities that serve to link them to divinity, Smith offers hope for the future integration of these young girls. However, at this point in her life and writing career, Smith cannot envision a fully integrated female protagonist who heals the split between sexuality and motherhood and embraces feminine sanctity.

The Last Day the Dogbushes Bloomed, a short novel developed from a series of short stories written from a child's point of view when Smith was nineteen to twenty years old, covers a pivotal summer in Susan Tobey's life. During these three months Susan's confusion about the nature of love and spirituality is exacerbated by her perception of the disjunction between sensuousness and motherliness. Susan's comments that "just about the only time[s] you see Queens" (4) are at meals and for haircuts suggest the young girl's distance from her mother. For Susan, Mrs. Tobey's open sexuality appears incompatible with her role as mother, so the young girl creates a fairytale world in which her mother becomes "the Queen," not a maternal figure at all, but instead beautiful and inaccessible. Unable to recognize and/or accept her mother's extramarital affair, Susan, in a created storybook explanation, labels her mother's lover "the Baron." Susan's reaction of wonderment to her older sister Betty's observation of their mother's attractiveness betrays the young girl's inner conflict. Early in the novel, Susan says that her mother "liked the Baron more than us" (5), but Susan has no problem with this obvious partiality since, after all, the Baron, as she has imagined him, is also royalty. Nine-year-old Susan perceives Mrs. Tobey as extremely selfish since ultimately her mother deserts her family to run away with the Baron.

In this novel, Smith focuses on the daughter, not the mother, and our only image of Mrs. Tobey comes from Susan's viewpoint. Furthermore, Smith depicts Mrs. Tobey, "the Queen," as a victim of patriarchy, trapped in an undesirable role from which she must eventually escape. We surmise that the disjunction between motherhood and sexuality invoked by society's codes at least partially contributes to Mrs. Tobey's eventual decision to leave her maternal role for a purely sexual one. The Tobeys' early marriage had been one of necessity (in society's eyes); as Mrs. Tobey tells Betty, "Sometimes people have to get married" (109). Throughout the novel, Mrs. Tobey displays irritation and discomfort with the demands of motherhood as she turns Susan away any time the young girl wants advice or needs an explanation. On the contrary, around her lover, the Baron, Susan's mother appears "soft and pretty" (44) as she drinks from a goblet held to her lips by the Baron; then, comfortable with her sexuality, she dances slowly and sensually with him as Susan watches. And since the Tobeys have separate bedrooms, Smith strongly suggests the asexual nature of this marriage. With this early image of mature female sexuality, Smith introduces a prototype that she later fully develops.

Throughout the novel, Smith identifies Mrs. Tobey as a sensual, sexual force, linking her to nature with imagery that suggests this woman's potency, imagery upon which Smith later builds in depicting female characters. Susan, fascinated and preoccupied with the Queen's appearance and gestures, consistently associates her mother with flowers, birds, and nature's cycles, a salient indication of the strong affinity between nature and female sexuality in Smith's imaginative vision. Comparing the Queen to a "red flower," Susan describes her mother as dressing often in pinks and reds, colors associated with passion, and as wearing flowing, full designs. Roses are linked to Mrs. Tobey throughout the novel, and on the day after the flood, the Queen's only concern seems to be for the roses that have sustained considerable damage. Susan compares her mother's laughter to "fairy music" and her hand movements to "fluttering ... birds" (4–5). Always moving in "a thousand ways at once" (44), Mrs. Tobey remains in a state of constant motion. She represents activity, mobility; neither husband nor children tie her down. On the night before Mrs. Tobey leaves her family when she enters Susan's bedroom to kiss her daughter, her movements are compared to the natural force of the wind, and as her mother leans over her, Susan says "all I could smell was summer" (87).

Nor Hall's *The Moon and the Virgin: Reflections on the Archetypal Feminine* discusses a necessary kind of silence that accompanies one's encountering "the holy." When in the presence of the divine, Hall argues, one is silenced by the sheer magnitude of the experience (59). Since Susan has elevated her mother to the status of royalty, even divinity, the young girl remains awestruck by her mother's mere presence. Like many of Smith's early female protagonists, Susan is silenced by both her mother and her environment, but her interest in and quest for language identify her as the first of a long line of female characters searching for a voice in a society that discourages girls from speaking up. Early in the novel, Susan informs us that one of the Queen's rules is that "you have to be quiet" (4) and act "like a lady" (32), thus reinforcing a Southern code calling for female passivity. In fact, Susan feels so lucky to have a Queen in her home that she remains reticent most of the time in order to avoid appearing stupid around royalty. In search of a voice and a suitable language with which to express herself, Susan often plays games associated with words and even decides to learn a new word each day over the entire summer. However, when she practices her spelling and pronunciation in front of the entire family, her mother responds, "Good heavens," and her sister echoes with, "Jesus!" as they burst into laughter (7), squelching Susan and diminishing her pride. Mrs. Tobey consistently trivializes Susan's questions and concerns, leaving her daughter unsatisfied and frustrated. A good example is Susan's puzzlement when Frank, the gardener, reports for work quite intoxicated. Instead of explaining Frank's condition, Mrs. Tobey sends her daughter to bed.

The old housekeeper, Elsie Mae, gratifies Susan's thirst for language and for accurate explanations. Providing rich and entertaining stories to feed the girl's curiosity about life and hunger for attention, Elsie Mae serves as the novel's maternal figure. Not once does Susan mention a one-on-one conversation with her mother, whom Susan considers to embody the mysteries of life and language. The Queen merely issues orders to her younger daughter. In contrast, Elsie Mae, in touch with the complexity and sacredness of life, tells the nine-year-old, "You don't have to marry somebody just because of you love them. And you don't have to love somebody just because of you marry them.... There isn't no rhyme or no reason to the thing at all" (112). While Elsie Mae's sensitivity to and affection for Susan are often expressed by a few words, a simple kiss or an embrace, Susan mentions only once Mrs. Tobey kissing her daughter and using endearing language with her, and this occurs when Susan is asleep on the night the Queen deserts the family.

Perhaps Susan's habitual silence in her mother's presence suggests the young girl's sense of awe at this ethereal creature seemingly from another world. Once her mother leaves the room, Susan attempts to articulate her feelings with the truncated explanation, "A Queen loves me.... I am loved by a Queen" (88). Although Susan feels privileged to have the love of a Queen, she dares not get too close to this mysterious creature or break the magic spell of make-believe with language. Susan's need for expression through language and gestures is further suppressed when her father leaves on a short business trip (presumably to see an attorney) and Susan has just told him good-bye. As she approaches her mother, Susan thinks, "I would like to kiss her but of course I didn't" (59). The key here is the phrase "of course"; Susan has internalized the code for proper language and behavior toward "royalty." As Susan later explains, "you get used to Queens and Princesses and things. Only you can't ever get too used to them. If you could get too used to them they wouldn't be royal, but you can't ever do it anyway" (98). Clearly Susan perceives a close relationship with her mother or sister as an impossibility, such that even a minor transgression like an unsolicited word or kiss could shatter her entire fairytale world.

After Susan's participation in the game called "Iron Lung" during which she is raped by Eugene (a visiting boy in the neighborhood) and Little Arthur (Eugene's imaginary friend who supposedly gives orders to the children), the young girl is again silenced, this time by the children's parents. When Gregory, who has been ousted from the club, catches the other children in their "game" and reports what he has seen to their parents, the children are brought home for disciplinary action. Ironically, the main concern is that Mrs. Tate's roses are ruined; no one even acknowledges that a brutal rape has occurred. The adults seem to adhere to what Smith, in an essay, calls "the traditional southern way to handle problems"—to "not mention them" or talk about them ("Southern Exposure" 3). Rather than facing the issue of sexual assault, the adults hastily dismiss the matter and insist that Little Arthur is dead, something Susan perceives as totally unrelated to what has just occurred. In desperate need of validation and consequent punishment, Susan asserts emphatically that she hurts "down there" and explains, "Little Arthur and Eugene were on top of me and they were the Iron Lung" that went up and down. Refusing silencing, Susan demands acknowledgment. The young girl's desire to communicate her experience represents not only her need to inform the adults of what has occurred, but also her longing to connect to other human beings in order to validate her pain. As Susan delivers her confessional and requests punishment, she speaks "faster and faster," attempting to find language to express the pain of her experience. Susan needs reassurance of the injustice of the rape. Ignorant of her own victimization, she insists on claiming her transgression and receiving chastisement from the adults. However, instead of reproach or even admonition, the adults offer consolation, patting her and telling her, "It's all right." Although she argues, "It's not all right" and asks, "Why won't you spank me?" the adults put her to bed with the words, "Hush, Susan" (170). Since her mother has disappeared with the Baron and left her family, everyone pities Susan. By withholding punishment and explanation from her, the adults squash Susan's voice and her fledging sense of her own validity. In explaining what has occurred during the "Iron Lung" game, Susan repeats the words, "I was dying" twice, linking the rape with symbolic death. Susan experiences not only the death of her innocence and virginity, but also the loss of her voice, since during the rape she had tried to scream but failed. She felt herself "going down and down into the earth" and the dirt "coming up from all around to cover me" (162). Just as her resistance was ignored during the rape, her cries for help afterwards are neglected by the adults.

As a means of survival, Susan learns to practice silence, and at the end of the novel, she remains to try to sort out her feelings about love, religion, sexuality, and motherhood. Unable to do so in any realistic way, she resorts to a "trick" to fool herself. She compartmentalizes her mind into boxes and places the Queen in one box, Little Arthur, who she says "is alive all the time," in another, and the things she likes, such as God, Sara Dell, Baby Julia, the dogbushes, and the wading house, into other boxes. Unable to openly express her anguish, Susan decides that her mother is "better off" and feels grateful to have had her as long as she did. Susan says, "Sure I missed her, but by then I didn't know exactly that I was missing the Queen and knew only that I was missing." Even Susan's nine-year-old mind can sense the overwhelming absence of sensuality and sexuality that her mother's presence in her life represented. This young girl has little chance of resolving her confusion about motherhood and sexuality now that such an important part of the puzzle is missing. And since Susan admits "there were some things that I never took out of their boxes at all" (173–74), Smith warns us of Susan's permanent silence and inability to find a voice.

If, as suggested by Nor Hall, "language evolves from the experience of being held by our actual and archetypal mothers" (28), Susan, having been deprived of a close relationship with her mother, may only hope to discover a suitable means of expression through reconnection with the feminine divine. Certainly Susan has acquired a new awareness of what she has lost—not only her childhood—but also her innocence and the fairytale world she has created, as she admits at the end of the novel, "Mother had left us," calling Mrs. Tobey "Mother" for the first time rather than the Queen (180). Susan's recognition and acceptance of Mrs. Tobey's abandonment shatters her make-believe world, filled with the sensual, sexual presence of her mother.

Because of Susan's inability to reconcile her mother's sensuality with her maternity, she remains outside of divine feminine experience. She feels like an outsider in her own home, "the castle," since Betty, remarkably self-confident, models with great ease the behavior and mannerisms of their mother. Susan calls Betty "the Queen's daughter" (3), and Betty, clearly a sexual being like her mother, imitates her mother's every move, even holding her little finger out in an affected way while sipping a drink, a duplicate of Mrs. Tobey. Betty's "sisterly" talk with Susan about the advantages of being female sounds like something their mother would say. Betty informs her younger sister, "girls, see, girls get to spend all the money and they don't have to shave and they can look beautiful all day long and make all the men fall in love with them" (39). At the time, these "advantages" do not seem at all attractive to nine-year-old Susan as she desperately tries to delineate the nature of love. Using her mother as a measure for marriage and maternity, Susan cannot imagine how "beauty" and "love" fit into the picture since the Queen doesn't appear to be "in love" with Mr. Tobey, but rather with the Baron, who stimulates her sexuality.

Susan's confusion about love occupies a large portion of her thoughts throughout the novel. She often muses about the definition of this obscure concept, eventually asking her only maternal source, Elsie Mae, to explain to her all about the mysterious phenomenon. Prior to their conversation, Susan has tried carefully to put the different types of love into their separate compartments in her child's mind. Confused with the "zillion things that you call love," Susan attempts to order the different types. Her thoughts about love reveal three major forms that confuse her: sexual love, represented by the black couple in the art book; maternal love, suggested by the mention of the Queen; and divine love, understood by Susan in her unquestioning acceptance of the often repeated phrase "God loved the world" (110–11). Adding to her bewilderment, Susan associates several important people (such as her mother, Little Arthur, Eugene, and even God) with the different types of love. Interestingly, Elsie Mae is not mentioned because the reciprocal love between this maternal figure and Susan in no way puzzles the young girl. Since she perceives the family housekeeper as strictly maternal and Mrs. Tobey as primarily sexual, Susan's dawning curiosity and confusion about sexual love do not involve Elsie Mae. It is, therefore, Mrs. Tobey's love for her daughter that perplexes Susan since she cannot conceive of maternal love and sexual love residing within the body of one woman. Susan feels assured of her mother's love, but the open sexuality of her mother disturbs the girl. The Queen's inaccessibility disallows Susan's turning to Mrs. Tobey for nurturance. Instead, she reaches for comfort in Elsie Mae, who rushes to the rescue, equipped with cookies or candy bars, hugs and kisses, even medicine and bandages, attending to Susan's physical and emotional needs each time Susan is upset or injured.

The apparent sexuality of both Mrs. Tobey and Betty causes Susan great discomfort as Smith explores the damage caused by the false dichotomy between the two complexes: sexuality and maternity. Remembering when her mother first told her about menstruation, Susan recalls thinking she would have to wear a bucket to catch the blood. When she told her mother this, Mrs. Tobey laughed at her daughter; later, Susan overheard her mother repeating Susan's words to "a golden lady in the Court." Even at the young age of nine, Susan recognizes her mother's betrayal, but she decides "Queens have the right." Thus, Susan's first sexual knowledge, delivered to her by her mother, is coupled with misunderstanding and embarrassment. It is, then, understandable that Susan dreads growing breasts, "big blobby things flopping around all the time in front of [her] chest," and kissing boys (41). Her experiences with sexuality continue to be confusing as she cannot connect the different types of love. When she witnesses her sister and Tom Cleveland's heavy petting, their "moving all around ... up and down and every way," she feels equal fascination and disturbance at the heavy breathing and "batting around on the sofa" (80–82).

Later, without any sense of the sanctity of sexuality, Susan associates Betty and Tom's actions with a picture of a naked woman she sees in an art book that Eugene brought to a club meeting. After Eugene has taught the club members the pronunciation and meaning of the terms "penis" and "breast," he demands that each must touch these forbidden areas on the page, himself taking the lead and punching at the woman's breast. Susan wonders "how it would be to be punched there" when she "got beauty" (grew up). Then she decides she doesn't want to "get beauty" at all, "if people punch at you." Susan's puzzlement about love, beauty, sexuality and male aggression escalates as she participates in the misogynistic ritual. After viewing the pictures in the book and being taught by Eugene that people embrace one another "before they fuck" (94–95), Susan thinks of Betty and Tom's petting on the couch. Then later, when she sees Robert (one of the club members) and recalls the awful grin he wore after punching the woman's breast in the picture, she speculates about the interrelatedness among love, sex, and violence, and wonders if Tom, her sister's boyfriend, was secretly smiling that way too.

The inveterate associations Susan makes among love, sex, and violence are striking. She mentally connects the violence of the children punching the pictures in the art book to Betty and Tom's sexual foreplay on the couch. The interrelation of violence and sex continues to confuse Susan as she tries to understand sexuality and its correlation to love. Any naiveté about love and sex she possesses is soon obliterated since Eugene and his imaginary companion Little Arthur serve as destroyers of the children's innocence and instructors of the sexual world. Early in the novel, when Gregory's cat is due to have kittens and the other children are anxious to witness the births, Eugene calmly comments that he feels nothing at watching a live birth since he once saw a woman deliver a child and "she yelled all the way through" (25). Although Susan does not associate Eugene's comment with her mother's having given birth to her, later in the novel while at the wading house, she watches a "mama fish" lead her baby fish around and interprets the fish's behavior as related to humans. Thinking of her own mother, Susan now finds her thoughts have immediately shifted to Little Arthur and "that green art book, and Little Arthur and the Queen got all junked up together in my summer head" (105). Again, disturbed by her feelings about love, she attempts to straighten them all out in her mind. The pattern of Susan's thoughts suggests her confusion. First she witnesses motherhood in nature by watching the fish. Then she relates this image to her own mother, the thought of whom reminds her of Little Arthur and the art book, her first experience with sexuality.

Later, Susan makes another arresting connection between her mother and open sexuality when in her father's basement room she finds a photograph of the Queen. Explaining that the picture seemed to possess a strange magnetism for her, she says she didn't want to look, but found the photo irresistible. In the photograph, her mother appears to be "breathing hard," and Susan experiences chest pain as she views the picture of Mrs. Tobey's enlarged face emerging from the darkness of the background. Describing the picture as "awful but ... beautiful too," Susan feels "messed up" after looking at it (119). Susan's description of the photograph of her mother conjoins several important related images. The mention of her chest hurting and Mrs. Tobey appearing to be "breathing hard" is reminiscent of both the "Iron Lung" game and Betty and Tom's petting session during which their breathing had gotten "louder and louder until ... [it] filled the whole room" (81). Susan's version of this sexual encounter is rife with references to Betty and Tom's breathing. Even though the photograph features Mrs. Tobey alone, her enlarged mouth suggests the heavy breathing of sexual passion. Additionally, Susan's explication of the photograph evokes the description of Eugene coming out of "black flowers" on the night he introduces Little Arthur to the children. Susan comments, "when there was only his [Eugene's] voice, I had wanted to see his face; but when I could see it, I didn't want to anymore" (62). This paradoxical view of Eugene, Susan's introducer to and instructor of the sexual world, relates to Susan's perception of her mother, whose eyes are almost but not quite visible in the photo, their limitless depth suggestive of the mystery of sexuality. Furthermore, the enlarged mouth that "opened and opened" (119), seeming to swallow everything, even Susan, appears cave-like in its darkness and mystery, the universally significant cave as representative of the womb, place for symbolic birth and regeneration. As Susan remains spellbound by the simulacrum in the photograph, her fears of being inside the mouth suggest her anxiety over the mystery of female sexuality. And since she feels equally attracted to and repelled by the image, she simultaneously longs for a return to the safety and comfort of the mother's womb where she can remain ignorant about sexuality, and yet dreads the painful process of acquiring the knowledge and experience necessary for the regeneration represented by the cave.

The associations among Mrs. Tobey, sexuality, violence, and Susan's need for expression culminate on the night Susan loses her spiritual and sexual innocence. It is Susan who suggests that the club of children obliterate the roses of Mrs. Tate, an innocent, afflicted old lady. Thus, since roses consistently evoke the Queen, Susan's wish to destroy the rose garden symbolizes her desire to attack her mother and the sexuality she represents. After the children have demolished the rose garden, they engage in the game that shatters Susan's sexual innocence. The many allusions to breathing, throughout the novel to suggest sexual passion and Susan's concomitant anxiety (her chest pain), reach their apex in the image implied by the name "Iron Lung." Susan describes the experience: "They jumped on me and pulled down my shorts and they were going up and down, up and down, up and down..., and the Iron Lung was hurting me between my legs" (163). A mechanical respirator used to provide artificial breathing, an iron lung totally encloses the patient's body, with only the head exposed. Helpless and trapped beneath the "iron lung" as Eugene and Little Arthur rape her, Susan feels unable to breathe as she is robbed of her air supply and her sexual innocence by male dominance and violence. Smith's choice of the expression "iron lung" serves to historicize the novel with reference to the 1950s polio epidemic, a time during which the term was a part of every child's vocabulary and held a very real terror.

This entire rape scene and the image of Susan's being deprived of her ability to speak and breathe on her own, then being forced to use the artificial device provided by the boys, suggest an account in ancient goddess mythology whereby a goddess called Ninlil, whose name means "Lady Air," was robbed of her maidenhood in a rape by Enlil, the god of air, based on the biblical father god Yahweh, who possessed the power to create words. Thus the female deity was forced to suppress her power of language and relinquish her breath of life to the imposing aggression of the male deity. This tale of female submission serves as a fascinating analog for Susan's victimization. Mythology holds that Enlil's punishment for such defilement of purity was banishment to the netherworld; Eugene is simply taken back to his aunt's house, but Little Arthur, the imaginary "master-mind" behind the "Iron Lung" game, is likewise symbolically banished by the adults with their insistence, "He's dead. There is no more Little Arthur" (169). The harm done to Susan is permanent, however, for she knows the adults are "lying" and that "wherever I went, for maybe the whole rest of my life, Little Arthur ... would always be there" (180). Even at age nine, Susan seems to sense the magnitude of the damage done to her as she accepts the eternal presence of male aggression and enforced silence and further compartmentalizes her feelings into "boxes," some of which will never be opened.

In Susan's search for answers and guidance, she grows increasingly disillusioned with a patriarchal God as she encounters mysterious forces in symbolic settings that have remarkable connections to the feminine divine and ancient maternal goddess. A spiritual child, Susan says she "loved God a lot that summer" (46) and often looked for Him up in the sky "behind the clouds" (18). Desperately seeking God's presence in her everyday life, Susan often spends time alone, either sitting under the dogbushes in her yard or at the wading house, her favorite spot. To get to this "special place," she must pass through a patch of blackberry bushes "which tried to grab me," and walk through shallow water up the middle of a small stream (11). At the wading house with a big rock inside, Susan reconnects to nature's creatures, all of whom have individual names and personalities. Here, she encounters divinity in nature, and Smith's description of the setting bears striking similarities to sites sacred to the ancient goddess. In goddess-centered religions, as Gimbutas explains, streams and stones are representative of the goddess's life-giving and health-giving powers (*Language* 324). Lotte Motz also stresses the sacredness of rocks and stones in goddess mythology (102). Struggling against forces that would attempt to keep her away from this especially feminine hallowed spot, Susan says she "got away" from the "hands" that were "reaching out" for her (12). At the wading house, Susan, frustrated and alone, finds renewal and strength before returning home to face more questions and doubts.

On the night she encounters a pack of dogs, Susan participates in another highly symbolic ritual that leaves her further addled about the patriarchal God, a confusion that escalates throughout the novel and culminates in Susan's recognition and acceptance of divinity in nature. When she wakes in the middle of the night with the light from the moon flooding her bedroom, Susan feels strange as a force propels her to walk outside, crawl under the dogbushes, and sit in the middle of a large open field where she says, "I was the only thing in the night besides the moon." Situated in a meditative and reverent position, she notices a procession of dogs approaching from out of the mountains, and although Elsie Mae has told her about these hungry packs of dogs that come in search of food, Susan remains unafraid as the dogs walk slowly "one by one" in a line and move "in a circle" around her, then retreat just as slowly back through the trees and up into the mountains (143–44). In *The Myth of the Goddess*, Anne Baring and Jules Cashford, while noting the ancient origin of the link among the dog, the moon, and the goddess, cite the dog as one of the earliest animals belonging to the female deity, serving as the guardian of her mysteries (72). Gimbutas interprets the dog's importance to the goddess as both an omen of death and as a guardian and stimulator of young life (*Language* 323), explaining that through millennia dogs appear in art as direct stimulators of the life force that promote the lunar cycle (233). Susan's mystical experience occurs at a crucial time in her life, on the night after she and the other girls in the neighborhood club (headed by Eugene and Little Arthur) have marched pantyless in a procession in front of the boys. The symbolic visit of the dogs may certainly be viewed as an omen of death due to the eminent loss of Susan's childhood, but the mystical midnight encounter also strongly suggests guardianship and protection of Susan by the pack of dogs since they neither bark nor frighten her as a magic circle seems to envelop her.

After this spiritual encounter that powerfully evokes the feminine divine, Susan returns to bed where she tries desperately to pray but can't remember how. Frightened, she says, "I couldn't pray to the God of the thunder, or the skinny Jesus walking on the waters, or even to the little pink Baby Jesus." No aspect of this male deity seems real to her anymore. She can only think "about the moonlight ... and about Little Arthur because I knew that he had been out in that moonlight somewhere too, and I thought about the dogs" (144–45). Linking the moon, Little Arthur, and the dogs, Susan makes an unconscious connection that epitomizes her confusion about sexuality and religion. From this attempt to pray but an inability to "remember" how, Susan gradually loses her desire for connection with God; after her rape, once in bed for the night, she admits, "I didn't even try to say my prayers" (171). Powerful implications exist in a scene soon after the rape when, at home alone, Susan thinks she hears someone call her name and imagines "it had probably been God or Little Arthur and I didn't much care which" (175). Little Arthur, her rapist, the thief of her childhood and her voice, is now interchangeable with God for Susan. Scholars in many fields of study effectively argue that the patriarchal deity did symbolically "rape" the ancient female divinity, robbing her of her mystery and multitudinous powers. At the end of the novel after the death of the gardener, when Susan realizes that all living things eventually die, her last attempt to pray to God again proves futile. In a fascinating scene that anticipates one in Alice Walker's *The Color Purple* when Celie begins to pray to the elements of nature instead of to the patriarchal God, Susan resorts to praying to a star, then feeling herself rise above the stars, she looks down to the tops of the trees and prays to them, then to the grass, the flowers, the rocks, "everything," sensing that each element responds to her prayers. Deciding "I could pray to anything," Susan affirms in the last few lines of the novel, "I wasn't afraid any more" (179–80).

However, the tragedy of Susan's young life leaves her unreconciled to her many internal conflicts concerning sexuality, violence, maternity, and religion. Having established "boxes" for every aspect of her life, Susan fails to weave the many threads together to create and discover an integrated selfhood. Although she professes no fear at the end of the novel, Susan appears to have accepted the "reality" of Little Arthur's presence in her life with her words, "nothing mattered" (180) anymore. In Smith's work, Susan Tobey is the first of many damaged female characters who suffer from the unrealistically imposed dichotomy between mind and body and the powerful need to connect to the feminine divine.

Smith's second novel, *Something in the Wind*, published three years after *Dogbushes*, also focuses on a daughter's perspective, and like Susan, seventeen-year-old Brooke Kincaid searches for her identity. Splitting herself into an authentic self and a fabricated self, she fails to mesh her own feelings and desires with the expectations of others, especially her socialite mother. Reminiscent of Susan's dubbing her mother "the Queen," Brooke avoids calling her mother by an affectionate title such as "mom" or "mother," instead referring to Mrs. Kincaid by her first name, Carolyn. Since Smith tells the story from Brooke's point of view, the reader only sees Carolyn from her daughter's vantage point, but Carolyn bears several similarities to Mrs. Tobey of *Dogbushes*. Smith's lengthier second novel allows for fuller development of the protagonist, but Brooke suffers from the same maternal/sexual conflict as Susan. Since she does attain sexual freedom and individuality, Brooke could perhaps be considered sexually liberated. By coupling expressed sexuality with the possibility for maternity in the question of Brooke's pregnancy, Smith moves a bit closer to depicting a sexual, maternal female in this novel, but Brooke's inability to recognize the interconnections among sexuality, maternity, and divinity prevents such integration.

In *Something in the Wind*, as in *Dogbushes*, the distant relationship between mother and daughter exacerbates Brooke's anxiety over her own developing sexuality and serves as an obstacle to Brooke's integration. Brooke says, "there was nobody, in spite of everything, that I liked better than Carolyn" (6), openly admitting her attraction to and fascination with her mother. Echoing Susan's thoughts about the Queen, Brooke's choice of the word "liked" suggests a relatively superficial friendship rather than a daughter's deep love for her mother. More of a casual acquaintance whose company Brooke enjoys, Carolyn Kincaid fails to recognize or connect with the needs of her struggling daughter. Although Carolyn does not desert her family like Susan's mother, her sexuality alienates Brooke, who describes her mother as "very distant" (33). Differing greatly from Carolyn since Brooke lacks interest in physical appearance and attracting the opposite sex, Brooke realizes her inadequacy in her mother's eyes. Before Brooke leaves for college, Carolyn provides her daughter the only "motherly advice" offered during the course of the novel. This counsel, reminiscent of Betty's guidance for Susan, chiefly consists of a number of tips on how to attract men. As Brooke recalls that summer, this lecture from her mother stands out as one of the few memorable events since advice was "out of character" for Carolyn, who "never said anything serious" (31). Carolyn cautions her daughter, "You ought to go out every weekend but you shouldn't go out two nights in a row with the same boy.... One thing you have got to remember ... is that boys don't like pale little egghead girls," reminding Brooke to get a nice tan to avoid becoming an "old maid." Warning her daughter of the dangers of intellectualism, Carolyn postulates, "A smart man is one thing but a smart woman is something else" (33–34).

This mother's advice to her teenage daughter embarking on a new life at college exemplifies de Beauvoir's argument that a patriarchal culture produces girls overly concerned with their bodies and equally unconcerned with their minds. Even at the end of the novel as the family prepares for Brooke's brother Carter's wedding, Carolyn's primary concern rests with Brooke's physical attractiveness; she insists that her daughter get her hair cut and literally pushes Brooke into the sun every day to work on her tan. Earlier in the novel with Brooke at home for Christmas break, her emaciated figure, sloppy clothes, and distant, apathetic attitude disturb the entire family. Carter, after expressing concern for Brooke, tells her that their older sister Liz thinks Brooke needs psychiatric attention. In the family's conversation about Brooke's welfare, Carolyn had said she "wouldn't hear of" sending her daughter to a psychiatrist, emphasizing, "Nobody in my family has *evah*." Carolyn, unable or unwilling to understand or communicate with her daughter, cursorily dismisses Brooke's physical and emotional problems, both a result of the girl's developing sexuality, as "a touch of growing pains" (120). Similar to the Queen in her denial of any family complication or problem, Carolyn casually glosses over Brooke's difficulties. Again in her second novel, Smith disallows the presence of both sexuality and maternal nurturance within the mother of the family, thus contributing to the antimony within the young protagonist.

Smith aligns Carolyn Kincaid, a potent, sexual force similar to but not as developed as the Queen, with nature, as the writer continues to explore the organic connections between nature's forces and female sexuality. Brooke compares her mother to "a moth heading for light" (9), reminiscent of the Queen's affinity with birds, but also suggestive of self-destruction. Often dressing in bright colors with flowing designs, Carolyn seems to spread sunshine wherever she goes. Brooke describes her mother as "swish[ing] out of the room ... with a noise like waves" (35) and directly compares Carolyn's presence to that of air, seemingly natural and necessary. In later novels, Smith further develops the idea of air movement and wind in their portentous function, signaling the presence of the feminine divine. Carolyn's sexuality appears less organic than Mrs. Tobey's, more imposed, and perhaps self-destructive (for example, her desire for Brooke to acquire a suntan) in her lifelong pursuit of youth and physical beauty. Brooke describes her mother's habits of excessive smoking and talking, wearing low-cut dresses, and often changing her hair color. Always hopeful of losing weight, Carolyn habitually purchases clothes a size too small for her. She epitomizes the mind/body split in her total devotion to and constant concern with appearance. As Brooke watches her mother primp, the girl's thoughts focus on Carolyn's apparent sexuality. Brooke imagines her mother giggling and leaning forward to expose "the blue shadow between her large white breasts" to her son Carter and his fraternity brothers (34). Carolyn's expressed sexuality and obvious pleasure in attracting men, even friends of her son, play a crucial role in Brooke's developing angst concerning her own sexuality since in her mind, maternity and sexuality exist in two different spheres.

Brooke's primary identification with her mother as a sexual being rather than a maternal one serves as the impetus for Brooke's plan to divide herself into two different girls: one shallow and interested in appearance, the other introspective and desirous of human connection and intimacy. Viewing her mother as sexual but not maternal, Brooke associates motherhood with artificiality and superficiality. Any time her mother has attempted "motherliness" or nurturance, it has felt to Brooke like a performance. Brooke knows she possesses greater depth of character than what her mother sees and condones; thus, she agonizes over her true identity. After the death of her close friend Charles, when she leaves for college, Brooke realizes that no one really knows her. Searching for a way to resolve her conflicting feelings, she arrives at a plan to split herself into two equal parts: a superficial half and a "real" half. Similar to Susan Tobey's defense mechanism of creating mental boxes for her feelings to avoid experiencing pain, Brooke invents a "plan" to dichotomize the two sides of her nature and avoid the painful integration that seems an impossibility in her culture. In Brooke's search for knowledge of self, she commits the worst possible error in attempting to separate her mind from her body, but as Smith explained, "part of the experience of Southern women for years and years ... would divorce you from your body" (qtd. in Loewenstein 501). Brooke's intentional splitting of self assists in coping with the enforced Southern prescription for appropriate female behavior, with the "daughter" half of her following the code her mother endorses. The genuine half, however, feels love and expresses it sexually. With the two halves constantly in conflict, Brooke practices "southern" behavior, trying to laugh in a lady-like way and hiding her innermost thoughts and feelings.

Brooke's struggle with her own sexuality begins early and continues throughout the novel, never to be entirely resolved. Her first kiss from John Howard, a young man of whom her mother strongly approves, awakens Brooke's sexuality. Feeling "remote and interested and sort of amazed," Brooke allows him to fondle her breasts. The separation of mind and body in full operation, she explains, "I felt my nipples rise of their own accord." John, frustrated with Brooke's lack of interest and response, abruptly withdraws his hand and demands an explanation, which Brooke fails to provide. Referring to herself in the third person, she thinks, "Do what you will with Brooke's body ... but please stay out of her mind" (38–40). When John invites Brooke to New York, Brooke declines the offer, wishing "my mind wasn't dead" and wondering why she turned him down (41). Brooke's alternating references to herself in the first, then the third, person saliently reflect her internal scission. Once at college, Brooke continues to battle with her split identity. Diana, her new roommate, turns out to be a younger version of Carolyn. When Brooke introduces serious discussion, Diana "pushed the little manners knob and turned

[Brooke] off" (59). Brooke soon realizes, however, that the more she "acts" like Diana, the way Carolyn would have her behave, the more men she attracts, so she suppresses her "real self" and allows her "false self" to take command. Katherine Kearns argues that Brooke wants to be "normal," attend college, not be too smart, and find a nice, handsome boyfriend who fits into society in order to gain the approval of her family (181–82). However, we never know for sure what exactly Brooke desires since she has been silenced by her society, her family, and even her friends at school to the point of numbness and acquiesence.

In Brooke's first intimate relationship with Bob Griffin, or "Houston" as she calls him, a "good old boy" (65) Brooke meets on a blind date, she initially hopes to achieve wholeness through sexual intercourse. However she soon discovers that Houston cannot supply the missing part of her identity. Smith provides early indications of the impending failure of this relationship by emphasizing Brooke's feelings of suffocation and shortness of breath when in Houston's presence. In later Smith novels, this somatic symptom signals the absence and therefore necessity of some sense the feminine divine. Brooke describes a room in Houston's fraternity house as filled with "heavy, communal breathing, coagulated," with Houston "breathing Purple Jesus [an alcoholic drink] in my face" (69). After their first petting session, Houston, in an effort to prove to Brooke his depth of character, initiates what he considers to be an intellectual discussion by asking her position on the subject of integration. Although Houston clearly refers to racial integration, Smith creates irony with the choice of topic. Brooke answers that she definitely supports integration, but readers know that she epitomizes a dichotomized female, unable to integrate her mind and body. Somewhat expecting sexual intercourse to help her achieve wholeness and a sense of the sacred, Brooke is surprised and a bit disappointed at the absence of physical pain the first time with Houston. She describes the experience as unimportant, "not a big deal after all" (81). Longing for some kind of transporting emotion through physical intimacy with another person, Brooke finds herself detached, "outside myself, watching some sort of game." With Houston in complete control, she realizes, "Houston was actually doing it" (84) as she lies passively waiting for him to finish, seemingly a nonparticipant—a recipient for Houston's sexual expression. Although Brooke has clearly consented to have sex with Houston, her words resonate with images of rape, recalling Susan's violation by Eugene and Little Arthur where she describes having her legs and arms held down. Brooke explains, "My feet were tied tightly together by the ski pants and I felt like a captive maiden" (83). Silenced by Houston during sexual intercourse, she is unable to "get [her] breath" or "speak clearly" (86). This loss of breath and language implies Brooke's spiritual death as she attempts to find wholeness in sexual union with another human being rather than looking within herself. After sexual intercourse, Brooke achieves a heightened awareness of her split identity. Referring to herself in the third person, she thinks, "I wished Brooke was different, but there was not anything I could do about her. For a little while, though, it had been great with Houston inside her and everything whole, but it was not that way any more" (88).

By connecting with Houston, Brooke follows the Southern prescription for female behavior in finding the "right man" to provide her with an identity; however, she soon discovers that Houston cannot supply her with the missing part of her self. As Smith continues to interrogate the inner sacredness of females and feminine experience, several of her protagonists manifest their confusion between sexual passion and spiritual ardency. The necessary reciprocal relationship for divine union is not possible for Brooke and Houston since for Houston, sexual initiative belongs solely to the male. The couple's break-up occurs when Brooke, quite intoxicated, plays the aggressor, pulling Houston down on top of her and tugging at his zipper, with the words, "Come on, come on, come on." Houston recoils in disgust and asks, "What the hell is wrong?" (99), then forces Brooke to her feet, silencing her one last time with, ironically, a question.

For the first time, the two disparate halves of Brooke begin to mesh in her relationship with Bentley T. Hooks, who introduces himself to her with, "Let's screw," then later offers, "I'll give you your first child" (133–34), words that, although crude, immediately serve to link sexuality with motherhood. A few months into their relationship, Brooke feels disappointment with the discovery that she's not pregnant. Bentley, like Brooke in his open sexuality, also struggles with his identity, often displaying a "lightning personality switch" (147). He has no problem openly admitting his love of sex. Comparing him to an "urchin," Brooke initially describes Bentley as possessing an "impish quality" (134–35). Smith's diction here evokes not only the image of a mischievous child or malignant spirit, but the word "imp," in its verb form, means "to extend, lengthen, enlarge, add to; to mend, repair" (*Oxford English Dictionary*), suggesting Bentley's curative effect on Brooke. He possesses the capability to help her "mend" or "repair" her split identity. When Brooke tells Bentley that he looks like an urchin, his comment that urchins, unlike him, "reproduce by fission" (135), reinforces his capacity for promoting growth and completion with a sexual partner as opposed to diminishing or minimizing the other person. Brooke feels their strong bond and senses the salvific nature of their relationship when shortly after meeting him, she senses the naturalness and ease of conversation with Bentley.

Throughout her writing, Smith uses blood, in its obvious link with females and feminine experience, to represent life and vitality and the concomitant potential for renewal and regeneration. Brooke's bleeding the first time she and Bentley have sex indicates the potential depth and possibility for permanent connection in their relationship. After her break-up with Houston, Brooke explains that she had "slept with just about everybody," assuring them all of her virginity, even referring to herself as a "professional virgin."

Brooke's only concern about her sexual vagaries is her failure to merge her mind with her body, symbolized by her inability to bleed during sexual intercourse. Concerning her active sex life, Brooke says, "I could do everything except bleed" (127). Bleeding symbolically represents penetration not only of her body, but also of her mind, which she has separated from her body. Accused (by her brother Carter) of not feeling anything, Brooke has thus far been successful at maintaining the dichotomy. Woman's blood, both in sexual intercourse and in menstrual discharge, holds the secret from which new life sometimes emerges. With the absence of blood during sexual intercourse, even in Brooke's first experience with Houston, Smith suggests Brooke's inability to recognize and accept the "new life" that awaits her in integrating her mind and body, in allowing her sexuality to complement her intellect. In her relationship with Bentley, however, Smith proposes integration for Brooke since she bleeds for the first time and even says of Bentley, "he made me a virgin again" (174).

Brooke's erotic ecstasy represents a divine, transformative power brought about when we question what we have been taught: that to feel good is wrong. If Brooke can recognize that satisfaction and joy are her birthrights, she may begin to heal the self-negation and numbness she has thus far accepted as normal and natural. Describing their first sexual experience, Brooke explains, "It hurt, then opened up, and I felt myself falling and falling and then I seemed to float around inside myself on the bed" (149). After intimate relations with Bentley, Brooke admits, "I felt real" (175) as she senses the curative quality of their sexual and spiritual union. Until Bentley, no one has been able to penetrate her carefully molded, protective exterior. Bentley has punctured the artificial Brooke and entered the "real" Brooke, meshing his own sexual love with hers. Now Brooke is fully able to feel, to experience, and to enjoy.

Smith's focus on the centrality of language emerges in Brooke and Bentley's relationship. Loving language but being silenced for so long by her parents, her friends, and even her other boyfriends, Brooke finally discovers her own voice in Bentley's presence. Although Brooke describes her mother's constant talking, Carolyn Kincaid has never listened to any of her daughter's words of expression. Even Brooke's sister Liz acts to squelch Brooke. At the funeral of Brooke's friend Charles, Liz instructs her, "Shut up and sing," when Brooke apologizes for standing up at an inappropriate moment (16). Moving on to a new life, Brooke takes her invisible muzzle to college with her, soon discovering in her roommate only a superficial acquaintance who refuses to participate in any serious discussion. Having been silenced for so long, Brooke assumes the inappropriateness and awkwardness of her feelings. Lack of a voice to express her innermost sensations and thoughts exacerbates the split in Brooke's identity. Like Susan Tobey, Brooke often plays word games, works crossword puzzles, and invents new words to suit the occasion. In desperate need of a language that speaks her feelings, Brooke often comes up short, such as the night of her break-up with Houston. Urging him to "come on, come on," Brooke thinks, "There were better words but I couldn't think of them" (99).

Not until her first conversation with Bentley does Brooke sense the potential naturalness of communication. She describes time with Bentley not only as a time when she feels complete, but also as the happiest period of her life. She says, "We used to stay up and talk for hours, but I can't remember now what we talked about" (175). With Bentley, Brooke says she feels "wide open" as she trusts him with her most important "secrets." Brooke wants to "make up a whole new language" (181) of love for the two of them since the usual English language seems inadequate to express their feelings for one another. Perhaps this new language would encompass "animal noises" like the ones Brooke described herself making during intercourse with Bentley, a primal vernacular closer to Kristeva's "mother tongue." Nor Hall describes divine experiences that are ineffable and therefore usually "undervalued in a world ignorant of the mysteries" (59). In Brooke and Bentley's sacred, sexual union, they have achieved a level of divine communion, and their mutual recognition of the absence of appropriate language to express their feelings indicates the mystery and depth of their relationship. They use physical language by playing "footsie" and even "tried to speak Spanish," but as Bentley observes, "There aren't ever enough words" (181). The words to describe Brooke and Bentley's mutual sexuality are muted by a lack of language. Patriarchal society leaves a disturbing void in the communication of sacred, sexual feelings, the vital flow that we feel in our bodies when connecting with someone. Later Smith protagonists, having embraced a divine feminine language that expresses these natural feelings, find communication ingenuous and invigorating.

Bentley's underground apartment, appropriately dubbed "the pit" (because of its symbolic connection with caves) functions as a world removed from other aspects of Brooke and Bentley's lives. Brooke describes the cool, damp, coziness of her new cavern-like home, with its "rare, strange air" (146) that turns golden when the sun sets. This highly charged emblematic setting that takes the couple into a cave "with its own odd air supply ... [and] underground source of atmosphere" (230) evinces the mystery of the feminine divine. Brooke and Bentley thrive in a place where they confront the possibility for symbolic birth and regeneration.

Once outside the mannered South and having fallen in love with a young man who shares with her a sensual, sexual nature, Brooke feels satisfied and happy, open and exposed, until she experiences ultimate silencing with Bentley, a final reminder that she will not find completion and fulfillment through another person, but only within herself and connection with the feminine divine. The loud music in a club ostensibly prevents Bentley from hearing Brooke when she tells him about her potential pregnancy. When he asks, "*What?*" she replies, "Nothing" (184). Bentley, in failing to hear and acknowledge Brooke's words, symbolically denies the reality of her possible pregnancy. As they leave the club, Brooke again attempts to exercise her voice and be heard when she sees Diana and tells her former roommate about her pregnancy. Diana's response, "Can't hear you" (186), serves as a final denial and muzzle for the open expression of Brooke's feelings. With her menses, the feasibility of pregnancy vanishes, but Brooke's inability to convey this vital information, at such a crucial time, signals the beginning of the demise of Brooke and Bentley's relationship. Smith seems to suggest that open acknowledgment of Brooke's possible pregnancy by both Bentley and Brooke would have provided hope for a permanent connection between the couple, a connection where divine sexuality and motherhood could be coexistent and complementary.

Brooke and Bentley's struggle with their deepening love and sexuality and their mutual search for spiritual fulfillment culminate in a series of seemingly unexplainable, supernatural occurrences that serve to illuminate the couple's increasing capacity for hatred and violence and the subsequent cessation of communication between the two. Like Susan Tobey, Brooke, throughout her early life, has searched for answers and guidance from the patriarchal God but has found traditional religion deadening. Longing for something in which to believe, Brooke feels envious of Diana's religiosity and "holy, mysterious thoughts" that seem foreign to Brooke (80). Diana's personality and actions remind Brooke of her own search for religious guidance at about age ten. As Mrs. Kincaid and her daughter were having lunch at a shopping mall tearoom, Brooke had asked her mother about God. Carolyn had continued eating, then she redirected her daughter's attention to a flower arrangement. Ignoring her young daughter's legitimate concerns, Carolyn changed the subject, dismissing the entire theological issue and silencing the puzzled girl. Later, disillusioned by the absence of any sign of guidance from God, Brooke tells her friend Elizabeth, "I don't believe in anything" (128). It is in her relationship with Bentley that Brooke has opened up enough to experience spirituality linked to the feminine divine through their sacred, sexual union. Although Brooke says as a child she was "big on Jesus," Carolyn demanded that her daughter stop embarrassing her by rededicating her life so often (158). Bentley, the son of a revival preacher, has likewise spent his younger years on a spiritual quest, admitting to Brooke that as a child, he had visions and heard voices, but now he has lost faith in any belief system.

In their womb-like cave, the pit, what Brooke and Bentley encounter as their love deepens and their souls bond is an inexplicable force that neither can accept. Brooke describes the first strange occurrence as "something standing in the doorway" for only a second in the middle of the night. In mentioning that this happens on the night after she and Bentley have seen children playing out the window (a sight that causes Brooke to cry), Brooke makes an unconscious association among children (her possible pregnancy), loss (her sadness at discovering that she is not pregnant), and the mysterious vision.

The nocturnal figure in the doorway portends the rift in Brooke and Bentley's relationship, caused by the impending closure of their once open line of communication. The crucial information about Brooke's possible pregnancy has been buried, left in the dark, and henceforward, the couple will become increasingly less able to communicate and more aggressive and violent in their dealings with one another. Subsequently, Brooke experiences difficulty breathing, representative of her loss of life and voice. Unable to speak, she says, "My voice was stuck somewhere deep inside" (197), but when she finally asks Bentley what he thinks, he denies that anything has happened, squashing her voice just as he has symbolically done by failing to acknowledge her potential pregnancy.

In an effort to understand the presence that has come to inhabit their apartment and in desperate need of spiritual reassurance, Brooke turns to Bentley's hidden Bible, but this effort offers neither consolation nor explanation. Continuing to read mostly the "red parts" (203) over the next couple of days, Brooke finally decides it is all meaningless and gives up. The couple's increasing capacity for violence and hatred and their waning ability to communicate seem to parallel Brooke's Biblical search for answers, a correlation suggestive of the disturbing lacuna and potential danger in a solely patriarchal text. When Bentley first discovers Brooke reading the Bible, he looks frightened as he retrieves the book and tosses it to the floor. Suddenly filled with apparent anger, Bentley, in a near rape, throws Brooke on the couch and bites her neck, then just as abruptly releases her and apologizes, proclaiming his love for her.

With the intensity of Brooke and Bentley's relationship, Smith explores the close association among sexuality, violence, and spirituality. In *Violence and the Sacred*, René Girard insists on the inseparability of violence and sacredness, explaining that the shift from violence to sexuality or from sexuality to violence is a "normal" one (35) since "violence is the signifier of the cherished being, the signifier of divinity" (151). Modern humans, considering sexual violence a pathological deviation from the norm, call this phenomenon *sadism* or *masochism* depending on its manifestation, but Girard asserts that this insistence on the normalcy of nonviolent sexuality is without foundation (144) and that sexual desire is "attracted to violence" and desperately attempts to "incarnate this 'irresistible' force [divinity]" (151). Bentley, having openly admitted to Brooke that he is "the world's only living original religious maniac" (Smith 159), struggles with ostensibly opposing forces, but the preponderance of evidence suggests the inextricability of violence, sexuality, and religion in the relationship between Brooke and Bentley. As communication continues to disintegrate and they stop talking to one another, they also attempt to silence the mysterious presence in their apartment by ignoring it, then pretending it doesn't exist. Their denial seems to manifest itself in their increasing capacity for violence. On an evening when Brooke questions whether she loves or hates Bentley, the couple visits a playground, and as Bentley pushes Brooke higher and higher on a swing, she becomes terrified. She finally jumps out of the swing, twisting her ankle, since Bentley ignores her screams to stop. Increasingly, Bentley's failure to acknowledge Brooke's words, his silencing of her, breeds more violence and separation. Again, as he had done after biting her neck earlier, Bentley apologizes and kisses her "too hard" (220), and they return to the pit to face the force that serves as the impetus for the destruction of their relationship.

The supernatural events—strange noises, blinking lights, and unexplainable drafts—occur only in the enclosed setting of the pit, for when the couple leaves their apartment, Brooke says, "everything was like it had been before" (205). This inexplicable presence seems to represent the spiritual strength of the couple's union. However, neither Brooke nor Bentley understands the enigma and neither possesses the willingness to complete the painful process of integration and regeneration. Instead, they deny, ignore, reject, and ultimately flee from the complexity and wholeness inherent in a permanent bond between them. Ironically, Bentley comes closest to recognition of the significance of the mysterious presence when he remarks that the "fairy godmother came in the night, maybe" (215), but his joking tone disallows a serious interpretation of his words. On the last night Brooke and Bentley spend together, although Brooke says, "neither of us ever mentioned the end of things" (218), she tries to pray to the patriarchal God one more time but finds herself unable to remember anything except "Jesus wept." Her futile attempt at prayer is reminiscent of Susan Tobey's effort on the night of the dogs' visit when she says she can't recall how to pray. A curious mixture of sexuality, violence, and spirituality again surfaces as Brooke massages Bentley's neck and shoulders and senses the opposition of forces with which Bentley has been struggling. She admits "for a minute I hated Bentley more than I loved him. I thought how easy it would be to strangle him"; then just as she moves her hands into position to do so, "pressing in harder all the time," she stops, horrified at the prospect. Brooke describes their lovemaking on this last night together as "violent, a consuming thing" and Bentley's face as "strained and cracked, possessed and almost holy." The interconnection of sexuality, violence, and divinity, manifested by the ethereal presence in the apartment, proves too complicated for Brooke to grasp. When she moves out the next morning, Brooke explains, "Neither of us said a word" (227–29) for "there was nothing left to say." She and Bentley have lost all capability of connection with one another; thus, appropriately, as he leaves her at her old apartment, she feels "unconnected all over" (231).

Brooke intuits that "something in the wind," some unnamed supernatural force, has prevented her from achieving total integration of the two Brookes and thus with another person. However, Smith seems to suggest that both Brooke and Bentley's inability or unwillingness to recognize the presence of divinity within themselves, and also in their union, obviates integration for either character. Just as Antipholus from Shakespeare's *Comedy of Errors*, from which Smith takes the title of the novel, senses some outside force in the wind preventing his entrance into his house, Brooke believes she has battled an opposing force rather than encountered an ally in achieving selfhood. Although subtle, there exists a sense of loss at the end of the novel at Carter's wedding as Brooke clutches her bouquet so tightly that an unwrapped thorn punctures her hand and causes a single drop of blood to fall. Brooke bleeds again, as during sex with Bentley. The thorn that punctures her hand poignantly recalls Brooke's initial penetration by Bentley and her potential integration, when not only Brooke's body was open and exposed, but also her heart and mind. Brooke says she has "come full circle" and resolves to take "new directions" away from the mannered South (243); however, this protagonist has fallen painfully short of completing her spiritual journey.

Although this novel's protagonist is older and comes closer to integration than Susan Tobey, Brooke Kincaid is equally damaged by the unrealistically imposed dichotomy between mind and body. Like Susan and future Smith protagonists, Brooke struggles with internal conflicts concerning sexuality, violence, maternity, and spirituality. Smith's next two novels, *Fancy Strut* and *Black Mountain Breakdown*, shift from the first person point of view of the first two and depict older female protagonists, but in these novels the author again takes the perspective of the daughter, not the mother. Dorothy Hill asserts that the self-destruction evident in Brooke's "accommodation to society" in leaving Bentley and rejecting the chance for integration continues in the next two novels, "where female passivity robs the developing female of her will as she allows cultural images to blot out her self" (31). Without an awareness of the feminine divine or any type of model for sacred integration, these protagonists remain unable to comprehend the complexity and richness of their female nature.

Chapter II

"VISIONS OF RAPE"

Patriarchal Assault in *Fancy Strut* and *Black Mountain Breakdown*

The protagonists of Lee Smith's third and fourth novels, Monica Neighbors of *Fancy Strut* (1973) and Crystal Spangler of *Black Mountain Breakdown* (1980), like the protagonists of Smith's first two novels, both suffer from a split identity based on their acceptance of an inherent incompatibility between expressed sexuality and motherhood and the societally imposed mind/body scission. Both Monica and Crystal search for validation; both are left disappointed with traditional Christianity; both find a path to divinity through sex. In these two novels, Smith uses imagery to suggest the presence of the feminine divine, but neither character achieves integration or embraces her own sacred sexuality to complete her spiritual journey. In her early novels, Smith disallows the coexistence of motherhood and sexuality as qualities within one character. However, *Fancy Strut* and *Black Mountain Breakdown* differ from the first two novels in that the protagonists grow to adulthood and marry during the course of the novels, unlike Susan Tobey and Brooke Kincaid. In all four novels Smith takes the perspective of the daughter, not the mother. At this point in her life and in her writing career, Smith saw the possibilities for women's lives as limited by social and cultural constructions, and her fiction reflects this vision. Only in her later novels will images of fully integrated women be presented and glorified.

Smith's third novel, *Fancy Strut*, breaks from the first person point of view of the first two books as the author begins narrative experimentation and also offers a view of women's limited positions within a community. The story is told by a shifting third person limited omniscient narrator, with each chapter related from a different character's point of view. Inspired by Smith's personal experience as a journalist in Tuscaloosa, Alabama, when she covered the town's 150th anniversary celebration, the novel provides a cross section of a small Southern town during the late 1960s. The "fancy strut" of the title is the actual name of a "stylized German goose step that requires troops trained to behave as a unit and not as individuals" (Hill 35). In the novel, all the members of the community of Speed, Alabama, effectively "strut their stuff," struggling to conform to the rigid conventional codes, thus eradicating the possibility for any individuality or even imagination. *Fancy Strut* indeed presents a dark view of the possibilities for females as the women in town play out their allotted roles in this patriarchal society. Whereas the protagonists of Smith's first two novels, Susan Tobey and Brooke Kincaid, do not within the scope of their respective novels grow to adulthood to become members of a community, the primary women characters of *Fancy Strut* are grown and married, settled into the superficial lives prescribed for them by their culture. They also struggle with sexuality, violence, maternity, and religion as both Susan and Brooke did.

In the novel, Smith explores the sexuality of four major female characters. Monica Neighbors, arguably the leading protagonist since of the novel's thirty-eight chapters a full nine are divulged from her vantage point, comes closest to continuing the development of female identity Smith began in *The Last Day the Dogbushes Bloomed* and continued in *Something in the Wind*. The reader only sees the three other women characters' points of view in two or three chapters each. Of the four major women characters, only one, Sandy DuBois, the oldest, becomes a mother, but Smith de-emphasizes Sandy's maternal role and instead focuses on her sexuality, maintaining the bifurcation between sexuality and maternity.

Expressed sexuality and acceptance of one's body are one facet of the feminine divine, and with her presentation of Sharon DuBois, a teenager and high school majorette, Smith toys with a mythological female archetype. Sharon openly takes pleasure in her body and seems to recognize the power implicit in female sexuality. Resembling Brooke Kincaid in her sexual interest and early exploration, Sharon masturbates in front of her mirrored door. Watching the undulating movement of her body, she wonders about sexual intercourse with an actual man and settles on a plan to seduce men. Nor Hall calls this archetype the "hetaera," an "awakener of desire" who may arouse positive excitement in a lover or, as temptress, may cause a dark side to emerge with great passion and even violence (40–41). Sharon DuBois seems to fit this pattern perfectly in her role as seductress of both her neighbor Bevo Cartwright and her boyfriend Red Hawkins. Bevo, a secret admirer of Sharon, describes her as possessing such vitality that it seems to be bursting through her skin. Smith often portrays sexual females as alive with such energy; they just may not understand yet how to best channel this force. Admitting that he has loved Sharon since the first day he met her, Bevo frequently daydreams of slowly undressing and enjoying Sharon's body. Bevo's sexual frustration leads to an act of desperation at the end of the novel when, in a violent display of passion meant to capture Sharon's attention and admiration, he sets fire to the football stadium during the sesquicentennial pageant. Sharon clearly revels in others' devotion to her (Bevo's as well as Red's), and Smith seems to highlight the normalcy and healthiness of Sharon's open sexuality and autoeroticism, in no way suggesting that Sharon will be trapped in total narcissism. As Hall acknowledges, only under Christian influence did masturbation become associated with shame. In matriarchal societies that worshipped the goddess, exposure of female genitalia was often considered an awesome exhibit of power.

Bevo's twenty-one-year-old divorced sister Ruthie, more like Brooke Kincaid in her sexual promiscuity, further develops Smith's interest in characters that transgress boundaries and embrace their sexuality. Smith describes Ruthie as "not exactly a whore, but ... not exactly not a whore either" (104), emphasizing her liminal position. Whereas Sharon plans to remain a virgin until marriage, Ruthie, the red-headed temptress (the first of a type Smith will use again in later novels), openly admits her sexual vagaries. One particular man, however, presents a new challenge for her when she is unable to manipulate him by withholding sex. Since "Ron-the-Mouth-of-the-South," the famous disc jockey in town to cover the sesquicentennial extravaganza, fails to respond to her sexual teasing, Ruthie is at a loss as to her next move. Although humorous, Ron's nickname suggests his gift for language that Smith consistently links to power and sexuality. Even though Ruthie is anxious to have sex with Ron and has always used sex as a means of controlling men in the past, since Ron doesn't seem particularly desperate, she decides to make him beg. Ultimately, to the great astonishment of her family and past lovers, Ruthie falls in love with Ron, the only man she can't dominate, and he finds in this temperamental tease a woman with whom he desires a permanent arrangement. The equality implicit in their relationship (neither can control the other) serves as an early indication of its longevity. By the end of the novel, Ron and Ruthie are planning a wedding, and Bevo notices something strange happening around his house: Ruthie and his mother Anne begin to fuse; he notes, "Ruthie was merging into Anne" (283). Smith often positions female characters at two extremes that function to illuminate society's imposed sexual dichotomy. The mother, Anne, divorced from her body, fulfills the role of the chaste Southern lady, while her daughter Ruthie openly expresses and embraces her sexuality. In mentioning the "merging" of mother and daughter, perhaps Smith anticipates an integrated female divinely in touch with both her sexuality and her maternal nature.

Smith carefully aligns Sharon's mother, Sandy DuBois, the novel's only sexually expressive mother, with nature and wildness as opposed to domesticity. Although Smith devotes only three chapters to Sandy, concentrating on her affair with Bob Pitt, her cousin's husband, Sandy clearly exemplifies a sexually aggressive adult woman. The name "DuBois," or "of the woods," directly links Sandy to Silvaney of Smith's later novel *Fair and Tender Ladies* and connects Sandy with nature and the feminine divine. To reflect a multifaceted and mysterious female psyche and also suggest the complexity of feminine experience, Smith frequently depicts sexually expressive female characters as simultaneously possessing seemingly contradictory qualities. Linked to divinity in references to her resemblance to a "holy angel" as a child and her choice of angel hair for decorating her house, Sandy also chooses the color "Fire and Ice" for her lipstick (13–14). Smith consistently shows interest in a mixture of the sacred and the profane, a combination which Sandy's character exemplifies. A free spirit who loves physical human contact, Sandy feels comfortable singing along with the radio in a car full of teenage girls, or breaking into a wild fit of laughter. Patricia Yaeger discusses the emancipatory quality of laughter as an advantage for the woman who can say "startling and audacious things," then "underscore their audacity with the madwoman's laughter"; the message is still delivered to the intended audience (196). Yaeger cites Mikhail Bakhtin's description of laughter as an unofficial language that disrupts the "official language of the status quo" (180). Sandy's wild laughter sets her apart from other women as she disrupts the status quo in her extramarital affair with Bob. Even Bob admits that Sandy laughs like no other women he has ever known. Julia Kristeva views laughter as a corporeal expulsion that removes inhibitions by "breaking through prohibition" to reveal an "aggressive, violent, liberating drive" (*Revolution* 224–25). Perhaps Smith's decision to focus on Sandy's laughter reiterates Sandy's sexual aggression as a liberating force. Bob Pitt describes Sandy's fondness for "doing crazy things" when he tells of the occurrence in the grocery store when she corners him and touches "his privates" (92). Although he calls Sandy's behavior "crazy," Bob later admits that this was the most exciting thing that had ever happened to him. Acknowledging that Sandy is "vain and mean" and even a "bitch" (96), Bob, however, knows he has always loved her, even in high school. Reveling in the intrigue of motel rooms and different sexual experiences, Sandy delights in sex with both Bob Pitt and her husband, Johnny B. Sandy's choice of a costume for the sesquicentennial pageant also reflects her wildness as opposed to domesticity. Rather than dressing as a staid Puritan like most of the wives, Sandy wears a scant Indian costume that resembles animal hide, and her red, full lips emphasize her sensuality. Sandy, comfortable with sexual expression and in touch with the sacredness of feminine experience, is the active, aggressive adult female that society finds difficult to accept.

Smith presents another desexed woman (similar to Ruthie and Bevo's mother) in Bob's wife and Sandy's cousin, Frances Pitt. Bob explains that he married Frances because she was "religious and serious" and should make a perfect wife and mother for his children (96). A common assumption that women are either sexual or spiritual (never both) is clearly evident in Bob's belief that Frances' religious nature explains her asexuality. As much a victim of patriarchal religion as his wife, Bob believes religion and sexuality exist in two completely separate realms. But after becoming a successful accountant

II. "Visions of rape"

and enduring years of ball games and family vacations, he realizes at age thirty-five that he has completely missed something. Bob has accepted long ago that his wife does not enjoy sex; "she undressed in the closet, and wore long-legged pajamas to bed" (290–91). Smith admits that women raised in the South were taught to hide their sexuality and that any bodily drive or function was "dirty" (Loewenstein 501–502). Frances Pitts' husband, however, feels left out, so he turns to Sandy, who brings out his animalistic nature and fulfills his sexual desires.

In the novel, Smith's major interest lies with Monica Neighbors, the young wife of the highly respected and quite wealthy newspaper editor, Manly Neighbors, since Monica suffers from a split identity not unlike Brooke Kincaid. Another sexual creature, Monica is drawn to natural, growing things, particularly roses (consistently representative of female sexuality in Smith's work), reminiscent of Susan's mother of *Dogbushes*. Younger than Sandy, Monica has been married only three years but already is restless, at first trying to use her overflowing energy in a socially acceptable way by repeatedly redecorating a brand new home. Monica represents a grown-up Brooke after a few years of marriage, with her identity even more divided. For three years, Monica has been a model wife, or so it seems, but suddenly she feels on the verge of madness. Like Brooke, Monica has split herself into a public self and a private self, refusing to even attempt to integrate the two. While presenting the outward appearance of a happy housewife, she secretly harbors fantasies of sexual degradation. Even though Monica's husband has made it clear that he wants children and doesn't understand his wife's desire to wait, Monica shudders at the thought of pregnancy.

Monica struggles with the separation between mind and body that earlier Smith protagonists battled in their efforts to achieve a sense of sacred wholeness. Monica's sexuality is revealed when Smith explains that the summer before Monica married Manly, while on a trip to Europe, she had casual sex with several Italians and one Swede, "just to prove ... she could do it." Although Monica rationalizes that sleeping with Europeans doesn't count as promiscuous behavior, she calls the experience "lovely, a lark." Away from the restraints of Southern society, Monica had enjoyed purely physical liaisons with strangers. However, upon returning home, she is plagued by guilt and feels extremely grateful to Manly for marrying her. She explains she had "especially needed somebody like Manly" (33), someone she believes can rescue her from her sexual vagaries. Never attempting to integrate her European experience and reconcile her sexuality with her role in Southern society, Monica marries a fatherly man whom she perceives as a "Teddy bear" (177), someone to save her from the burden of self-discovery. Since her lifestyle demands that she have a lovely home and a full-time maid, she does, even though she despises the meddling housekeeper.

Although Manly seems the perfect husband in all outward respects, he reifies the mind-body split and therefore fails to assist Monica in her spiritual search for integration. Monica desperately wants to be needed by her husband, but Manly, the victim of an overactive rational mind and undeveloped sexuality, thinks he has no problem he cannot logically solve by merely analyzing it. He loves Monica, but he doesn't need her sexually or in any other way, and her behavior puzzles him. He resolves that women are not meant to be understood anyway, but rather they are to be "reverenced and protected," perfectly articulating the age-old (Southern) practice of placing women on pedestals to be admired but not touched. Manly's inability to understand his wife is captured when he notices Monica daydreaming and thinks, "What did she have to daydream about? What could she be thinking of that was not real and present and accounted for?" (172). The obvious irony is that she dreams of something Manly could never imagine: driving to a sleazy motel to meet a lover with whom her sexuality is unrestrained, even secretly harboring the "wild hope" that Manly will "burst through that door" and "rip off her Tanner dress so violently that the buttons would sound like bullets," or perhaps "strip her and set her up on the coffee table and make her do terrible things" (177–78). But Manly only stands and stares at his wife, wondering what's for dinner, not recognizing his wife's starved expression since the only starvation he understands is caused by a need for food. Dorothy Hill insightfully describes Manly as one of Smith's "self-consciously desexed and self-castrated" men, "cut off from their sexuality and aggressiveness" (38), a man who, due to his own acceptance of the dichotomy between mind and body, reinforces his wife's bifurcated view.

When Monica encounters Buck Fire, an out-of-work actor and the professional manager of the pageant, the conflict between her mind and her body begins. Monica and Buck literally collide on the stairs of the pageant headquarters, and even at this first meeting, Buck grasps her buttocks for a "quick feel." The ambiguity of Monica's response prompts Buck to "lick her belt buckle experimentally" (43). Buck, also a sexual being, as his name clearly suggests, thinks there's "no risk in screwing the married" and plans to "love-'em-and-leave-'em panting" (36). At first, he considers Monica boring and unattractive, but after their collision when she turns red with embarrassment, Buck decides she harbors a secret desire for him. Sexually aroused by her first brush with Buck, Monica feels uncomfortable and desires the safety and assurance of her husband, so she rushes home, "the thought of Manly fill[ing] her with love or something close enough" (45). She still thinks she can suppress her sexuality as long as she stays away from Buck Fire, but soon she begins to fantasize about him. Monica's thoughts reflect her confused feelings: "She realized that she was real in her daydreams, and real in her house with Manly. But not here. She was not at all real" with Buck (133–34). So, reality encompasses life with Manly and she can daydream within that reality, but when the fantasy comes to life, it doesn't seem real. Monica's awareness of the sacredness

II. "Visions of rape"

of feminine experience and its concomitant sense of wholeness are blocked by this false scission between flesh and spirit.

Smith often investigates a character's capacity for sacredness and connection with the feminine divine by exploring her dreams or fantasies. Recalling fantasies or daydreams is crucial in the emergence into consciousness for a woman. Monica's daydreams supply her with vital information to fill the gaping void in her life. Monica's sexuality emerges with increasing intensity as her affair with Buck progresses. The first time he puts his arm around her and fondles her breast, she flushes, saying she "felt like she was crashing and burning, a way she had not felt for years" (137). Smith consistently associates fire with the open expression of sexuality. Very soon after their first sexual encounter, Monica perceives there is no longer a dream lover, but rather a combat within her between Manly and Buck, a contest between the two sides of herself. With no hint of integration, Monica allows her mind to struggle against her body in a battle that ensures defeat for her, either way. Buck calls Monica "wild," admitting "she can wear him out" (243). Monica, like Sandy, is linked to wildness rather than domesticity, as are many of Smith's sexual females. As Monica lives out her fantasy of an illicit love affair and performs sexual acts she's never even considered with her husband, Buck satisfies in Monica the need the ironically named Manly leaves unfulfilled. Monica thinks with satisfaction she'll go straight to hell, having given in to the desires of the flesh, but then she decides she doesn't believe in the existence of hell anyway.

Smith's description of Monica's lover, Buck Fire, is rife with religious connotations and foreshadows the full development of the sacred male with Honey Breeding of *Fair and Tender Ladies*. In a personal interview, Smith explained her feeling that sexual passion has a power similar to religious passion; therefore, a character often searches for spiritual intensity in a sexual relationship since both sexual and religious ecstasy take a person "totally outside yourself" (Byrd 100). Often, after a sexual experience, a female character feels "born again"; by expressing her sacred sexuality, she has reclaimed her body. When Buck walks around in and out of a patch of sunlight, "it had seemed to Monica that he was not only illumined but transfigured," and her sexual experience with him proves both illuminating and transformative. With the description of his hair glowing "a thousand colors in the sun ... from palest yellow to brightest red to black" and his "astonishing gold shirt" reflecting the sunlight and "sho[oting] it back in rays," Smith establishes Buck's divinity and even evokes the image of Christ with a glowing halo. When Monica first sees Buck, she perceives him as a "new and startling dimension ... unlike any man she had ever known.... Like a damn Annunciation." Smith's diction clearly implies Buck's association with Christ, his arrival in Monica's life signaling the opportunity for sacred union, or salvation. Observing Buck, Monica says, "Oh Jesus" (41–43); then, at the sight of his bare chest, she thinks "Oh Christ" (208). When Monica goes to Buck's apartment for the first time, she feels she's entering another world. Establishing his close connection with Monica, Smith describes Buck's hand as "almost exactly the same size" as Monica's (210). Monica and Buck are the first of many couples in Smith who are described as being the same physical size, suggesting their equality in a reciprocal, nonsacrificial relationship. Like Ruthie and Ron, neither Monica nor Buck dominates; rather, they divinely complement one another in their mutual enjoyment of sacred sexuality.

Smith's interest in language and women's need for expression in a patriarchal society most strongly emerges in this novel with her portraiture of Monica. Like Brooke, having been silenced for so long, her voice not heard or acknowledged by anyone, Monica kicks the chaise lounge in her bedroom and orders it to speak to her. Smith emphasizes Monica's sense of aloneness with the understatement, "It was silent" (29). Nor does she get any direct reaction from Manly no matter what she says or does; he is too much in control. Monica's daydreams of illicit sex usually involve a different kind of silence, however. Envisioning silence, Monica imagines "no words spoken..., just the fierce crush of their violent embrace" (33). Reminiscent of Brooke who wanted to invent a whole new language for the sexual love between her and Bentley, Monica finds the English language inadequate to express sexual feelings.

Historian and pioneer of women's studies Gerda Lerner explains the language of spiritual union as a conundrum, "words that manage to express the inadequacy of words" (67); perhaps Monica senses such an insufficiency in patriarchal language. Because women's sexuality has been muted by a lack of language, females have long remained silent. At one point in the novel, Monica even admits her dislike of conversation; conventional language cannot convey her feelings. With Buck Fire, Monica finds herself "off in a new place where she [does]n't think at all and everything [is] touch" (Smith 210). Separating her mind from her body, she rediscovers sexual pleasure. The inability of language to capture the essence of the sensual is reiterated at the end of the novel when Miss Iona Flowers, the self-appointed "custodian of beauty and truth in Speed, the champion of the pure and good" (4), has a vision of the perfect pageant that is far removed from the actual one. She stresses the impossibility of articulating "through normal language" what had "no recognizable form." She says that instead, the pageant's meaning was "assimilated directly into the senses without being translated into blocks of language and forced through the mill of the mind" (278). The mind, where language originates, seems to be a world away from the body, which can feel and express the sensuality of certain experiences. Smith's diction also suggests the difficulty and pain of forcing "blocks of language" through the "mill of the mind," hinting that sensual experiences cannot be translated into language. As Smith's spiritual journey of writing continues, she and her characters find an available language, one that encompasses the feminine divine.

As another protagonist whom patriarchal religion leaves unfulfilled, Monica, in search of selfhood, makes the conscious decision to wallow in what she believes to be the degradation represented by her sexual relationship with Buck. She describes the affair as merely "[f]ucking Buck" (285), while, ironically, Buck Fire, the carefree ladies' man, has fallen in love with Monica. Unable to integrate her sexuality into her life with Manly, Monica believes she must choose either Buck and the physical pleasure he provides, or Manly and the stability and boundaries he represents. Even though the affair with Buck transforms Monica's understanding of her own sexuality, at the end she chooses what Anne Goodwyn Jones calls the "permanence and guilt" of her relationship with Manly (127). After sleeping with Buck for the last time, she decides that perhaps she has successfully lived out a fantasy that will now vanish. The affair quickly fades into a past separated from Monica's "real" life. At the end, with neither fantasy lover nor real one, she feels "worn out and empty and suddenly brittle and just a little bit old." She does try to express her sexual passion with Manly, but he doesn't understand, respond, or accept it, reminiscent of Houston's rejection of Brooke's sexual advances. But unlike Brooke, who ends the relationship with Houston, Monica resolves to stay with Manly, thinking, "At least he can always get it up." Surely Smith intends for us to note the puns with her choice of characters' names; Monica's husband will never have the "fire" of a "buck," but after all, he is at least "manly" at some basic physical level. The futility Monica feels about being misunderstood and her final resignation to it are illustrated in a vision she has of Manly finding a note inside a bottle that has washed up on the shore: "It was as though Manly had found her, picked her up off a beach someplace where she had drifted, and dusted her off and kept her carefully among his most prized possessions. But he couldn't read the note" (322–24). In contrast to Buck, Manly owns Monica as he would a treasure, all the while unable to "read" or understand her sexual nature and desire for passion and physical aggression.

With no hope of ever expressing her sexuality with her husband, Monica chooses the community-validated path that had been so disgusting to her earlier; she tells Manly that she's ready to have a baby. Ironically, earlier in the novel, just after Monica has met Buck Fire but before their affair, she makes an unconscious connection between sexuality and motherhood when, bursting with pent-up sexual frustration, she admits that she feels "pregnant" with things "building up and preparing to explode" (199). At this time she sees motherhood as a grim alternative. Monica views pregnancy and motherhood as totally separate and apart from sexuality, and in choosing to remain with Manly, suppress her sexuality, and become a mother, she has opted for an unfulfilled life that she believes to be a secure one. Monica, not yet ready for self-knowledge and divine integration, falls victim to the popular notion of the antinomy between erotic nature and the maternal feminine.

As in the first two novels, in *Fancy Strut* Smith associates sex with violence, and Monica, torn between mind and body, is the character who most often makes the connection. Feeling like an "impostor" (32) married under false pretenses, Monica secretly revolts against Manly's "goddamn Boy Scout" (34) ways by driving too fast without a seat belt while imagining meetings with a fantasy lover. In her daydreams, Monica fantasizes about passionate but violent sex with Manly. She longs for the intensity, the passion, the sexual and spiritual connection. Monica's attraction to violence again surfaces after a rendezvous with Buck. As Monica leaves Buck's apartment, she remembers an experience she had in Atlanta of walking down the street wondering what was happening behind people's windows. She imagined scenes of murder and other forms of violence. Now, after beginning an affair with Buck, she feels she has "done it herself, committed the unusual, the illicit, the extraordinary act" (213), directly associating her sexual act with these violent crimes. Trapped within patriarchy and its stereotypical view of female passivity, Monica can understand sexual aggression only in terms of violence, not in a positive way. At the end of the novel when the football stadium fire has ended the sesquicentennial pageant and rioting has broken out in the town, Monica, safe with Manly in his second story office, remembers her "old dreams of rape [that] had often included riots" (321). With rioting, Smith suggests people's common need for disturbance and disruption in this small Southern town's rigidly prescribed codes of behavior that so stifle imagination and individuality. The concatenation of Monica's propensity for aggression (now receded to her daydreams) and the citizens' uncontrolled violence deliver a salient message about the hostility bred by suppression. Now, resolved to stay with a husband who never questions anything, Monica ignores the "visions of rape danc[ing] in her head" since she thinks she won't "need them any more for a while" (323). Monica obviously feels that to express her sexuality and receive any sexual satisfaction, some sort of violence must be present, and with calm, collected, and controlled Manly, this hardly seems possible. Crystal Spangler, of Smith's next novel, will share Monica's fascination with and attraction to violence, particularly in its relation to sexuality. Victims of patriarchy's dichotomized view of women, Monica and Crystal stand in stark contrast to their respective Southern societies in their alignment with what René Girard calls the normalcy of "violence in awakening [sexual] desire" (144). In their longing for intense passion, Monica and Crystal are equally drawn to violence and aggression, but both are willing to settle for unfulfilling lives void of the fervor they so desire.

In *Black Mountain Breakdown,* Smith continues her journey, writing a protagonist who epitomizes the passive female torn between society's conflicting values. Eventually permanently silenced, she is paralyzed by her inability to achieve integration. Originally a short story entitled "Paralyzed: A True Story" and told from the unsympathetic point of view of Agnes McClanahan, *Black Mountain Breakdown* tells the story not only of a young girl's stunted maturation process, but also of a changing community. Smith's interest in cultural change and the effects of the passage of time in small secluded mountain communities persists in much of her writing. Smith said that one of her aims in writing the novel was to capture the way it was growing up in that time. The novel is set in rural western Virginia in a small town named Black Rock, a town loosely based on Smith's hometown memories of Grundy. With a tragic tone, Smith couples the third person point of view with present verb tense to achieve a careful tension. So, although Crystal doesn't tell her own story, the omniscient narrator's present verb tense creates a striking sense of immediacy. Crystal's experience echoes those of Susan Tobey and Brooke Kincaid, and to a lesser degree Monica Neighbors, but Crystal is, by Smith's admission, a more extreme case than the lost female characters in the earlier novels. Agnes, Crystal's best friend and foil in the novel, observes, "Crystal seems to lack something, some hard thing inside her" that others are born with (16). Crystal is a striking contradiction, a reflection of what others want her to be. Thus, Crystal embarks on her journey to adulthood caught within the same conflict as previous Smith protagonists. Her sexual nature is unacceptable in society's eyes, but it is only through her sensuality, her sexuality, her divine connection to nature, that she even approaches an identity of her own.

Crystal's name describes her nature perfectly. Feeling totally transparent, she must stand beside or opposite something to gain any substance at all. As Crystal studies herself in the mirror and imagines different identities, she cannot settle on one image, but constantly changes identities as she searches for her selfhood. In mythology, mirrors, common tools in initiation ceremonies, provide entrance into the spiritual world of self-discovery. Crystal's gazing into mirrors throughout the novel represents her deep longing for self-discovery as she imagines various identities for herself. Even other people become Crystal's mirrors as she continuously looks to them for self-definition. Smiling at everyone in order to gain easy popularity, Crystal becomes what people want her to be, not retaining enough individuality even to adopt her own unique handwriting. (Brooke Kincaid also changed her handwriting as she changed identities.) As a crystal refracting light, Crystal deflects all individuality away from herself and onto those around her. Crystal feels alive only when people are pleased with her and notice her. The sole ninth grader chosen for cheerleader, Crystal quickly attracts the attention of high school boys, and like Brooke, she begins to define herself through them; "it's only when she's with boys that she feels pretty, or popular, or fun. In the way they talk to her and act around her, Crystal can see what they think of her, and then that's the way she is" (136). However, unlike Brooke who perceives her real self as hidden inside her, Crystal sees her real self as something supplied to her by a force outside herself, usually a man. For Crystal, no connection exists between the outside and the inside.

For her protagonists, Smith consistently imagines male counterparts who are nonconformists, often shocking and unusual in appearance and manners, in order to suggest the necessary disturbance of the status quo in awakening a female character's sacred sexuality. Mack—like Bentley and Buck before him, and *Fair and Tender Ladies'* Honey Breeding, *The Devil's Dream*'s Wayne Ricketts and Black Jack Johnny, *Saving Grace*'s Randy Newhouse, and *On Agate Hill*'s Jacky Jarvis after him—represents the sexual, physical component of love as he arouses the erogenous aspects of Crystal. Crystal begins to feel a connection between her two worlds when she starts dating Mack Stiltner, the high school dropout with a bad reputation, but after the couple's break-up, her split identity resurfaces with even greater force. Since with Mack Crystal says she can be her true self, she would rather be with Mack than anyone else. Considering the sexual freedom her relationship with Mack offers, Crystal decides, "it means she can fuck him if she wants to, which she does" (97). Following her break-up with Mack, she experiences religious salvation at a local revival, but she admits that her relationship with Mack seems to have more connection to real life than does her salvation. Crystal's communion with Mack, in fact, serves as a type of salvation for her; he houses the potential to "save" her from her own passivity. The divine nature of their mutual sexuality is more "real" to Crystal than experiencing salvation in the imposed patriarchal religion that denies women both physical pleasure and a voice. Without Mack, she resumes imagining other selves.

Similar to several of Smith's earlier female characters who exhibit open sexuality, Crystal's sexuality is likewise related to her love of nature and her acute senses. Smith has said the most sacred experiences occur in nature. Like Sandy DuBois, whom Smith associates with nature rather than culture, and even Monica Neighbors, who loves growing flowers, the author aligns Crystal with the natural rather than the cultural, revealing Smith's continuing interest in the intricate connection between female sexuality and nature. As Crystal wraps Christmas ornaments for storage, her hands "move silently like birds" (63), reminiscent of *Dogbushes*' Queen's fluttering movements. On her first date with Mack, not only his presence, but also the sweet smells of outdoors and warm wind blowing across her face awaken Crystal's senses in a scene conducive to the feminine divine. Crystal feels intoxicated with the profusion of nature, the smells which always remind her of Mack and are consistently associated with Crystal's sexuality. Later, when she and Agnes go swimming after Crystal has been cooped up reading the Bible for days, the colors of the mountains and sky excite her. As she sunbathes, Crystal loves the sensation of the hot cement burning her body through the towel and the "grainy scratchy" feeling when she moves (127). Throughout the novel, Crystal's continuous interest in textures and patterns manifests her elevated sense of touch. Part of her "crystal"-ness seems related to not only her receptivity to other people, but also her sensitivity to sensory stimuli. As a child, she fingers her father's bathrobe hem and the lace on the armchair in the parlor as Grant reads poetry to her. The first scene of the novel describes Crystal tracing the raised lettering on a Mason jar she plans to use for capturing fireflies. Later, at the old homeplace at Dry Fork, she touches the carved initials of her father on a window sill and fingers Uncle Devere's flannel shirts that hang in the closet. Crystal's sensuousness connects her to her body, thus to nature, and offers an awakening to the divine in everyday feminine experiences.

In Smith, women divorced from nature and their bodies remain at odds with their own feminine nature and never achieve divine integration. Unconnected with nature or the senses, Crystal's mother, Lorene Spangler, has difficulty understanding Crystal's desire to stay outside at night catching fireflies and enjoying the outdoors. Like Carolyn Kincaid, Lorene's primary concern lies with appearance; she insists that her daughter start rolling her hair at age twelve. Lorene considers her husband a fool and a bad influence on Crystal, but she ignores this and anything else she doesn't like, consoling herself by spouting off empty platitudes. Even though Lorene calls Crystal the "child of her old age, the joy of her heart" (21) and centers her whole life on this beautiful, perfect little girl, Lorene is only satisfied when Crystal conforms to her mother's expectations. Lorene wants to shape Crystal into her version of the perfect woman—a beauty, a trophy, a prize, reminiscent of Manly's image of Monica as a treasure.

Like earlier Smith protagonists, Crystal initially tries the conventional path of Southern women, the one validated by those around her, but her emerging sexuality, a source of confusion and fascination, prevents her from finding contentment. Crystal "decide[s] to be in love with Roger Lee," the football star and high school hero, at first ignoring Mack Stiltner, the "mean country boy" who keeps staring at her (51). Although Roger promises to provide Crystal with a lifetime of happiness, she senses a void in their relationship. Exaggerating the dichotomy between mind and body, Smith aligns Crystal's thoughts of sexuality with the animal world, a mindless world. What is absent with Crystal and Roger is the naturalness of physical, sexual love. In invoking her mother's injunction against premarital sex, Crystal adheres to the socially validated notion of separation of mind and body. Ironically however, despite her mother's warnings, Crystal soon engages in premarital sex with not only Mack, but also anyone she happens to date. Whereas Crystal cannot imagine "petting" with Roger (although she thinks she's in love with him), with Mack later she never considers the matter; her sexuality is awakened with no analysis of the situation.

Smith suggests early Mack's potential for healing the split between Crystal's mind and body when, by merely thinking of Mack, Crystal's feels stomach discomfort she describes as "weird" (57). When Crystal goes on a picnic with Roger Lee and considers petting with him, she thinks of Mack Stiltner, though they have not spoken to each other at this point. Crystal's somatic symptoms, brought on by thoughts of Mack, link to Crystal's childhood rape when afterwards, although she has suppressed this traumatic experience, she compares the pain to menstrual "cramps" (71). From this point on in the novel, a strange, uncomfortable sensation in her stomach marks the emergence of her sexuality, and later it signals her ecstatic religious experience, thus establishing a connection between the sexual and the religious. With Crystal Spangler, Smith initiates the body-spirit connection that continues to shape the feminine experience in her writing.

Crystal finds a sacred spot, a hallowed feminine space, in the cave-like parlor of her father. Grant Spangler represents Crystal's gateway to the mysterious world of fantasy, poetry, and language, and her fascination with stories, both true and made-up, ties her to both Susan Tobey and Brooke Kincaid in their common desire for a voice of their own and a language in which to express themselves.* Capturing his young daughter's imagination with tales of the past, Grant tells romantic stories and some that Crystal considers grotesque—of men being shot and hanged. As Grant's health deteriorates, he increasingly craves the company of his daughter; however, when others try to communicate with him, he "turns his face to the wall" (53). Even though Grant is slowly dying, Crystal won't allow herself to believe it and finds within his darkened parlor, where he has secluded himself, a warm and protective environment, a retreat into the symbolic womb of the cave where she receives nourishing words from her father. Nor Hall explains the ancient belief that wild honey, called "divine amniotic fluid," could be found hidden in divine caves attended by giant bees. In the cave, one might partake of the sweet manna and receive "the gift of honeyed speech, a golden tongue, a promise of nourishing words" (25–26). In the cave-like parlor where Grant reads to Crystal, she experiences regeneration, thriving on the words her father provides and discovering a voice with which to express her innermost feelings. As father and daughter share a love for language, Grant reads poetry to her, eliciting Crystal's deepest emotions.

Smith links the "nourishing words" of Crystal's father to Crystal's literal survival. With the double tragedy of her father's death, immediately after her brutal rape at age fourteen, Crystal is forever damaged. The memory of Crystal's rape at Dry Fork by Uncle Devere submerges deep in her subconscious mind right after it occurs, not to resurface until sixteen years later. Like Susan Tobey, Crystal is silenced by the assault, robbed of the language to express her pain. After the rape, which initially the reader only suspects, Crystal feels sick and faint; all she knows is that "something hurts her so bad" (70). Mistaking the discomfort for symptoms of a virus, Crystal takes aspirin and drinks her Aunt Nora's hot mint tea before sleeping a heavy, dreamless sleep. Perhaps Crystal's failure to dream from this time on suggests her inability to go beneath

---

*In light of Smith's consistent association of breath and wind with goddess imagery, it is interesting to note that Grant's emphysema deprives him of the ability to breathe normally. Grant's desire for Crystal's presence suggests his need for his daughter to provide him with the breath of life, the inspiration to survive. Lorene ignores anything she doesn't understand, so her blindness to the relevance of Grant's relationship with Crystal comes as no surprise.

the surface of ordinary experience and achieve self-knowledge through remembering and acknowledging the rape. Without dreams, Crystal lacks an important tool that could allow her to achieve integration. The nightmare that has just occurred is soon followed by another, perhaps even more painful one, when Crystal returns home the next morning to discover her dead father alone in the house. Crystal feels "the whole world fall away from her by degrees until nothing at all is left" (72), once more robbed of a voice since her father was her source of and inspiration for language. As her aunt attempts to silence Crystal, shouting, "You shut up that hollering, now" (76), Crystal, her eyes "full of fire," clings to her father's body and begs to remain with him. Then, turning on her mother, Crystal spits and screams, "Get away from me. Get out of here. Don't you *think* about touching me!" (78–79). Crystal manages to attend the funeral without saying a word or shedding a tear, but she "feels as empty as light, somewhere outside herself" as her mind and body separate and she watches "herself walk up the aisle, then sit, then walk back out at the end" (81). Despite her cool exterior, Crystal is consumed by rage when her family tries to remove her from her father's grave. Once again, just as she remained by her father's side in the parlor, she feels paralyzed and refuses to leave the site. As her family forces her from her chair, Crystal finally finds enough voice to scream, expressing the pain that she alone seems to feel.

In her portrayal of Crystal, Smith dallies with the medial feminine, an archetype possessing the ability to foresee change. Crystal's eyes, described as "lakes" holding mystical reflective power, betray painful "secrets in them" (91). In mythology, crystal formations (an idea that surfaces in the modern world with the debased crystal ball) hold essential mysteries that are revealed in what Jung came to call "crystal language." Crystal exhibits an instinctual sense of the future on several occasions, most notably at the revival when she experiences religious salvation and again at Girls' State where she encounters an enigmatic presence. This "gift of discernment," always powerfully linked in Smith's work to spirituality and the feminine divine, reaches full development in Florida Grace Shepherd of *Saving Grace*. As Crystal is drawn to Mack Stiltner, she seems for the first time "self-possessed" (87). From the outset, when Crystal sees Mack staring at her, she intuits their magnetism. Even before they go out, when Crystal encounters Mack in town, she feels weak, "the way she feels when she considers the circulation of the blood" (55). Her intuition immediately connects Mack to a life-giving force, a natural process that Smith consistently ties to sacred feminine experience.

Similar to Brooke and Bentley, then Monica and Buck, Crystal and Mack offer another early version of the divine couple in Smith's fiction. Crystal and Mack also struggle with language in its inability to convey sexual feelings. After they make love, "they lie on the mattress all tangled up, not talking, and the fresh air from outside blows in across them as softly as breath" (98), Smith's diction here suggestive of the feminine divine. No words are necessary between

Crystal and Mack; they are soul mates. The only person who understands Crystal's desire to "*have it all*" (102), Mack admits his similar aspirations, then explains that the only difference between Crystal and him is that he realizes the impossibility of this goal and Crystal doesn't. When Mack shares with Crystal a song he wrote about her "angel hair" and its sharpness, keeping him at a distance from her, Crystal becomes uncomfortable and confused, feeling "all lost inside" (100). Although attracted to Mack as to nature itself, Crystal feels exposed and becomes vulnerable in his presence. Smith often describes a protagonist's openness to her sacred sexuality and the divinity in feminine experience in terms of an exposed wound that needs healing. Around Mack, Crystal feels the same way she does in biology class when studying the circulation of the blood and she has to run out of the classroom to avoid screaming. Crystal's behavior confuses even Mack. On their first date, with his constant reminder to slow down, "she was all over him immediately, like somebody from up in the hollers" (95). Able to express openly her sexuality with Mack, Crystal admits she usually "comes before he does" (98) and even achieves orgasm at home alone while just thinking about him.

Crystal's relationship with Mack and its concomitant intensity and exposure elicit from Crystal fear of the symbolic cave and rebirth. In Mack's song, Smith again mixes the sacred with the profane in her depiction of Crystal's divine, "angelic" qualities that are equally extremely dangerous. The words of the song demonstrate Mack's understanding and acceptance of Crystal, but she, like Brooke, is unable, or unwilling, to face self-knowledge and regeneration represented by the cave. In the ensuing argument between Mack and Crystal, he challenges her to own for once her passion, but Crystal, extremely distraught, wishes for a minute that Mack were Roger, longing for the safety of a distant arrangement like the one she and Roger had. In his song, Crystal recognizes immediately Mack's ability to penetrate her soul. Mack is symbolically capable of making Crystal "bleed," further explaining his consistent association with blood throughout the novel and the attendant opportunity for new life and regeneration. Crystal's relationship with Roger offered safety since it did not threaten to disturb her carefully constructed exterior, but with Mack, the danger of exposure and penetration proves too great. Mack asks Crystal to marry him and go to Nashville with him, but Crystal cannot make any decision; instead, she chooses to allow others to determine her identity and her desires.

The communion between Mack and Crystal is suggested by not only their similar physical sizes, like other couples in Smith, and their mutual link to nature (his mouth is compared to a bird's and Crystal consistently associates him with nature), but also Mack's blatant remark to Crystal, "we're two of a kind, baby, we're just alike, you and me" (102). Unlike Bentley who denied the depth of his bond with Brooke, Mack recognizes and accepts the sacredness of the union between Crystal and him. He realizes that Crystal's unwillingness to risk the pain of self-knowledge remains an impervious barrier between them. Perhaps it is Mack and his piercing song that Crystal thinks of years later, long after Mack has gone to Nashville and become successful, when her older brother Jules calls in the middle of the night to share his sadness at the limitations of his own love life. Crystal feels as though her brother has "reached down inside her and plucked one note on an antique musical instrument, and the echo goes on and on, a high painful keening note" (186). The antique instrument suggests Mack's song and recalls a moment early in the novel where his mouth is compared to a "musical instrument" (97). Jules' phone call painfully reminds Crystal of the kind of love she felt for Mack and the potential union that offered integration and regeneration.

The strong link between sexual passion and religious intensity apparent in most of Smith's works surfaces in Crystal's experience of salvation at a local revival. For Crystal, religious salvation becomes tied to the intense feelings she had with Mack, consistently associated with nature. As Crystal sits on the porch with Agnes and Jubal Thacker (the young Holiness preacher), she wonders if Jubal ever "hears voices" or has "seen God's face" (112), then remembers Mack as she notices the sweet smell of the trumpet vine and feels "she's going to die" (115). It is, in fact, fear of metaphorical death (of her passivity) and the accompanying pain of rebirth that the sweet, sacred union with Mack offered that halted their relationship. As Jubal talks about salvation, Crystal once again experiences the same sensations she felt with Mack: "the hair along [her] arms rises at the sound of Jubal's voice," and she "feels funny in the pit of her stomach, and the trumpet vine smells sweet." In this setting, the ingredients that have come to suggest the presence of the feminine divine in Smith's writing are interwoven: the power of language in Jubal's "soft, disembodied voice" (116), the preponderance of sexuality represented by the sensation in Crystal's stomach, the sweet sensuality of nature, and the concept of death and rebirth in Crystal's thoughts of dying.

Smith beautifully weaves together images of Crystal's sexual nature with traces of her spiritual self when Crystal attends a local revival. Crystal continues to experience a strange sensation in her stomach on her way to the worship service, where she is drawn physically into the ecstatic ritual. As the choir sings and Crystal, unsaved, considers her own death, she feels "fear shoot[ing] straight through the middle of her like a sweet sharp knife" (119). Smith's diction poignantly captures the dualism that has become second nature for Crystal. Although "sweet" and "sharp" at first seem incongruous, the two adjectives sharply recall the words of Mack's song about Crystal's "angel hair" and also demonstrate the complexity of the sensation Crystal experiences as she is equally drawn to, and terrified by, the spirituality that envelops her. Smith explains ecstatic religious conversion as a person's being "compelled and repelled in almost the same measure," that this "sort of giving over" initially feels like the loss of self, which is "absolutely terrifying" (Byrd 97). Ironically, Crystal feels no fear at this prospect since she finds comfort only outside herself in self-definition from external forces. In her salvation experience, in the giving of self in spirit as much as in flesh, she feels truly alive. Crystal's stomach "feels funny" again as she "tastes death in her mouth all sugary and metallic, like sucking a scab." Connoting electricity, the sensation begins "shooting straight into her head and all down her body." She feels again "like she felt when she was with Mack—alive, fully alive and fully real, more than real" (123–24). The physical sensations Crystal's ecstatic religious experience incites directly parallel her feelings of sexual euphoria with Mack.

Even the description of the people and setting at the tent revival teems with sexual imagery. Smith writes, "Something is going to happen here, and they're ready for it. They want it. It's hot and dry ... and Crystal licks her lips" (122). As Crystal stands to approach the altar, she notices a woman nursing her baby, and the sight of the "swell of fat veined breast and the baby's mouth on it and its moving cheeks" causes Crystal's stomach to hurt again. In associating Crystal's stomach pain, linked to her sexuality, with the sight of a nursing mother, Smith evokes the image of the feminine divine in her incarnation as goddess of both sexuality and maternity. Female sexuality, motherhood, and religious ecstasy are interwoven to evince the essence of the fully integrated female deity. As Crystal walks down the church aisle, falls to her knees, and makes her conversion experience public, she feels "every part of her mind and body ... on fire, flaming, a keen high white flame" (124), the image of fire consistently associated with sexual passion in Smith's work. Crystal will continue to crave this level of fervidity, but for her, it will not endure.

When Crystal attends Girls' State after her senior year of high school, her encounter with the divine approaches the intensity of her earlier religious conversion and sexual union with Mack. Constantly searching for something or someone to give her substance, she wants to feel "the way she felt with Mack or the way she felt the night when she was saved" (135). At camp, she awakens in the early morning hours "tingling from head to toe" and "runs her fingers over her breasts and down over her pelvic bones sticking up, down over the length of her body" (138). In a setting permeated with imagery of the feminine divine, Crystal experiences the power of her own sacred spirituality. As "the air around her seems to move," Crystal notices the "sounds of breathing intensify" as the air appears to make "a swell, rising movement." Crystal's initial sensation is one of "disconnect[ion]," like she had felt when her father died and again when Mack got too close to her. Then, she feels "oddly terrifyingly buoyant" like she is floating, exactly the way Brooke described feeling during sex with Bentley. Suddenly, the wind begins to roar and Crystal feels "the blood run[ning] like a creek in her veins." Just when she expects to "plummet down some awful immediate spiral," she feels suspended and watches the early morning light fill the room (139). Following what she believes is the sound of a deep, sad, familiar man's voice, she rushes outside only to be disappointed at finding no one there. Instead, she sits on the damp lawn, enjoying the sensation and chewing on a blade of grass, again aligning herself with nature rather than culture. Crystal tries to explain to Agnes "this vision" that she has decided was sent by God, but Agnes' response silences Crystal. With her heart beating rapidly, she wishes she could feel "this much alive" forever (142). The only time Crystal can feel this life pumping through her veins, however, is with religious or sexual passion. Smith's description of Crystal's mystical experience encompasses several striking appurtenances of the feminine divine: Crystal's prophetic feelings when she awakes, her heightened sensuality both inside her room and outside on the wet grass, the strong presence of the wind with emphasis on breathing, Crystal's awareness of her own blood flowing, and her sudden ability to speak.

Crystal finds briefly in her relationship with Jerold Kukafka, whom Agnes calls a "wild-eyed hippie agitator of some sort" (149), another opportunity for divine integration. Noticing that Crystal's eyes "look exactly like they did that time at Girls' State ... all starry and wild and blue" (155), full of the necessary passion for Crystal, Agnes attributes the look to Crystal's illicit lifestyle. Even angry and repressed Agnes perceives the communion between Jerold and Crystal as she imagines the two making love on the beach. Crystal senses that her relationship with Jerold insists on the present only and never considers a future with him. In fact, the "blank spots" about Jerold's past thrill her. The important quality about Jerold is that he makes Crystal feel alive with the old fervor; "When he was on top of her, then all the old intensity came back and the way he made her feel was wonderful again, was like it used to be back at the beginning ... when she never felt so much alive." And Jerold, like Mack, tells Crystal that they are alike, but he also insists they are both "doomed" (181), something she refuses to believe, just as she had denied Mack's poignant observations about her.

Nor Hall notes that in the feminine quest for self-knowledge and integration, a girl is often attracted to "priests, poets, and artists—creative men who represent the spiritual father." The girl, however, runs a great risk of becoming fixated with this artist figure, in which case she must be rescued by a hero, "either a real person or her own other side" (139). Drawn first to Mack, a musician, then to Jerold, a writer, Crystal follows the archetypal pattern for the feminine quest. Although she gravitates toward others who might assist her on her spiritual journey, Crystal denies the possibility for such closeness in her relationship with Mack, and Jerold's suicide prevents any permanent bond there. It is doubtful, however, even if she had become fixated with one of these young men, that Crystal would have summoned the inner strength to save herself.

Just when we think she may be "saved," with a newfound sense of self-worth and a voice of her own (she has begun teaching), Crystal's world is shattered by the reappearance of Roger Lee Combs. In "The Second Rape of

Crystal Spangler," John Kalb argues convincingly that the juxtaposition of part one of the novel, in which Crystal is raped by Devere and returns home to discover her dead father, and part three, in which Crystal returns home from Dry Fork to have Roger tell her, "I'm not going to rape you" (197), suggests the pattern of violation in Crystal's life. She again becomes a victim of assault, not physical this time, but emotional. Roger, now married with twin daughters, resurfaces and insists on delivering Crystal from her present existence. Crystal assures Roger of her happiness and her lack of need for his assistance or attentions, but Roger argues that even though she believes herself to be happy, she's really not; she needs a man, love, a home, children, and "a position in the community," and all he's ever wanted in his life is to provide her with these things. Although Crystal puts up an argument, the temptation to return to passivity proves irresistible for her, and Roger convinces her of her basic unhappiness and real need for a man. With Roger to take care of her, she won't be required to make any decisions, suffer any consequences, or feel any pain. Her weak constitution cannot stand up to Roger's entreaties; Crystal dismisses her newfound sense of wholeness and submits. When Roger says "I want you" and "grabs hold of her and kisses her," Crystal feels the old intensity return, recalling with both delight and anguish what she had felt with Mack and later with Jerold. Vulnerable in Roger's looming presence, Crystal succumbs. Even as Crystal relinquishes her fledgling selfhood to Roger, "some part of her is screaming" (199–200), but her silent rebellion is squashed. Just as her screams went unheard at her father's death, she ignores the screams of her inner self now as she surrenders a vital part of her self. Agreeing to quit her successful and satisfying teaching career in order to please Roger by going away with him, she slips into a role he has designed for her, much like Monica's acquiescence to Manly's desires at the end. To represent his love for her (or rather, his desire to "own" her), he gives her a parting gift, a Valentine present—a gold ring with a dark red ruby.* Now alone, Crystal stands in her bathroom holding up her hand while "the ruby flashes red in the mirror, red as blood in the mirror, holding secrets" (202) that will only be revealed when Crystal comes face-to-face with her passivity. Again, Crystal searches the mirror for a reflection of her identity, only to discover it hidden beneath the painful secret of her rape.

Nor Hall insists that wounded women must seek healing "in the blood

---

**Crystal's mention of Roger's gifts of rings saliently reflects Roger's desire to possess Crystal as he would a treasure (reminiscent of Manley's feelings for Monica). In* Sacred Sexuality, *A.T. Mann and Jane Lyle explain the original wording of the Anglican marriage vows (which was based on an older Anglo-Saxon tradition) in which the groom vowed, "With this ring I thee wed, and this gold and silver I give thee, and with my body I thee worship, and with all my worldly chattels I thee honour." The bride then replied, "I take thee to my wedded husband ... to be bonny and buxom in bed and at board, till death us do part" (34). With Roger, Crystal will remain safe; she will not be forced to experience anything too deeply because Roger will "worship" and "honour" her, protecting her from the world.*

of the wound itself"; the void cannot be filled by another but must be filled by the integration of a "divided self" (68). Crystal's perception of the ruby red ring as blood in the mirror identifies her wound, the source of her division, but Crystal lacks the strength and volition to pursue the necessary journey to self-knowledge. Echoing Jerold's fatalism that also led to a "death," Crystal sees Roger as "inevitable" and allows the thought of him to "slide all over like body lotion, covering her, working in" (202). Comforted by the sense of absorbing Roger's identity into her own "crystal-clear" one, she feels relieved to have someone once more making her decisions for her. At this point in her life and in her writing career, Smith sees no other options for Crystal but to follow the community-validated path of becoming a wife and losing her own struggling individuality.

During Roger's political campaign for a congressional seat when Crystal tours a psychiatric hospital, she confronts the repressed memory of her rape by her retarded uncle. At the hospital, Crystal wanders off alone into a room with a young man in a crib, "hunched in the corner ... struggl[ing] to hold up his wobbling oversized head." As he reaches his hand through the bars toward Crystal, she is struck immobile by the face, which is described as "a moonface, white and smooth, a moonface like Devere's." The face of the encephalitic patient immediately transports Crystal back to the rape she suffered when she was fourteen. Reliving the entire experience, Crystal can now see Devere moving toward her with a wrench in his hand, "bent over, mak[ing] queer crablike motions toward her ... his face pucker[ing]up and twist[ing]." Then Crystal remembers "his penis stick[ing] out thick and red" and how gently he picked her up and laid her on the tool shed floor. The image of the thick red penis, erect with the flow of blood, reminds the reader of Crystal's earlier discomfort with any thought that related to the circulation of the blood and perhaps helps explain her reaction to her own menses. While Devere violates her, Crystal, although experiencing physical torture, remains motionless. Smith describes the pain Crystal feels "traveling up her whole body into her shoulders and then pinpointing itself somewhere up at the very top of her head, like somebody driving in a nail up there" (217–18). The imagery here clearly suggests a crucifixion, with Crystal being sacrificed at the hands of a mentally-disturbed man.

Crystal's paralysis during and even after the rape is an early key to the crisis of her passivity and an indication of the behavioral pattern that follows. Never moving, she waits for the brutal assault to end, subconsciously connecting with her father and the past by occupying her mind with lines of poetry and imaginary ghosts until all she feels is "pressure and this nail in the top of her head." By recalling lines from poems and stories read to her by her father in order to block out the agony of the rape, Crystal uses language as a tool for survival until the violation ends and the torment stops. And since "she can't breathe" (like her emphysematic father), language is Crystal's salvation, her only means of sustenance, just as her father's words nourished her in the private world of his parlor. As her body is assaulted, she divorces her mind from her body and imaginatively travels elsewhere in order to endure the immediate physical abuse. The second mention of "the nail," the source of Crystal's pain, along with Crystal's name itself, strongly links Crystal's experience to Christ's suffering. When the rape ends, Crystal, thinking her legs and back are broken, watches Devere calmly dress and leave; "his deep set eyes, those Spangler eyes, don't seem to see her at all." By his calm, smooth face, Crystal sees that "he doesn't know.... He doesn't know anything about it" (218-19). Again, Crystal's thoughts remind the reader of the Biblical account of Christ's request, as He was dying on the cross, that God forgive his persecutors, since "they know not what they do." Although she doesn't ask for Devere's exoneration, Crystal, as victim, accepts Devere's ignorance of his actions and the great pain Crystal will suffer. Nor does Crystal remember anything about the rape until sixteen years later when she tours the psychiatric hospital. Just as Crystal had been unable to move during and after the assault, and as she felt paralyzed at her dead father's side and again at his funeral, now her hand remains glued to the hand of the mental patient, and she sits beside his crib until the hospital staff forces her to leave.

With the emergence of the memory of her rape serving as the ultimate deprivation of Crystal's voice and identity, her capacity for language and integration is completely lost as she sinks into what will prove to be permanent passivity. Back at her childhood home in Black Rock, "Crystal paralyzes herself. She just stops moving. She stops talking, stops doing everything" (225). Smith's choice of the active rather than the passive voice here emphasizes Crystal's willful decision to be paralyzed; she is not a victim this time. She chooses silence over language. No medical explanation exists for what has happened to her; the experts agree that it's all in her mind. Lying in bed all day every day looking out the window at the roses in full bloom and the green mountain, Crystal remains closely attuned to nature, but she lacks the ability, or the will, to participate in life anymore. Even in her state of catatonia, Crystal is aligned with roses, suggestive of female sacred sexuality in Smith, and with the mountains, the strongest symbol of the feminine divine. On her frequent visits, Agnes feeds Crystal's hunger for stories as she reads to Crystal while Crystal stares out the window as "the seasons come and go and the colors change on the mountain" (228), connecting Crystal once more to the cyclical pattern of nature and feminine experience.

Craving stories and connections from the past, Crystal has always harbored fascination with violence and its connection to sexuality. Stories of Chester Lester, the neighborhood hoodlum (and later convict) who as a child forced Agnes and Crystal at knife point to pull down their pants for him, "excite her, knowing how bad he is" (115). She has been drawn consistently to the exotic, linked to wildness as opposed to domesticity. As a twelve-year-old, she dreams of wild and faraway places and fantasizes about the "wild and mysterious" Pearl Deskins. Although Agnes says Pearl has a terrible reputation, Crystal feels "a thrill shoot through her [that] makes her tremble inside" when they talk about Pearl (18). And Mack Stiltner, at their first chance meeting in town, thrills Crystal with his temerity when he grabs her and "roughly ... kisses her on the mouth" (55). Instead of fighting or pushing him away, she kisses him back. Crystal's preoccupation and fascination with violence is reminiscent of Brooke and Bentley in their growing capacity for violence, and of Monica and her thoughts about the dangerous streets of Atlanta. At a beauty pageant in Richmond, Crystal, in her hotel room, thinks, "Somewhere down there, people are stabbing each other, people are killing other people, robbing stores, fucking each other, people are yelling and screaming, houses are burning down to the ground. All of life is going on down there without her" (133). Interestingly, Crystal places sex in the same category with other violent and destructive behaviors, and even more striking is the sentiment that she is left out of the goings on, suggesting Crystal's need for intense passion to feel alive. She likes to visualize near-rape scenes, much as Monica did. Before Crystal marries Roger, when she imagines the ideal life, married to a man for whom she feels "a magnetic attraction," she envisions being in Nashville with Mack tearing off her "cowboy suit, scattering sequins all over the white shag carpet." This imagined scene of male sexual dominance that Crystal describes as "wonderful," with the scattered sequins (131), recalls Monica's fantasies of Manly coming home and violently ripping off her clothes. Both women crave the intensity of sexual and spiritual passion often associated with violence, and both desire and dream of male aggression. Girard postulates that "sex and violence frequently come to grips in such direct forms as abduction, rape, defloration, and various sadistic practices" (35). Both Crystal and Monica, victims of patriarchal assault, suffer the consequences of a limited sense of female sexuality in their lack of any understanding of the feminine divine.

Sexual beings that have great difficulty expressing their sexuality in their respective community-validated roles, Monica and Crystal, without any sense of the feminine divine, struggle with the same issues Susan and Brooke did. At the end of *Fancy Strut,* Monica, however, has decided to try the role of mother, but we anticipate her eventual breakdown brought on by the suppression of her ebullient sexuality. Crystal, however, serves as the culmination of Smith's unintegrated female characters, her mind so completely severed from her body that she is unable even consciously to make a choice. Crystal is by nature sensual and sexual, but she never mindfully makes a choice to be so. With only a partial self of her own, she desperately needs sexual love to feel complete. For Monica and Crystal, "no middle ground" (*Black Mountain Breakdown* 103) exists. Both females are damaged by the "visions of rape" (*Fancy Strut* 323) that come to dominate their lives and leave them unfulfilled. In their limited visions, neither Monica nor Crystal understands the richness and complexity of the possibilities for their lives. Without any sense of the feminine divine for self-validation, they remain in their confined roles, believing they have no choice. Only in Smith's next novel, *Oral History* (1983), will the author envision a fully integrated divinely sexual female.

Chapter III

"ENCLOSED ... IN GOD'S WOMB"
The Chance for Rebirth in *Oral History*

In her influential essay "Stabat Mater," Julia Kristeva argues that the myth of the Virgin Mary fails to provide an adequate model for women and has lost its power in the modern world since it obliterates the human truth of the inextricability of sexuality and motherhood. The image of the Virgin Mary leaves a disturbing void in the female psyche because it silences the female body, denying integral parts of women's lives (312–13). Lee Smith's fifth novel, *Oral History* (1983), reclaims the female body and gives women voice as the author continues to explore the healing presence of the feminine divine in providing women with an alternative spirituality. By attributing mythic qualities to female characters, Smith explores her own spirituality as she moves closer to a mythology she can embrace.

Oral History presents several liminal female characters who exhibit open sexuality and also become mothers and thus offers a new myth that encompasses a multifaceted sexual mother. With her depictions of powerful female characters, as Rebecca Smith has convincingly argued, Lee Smith "implies that recapturing the power of the goddesses is possible" (60). *Oral History* covers more than a hundred-year time period and utilizes thirteen different points of view: seven first person oral narratives and one first person written narrative interspersed among four pieces told by third person narrators, sometimes omniscient and sometimes limited to a single perspective. Smith moves smoothly from one vantage point to another, providing the fabric to be pieced together by the reader who then learns the past, present, and even future of the Cantrell family. Choosing to center the novel on the powerful presence of the sacred sexual Dory Cantrell, Smith attributes mythic qualities not only to Dory, but also to other female characters in the novel as the writer continues on her spiritual journey.

From the first female voice in the novel to the last, the reader can detect Smith's gravitation toward characters who are both mothers and sexually expressive women. Smith heavily populates the novel with female characters, some who, like Frances Pitt of *Fancy Strut*, suppress their sexuality in order to conform to society's expectations. Among this group are Granny Younger, the first narrator and in a sense the voice of the community; Rose Hibbitts, an emotionally disturbed woman; and Ora Mae Cantrell Wade, a key player in the drama of the Cantrell saga. However, many more women choose to express their sexuality, even though most of them suffer for doing so. To this group belong Red Emmy, the archetypal temptress; Pricey Jane Cantrell, the mysterious gypsy-like woman; Dory Cantrell Wade, the golden girl; Justine Poole, the proprietress of the local hotel; and Pearl Wade Bingham and Sally Wade, two of Dory's daughters.

Finally able to give women a mythic role, in *Oral History*, Smith moves to the mountains of West Virginia for the setting of this novel, signaling her readiness to plumb the depths of the region for stories that empower sexual females as she returns to her roots in search of a mythology that accepts and honors women. In her first novel, *The Last Day the Dogbushes Bloomed*, mountains only fringed the novel, and in *Something in the Wind*, the action shifts to Tidewater Virginia and Piedmont North Carolina; in *Fancy Strut*, Smith moves to the foothills of Alabama. Crystal of *Black Mountain Breakdown* is the first character who begins to look to the mountains and the past for some clue to her identity. Now ready to examine the area of her childhood, Smith carefully places *Oral History* deeply in the mountains, moving behind Black Rock Mountain to the three mountains that envelop Hoot Owl Holler: Hurricane, Hoot Owl, and Snowman, an area rich in Celtic mythology and full of both tragic and heroic stories that ennoble women and offer them an alternative to the fate suffered by Crystal Spangler. Smith frames the novel with italicized sections that take place in the modern-day present with the visit of Jennifer Bingham, a descendent of the Cantrell family, to Hoot Owl Holler. In order to complete a project for her college oral history class, she has come to tape-record the sounds of the haunted homeplace and to talk to her presumed grandparents about the family's past. Between these bookends that comprised the short story from which the novel originated, we find several versions of the Cantrell family's history. As Smith herself admitted in a 1983 interview with Edwin T. Arnold, the truth about the past is never really known; "when you go back to look for it, all you ever get is your interpretation of it. And it changes so that what really happened is not what anybody thinks happened by the time the story gets all weakened and changed" (245). In her evocation of the image of the goddess of ancient mythology, Smith "wrote her way through patriarchy to get to a sacred-sexual imaging of the female" (Hill 80). What has resulted in Smith's characterizations are women who are endowed with divinity and sacredness.

Granny Younger, the village midwife and healer, continues the mountain tradition of the "Granny woman" (given only cursory treatment in *Black Mountain Breakdown* with Crystal's two aunts at Dry Fork) in Smith's depiction of

Granny as a wise old storyteller who has, in a sense, lived beyond sex. Granny opens the saga with the story of the first Almarine Cantrell (born in 1876), described as a "pretty," god-like child with "pale-gold hair" (28) and an affinity for nature and all living creatures. Glad to accept her role as storyteller, Granny warns the reader that she plans to tell the story the way she wants to, and "iffen you mislike it, you don't have to hear." Granny attempts to establish her reliability by informing us of her age and experience, with assurance that the story she tells is "truer than true" (37). However, despite her gender and verbal acumen, her collusion with the patriarchy in her judgment and condemnation of Red Emmy is obvious early in her narrative. In fact, Granny exemplifies one of Smith's female characters who has chosen to suppress her own sexuality. She admits that when she was younger, she had "knowed him [Isom, Red Emmy's father] bettern I ever knowed ary a soul" (46), but, stopping in mid-sentence, she elects to omit this story, instead focusing on the one about Almarine and Red Emmy. Granny lucidly reveals what she has sacrificed when she describes her experience of one day stumbling upon the two lovers kissing, which "[m]ade me feel like I had not felt for years.... Now a person mought get old, and their body mought go on them, but that thing does not wear out. No it don't" (52). Granny's comments elucidate her capacity for passion, and even in old age she acknowledges her sexuality, but ironically, she refuses to interpret another older woman's sexuality as normal; instead, she adheres to the community-validated explanation for Red Emmy and Almarine's behavior in labeling Red Emmy a witch and insisting that she has cast a spell on Almarine. Paula Gallant Eckard sees Granny Younger as representative of "time in all its dimensions" and symbolic of "Smith's efforts to reconcile maternal time with patriarchal time" (144–45). Perhaps more salient than the timelessness and "nurturing force" Eckard attributes to this character is Granny's immoveable position within the patriarchy that judges and condemns Red Emmy for her open sexuality.

The imagery Smith employs in Granny's description of Almarine and Red Emmy's first meeting, then their subsequent love affair, certainly suggests divine intervention. Smith draws on imagery of the feminine divine in creating Red Emmy, a sacred sexual female that will begin to bridge the gap between motherhood and sexuality. As Conrad Oswalt has noted in his article "Witches and Jesus: Lee Smith's Appalachian Religion," Smith often endows her female characters with "a mystical ability to harness a bewitching connection with the elemental powers of nature" (104). Thus, a mysterious redbird "pull[s] on Almarine's heart" and leads him "offen the trace." Guided by some unidentifiable force, he follows the bird without even thinking. "He don't have a choice in the world" but to experience what will place a "stamp on the rest of his life." Almarine comes upon Red Emmy bathing in a circular pool of water, and the description of her at this first meeting clearly establishes her divinity: "She was naked from the waist up.... The skin of her back showed the whitest white that Almarine ever seed, and her hair fell all down her back to her waist. And that hair! Lord it was the reddest red, a red so dark it was nigh to purple, red like the leaves on the dogwood tree in the fall" (42–43). Dorothy Hill argues that with Red Emmy, Smith attempts to restore sexuality, to redeem the color red which, in modern times, fades to the more "feminine" color pink, just as female sexuality has been "muted and suppressed" (63). This reference to Red Emmy's hair as almost purple takes us back to the Queen of *Dogbushes,* the sexually expressive mother that Susan cannot imagine becoming. Red Emmy, like the Queen and other of Smith's sexual female characters, is closely aligned with nature, but she takes on even more importance with further description. Once Red Emmy becomes cognizant of Almarine's presence, she turns around to face him, and "everything that happened, happened real fast of course, but for Almarine it was like it taken a hundred years." As Red Emmy turns, "her hair whirl[s] out slow ... like a red rain of water around her head. In his mind he would see her again and again, the way she stood up so slow and how she turned" (44). Time seems to stand still as Almarine views the naked goddess bathing. Only when she turns around is the vortical halo of hair apparent. Kathryn Rabuzzi notes, "Meeting the Goddess comprises one of life's transcendent moments, which no one is privileged to experience often" and one that "exist[s] outside the ordinary time frame" (175). Almarine, a mortal, even upon viewing the nudity of this divine female, however, does not die or even go blind as mythology indicates he should, suggesting his divine characteristics and connecting him to both Red Emmy and his daughter Dory who will also be linked to the feminine divine.

Almarine's name, of course, connotes water, and since Red Emmy emerges from a circular pool of water and her hair is described in terms related to water, the divinity of the couple and their powerful communion are immediately established. Smith will return time and again to the image of a halo to suggest a character's divinity. Just as Red Emmy's hair appears to form a halo, Almarine is later depicted while sleeping, with "his light hair splayed out on the piller" like an angel with a halo (48). Water imagery is prominent in relics of ancient goddess worship; the belief in the sacredness and regenerative power of water extends from prehistory to this century. Red Emmy's "red rain of hair" and her first appearance to Almarine in the water indicate her ebullience. Furthermore, Smith describes the "freshets of water ... busting outen the rocks" as Almarine follows the redbird down the mountain to finally discover that the "streams had all flowed into a pool which was set in a little circle of rocks" (42–44). The circular shape of the pool from which Red Emmy emerges reflects "a transmitter of the concentrated divine energy" of the goddess (Gimbutas, *Language* 322). In her article "*Oral History*: The Enchanted Circle of Narrative and Dream," Rosalind B. Reilly examines the frequent use of the image of the circle in this novel. Pointing out that circles mark spots where "the imagination confronts its own dream of perfection," Reilly posits that this dream tends to be "embodied by someone of the opposite sex so that the magic circle of the imagination is also a magic circle of union with another person" (82).* Thus, Almarine meets his dream of perfection in the flesh. Mesmerized, he stares at Red Emmy as "she made no move to cover her glory and Almarine looked his fill" at this woman "as big as he was, a woman nearabout six feet tall.... Her mouth was as red as a cut on her face and the color flamed out in her cheeks.... Her hair hung all down her back like one of them waterfall freshets along the path and her breasts were big and white with her nipples springing out on them red as blood" (44).

Several aspects of Smith's careful delineation of this initial image of Red Emmy deserve examination. In many of the Paleolithic sculptures, the breasts and buttocks of the female were exaggerated, symbolizing the great mother goddess as the divine source of nourishment—milk/rain—and as giver of life in general (Gimbutas, *Language* 31). With the dual emphasis on Red Emmy's nakedness and exposure of large breasts and on her hair, twice directly related to rain, Smith depicts a divine female powerfully linked to goddess mythology. Once again, as with Monica and Buck, and then with Crystal and Mack, Smith creates a male and female character approximately the same physical size, thus establishing the inherent equality and reciprocity in their divine union. Smith calls this technique "twinning" and explains that often a woman gravitates toward the "other" that reflects something of herself (Per). The "reddest red" of Red Emmy's hair, mouth, cheeks, and nipples closely links her to the life force and also establishes her strong sexuality. Granny further emphasizes Red Emmy's association with blood and female sexuality when she points out that Red Emmy's age (around forty), compared to Almarine's (twenty-two), is not a problem since "a witch don't show age like a regular gal, her body's too full of blood" (47). The blood motif surfaces in many of Smith's works, consistently signaling a woman's expressed sexuality and intense passion. In earlier novels, Smith has tied female protagonists such as Susan Tobey, Brooke Kincaid, and Crystal Spangler to the flow and circulation of blood. Rabuzzi relates female blood to the "great power" of women, "the secret" of their sacred sexuality (27), and the "source of life" which today "remain deeply hidden from consciousness in a culture which finds sanitary napkins embarrassing" (201). In Smith's fiction, the transformative power of women's blood is restored.

The cave as symbol for the regenerative womb of the feminine divine again appears in *Oral History* in Granny's explanation of Red Emmy's background and at other crucial moments in the novel. Acknowledging Red Emmy's mysterious nature, Granny suggests that Isom, Red Emmy's father, "just drempt Emmy up outen the black air by the Raven Clifts" and raised her

---

*For an engaging discussion of sacred circle imagery in this novel, see Rosalind B. Reilly, pp. 79–92.

"with ravens, in caves" (46). Red Emmy's arcane origin links her to such Greek goddesses as Athena, who sprang from Zeus's head, and Aphrodite, who emerged from Uranus's testicles. Dorothy Hill postulates that the plot of *Oral History* leads back to the cave "for recovery of lost meaning, [and] search[es] for lost sacred names obliterated by the patriarchy" (62). The "lost sacred names" for which Smith's imagination searches reflect a language that expresses the sacredness of females and the divinity of feminine experience. Granny's mention of Red Emmy's origin as a cave suggests that her presence offers the potential for healing and restoration of female divinity. Rebecca Smith discusses Red Emmy's link to the archetypal sibyl who wanders the mountains and "is associated with the Old Goddess" or mother goddess (63). Red Emmy takes on additional mythological significance with the "death-and-resurrection symbolism of the raven" (Walker, *Women's* 847), a bird described by Gimbutas as an epiphany of the goddess in her sovereignty over death and regeneration (*Language* 324). Although Red Emmy presumably dies, regeneration exists in the novel's other sacred sexual females.

Later in the novel, Smith returns to the cave motif when Parrot Blankenship shares a humorous tale that poignantly reveals society's fear of women's sexual appetite to a group of men during the male initiation rite at an annual hog killing. The story's principal character, a witchlike "widder lady" (201), rides Parrot mercilessly at night (the way the mountain people claim Red Emmy rides Almarine) until eventually, upon detection of an opening through a "brushy-thicket" in a mountainside cave, he discovers treasure. Parrot explains, "I ... pushed through with my nose until I got my head inside that cave ... [where] it was hot ... and had a funny smell to it, and it was black as the blackest night you ever seen or ever imagined in all your life"; then he wakes up and discovers he "was in the widder's bed with my face in her crack, and I had done benastied myself!" (204–205). The cave of Parrot's joke metaphorically depicts that most mysterious part of a female, the womb. Ironically, however, in this debasing story told to incite laughter among a group of men, Parrot admits to discovering treasure in the mountainside cave, thus unconsciously acknowledging the regenerative power of the symbolic womb. Parrot's name clearly suggests that his voice, his jokes, "parrot," or repeat, the biases of the mountain people, his story powerfully reflecting the fear of the older sexually expressive woman.

The cave serves as a positive, healing force for Sally later in the novel when she discovers and metaphorically obtains great treasure there. After her mother Dory's death, Sally experiences symbolic rebirth when she escapes to a "special place" that is hers alone, "a kind of cave" where she feels no one can see her (253), reminiscent of Susan Tobey's wading pool and Crystal Spangler's father's parlor. Sprawled on the dirt floor of the cave, Sally cries uncontrollably then suddenly decides to take possession of her life and get up and leave the cave. She lies down on the shiny rocks in a nearby creek and allows the water to run over her whole body, then sits up on her elbows and lets the sun dry her face. Just when Sally is suffering most over the death of her mother, her retreat to and emergence from the cave, the symbolic womb of her mother, represent her experience of reunion, rebirth and regeneration. The spring water running over Sally restores sustenance to her, allowing her to move ahead with her life. Sally's experience also links her to Red Emmy, the first sacred sexual woman in the novel who likewise emerged from a cave and was discovered in a pool of water.

The passionate, sexual goddess manifests herself not only in the brief relationship between Red Emmy and Almarine, but also in Granny's words of explanation. Granny informs us that the couple stayed in bed for two complete days, after which "they had them a spell of ... froze-time on Hoot Owl Holler. Everything stood still.... But he moved like a man set under a spell." Almarine's encounter with the feminine divine removes him from the ordinary world. The otherworldly nature of the relationship between Red Emmy and Almarine is apparent even to Granny, but she attributes all the mystery to Red Emmy's "witchery." Even though Almarine appears happy, always smiling as he does his chores, Granny insists that he is "bewitched," and no one in the holler will have anything to do with him; "you don't want no truck with a witch" (49–50). When Almarine becomes ill, Granny readily explains that "a witch will ride a man ... to death if she can" and Red Emmy's nice daytime behavior causes her "to go hell for leather all night to make up for them long sweet days." Openly acknowledging that Red Emmy did all the farm work while sick Almarine rested most of the time, the biased old mountain woman adamantly refuses to praise Red Emmy's love for and devotion to her husband. Granny insists, "He was servicing her, that's all, while she liked to rode him to death" (53), recalling the myth of Hekate (an ancient goddess predating Olympus) who ostensibly "rode men to death."

Red Emmy's banishment by Almarine encodes society's reaction to and even fear of the sexually expressive adult female and represents patriarchal religion's consistent denial of female sexuality. When Almarine eventually seeks medical attention from the area's "healer," Granny insists that he reinvoke the patriarchal religion by making "the mark of the cross on her [Red Emmy's] breast and her forehead with ashes" and uttering "the name of the Father and the Son and the Holy Ghost" as loudly as he can. If that doesn't work, Granny tells Almarine he must "cut her ... and make the mark of the cross with her blood." The damage done to the ancient sacred goddess parallels Granny's instructions since she was "cut" as her multitudinous qualities were splintered and redistributed to various divinities before she was eventually totally eclipsed by the male patriarchal God. Almarine's love for Red Emmy is clear when he begins to sob and then protests that he can never harm her. Granny describes his wailing as "one of the awfulest sounds I ever did hear"—and appropriately so since he will expel the divine female presence from his life. Almarine, however, a victim of the society that produced him, eventually agrees that he must banish the red-headed goddess from his home in order to regain his own strength and masculinity. Granny explains Almarine's feelings: "Almarine loved her, is what it was. You know a man can love something he don't even like, and Almarine loved her as much as he disgusted her, and scared as he was" (54–55).

Granny's words echo those of Smith during a personal interview when she described "this incredible being compelled and repelled in almost the same measure" by the more ecstatic forms of religion (Byrd 97). They also bear striking similarities to Susan Tobey's conflicting thoughts about both her mother and Eugene, Brooke Kincaid's disturbing feelings about Bentley, and Bob Pitt's ambiguous perception of Sandy DuBois. Almarine senses this same antinomy in his relationship with Red Emmy, which for him has certainly been a religious experience. Granny's simplistic words also seem to allude to the frequent treatment of women who are equally attractive and dangerous, invoking the old Puritan desire to taste the "forbidden fruit." Almarine has tasted and even found happiness, but Granny's "words of wisdom" convince him he has made a terrible mistake. Linda Tate notes that Granny's "intolerance for Red Emmy's divergence from community standards for appropriate female appearance and behavior" reflects the entire community's desire to erase the truth about Red Emmy (107). Thus, Almarine, as a good citizen, agrees to accept Granny's diagnosis and prescription for recovery without even considering the effect on Red Emmy, much as Richard Burlage will later desert Dory without thinking of her anguish. And even though he's told Granny of Red Emmy's pregnancy, Almarine accepts the old woman's advice to exile her and soon even begins to think about finding another wife. Giving no explanation of the exact means by which Almarine banishes Red Emmy, Granny says, "the long and short of it" is that Red Emmy disappeared (56).

Supplanting Red Emmy, the presence of the full-powered feminine divine, Almarine's next wife, Pricey Jane, serves as a domesticated version of the goddess. Eckard discusses Pricey Jane and Red Emmy as together embodying "the dualities of the total female principle: maternity and sexuality, procreation and destruction, passivity and power" (147). Like Red Emmy, Pricey Jane also has mysterious origins, and Almarine meets her while she is traveling in a wagon with her gypsy-like relatives. Nor Hall connects the image of the gypsy wagon with the idea of a roving *temenos*, a sacred enclosure or space where "individuating or unfolding life is protected." Hall argues that in today's world, where we no longer revere fixed symbols of divinity—"sacred stones, groves, mountains, or altars"—these protected spaces must be roving, moving at all times (168). Pricey Jane's origination from just such a space intimates her sacrality. Pricey Jane's name itself indicates her value, but the fact that Almarine trades a mule for her hand in marriage betrays his view of her as a possession, unlike his perception of Red Emmy, who could not be owned by anyone.

With Pricey Jane, Smith introduces a scheme of color symbolism that will remain consistent throughout her writing from this point forward. Paul Friedrich defines golden as the most common epithet for Aphrodite, a descendant of the original great mother goddess, the color representing not only the beauty of the goddess, but also the other attributes such as procreation and verbal acumen (78–79). The Chinese "Golden Flower" of Eastern philosophy serves as a symbol for the integration of soul, spirit, and body, an ideal balance either achieved or denied through sexuality. The Taoists understand the "Golden Flower" as a "psychological and spiritual centre" discovered through integration reached by means of the sexual act, sexuality viewed as a "catalyst for higher integration" (Mann and Lyle 93). One of the first aspects of Pricey Jane mentioned is her golden earrings, which her mother gave her before she died. These symbolic earrings will accompany the Cantrell women through several generations of sexually expressive females. The "flash of gold at her ear" (59) immediately captures Almarine's attention and interest, just as later in the novel Richard Burlage is likewise taken by the sparkle of the earrings on Pricey Jane's daughter Dory's ears. Both the color and the design of the earrings signal their salience in the novel. The importance of the golden earrings that will be passed along to Pricey Jane's only daughter Dory (whose name means "gold") cannot be overemphasized in their symbolic association with such goddess-related attributes as sexuality, procreation, and integration. To compound their significance, the earrings have "roses traced in gold around the loops" (61–62), roses serving as a consistent symbol for female sexuality in Smith.

Barbara Walker directly connects the rose to the pre–Christian images of the goddess, calling it an obvious sexual symbol of goddess worship. Walker also explains the ancient belief that Venus's sexual mysteries were spoken "under the rose (*sub rosa*)" (*Women's* 866–68). In Pricey Jane's portion of the narrative, as she remembers her long-dead mother, she recalls that her mother "never said a word about love" (68), always pretending not to hear her daughter's questions or acting as if love were an unfamiliar term or something shameful. Pricey Jane's mother withholds the mysteries of female sexuality from her daughter, but ironically, in tendering the earrings to Pricey Jane when she dies, the old woman has provided her daughter with a symbol for a potent sexual force, an appurtenance of the feminine divine.

With the active, energetic, and sensual Pricey Jane, Smith continues her exploration of chimerical versus corporeal. Pricey Jane's love for Almarine is obvious; "she follered [him] around, and ... she'd reach right out and touch him whenever they passed in the house" (64). This open expression of affection seems odd to Granny as she describes it like it were unusual behavior for a wife. Shifting from Granny's first person narration, Smith chooses to relate the second section of the novel in third person omniscient point of view from Pricey Jane's perspective. In this section we learn that Pricey Jane "loves Almarine so much it's like she made him up out of her own head, the perfect only man for her to love" (68). These words reverberate with echoes of Granny's description of Red Emmy's genesis—that her father dreamed her up in his head—and Smith's later novels, most notably *Fair and Tender Ladies* and *On Agate Hill*, in which the protagonist harbors the same sense of having created a lover in her own mind. With the idea of imagining a perfect "other," Smith works toward filling the void of the lost feminine divine. When this wound is healed, all scissions between body and mind, flesh and spirit, sexuality and motherhood also disintegrate.

In a poignant image of divine motherhood, Smith combines the maternal with the sexual in her depiction of Pricey Jane thinking of her husband while nursing her baby. As Pricey Jane breastfeeds Dory, her sensuality replete, she feels a connection to her dead mother; "the steady pull on her nipple is like a chain, somehow, linking her to Dory and more than that to Almarine" (70). Sally, one of Dory's daughters, will later feel this same sensation as she breastfeeds her child. A sensual creature, Pricey Jane, while sitting on the front porch, opens the front of her dress to let the fresh air hit her breasts, so full of milk that they hurt. As the breeze blows across her skin, her breasts leak. "She wipes at the watery milk with her hand and tastes it experimentally, giggles, and makes a face" (73). Almost eighteen, Pricey Jane is free to experience and enjoy her own sensuality and sexuality. One day she watches as two dragonflies mate; "they fly together, a single enormous glittering dragonfly, and Pricey Jane smiles. *'Hit's a woman's duty and her burden,' Rhoda said.* Pricey Jane smiles and fills her buckets at the spring" (71). Smith's depiction of Pricey Jane and the imagery surrounding her powerfully links her to goddess mythology, the wind and the spring of water signaling the presence of the feminine divine. For Pricey Jane, sex is not at all a duty or a burden as Rhoda has described it; instead, she views it as the sacred union of two to form "a single enormous glittering" body, a Taoist image of integration and elevation. Had Pricey Jane lived, she would most likely have continued to enjoy fulfilling the roles of both wife and mother. However, Smith is not yet willing to allow this sexual mother to survive. Both Pricey Jane and her son Eli die, leaving only Dory and Almarine. And likewise, Red Emmy disappears from the novel.

Pricey Jane's replacement represents another stage of the goddess's decline from the full-blooded and powerful Red Emmy, to the gentle, domesticated Pricey Jane, and finally to the asexual, dutiful Vashti. Almarine once again marries, but this third wife approaches him, unlike his first two wives whom he pursued. His relationship with Vashti, as Anne Goodwyn Jones explains, "has little of love—and little of death.... [The] intense sexuality—has disappeared, to be replaced only by loneliness and isolation" (17). The mysterious Vashti, the widow of Almarine's estranged brother, appears at Almarine's door with her four-year-old daughter Ora Mae and takes control of the household and Almarine's life. Resigned to live without the passion and vigor he has known as a young man and after losing two women he has loved intensely, Almarine now simply accepts what fate assigns him. The account of the Vashti of the Bible clearly describes the subjugation of women when Ahasuerus, a Persian king, ordered his beautiful wife Vashti to expose her naked body to his drunken guests. Her refusal resulted in banishment and the king's marriage to the obedient Esther. Dorothy Hill posits that this story may "well encode the rise of the patriarchy, the fall of the goddess, and the ascendency of the male-imaged monotheistic tradition" (71–72). Ironically, however, Smith chooses the name Vashti for the most domesticated of the Cantrell women; she gives birth to Almarine's four sons and another daughter, and raises Dory, Ora Mae, and all five other children in a loveless home where she performs the necessary chores.

The embodiment of the union of spiritual love and sexual passion, Dory Cantrell, Smith's first totally integrated female character, serves as the center of the Cantrell family history, but the writer disallows Dory's telling her own story. Smith has not yet found a voice for the sacred sexual female. We are provided details about this "golden" girl by several other characters, especially her lover Richard Burlage, but Dory's personality remains the central mystery of the novel. With Dory, Smith continues a motif that has informed her earlier fiction, the idea of yearning, of longing for some nebulous belief system that will guide or support a woman in her search for meaning. In Western civilization, this quest proves difficult since the concept of self has long been masculine. As one might expect, Dory's quest will prove a fruitless enterprise since neither Richard Burlage nor society as a whole is prepared to accept her power and sacredness. Dory becomes heir to her mother's golden rose earrings and wears them until her death, just as Pricey Jane and her mother both did, thus inheriting her mother's potency and sexuality, Dory also continues the line of female force and power begun with Red Emmy.

Smith describes Dory, like earlier sexual female characters, in terms that relate to nature and feminine divinity. Along with Red Emmy, Dory is linked to fire, suggesting both the heat of her passion and also the eventual destruction she will suffer because of it, a theme introduced with Bevo's incineration of the football stadium in *Fancy Strut*. When Richard Burlage encounters Dory for the first time, the image he sees remains with him forever, much as Almarine never forgets the way Red Emmy looked when he first encountered her in the pool of water. For Richard, Dory personifies "that wellspring of naturalness" (103) he has expected to find here in the mountains. As Rosalind Reilly has noted, the mountains constitute a sacred space where "supernatural enchantment" is possible, where events may take place in a sacred, timeless world (82). Smith's diction leaves no doubt about Dory's divinity, joined as she is with nature, water, the mountains, and with Red Emmy. As Dory stands on the swinging bridge, Richard observes that "behind her, the woods were aflame with color" (121). Her honest passion and closeness to nature invigorate Richard, and he is unable to think of anything else until he visits her at Hoot Owl Holler and finds her to be even lovelier than before. Dory's "oneness with the natural things of the earth" shocks Richard (130). Smith's sexual females consistently possess an affinity for nature and its creatures. One is reminded of Crystal Spangler and her practice of catching fireflies that so disturbs her mother. And just as Crystal makes an unconscious connection between nature and Mack Stiltner and views their love-making as completely natural, Richard compares sex with Dory to "coupl[ing] like animals, there in the woods" (158).

The full embodiment of the sacred sexual female, Dory immediately transforms Richard as he undertakes the arduous task of analyzing her behavior. When he visits her at Hoot Owl Holler and comes close to her physically for the first time, he describes her presence as "intoxicating." As Dory leans toward Richard, at his request, to display her golden earring for him, he describes his loss of control: "suddenly I found myself pressing her against me urgently, covering her neck, her hair, her cheek with kisses. I couldn't stop myself!" Richard explains that he kissed "her full red lips" and "stroked her amazing hair, which sprang up under my fingers like something alive." Stopping himself just before losing his self-control, Richard "clasped her hands together firmly and kissed them, then stepped back." Richard's description of Dory's hair as springing up and seeming alive echoes Bevo Cartwright's account of the extremely sexual Sharon DuBois. The sexuality of these females exists just beneath the surface of their appearance, seeming to possess a life-force of its own in its inclination to express itself. After such an arousing embrace, which Richard ends out of a sense of duty, Dory disappears into the "golden woods" (132). Never having experienced sensuality without analyzing it, Richard is left in a quandary about what to do. He makes a list of reasons for and against continuing to see Dory. Admitting that his "intellect *trembles with [his] body*" (135) when he thinks of kissing her, Richard consciously acknowledges the "elevating" effect Dory has on him; she joins the two separate spheres of his essence: the body and the intellect. Unlike previous Smith novels that depicted female protagonists struggling with a mind-body split, *Oral History* initially presents Dory as the healing presence that serves to unite these two spheres. Even Richard acknowledges the symbiosis implied in their relationship.

Dory's power over Richard directly relates to her expressed sexuality. The first time he sees her, he experiences a "feeling of recognition," imagining that they have "known each other for hundreds—no, thousands!—of years" (129). However, unfortunately for both Richard and Dory, he senses that this feminine divinity exists "only in that shadowy setting—those three mountains, that closed valley—whence she came" (148). Richard's intuition that informs him of the sanctity of Dory and her existence within the setting adorned by three mountains resonates with the presence of the feminine divine, but he ultimately deserts Dory, refusing to take her from the mountains. Barbara

Walker relates that in most cultures, mountains were identified with breasts, or "*mons veneris* of the Earth," *mons* meaning both mountain and vagina, also viewed as "paradise" (*Women's* 695–97). Richard's belief in the confinement of such sacredness to the mountains and his unwillingness to take Dory to Richmond with him as he has promised encode society's denial of the existence of the feminine divine. The first time Richard and Dory come extremely close to having sex but are interrupted by the sudden appearance of her brothers, Dory's honesty, her "transparency" surprises Richard. Just as Red Emmy, with no feeling of embarrassment or shame, had revealed to Almarine her bare breasts, Dory exposes her breasts to Richard, who calls them "the most perfect breasts which exist in all the world," and as she pulls him to her, she says "Suck me" twice before Richard is able to respond to her directness (146).

French feminist Hélène Cixous addresses the problem of shame that most women feel in regard to their bodies: "We've been turned away from our bodies, shamefully taught to ignore them, to strike them with that stupid sexual modesty." She urges women to reclaim their bodies and openly express their sexuality (256). Kathryn Rabuzzi asserts that only when a woman can see the "natural beauty of women's natural bodies" will she acknowledge the "Goddess in all Her radiance" (184). Unashamedly, Dory exposes and claims pleasure from her own body, offering her breasts, what Nor Hall calls her prized treasure, swollen "with the importance of transformation," to Richard, for him to take nourishment from "the milk of immortality" (56–58). As she asks Richard to suck her breasts, Dory not only desires sexual satisfaction for herself, but also, according to the Taoist precept, she offers Richard a healthy substance. Richard explains, Dory "took my head and drew me to her breast, offering it up with her hand" (146). The way in which Dory gives herself to Richard (presenting her breast to him with her hand) resembles a sacrificial ritual of some sort, and indeed, ultimately, she makes the supreme oblation for him. Richard, however, is not yet able to partake of Dory's divinity; he is forced to "relieve [him]self by [his] own hand" since Dory's brothers arrive to take her home because of the symbolically significant rising creek. When Dory comes to Richard again after several days, they "ma[k]e love as no mortals have ever made love before," creating a divine union. Dory awakens Richard's passion and takes him "beyond all boundaries of physical sensation" (147).

The sacred union of Dory and Richard echoes that of Red Emmy and Almarine and further develops Smith's treatment of divine integration as the sexual and the intellectual merge. From the first moment Richard sees Dory, he knows, as Almarine knew about Red Emmy, that "something in [his] life w[as] decided at that very moment" (119). Just as Red Emmy and Almarine were described as being the same physical size, Richard discovers only after sex that he and Dory are "almost exactly the same size, toe to toe," that they complete one another and are "truly one" (155). He had experienced this same sense of oneness earlier on Hoot Owl Holler the second time he saw Dory when they walked down the mountain together "as one, flawlessly" (129). In their relationship, mind and body merge, unlike the union of Crystal and Roger where she sublimates her selfhood to him. When Dory and Richard spend Christmas together at the schoolhouse and remain snowed in for several days, again Richard has the sensation that Dory is not "separate" from him, that indeed they are "truly one." Increasingly entranced by Dory and less and less able to perform his teaching duties, Richard says, "always in those days I smelled of sex, of her body, of our juices which flowed together into one" (156–58). In Richard's perception of their "juices" becoming one, he seems to sense the deep connectedness and reciprocity of this relationship. However, in Richard's frustrated attempt to codify all experiences, he ignores the magical, mystical nature of his union with Dory.

In *Sacred Sexuality*, A.T. Mann and Jane Lyle note that in the ancient subculture of alchemy, when the "vital essences" of male and female blend, the magical mixture is usually regarded as a liquid (174), lending further support for the divine, elevating essence of Richard and Dory's bond. In later novels, other protagonists will likewise perceive particular lovers as vital "parts" of themselves, feeling that the two are one in sacred sexual union. Isolated from the outside world as he learns to live in and enjoy the sensual one, Richard writes in his journal that Dory has brought him "*to [his] senses*" (156). However, after only a couple of months, Richard begins losing weight and becomes fragile and weak, like Almarine had done with Red Emmy. The forceful sexual female eventually takes her toll on the male lover, which ultimately drives him away. Both Almarine and Richard are products of a society that denigrates and exploits sexual women. Although they love Red Emmy and Dory, respectively, these men lack the necessary strength to deny convention and act on their deepest feelings. Their eventual sickness represents the illness that pervades a male-dominated culture, one blind to the presence the feminine divine.

Smith further links Dory and Red Emmy with striking imagery of the divine. Just as Red Emmy first appeared to Almarine wearing a halo of hair around her head, when Richard sees Dory for the first time, he says her face "is framed by the finespun golden curls, almost like a frizz, about her head — hair like a Botticelli!" (118). Smith powerfully associates Dory with divinity in the comparison Richard makes of her hair to that of female figures in paintings by the Florentine artist Sandro Botticelli. One of Botticelli's most famous paintings, "Birth of Venus," depicts the goddess as she is blown ashore by the winds, and in fact, later Dory will appear at the meeting house door accompanied by a blast of wind. In addition, Smith's reference to Botticelli adds another dimension to Dory — an association with the Virgin Mary, the subject of many of his finest paintings. Since Botticelli, often considered a Platonist in his attempt to combine and blur the Christian and Platonic traditions, draws parallels between Venus and Mary as symbols of spiritual, divine love, Dory's characterization deepens with this interconnection to her divine mythological foremothers. When

Richard describes Dory standing at the schoolhouse door, he notices in particular her hair making "a flaming gold halo around her head" (119). Later, when the two spend Christmas together, Richard observes Dory on the bed and notices her hair "in a tangle like a golden halo across the pillow" (156). Dory clearly offers the salvation for which Richard searches, and all Richard's senses inform him of this truth. The last picture of Dory that Richard paints, reminiscent of the first, highlights her divine qualities: "a girl so lovely as to take your breath away, and all the leaves of autumn swirling about her, red and orange and gold" (167). Richard's ultimate impression of Dory, adorned with a halo of fiery colors, emphasizes not only her connection to Red Emmy, but more importantly, her affinity with nature as she serves as the apotheosis of the feminine divine.

Once again, as she has done with Brooke and Bentley, then with Monica and Buck, and Crystal and Mack, Smith explores the inherent limitations of language to encompass the infinite at sacred moments. At first, Richard feels the easy conversation between Dory and him connects them and believes the vast differences between them and their manners of speech will "melt and blend together into some single tongue" (129). This tongue would undoubtedly speak the language of love, perhaps the new language that Kristeva says "would be closer to the maternal body, its experiences and psychology" (qtd. in Parker 163). Kristeva calls this means of expression the *semiotic modality* or *chora** which is "analogous only to vocal or kinetic rhythm." Kristeva insists that we must restore this language's "gestural and vocal play" in order to achieve integration and wholeness ("Semiotic" 34–36). Even the verbose and eloquent Richard Burlage admits that in Dory's presence, he feels "for possibly the first time in [his] life ... *at a loss for words!*" Sexually aroused while holding her close and stroking her hair, he confesses, "For once I had nothing to say," so he simply whispers her name (145).

Smith also emphasizes the inadequacy of the spoken language at the divine moment when Richard and Dory finally rendezvous to make love. Dory comes for Richard while he attends a revival service of the Freewill Followers, a Holiness congregation similar to the one where Crystal is "saved," complete with serpent-handling and speaking in tongues. Nor Hall calls the "tongues of fire at Pentecost" an evocative language akin to the fresh new feminine language we all await to fill the void left by patriarchy (29), and feminist scholar Elaine Showalter identifies glossolalia as a female means of claiming voice in a patriarchal religion that consistently silences women (536).†

**Kristeva borrows the term* chora *from Plato's* Timaeus *in which it denotes an "essentially mobile and extremely provisional articulation constituted by movements and their ephemeral stases." Interestingly, Kristeva notes that Plato himself calls this means of expression "nourishing and maternal" ("Semiotic" 35–36).*

†*In "Feminist Criticism in the Wilderness," Showalter acknowledges ethnographic evidence that in some cultures women have "evolved a private form of communication" out of their need for language. Showalter further notes that in ecstatic religions, women, more often than men, speak in tongues, a phenomenon anthropology attributes to women's "relative inarticulateness in formal religious discourse" (536).*

While listening to such "feminine language," Richard senses "something real" in this church and resolves to "'open [his] soul to God' and 'let him in'" (Smith 141). However, instead of allowing the male God into his soul, Richard joins Dory and they leave the meeting house together. Richard repeats twice, "We did not speak," as he explains their passionate love-making that evening (154).

Gerda Lerner describes the "paucity of language in the face of mystical revelation" (68), reinforcing the contention that for both Richard and Dory, sexual union represents elevation to a higher level of consciousness made possible by the presence of the feminine divine. Rabuzzi suggests that "patriarchal filters" have hidden the female deity for so long that we possess neither the vocabulary nor the language to acknowledge her (179); thus, silence prevails in her presence. Even as Richard abandons Dory to return to Richmond, realizing he leaves behind his "only hope of salvation in the world," he betrays the knowledge he has acquired with his thoughts that he has "passed beyond believing in retribution, beyond morality ... beyond belief in any God but that mountain God who traffics not in words and acts but in the heart" (Smith 162–63). That "mountain God," the sacred sexual maternal goddess, anthropomorphized in Dory, has been silenced for so long by patriarchal religion that her language is one not of words but of sensuality.

Richard's flirtation with the rural church of Tug runs parallel to his relationship with Dory, serving to highlight his mind-body split and also the link between Dory and religion. Soon after his arrival from Richmond, he tells the Rev. Aldous Rife, an old family friend, that he has come to the mountains "to find in Nature the source of that religious impulse that has been stifled rather than nurtured by the rigid disciplines of the Episcopal Church" (123). In the natural, sacred, sexual Dory, he finds this source, but even though he admits that his relationship with Dory "may in the end prove to be [his] salvation" (125), his desire for control ultimately prevents him from succumbing to his strong spiritual passion, both during the revival service and in his relationship with Dory. Tate points out that Richard's attempt to explain and categorize his experiences with "lists, memoirs, [and] photographs" results in a limited vision (100). He refuses to allow for the possibility of mystery implicit in the feminine divine. Even Aldous, who for over twenty years has been involved in a sexual affair with Justine Poole, the sexually accommodating proprietress of the local hotel, is blinded by the patriarchal mind-body split. He prays for Richard's ability to "forgo the temptations of the flesh and to cleave to the purity of ... spirit" (134). Aldous fails to see the inherent union of flesh and spirit in Richard's relationship with Dory and that Dory's presence in Richard's life, rather than "leading him unto temptation," keeps him "attuned to [his] soul" (136). Aldous' belief in the impossibility of integrating flesh and spirit corresponds with both Freud and Lacan's theories that insist on the unbridgeable gap between nature and culture in which nature is associated with the body and culture with the intellect.

In light of Dory's later pregnancy by Richard, Kristeva's contention that pregnancy represents "the threshold of culture and nature" ("Stabat Mater" 327) suggests that Richard and Dory's union and offspring represent the junction of nature and culture, of body and mind, flesh and spirit. Although unrealized by either character, the healing union of Richard and Dory symbolically produces hope for integration. Smith pointedly joins divinity/spirit and sexuality/body with her careful choice and description of setting when Richard and Dory finally engage in sex. At the revival service, while experiencing "the sense of majesty and trepidation—of awe at the literal presence of God" (Smith 137), Richard cannot determine whether what he senses indicates "a true religious impulse" or simply "anxiety over her [Dory]." Richard fails to realize that Dory's sacred sexual presence offers him both spiritual salvation and divine union of flesh and spirit. Just at the moment when Richard prepares to declare his religious "salvation" at the revival, Dory suddenly appears at the meeting house door, accompanied by "a blast of cold air" (153–54), her image recalling the Botticelli painting. In the careful alignment of Dory's appearance at the door with Richard's decision to profess his acceptance of the patriarchal God, Smith creates a scene of allegorical proportions that reveals saliently the salvific nature of the feminine divine.

When at Christmas Richard and Dory spend three days snowed in together at the schoolhouse, the religious/sexual/mythological significance of their experience reaches its apex. Nor Hall describes the archetype of rebirth as "entry into darkness" with closed eyes and mouth, a time when ignoring the external world "permits an inward focusing" as the initiate remains in the "incubation cave." Before entering the sacred cave, however, the "incubant had to first go through baths of purification," then drink from the streams of Lethe (forgetfulness) and Mnemosyne (memory) in order to both forget the past and remember what was about to happen. In psychotherapy, these streams are called *amnesia* and *anamnesis*, amnesia representing the sacrifice or death of the old self, and anamnesis signifying the narration of the experience as the process of passing through the birth canal, out of darkness and into light. The "proper ritual prescriptions" must be carried out and "the desire to descend into the incubation chamber must be prompted by an authentic searching rather than mere curiosity." After three days of "visionary solitude," the initiate, in a "rather dazed condition," emerges and receives a "freeing of tongues" and ultimately learns the "power of laughter" (24–27). Richard Burlage's three days with Dory strikingly parallel this archetypal voyage. It is not mere curiosity that leads Richard to the mountains or to Dory; he openly acknowledges his spiritual search. Describing his experience with Dory as "the nativity of me!" (159), Richard feels reborn in a "veritable new world! which corresponds ... with the state of my soul." In silence (with closed mouths), Richard and Dory enter the dark schoolhouse, where each moment is "a moment torn from time," in their sacred cave, with snow piled up all around the building. Richard describes the setting in striking terms that connote the feminine divine: "We are all enclosed here, as in God's womb (intriguing image!) surrounded by the rounded mounds of icy snow" (156–57). Even Richard is "intrigued" by the implied gender reversal with his choice of the words, "God's womb."

The couple undergoes a bath of purification when they bathe together. As Richard soaps Dory's body, "she squeals and giggles" (157), her musical laughter echoing that of Smith's first sexually expressive female, the Queen of *Dogbushes*, and signaling her freedom from the constraints of patriarchy. Richard, however, does not laugh, nor does he allow the "freeing of tongues" that would prove indicative of his acceptance of what Hall calls the feminine language (27–29). Although he describes the sensation Dory incites in him in terms of resurrection, "as if I were Jesus and the stone door to my tomb was rolled away!" (119), Richard, in fact, exchanges "womb" for "tomb" in his choice of spiritual death. Though "dazed," he re-emerges from the "goddess's womb" having followed the "ritual prescriptions" for the attainment of self-knowledge, but in denying the validity of his spiritual voyage, in refusing to acknowledge what he has discovered, he obviates his own rebirth and regeneration, instead becoming weak, fragile, and physically ill.

In examining the mystical union of sexual intercourse, Mann and Lyle add further layers of meaning to Dory and Richard's symbolic three-day incubation period. During the alchemical wedding, after the ritual bath and "awash with alchemical liquids, the mystic couple literally and symbolically 'drown' in the unconscious moment of orgasm, the 'little death' of all worldly concerns which transcends all man-made boundaries and dualities" (174). So goes the experience of Richard and Dory as they briefly exist in an "ethereal, timeless, other-worldly" haven (Smith 117). Mann and Lyle relate the alchemists' insistence on the "presence of the goddess" and the call for recognition and acceptance of her, the proprietress of "vast unknown Nature" (170).* Richard's instincts seem to inform him of Dory's divinity when after love-making he touches her breast and utters the single word, "Jesus" (155) as this "girl from another world" (119) begins to exert her sexual force, the force of the sacred feminine divine. Like Monica Neighbors who decides she'll "go straight to hell," Richard resolves, "If this is sin, then I am Christendom's worst (or best!) sinner. If I be damned, then let it be. But I think otherwise." All Richard's senses, both physical and intellectual, inform him that with Dory, he exists "in a state of grace"; he even acknowledges finding "all the grace [he] ever hope[s] to see" (156–58), but when he tells Dory about the train and makes plans to take her to Richmond with him, he still suspects he is fantasizing about an event never to occur.

*Mann and Lyle relate that Carl Jung spent many years of intense study examining alchemical texts and perceived them as "an allegory of man's quest for wholeness and spiritual development." Jung, according to Mann and Lyle, found Christian teachings insufficient in meeting the needs of humankind (170).

Although Smith's imagination creates in Dory a fully integrated sacred sexual adult female, the author's vision is not yet able to allow such a woman to flourish or even to survive. Richard's abandonment of Dory, not unlike Almarine's banishment of Red Emmy, reifies society's denial of the existence and power of the feminine divine. As Rebecca Smith points out, "the goddess who unites sexual passion and spiritual love and purity is rejected by learned society" (68). Lee Smith commented that she has been accused of being "anti-intellectual" and "anti-education," probably because many of her "educated characters are so out of touch with themselves," having been conditioned to exist inside "the box" (Per). Briefly, with Dory, outside his "boxed" way of thinking, Richard knows "that no purer physical and spiritual union ever has or ever shall exist on earth" (Smith 161); however, he leaves Black Rock and virtually destroys Dory. Left pregnant with his twin daughters, she renounces her physical body as her mind begins to wander aimlessly, literally divorcing herself from feeling of any kind. Formerly integrated, equally spiritual and sexual, Dory now splits herself in order to survive. Her brother Jink describes Dory as she grows larger and larger in her pregnancy: "it was like somebody else had come in and took over her body." Noting Dory's silence around everyone in the family, Jink says, "In her mind, she'd gone off from us all" (192–93). Words are insignificant for Dory now. Dory possesses neither the need nor the desire to connect with anyone after the ultimate communion she felt with Richard. Dory closes her heart to everyone, although other people are automatically drawn to her—everyone except Ora Mae, that is, who says Dory was "the worstest one of them all [Cantrells]" (210). Ora Mae cannot understand Dory's inability to love the loyal, dependable, persistent Little Luther Wade even though she agrees to marry him in order to give her twins a name. But no one succeeds in healing the wound or replacing the missing part of Dory's heart that went on that train to Richmond with Richard Burlage.

Dory's divinity, however, continues to permeate her surroundings until she makes the desperate choice to join Richard the only possible way. In the last section of the novel, Sally, Dory and Little Luther's daughter, describes how her family was like a kaleidoscope with Dory in the middle. She explains how the whole family senses the divinity of Dory. Even Little Luther, whom Sally calls "Pappy," had "everything he wanted. Which was Mama [Dory]," Sally tells us, but no evidence exists that Dory ever loved Luther at all. Dory's divinity infuses the family with beauty and love although she seems removed from all of them, "caught up in a waiting dream" (238–39). Her beauty never diminishes, and even as she goes about her domestic chores, Jink notices how her hair curls around her face, halo-like, as she offers her little brother a piece of "divinity fudge" (192). Smith's diction powerfully reveals Dory's innate sacredness as she metaphorically provides nourishing divinity to her family members. Until her suicide, Dory remains with her family, offering them a small piece of the divinity she possesses, always, as Sally explains, making "a real big deal out of Christmas" (252), a holiday that will forever hold the memory of her first and only love. Perhaps the goddess tries her best to be domesticated; after all, Ora Mae informs us that Dory made all the clothes for the entire family, but as Sally clarifies this action, "it was like she [Dory] was listening to something couldn't none of the rest of us hear" (239). Sally's feelings concerning her mother echo those of Susan Tobey about the Queen. Susan felt lucky to have had a Queen live with her as long as she did; likewise, Sally says, "I knew we had Mama with us on borrowed time[;] she was so clearly waiting—and patiently, too, not troubling us at all—but a place inside her was empty that we couldn't fill" (244), the place left empty with Richard's departure.

Dory's sacred power affects the entire family. Sally says it made Maggie, one of the twins, "nicer than nice"; Pearl, the other twin, wilder; Billy, Ora Mae's son by Parrot Blankenship, "sissier"; Lewis Ray, Sally's brother, more contrary; Pappy, more foolish in his song-writing, singing, and undying devotion to his wife, and herself, driven to work harder and "cover up" more for her mother during Dory's frequent disappearances. Only once when Sally follows her mother does she discover that Dory wanders down to the railroad tracks with her "head cocked" like she's listening for a train (244). In later novels, Smith repeats the idea of a head cocked to one side as representative of damage done to a character, most prominently present with Zeke and Rose Annie Bailey of *The Devil's Dream*. Dory's yearning and wandering serve to illustrate the wild passion now absent from her life; later Smith protagonists will likewise be described in similar terms. The motif of longing, of yearning for the intangible, symbolizes the deep need for the presence of the divine feminine as the idea of a patriarchal God becomes more abstract and unattainable. At age thirteen, Sally learns that the train whistle and squealing brakes she and her family hear signal her mother's suicide; Dory has lain down on the tracks and been decapitated by a train. Now, quite literally, Dory's head (mind) is brutally severed from her body, unlike the metaphorical separation of Crystal Spangler's mind from her body. Smith thus ends Dory's life, but not her portrayal of the sacred, sexual mother and the damage caused by society's insistence on a scission between mind and body.

Ora Mae, another mythic female, supplants Dory and marries Little Luther, just as her mother Vashti had replaced Red Emmy and Pricey Jane by marrying Almarine. However, Ora Mae exemplifies one of Smith's desexed females who chooses to separate her mind from her body, a degenerated goddess who represents the decline the female deity suffered. Only in a section of the novel narrated in first person by Ora Mae does Smith reveal that Ora Mae had never delivered Richard's letter to Dory. Ironically, Ora Mae imparts this information in order to credit herself for Dory's having "such a fine husband [Little Luther] she don't deserve" (216). Even as Richard gave Ora Mae the letter, he had perceived her as "the embodiment of something timeless and mythical, something as old and uncompromising and unchanging and hard as those ancient mountains themselves" (164). Like her mother Vashti, Ora Mae appears asexual, but echoing Granny Younger's earlier confession about love, Ora Mae betrays a once-open heart in the account of her first sexual experience with Parrot Blankenship. Her use of sexuality as power, her treatment of Parrot, and his reaction to her asexuality reverberate with similarities to *Fancy Strut*'s Ruthie Cartwright who teased Ron-the-Mouth about sex so much that it nearly drove him crazy. Ora Mae knows that what attracts Parrot to her the most is her lack of interest in sex; however, unlike Ruthie and Ron who finally come together in their mutual sexuality, Ora Mae rejects Parrot to the end, refusing to acknowledge her own sexuality and instead suppressing it behind a hard, impervious exterior. Smith's choice of names for these two male characters from extremely disparate novels reflects the writer's belief in the inherent power associated with language. Whereas Ron-the-Mouth takes control of language and uses his own individual voice, Parrot merely mimics the attitudes of patriarchal society, never displaying any individuality. Only once is Parrot able to penetrate Ora Mae's facade, but just briefly. As he kisses all over her body and asks her to leave town with him, Ora Mae sobs. She explains to the reader that she saw the mountains "open up there for a minute" as she imagined herself in Charleston with Parrot. Then she explains that she knew Parrot would leave her "as sure as the world." So she lay there crying, allowing him to kiss all over her body; "every kiss burned like fire on my skin, I can feel them kisses yet if I've got a mind to" (215).

Kristeva calls women's tears "metaphors for nonspeech, of a 'semiotics' that linguistic communication does not account for," suggesting that tears represent a "'return of the repressed' in monotheism" ("Stabat Mater" 320). Ora Mae's sobbing as Parrot excites her indeed replaces words that could express linguistically the exposure of this woman's repression. Making the conscious choice to split her mind from her body, Ora Mae claims the ability to "feel" when she has "a mind to." Ora Mae willingly relinquishes an opportunity for love, the only one she will ever have. Instead of experiencing love, with its equal measure of joy and pain, she chooses to play the martyr with her "hands full of Cantrells who can't do a thing without" her (Smith 215). Ora Mae's description of kisses feeling like fire links her to the goddess figures, Red Emmy and Dory, and obviously she has experienced strong sensuality, but like Granny Younger, she seems to forget how it feels, constantly arguing that Dory has no "sense" whatsoever and is only being stubborn by acting so distant and removed. Perhaps Ora Mae does remember, at least momentarily anyway, the power of sexual love and realize the magnitude of what she has missed when, many years later, after Pearl's death and burial next to her mother Dory, she cries out with "the awfulest low sad wail ... ever heard..., rising up of age and pain" (277) and throws the golden earrings, symbolic of sacred female sexuality, into the gorge. Eckard posits that only when Ora Mae discards the earrings does "Red Emmy's curse seem to be broken" (140). If the curse is rooted in female sexuality, then Ora Mae only attempts to break it by eliminating the earrings, just as she has tried to bury her own sexuality. Dorothy Hill suggests that by destroying the earrings, Ora Mae is throwing away the possibility of the powerful, full female among her people (56). However, Ora Mae is unsuccessful at discarding the possibility of female sexuality since Sally retains the sacred sexuality of her female ancestors and offers hope for future generations of Cantrell women. Sally compares Ora Mae, as she jettisons the earrings, to "a big black statue in a church" as she stands "with her arms flung out," appearing almost superhuman; then, once the earrings are gone, she shrinks "back from whatever she was to old Ora Mae again" (277). The implication is that this old woman recognizes and experiences at least momentarily the power of the feminine divine associated with the golden earrings previously worn by Pricey Jane, Dory, and Pearl, all of whom have died prematurely, each having paid the ultimate price for her open sexuality.

Dory's daughter Pearl continues Smith's exploration of the sexual female, but again, like Dory, Smith disallows the survival of an integrated woman. Pearl, the twin Sally describes as always having been "out for blood" (241), inherits the golden rose earrings, but for Pearl, "nothing was ever going to be enough" (267). In mentioning Pearl's desire for "blood," Smith not only connects Pearl to her mother and Red Emmy, but also establishes early on Pearl's sexuality and intensity. Sally explains that Pearl always had the feeling she was missing something. Pearl, like Crystal Spangler before her, is drawn to an artist, a creative young man who offers an opportunity for self-knowledge. Describing Donnie "like a Greek god," Pearl explains her love for this beautiful, shy, talented, and sensitive teenage boy. Once the two have run away together, Pearl leaving her upholsterer husband and young daughter Jennifer (the college student introduced in the present of the novel), Smith transgresses boundaries and cleverly mixes maternal and sexual love with Pearl's comment to Donnie while they are eating at a restaurant: "You know, you really ought to order some vegetables. You know you're a growing boy" (272–73). Although humorous to the reader, this is the point where Pearl realizes she must take Donnie back home.

Paul Friedrich's research provides a helpful backdrop for examining Smith's depiction of a maternal sexual female. Questioning the suppression of the ancient archetype that combines "the erotic with the motherly," Friedrich attributes the dichotomy to our collective world view. Friedrich acknowledges that a significant minority of European and American women ever achieve and reflect such integration of sexual and maternal love since our Western value systems operate on a falsely imposed bifurcation (181–84). Pearl, in her sexual love and maternal concern for Donnie, exemplifies such an integrated female. In her depiction of Pearl, Smith advances toward the psychic and social change in the image of the non-sexual mother upon which feminist theorists insist. With Pearl's desertion of husband and child to join her lover, Smith introduces a pattern of behavior she develops further in later novels as the writer begins to increase alternatives for women's lives. Pearl's affair with Donnie, much like that of Dory and Richard, and even Red Emmy and Almarine, has been impregnating in the sense that Pearl has felt and experienced sexual love. She has learned about what she says "Mama [Dory] knew about and never told us" (265). Now Pearl has felt what she thinks her mother must have, and just as Dory's life was destroyed, Pearl's is also. At this point in her life and writing career, although Smith can imagine and create an integrated female, she disallows the survival of such a woman within society. Pearl had always said she wanted "things to be *pretty*..., to be *in love*" (258), but the two ideas are not necessarily coexistent. With her husband, Pearl had a "pretty" life, all the nice belongings one might desire, but she needed to experience the "killin'" kind of love in order to feel fully alive. Once she does, her life virtually ends, soon giving birth to a premature baby, then dying of "complications." As Sally notes, Pearl's being buried next to Dory is "fitting" (275–76); they both wanted more than society was ready to allow them.

The last section of the novel reconnects to the first part told by Granny Younger since both narrators relate stories of strong, sexual females. This time, however, Sally tells her own story whereas Red Emmy's story was delivered by Granny. In her article, "The Power of Language in Lee Smith's *Oral History*," Corinne Dale notes that Sally empowers herself both sexually and linguistically by taking control of the story (21). No longer is the sexual female silent or apologetic. In Smith's creation of both Dory and Sally, she offers alternatives to the selfless, passive mother. Unlike Dory, however, Sally exerts a salient force of control over her life and her choices through her power of language. As Dale points out, Sally, more than any other character, accommodates "the sexual and the intellectual, the primal and the cultural" (32). Sally begins her section by boldly stating, "There's two things I like to do better than anything else in this world, even at my age—and one of them is talk. You all can guess what the other one is" (233). Kristeva's idea that bodily drives are manifested through language challenges the traditional dualism between body and mind and works to reconnect the body to language. In Smith's creation of Sally, Kristeva's ideal integration is actualized. Kristeva insists that the body, the maternal body in particular, does not have to be sacrificed to culture (Oliver 112). Though Dory suffers such a sacrificial death, her sacred sexual daughter remains to seize control of both body and language, boldly relating her own story and that of her mother. Sally explains, "Roy [her husband] can fuck your eyes out, Roy can, and talking all the time" (233), further establishing the relationship between sexuality and language.

Healing is suggested by Sally and Roy's marriage, one based on equality and communication. Unlike the sex between so many before her who could find no words to express their erotic feelings, Sally is filled with words and shares all of them with her husband in a reciprocal, nonsacrificial relationship. Even Freud called the practice of psychoanalysis "the talking cure," admitting the salvific nature of language. Sally tells Roy the story of her life, centering, of course, on her mother and how Dory affected the whole family. Sally was the child who tried to foster family harmony by working hard and being "good"; she thinks this may be the reason she "turned bad" (240). What she describes as "bad" is her openly sexual behavior, sleeping with various men and eventually running away to Florida with a disc jockey she thought she loved. Unlike Monica Neighbors and Crystal Spangler, Sally willingly explored her sexuality and experienced the wildness so common for Smith's sexual females. Now, with Roy, Sally says she can be herself and doesn't need to put up a front. She looks back over her life and observes, "All that time of working so hard and trying so hard and not talking had passed away like a dream" (267). Until she met Roy, she was silent, unable to express her true self both sexually and linguistically. Similar to Dory and Richard who are described throughout as being one, as completing each other, Sally says she and Roy are "two of a kind" in bed; "it's like it all gets mixed up some way, like you kind of forget where your body stops and his starts or who did what to who and who came when and all that" (234). Her description is reminiscent of Mack Stiltner's appeals to Crystal when he tells her, "we're two of a kind, baby" (102), but Crystal is not ready to embrace his honesty whereas Sally and Roy are accepting of each other and complement one another. The union of this couple looks forward to Smith's representation in later novels of an androgyny akin to what theologian Rita M. Gross calls "the original creature [who] was undifferentiated humanity, neither man nor woman" (*Feminism* 119).

In her depiction of Sally, Smith moves a step further in imaging the feminine divine, exposing and examining the deep and natural connections among sexuality, motherhood, and spirituality. When Sally nurses her son Davy, she consciously links motherhood and sexuality: "There is something about a baby's pull on your nipple that puts you in mind of a man, but it is entirely different from that—it's different from everything else. And there's a lot of things ... you can't explain" (266). Sally's contemplations powerfully tie her to not only Dory, her own sexual mother, but also her grandmother, Pricey Jane, as well. As Pricey Jane nursed Dory, she too was conscious of the sensuality in "the steady pull on her nipple" (70). To all three women, the union of sexuality and motherhood is natural, but to most of society, "maternity is understood to be the end-product, *not* the site of sexuality" (Parker 260). Paul Friedrich acknowledges the close harmony between maternal and erotic love, citing in particular the maternal experience of breast feeding as erotically arousing for a woman as well as a woman's milk "let[ting] down" during erotic play, arguing that these sensations are normal and natural (184–86). Freud, however, believed that a mother's deriving sensual/sexual satisfaction from nursing her child suggests gratification of perverse repressed desires. Even in the twenty-first century, while nursing is much more common among new mothers and imposed feeding schedules have virtually disappeared, the hegemony of patriarchal culture supports oppression and dichotomization of women's sexual and maternal drives, reflecting the limited understanding our culture has of maternal sexuality. Rabuzzi suggests that breast feeding represents a "subtle transformation" in which the mother achieves "motherselfhood" and follows the pattern of the goddess (220). Clearly not only Sally, but also those before her, in their consistent alignment with the feminine divine, integrate the two complexes of motherhood and sexuality.

In her narrative, Smith creates what Patricia Yaeger calls for—new space—where "not only [woman's] body ... must be reimagined, not only the inseminated womb, or the female genitals, but 'patriarchal' language itself must be given a new dimension, must be brought back to earth and made playful" (210–11). By ending her novel with Sally's voice, openly conceding the ultimate mystery of maternal sexuality with her acknowledgement of the inexplicability of life, Smith insists on the survival and proliferation of the sacred sexual mother. As Sally and Roy are "fooling around ... [and] laughing" (Smith 278), Smith offers a challenge to present hierarchies and codes for appropriate female behavior. Roy rests his hand on Sally's breast and asks his wife to talk to him more, desiring the nourishment her stories offer. In mentioning the placement of Roy's hand, Smith connects this scene with earlier ones in the novel where sacred sexual females unashamedly exposed their breasts to their lovers. In each case, female breasts symbolize the goddess's regenerative power through literal and metaphorical nourishment. Although Sally's importance in the novel is sublimated to Dory, in her portrayal of Sally, Smith offers a speaking mother, one who openly expresses sacred sexuality. In Sally and Roy's divine union, neither partner desires escape whereas in Dory's union with Richard, the male deserts the female and the opportunity for salvation she offers. In earlier depictions of divine couples such as Brooke and Bentley, Monica and Buck, and Crystal and Mack, the female is consistently denied the opportunity for integration and abandoned the relationship. Only at the end of *Oral History* and in later novels is Smith ready to allow the female to embrace her divine sexuality and survive. Rebecca Smith argues that the females in this novel " help to redeem the ravaged Crystal Spangler," but that Sally "is not interested ... in reviving strong mythical goddesses" and is complacent in "suppress[ing] this feminine myth and let[ting] it lie unexamined" (80–81). However, Lee Smith, far from being satisfied to "let it lie," charges forward with her spiritual journey in the novels that follow *Oral History* as she continues to exhume and explore the feminine divine.

Chapter IV

"UPENDED AMONG THESE ROSES"

Damage and Hope for Healing in *Family Linen*

In *New Woman New Earth*, Rosemary Ruether explains how patriarchal religion split apart the "unities of mother religion into an absolute dualism," a bifurcation that elevates male consciousness and negates and denigrates female consciousness. Ruether goes on to suggest that this dualism insists on the "transcendent divine sphere" of the male and the posteriority of the female who is "created by, subject to, and ultimately alien to the nature of (male) consciousness, in whose image man made his God" (194–95). In *Family Linen* (1985), Smith presents a host of damaged characters, both male and female, who suffer from the cultural absence of the feminine divine and the resultant dichotomy between mind and body. Female characters in particular continue to search for something to believe in. Like earlier Smith characters, some choose to deny their sexuality in an effort to conform or just to survive and function within society, while others come to terms with their internal conflicts among sexuality, motherhood, and spirituality and find healing in self-acceptance. Again reflecting appurtenances of the feminine divine in her portrayal of female characters as sacred creatures, Smith works to restore females to what Ruether calls the "transcendent divine sphere" typically reserved for males in Western patriarchal religious traditions.

Family Linen offers a more accepting, forgiving view of humanity than previous novels, with a more immediate plot in the sense that all the narrators are alive in the story's present. Smith does reveal, however, a version of the family's distant past in the written words of the family matriarch's journal. Reminiscent of similar treatment of the recorded past when Crystal Spangler likewise finds comfort in reading the journal of a distant relative, Lacy Hess's fascination with her mother's journal illustrates Smith's continued insistence on the importance of the past and family history in the attainment of self-knowledge. *Family Linen* demonstrates Smith's on-going experimentation with point of view and plot as she successfully blends several genres in the work's diverse readings as a family-history novel, a psychological thriller, and a murder mystery. Smith has admitted that she struggles with plot, but with all these characters "walking around in [her] head wanting to talk," she sometimes just appropriates one (qtd. in Loewenstein 491). The real-life story behind the novel, called the "outhouse murder," featured a North Carolina woman who was suffering from migraines and visited a hypnotist. Through therapy, the woman regained the memory of witnessing her mother killing her father with an ax before dumping the body into the outhouse. Once police discovered the remains of the long-dead man, the woman's story was verified. In the novel, Smith replaced the outhouse with a well, so metaphorically, the family's life is poisoned at the source. In goddess mythology, a well provides the life-giving source of the goddess, and the washing motif runs throughout the novel with the "family's linen" being cleansed by the revelation of a dark family secret and the suggestion of symbolic rebirth at the end when family members, along with several wedding guests, jump into the swimming pool, immersing themselves in the magical life-giving water of the feminine divine.

In *Family Linen*, Smith treats the lives of women as important in numerous ways, showing great compassion for her female characters in particular. In *Oral History*, the sacred, sexual, maternal female was possible only in an imagined past; in *Family Linen*, this female exists in the present. Like *Oral History* before and *The Devil's Dream* after, *Family Linen* uses multiple narrators and shifting points of view from first person to third person omniscient. By the fourth section, which is delivered by the youngest daughter Lacy in third person limited omniscience, the shifting perspectives from various family members captivate the reader. The alternating blend of first person chapters and third person limited omniscient chapters eventually shifts to omniscient sections on the two occasions when the entire family is gathered together: first, at Elizabeth's house when the family divides her belongings; and second, during the wedding at end of the novel. Like *Oral History*, *Family Linen* focuses on family, emphasizes remembering and preserving the past, uses a gothic Appalachian setting, and places importance on love or the lack thereof. The possibilities for women's lives can be traced in the novels as Smith gradually imagines more options for growth and fulfillment in women's lives. By drawing on the mythic past in *Oral History*, Smith constructed the female character differently from earlier depictions, seeing her simultaneously as sexual, divine, and maternal; however, Dory is sacrificed since society is unable to recognize or accept her multifaceted nature and therefore contributes to her destruction. As noted by Dorothy Hill, with *Family Linen*, Smith takes her characters further, more deeply into their pain, and begins to find ways of healing their wounds (85).

Similar to Dory's centrality in *Oral History,* the central mystery of *Family Linen* also revolves around a damaged female, Elizabeth Bird Hess, the *grande dame* of Booker Creek, Virginia. Miss Elizabeth, like Dory, suffers from limitations placed on her by her environment, but, unlike Dory, she seizes control of her own life. Elizabeth, caught up in her own pretense, holds her head high and denies any problem, adopting her husband's illegitimate daughter and remarrying to give birth to two more children. The tension between internal reality and external facade distances Miss Elizabeth from her family so that when she dies, none of her children feels they have really known her. Throughout her life, she has remained blind by choice; her inability to face reality leaves the terrible burden of confronting the truth to her family members, primarily her children, who serve as the principal narrators of the novel.

Throughout Smith's novels, a recurrent motif surfaces in which a woman defies her family's wishes, marries for love, and lives a short and difficult life. Elizabeth's early struggles with her own sexuality and the damage done to her as a young girl are revealed after her death when her daughter Lacy finds her mother's fifty-year-old journal at the bottom of a dresser drawer. In a flowery, poetic style, the words in the old-style composition book titled *Days of Light and Darkness:—Memoirs by Elizabeth Bird, 1928* relate the story of Elizabeth's parents' meeting and marriage and Elizabeth's life until about age twenty-five. Similar to Ivy Rowe's mother Maude of *Fair and Tender Ladies* who married John Arthur and left her family, Elizabeth relates in her journal how her mother Mary, with her "flaming hair," was charmed by the "wild young buck" Thomas Lemuel Bird and left her family to travel across the state of Virginia and live with her new husband. By mentioning Mary's red hair and the feeling Thomas has of entering "a different world" when he encounters her, Smith links their meeting to that of earlier divine couples. Additionally, the courtship of Mary and Thomas takes place "by the deep, still waters of Lake Junaluska among the solemn Mountains" (168–69), water and mountains signaling the presence of the feminine divine in Smith's work. After years of hard work and giving birth to *three* daughters over a period of seven years, however, Mary begins to lose her youth and energy, especially after the extremely difficult labor and delivery of Fay, the youngest. Elizabeth notes that a "certain sadness" sometimes seemed to overtake her mother as she longed for her family back home although Thomas "lavished her with attention and sweet solicitous Care" (170). Despite the "sweetness" and devotion of her husband, Mary experiences the longing characteristic of so many of Smith's female characters, a yearning for what Kathryn Rabuzzi terms "motherselfhood," a selfhood equipped with a voice "authentic to women's experiences" (12).

With her portrait of Elizabeth, Smith depicts another damaged female in a world devoid of any sense of the feminine divine. The first of several broken female characters in the novel, Elizabeth experiences pain early in life in a relationship that awakens her sexuality. At age nineteen, she encounters physical passion for the first time with Ransom McClain, a delicate boy with "springing pale hair" who captures Elizabeth's imagination and seems to her "the masculine counterpart of Grace Harrison" (185), a dear friend of Mary's who had taught Elizabeth literature and language when she was young. With the entrance of Ransom, Smith seems to suggest a similarly healing divine presence for Elizabeth, as this young man symbolically offers "redemption" or "ransom" for Elizabeth. Elizabeth describes Grace's correlation to Ransom; she is "willowy" and "elongated" (176), with fine blonde hair appearing to "spring up even more angelically around her face, floating, it seemed" (179). In Smith's attribution of divine qualities to both Ransom and Grace, who offer Elizabeth a chance for a life very different from her mother's, with their halo-like hair and the mention of their energy and liveliness, she seems to gravitate toward an androgynous image of healing, equal parts male and female. After Mary's death and an unexplained experience with Thomas for which Grace permanently suffers, Grace refused ever to visit the Bird household again, leaving Elizabeth feeling abandoned and alone, robbed of what she senses represents the "grace" of God.

As in earlier novels, language plays a crucial role in divine union and the expression of sacred sexuality. Ransom, like Grace and other deific figures in Smith, shares with Elizabeth a love for language. Suffering from estrangement from Grace, Elizabeth senses that Ransom understands her spirituality that has been "suppressed in [her] by Duty and Tragedy." Elizabeth describes the "sweetness" of the summer spent with Ransom, during which she reconnects with both her sexual and spiritual selves. She explains, she and Ransom "fell into a summer of sun-drenched Abandon and the Purest form of Love" (186–87). Although Elizabeth expresses shame at the pleasure she derives from Ransom's presence, she also claims the right to what Luce Irigaray labels *"jouissance,"* expressed passion necessary for fulfillment ("Bodily Encounter" 43). Smith's diction, with the words "tastes," "voracious Appetite," and "Thirst" (187), reverberates with allusions to Lévi-Strauss's "honey-mad" woman who feeds on honey wildly and to excess, representing her desperate need for both language and the open expression of her sexuality. Ransom awakens not only Elizabeth's physical passion, but also her long-submerged passion for language as the two read to one another by the river. When Ransom leaves and abruptly stops writing to Elizabeth with no explanation, she begins wandering the mountain, much like Dory before her. However, instead of eventually ending her life as Dory does, Elizabeth turns to patriarchal religion for comfort, converting from Methodist to Episcopalian where the Priest "does not make so much of the unrefined elements of Christianity such as the Blood and the Cross" (Smith 190). Without any means of sexual expression, Elizabeth squelches her love for language and her ebullient sexuality, becoming a member of the Holy Fellowship of Saints. In her journal, Elizabeth offers a metaphorical description of herself during this time of her life as she faces a "dark and wild" night with the "moon ... scarcely visible" and the "antic wind in a frenzy," blowing her skirt about her ankles and extinguishing her candle (192). The seductive power of the wind, in Smith consistently representative of female sexuality and the feminine divine, remains strong around and within Elizabeth although she suppresses these feelings for several more years.

Elizabeth's buried passion resurfaces only briefly late one afternoon in a highly charged symbolic scene. When Elizabeth comes inside after working with the day lily bulbs, she sees in the flames of the fireplace "strange birds with fiery plumage" and "dancing men" (202), a mirror image of the fiery passion she feels burning inside. In *She Who Is: The Mystery of God in Feminist Theological Discourse*, Elizabeth Johnson re-envisions a female deity who resonates with overflowing energy and incarnates "words and deeds of liberation." Johnson explains that fire, in its non-destructive capacity, symbolizes this feminine divinity in her transformative and regenerative power (243). As Elizabeth gazes into the flames, she encounters the potential source of her liberation, a sense of her own sacredness and the sanctity of her life, but she lacks the ability or willingness to view spirituality in any terms other than patriarchal. Noticing the "climbing roses" on the trellis and the "purple asters" along the walk, Elizabeth once more goes to work digging in the soil to find the bulbs. With the breeze chilling her, she observes the fresh new bulbs and describes them with strong erotic imagery. Elizabeth's pondering the mystery of such a "frail form" holding sap within it that suddenly "spring[s] forth so abundantly ... with such vigor" (195–96) evinces a fascination with male genitalia and ejaculation. Her weeping indicates her sense of loss at the absence of expressed sexuality in her life. Even though Elizabeth says she can't imagine what she was thinking, the reader certainly can. After this experience, Elizabeth rushes into the house and bathes, an unconscious purification ritual. Even after having eaten the "nourishing honey" in her relationship with Ransom and cleansed herself, both necessary rituals for archetypal rebirth, Elizabeth remains trapped in self-ignorance.

Elizabeth experiences another chance for sexual and spiritual integration in her short-lived marriage to Jewell Rife. The reader learns about this time period of Elizabeth's life toward the end of the novel in a section narrated in first person by Nettie, Elizabeth's sister. Nettie compares Elizabeth, at age twenty-three, to "an apple hanging on a tree, waiting for somebody to come along and pick it, and Jewell was the right man for the job." A charmer and a big talker, Jewell looks like "something wild," like "all outdoors." Jewell's wildness, even as it clashes with Elizabeth's pure domesticity, is what attracts her to him, but one suspects the marriage will end disastrously. Smith builds upon her earlier fire symbolism with Elizabeth and Jewell's first meeting. On his first visit to her house, Jewell builds a fire in the fireplace to warm Elizabeth and Fay. Nettie's comment that no one "had made a fire in that fireplace for years and years" (216–18) clearly has more than just a literal application, as

Smith has consistently associated fire with expressed sexuality. Additionally, Jewell's hair is described as "black curls, which popped back up no matter how hard he tried to slick them down" (232), suggesting his irrepressible sexuality and bringing to mind both Ransom McClain and Grace Harrison, two other people Elizabeth has loved.

Jewell's ability to make Elizabeth laugh suggests his function as a potential tool for her emancipation from patriarchal constraints as she opens up to express her sacred sexuality. Nettie concludes that the reason Elizabeth fell in love with Jewell was because he could make her laugh a certain kind of "silvery laugh," and she had experienced "precious little laughter" in her house for many years (218–19). Just as Ivy Rowe feels intoxicated by the presence of Honey Breeding, Nettie describes Elizabeth as being "drunk on" Jewell, giggling, humming, and blushing when he's around. Jewell's wild spirit cannot be tamed. Nettie describes the change that comes over Elizabeth when she's with Jewell, how Elizabeth, "so full of life and joy," seemed "like three people," appearing to "bust right out" of her skin (221–22). As villainous as Jewell seems, his name and the effect he has on Elizabeth certainly suggest his divinity as Smith once more mixes the sacred with the profane since Elizabeth, one of *three* daughters, seems like "three" people, her sexuality seemingly bursting through her skin like many of Smith's earlier female characters. And through the years of their unhappy marriage, Jewell periodically orders a dozen red roses for Elizabeth, a reminder to the reader of her hidden sexuality and the sacredness of her femininity.

Elizabeth's way of coping with Jewell's infidelity and irresponsibility exemplifies what Smith calls the Southern art of *"denial"* ("Southern Exposure" 3); Elizabeth is not prepared to accept her own complex nature. Only once in her six years of marriage to Jewell, which produces two children, does Elizabeth even hint that a problem exists (presumably related to her husband's sexual demands). Elizabeth's fragmented statement to her sister Nettie— "Things are not—... It's just not—" (224)—indicates the extent to which denial is her only tool for survival. Nettie later witnesses the brutal truth that Elizabeth will repudiate: in Elizabeth's absence, Jewell rapes his sister-in-law Fay. Nettie says, "it's probably been going on for years" (235), but Elizabeth's response to Nettie's tactful confrontation is denial.

Although with Elizabeth's strength and determination, Smith offers hope for survival, Elizabeth (unlike Dory, for example) is not the sacred, sexual, maternal goddess, for Elizabeth fails miserably in integrating her sexual and maternal instincts and recognizing the divinity of feminine experience. Rather than incorporating her sexuality, obvious at a young age, into her later roles as wife and mother, she chooses to lock away the physical passion she once felt, making herself untouchable for all who love her and in effect becoming a complete stranger in her own home. The depth of her seclusion is best illustrated in a scene at the hospital after her stroke when Elizabeth lies in the bed under an oxygen tent and her daughter Myrtle looks at her and reflects on her own inability and lack of desire to touch her mother. Not even Elizabeth's husband Verner Hess can touch her. Smith offers a redeeming view of this male with her portrayal of Verner, described in terms of his "sweetness" and also as having red hair (251), which is often linked to divinity in Smith. In a powerful memory, Lacy recalls her mother, dressed in "flowered voile," sitting at the head of the table at Sunday dinner, stiff and untouchable. Verner would slip out the back door where all the children came to him, one by one, with their problems, while their mother slept in her bed "fully dressed and perfectly rigid" (161). In the section of the novel narrated by Arthur, Elizabeth's only son, he admits that he has always envisioned his mother as a queen, calling to mind that in ancient mythology the queen bee was served by all others and considered an epiphany of the goddess, but this "queen"—Elizabeth—lacks the sweetness of honey that would allow her integration.

The perfect image of the Southern lady on a pedestal, Elizabeth remained pure and protected from reality as Verner dealt with the many problems, all the while discouraging the children from disturbing their mother, so that eventually Elizabeth was completely insulated from their lives. In his great love for his wife, Verner contributed to Elizabeth's inability and unwillingness to face the truth in any situation, for as Lacy explains, he "worshiped her." Lacy admits her inability to understand why her father possessed such a love for her mother, but she knows "there doesn't really have to be a reason, you worship what you worship, you love what you love, and can't help it." Lacy's comment looks forward to both Ivy Rowe's and Molly Petree's observations about the inexplicable nature of love. Lacy determines that the whole house revolved around the "secret, the hidden beast," that Verner Hess worshiped Elizabeth and loved her obsessively. Lacy finds it odd that such a small, unobtrusive, "red-headed" man should be capable of possessing such a great love (161–62). Although Smith's diction hints at the possibility of Elizabeth's divinity (Verner "worships" her), she falls miserably short of achieving the level of self-knowledge that the feminine divine would allow. Elizabeth does, however, survive.

In her depiction of Elizabeth's oldest daughter Sybill, Smith probes the issue of self-knowledge or lack thereof, in portraying another female damaged by the absence of the feminine divine in her life. Irigaray explains somatic pain as symptomatic of women's paralysis "in their relationship with their bodies" and the absence of a real identity ("Women-Mothers" 52). Sybill, with her increasingly painful migraines, clearly exemplifies a woman disconnected from her body and struggling in her search for an identity. Sharing with her mother and many of Smith's earlier female characters an overwhelming concern for appearance, Sybill has become a frigid, compulsive perfectionist who refuses to involve herself in any relationship that might prove unpleasant. Although Sybill tells the hypnotist that her mother is "a *real* lady" (35), one already suspects that in Sybill's estimation being a "lady" means distancing oneself from pain. Merely being in the same room with her younger sister Candy embarrasses Sybill, for Candy is a sexual, sensual, "unladylike" woman who acts on her feelings. As Sybill sits with the hypnotist examining her fingernails, her nails suddenly appear "funny and ragged, red and flesh," reminding her of Candy (21). Smith's choice of the color red and the word "flesh" to remind Sybill of Candy links Candy to the aspects of womanhood that make Sybill so uncomfortable, such as love, sexuality, and sensuality. Though disgusted by the ideas of sexuality and sensuality that Candy exudes, Sybill also has suspicions that her parents "*liked Candy better*" than her but then remembers that her mother hadn't actually liked Candy at all since Candy was "too wild." Sybill congratulates herself that her mother "always approved of her" (148–49). Linked to her own lack of self-identity, the paradoxical image of her mother that Sybill holds encompasses the "overly careful, sensitive, sweet mother" she remembers from childhood, alongside the "mythic figure in the streaming rain, with ax upraised" that she sees in her dream (146).

The provocative mixture of sweetness and flowers in one image of Elizabeth, and water and an ax in the other, calls for further speculation as to Smith's intent. Three of these ideas have previously been linked to the feminine divine, female sexuality and rebirth (sweetness, flowers, and rain), but the ax, a weapon of death, breaks with this pattern, unless we return to the image of the original mother goddess who encompassed all of life, death, and regeneration in her many symbolic forms. Triangles and double triangles resembling hourglasses, which were symbolic of the goddess, are common designs on tomb architecture dating back to 5000 B.C. Then around 4000 B.C., the bull's head and horns with its obvious uterine shape became a common symbol at the entrances of tombs. Often between the horns of the bull in the middle of the forehead was a butterfly, or a double triangle or hourglass turned sideways, which also resembles an ax. The images are complex and varied, but these symbols for the goddess were predominant throughout the prehistoric, pre-patriarchal cultures of Old Europe (Gimbutas, *World*). Anne Baring and Jules Cashford cite the Minoan focus on the dynamic energy of the goddess, who was often represented in a standing position, with arms upraised, "holding the double axe in her hands" (107), an image almost identical to the one in Sybill's mind. Furthermore, Cretan vases were decorated with semblances of double axes "patterned with roses and ... lilies, both flowers that call forth the goddess" (113), recalling Sybill's memory of her mother's "smelling always of lilac" (Smith 146). Perhaps Sybill's dichotomized simulacra of her mother are not as oppositional as one might originally think, considering the imagery of the feminine divine that comes to increasingly permeate Smith's fiction.

Irigaray's insistence on the damage caused by suppressed sexuality ("Bodily Encounter" 44) is reflected in Sybill's fascination and preoccupation with roses, consistently a sexual symbol of the feminine divine in Smith. One of the first observations Sybill makes in the hypnotist's yard is of the rose bed, and although she usually appreciates roses, today her head begins to ache when she merely looks at the blurred colors of the Peace rose. Sybill likes a "solid rose ... something definite" (Smith 18), and up until she began to have the migraines, she has been in control of everything in her life. Smith immediately introduces the conflict for Sybill between maternity and sexuality with her description of the setting in the doctor's yard where a swing set, obviously evidence of children and possibly a mother, stands juxtaposed to a rose garden, a consistent representation of female sexuality. As Sybill tries to imagine being the hypnotist's wife and where she would have placed the rosebed, she thinks of how she has always disliked children but then decides that she admires the imagined wife since "[e]ven if she has children, she keeps order" (16–17). To Sybill, maternity and children are associated with disorder and chaos, conditions of which she wants no part, a position that looks forward to several female characters in *Fair and Tender Ladies*. At the hypnotist's office, Sybill thinks of her brother and sisters and how they live such "messy lives," the way she thinks hers will be if she "*take[s] up with Edward Bing*" (39), the neighbor whose dinner invitations she has declined for fear of the aggravation of involvement.

Nor Hall acknowledges the archetypal sibyl's association with "the Old Goddess and tremendous Mother" (183) who possess the "gift of being able to give shape to what lies beneath the surface" (173). Sybill functions precisely in this way, since she alone retains the knowledge of what literally "lies beneath the surface" of the yard, her father's murdered body. Additionally, streams and water were always present where the sibyl dwelled, adding further implications to the rain-drenched setting of not only Sybill's revelation of the murder, but also the actual crime scene itself. On Sybill's second visit to Dr. Diamond, when rain falls and the "roses droop" (Smith 36), Sybill undergoes hypnosis and relates her dream of seeing her mother murder her father (Jewell Rife) with an ax and dump his body into a well. She describes the "rose-flowered rug" in her home at the bottom of the stairs, the lightning flashes sending out "sparks of light in every direction," creating a halo image, and her father's "face and hair all red with blood" in the pouring rain (41–42). The long-submerged memory, powerful enough to permanently damage Sybill's ability to love anyone, surfaces in language rife with sexual connotations. As she leaves the hypnotist's office, after having exhumed the dark family secret, Sybill experiences a "vision of Edward Bing, upended among these roses" and feels overwhelmed by "the sweet moist air so heavy with roses and rain" (45). With the source of her sexual frustration now exposed and the image of her mother as "the perfect lady" destroyed, Sybill possesses awareness of and susceptibility to the presence of female libido in the world. Edward Bing, a possible lover, appears "upended among the roses," not just one of the roses, but completely inverted, the opposite of what she thought of him before the hypnosis. And the air is saturated with sweetness, water, and roses, three important representations of female sexuality and the feminine divine.

Smith links Sybill's denial of her own eroticism to her repudiation of men. Having excluded men from her life and sculpted herself as an attractive, precise, efficient woman, Sybill seems the direct opposite of both Brooke Kincaid and Crystal Spangler. Sybill has embraced society's imposed virgin-whore dichotomy. She wants order, efficiency, simplicity; anything she doesn't understand, she denies. Sybill's feelings about her sexuality are best revealed in her thoughts about her unconscious, which she regards "like she regarded her reproductive system, as a messy, murky darkness full of unexplained fluids and longings which she preferred not to know too much about" (17). A perfect example of Irigaray's damaged female for whom even menstruation is a "horrible sight, bloody," Sybill is "repelled by all fluence" ("Volume" 64). As a survival mechanism after her traumatic childhood experience, Sybill has split herself, as her name clearly suggests, completely blocking passion from her life, much as her mother has done. So when Edward Bing moves into her apartment complex and Sybill, still a virgin, begins to harbor passionate thoughts about him, headaches and dreams begin. Like Ivy Rowe, she initially attributes these strange feelings to "the Change of Life" (24). When Sybill tells Dr. Diamond about Edward, the doctor, trying to determine the reason for the headaches, questions Sybill's virginity, to which she abruptly replies, "None of your beeswax!" (26). Smith's diction in Sybill's trite response emphasizes her refusal to allow any "bee" to pollinate her "flower" and the concomitant absence of the sweetness of honey in her life.

Sybill's sister Myrtle reifies Irigaray's observation that "mothers feed but do not speak" as they remain trapped in the role of satisfying the needs of others and have no access to desires of their own ("Women-Mothers" 51). Smith has often discussed the dangers of a female's losing her individual identity in the busyness and complacency of caring for others. For these women, achieving a sense of feminine divinity can prove extremely difficult. Although the *Oxford English Dictionary* states that the fragrant myrtle was sacred to Venus and was used as an emblem of love, Smith chooses not to attribute these qualities to her character by that name who, although blonde, beautiful, and mother to *three* children (like her grandmother), shares with her mother and sister an obsession with appearance. Myrtle has always used her family to shield her from any real self-knowledge; like *Oral History*'s Richard Burlage, Myrtle won't allow herself to explore too deeply or to feel too much pain. So she reaches for the jolt of sensation that her marriage lacks in her meaningless affair with Gary Vance, someone she "wouldn't be caught dead with" (Smith 4), an exterminator who spends his time going to movies, drinking beer, and smoking marijuana. Similar to *Fancy Strut*'s Bob Pitt, who felt he had missed out on something and therefore engages in an affair with Sandy in an effort to fill the void, Myrtle needs a break from the boredom of her mundane life as a housewife and mother and uses Gary as an opportunity to explore her purely sexual self. With Myrtle and Gary's affair, Smith again explores a purely physical relationship, one that lacks the necessary depth and complexity to provide sacred union. After spending much of her life birthing and caring for children, Myrtle begins to experience the internal conflict present in many of Smith's female characters, somehow "hold[ing] two opposite things in her mind at the same time" (48); she loves her husband and her children, but Myrtle shares with Brooke Kincaid and Crystal Spangler a sense of unreality, "like her life ha[s] happened to somebody else" (61). Realizing she has no real identity of her own, she knows her existence is defined by her various roles in her family and in the community.

With Myrtle's two love relationships, Smith mixes the sacred and profane as she continues to explore the dichotomized male also. In her marriage, Myrtle possesses the sanitized, socially-acceptable position of wife; in her affair with Gary, she hungers for degradation, much like Monica Neighbors in her fantasies of illicit sexual encounters even before she met Buck. Whereas in her life as wife/mother, Myrtle feels disgust at the sight of an unclean object or inappropriate clothing, these details don't concern her in her other world of illicit sex, a world in which she invests no emotion. Myrtle simply cannot feel pain, or *anything* for that matter, and this lack of genuine feeling not only drives her to the arms of a younger man, but also contributes to her husband's finding comfort in the company of the softer Candy. Although she has failed to integrate her sexuality with her roles as wife and mother by the end of the novel, Myrtle's realization of this void in her life offers hope for a positive change in the future. Like her mother who decided to bury her sexuality and live out her life with Verner Hess as a "real lady," Myrtle opts for the comfort and security represented by Don and her newly refurbished mansion.

Candy, "love child" of Jewell and Fay (139), "wild" sister, according to both Sybill and Myrtle, serves as the novel's primary goddess figure, successfully integrating maternal and sexual love. Of all Elizabeth's children and all the narrators in the novel, only Candy seems satisfied with herself and her life. In an interview with Michelle Lodge, Smith described Candy as the heroine of the novel, the most important character and the most successful, well-integrated person (310). Since Candy is not actually the daughter of Elizabeth, she possesses a certain freedom from conformity that allows her to lead a life very different from her brother and sisters. Dorothy Hill notes that Candy, a "child born of male violence and female submission," goes far beyond the other female characters in her choice of lifestyle (91), a beautician who explores her sexuality while successfully fulfilling the role of mother. Sybill and Myrtle consider Candy their inferior due to Candy's occupation and promiscuity as a teenager and young adult. Although Candy has given her children the freedom to grow and become successful adults, Myrtle labels Candy a "terrible mother" (Smith 58), and both sisters express amazement that one of Candy's children attends law school and the other teaches art. Sybill and Myrtle's opinion of their sister reflects the views of society that, in most cultures, are based on an unrealistic dichotomy between maternity and sexuality.

Smith emphasizes not only Candy's sexuality but also her link to the feminine divine with the imagery the writer uses to describe Candy's home. The street lamp outside Candy's window "makes a lavender pool on the sidewalk that's magical" (118); indeed, Candy's home possesses the mystery and chimericalness of divinity. Smith's diction demands notice since the water image with the "pool" of light, consistently associated with female sexuality and the feminine divine, is assigned the color lavender, a light shade of purple, the color connoting royalty. Even Candy's beauty shop sports "rose-pink" shag carpet and smells "sweet" with the mixture of the scents of perfume, shampoo, formaldehyde, and pine Lysol in the air. Candy, a complex woman, exists as the only female in the novel linked to both life and death, the cycle represented by the feminine divine. With Smith's wording, "formaldehyde" alongside "perfume," the author suggests the antinomy implicit in the feminine divine. Again, life and death are juxtaposed when Candy prepares Elizabeth's hair and make-up for the funeral and she notices the smell of the many flowers at the funeral home.

Katherine Kearns views Candy as the "impossible reconciliation of the mother and the whore as she nurtures and satisfies every need, the figure of the happily sensual woman" (180), reminiscent of *Oral History*'s Justine Poole, *Fair and Tender Ladies*' Geneva Hunt, and *On Agate Hill*'s Martha Fickling, sexual women who nourish others but also satisfy their own needs. Interestingly, Smith often treats such ebullient and integrated female characters as ancillary. Even Candy provides just one voice of the novel's four female protagonists. These women, in touch with not only their sexual nature, but also their maternal and spiritual capacities, seem a rarity in the Southern society of Smith's fiction. Candy's warm, life-affirming nature manifests itself throughout the novel in her response to and treatment of family members. After Elizabeth's stroke when Candy visits her in the hospital and holds the dying woman's hand, Myrtle, although shocked, acknowledges Candy's "good intentions" and "big heart" (59). Unlike her sisters, Candy accepts and enters human suffering; she responds to life. As the entire family stands gathered at the hospital awaiting the news of Elizabeth's imminent death, Candy's brother Arthur thinks about his younger sister, "Candy's a toucher"; she "always makes you feel better" (106). Despite Candy's own apparent anguish at losing her mother, she manages to pat, stroke, or touch each of her siblings in an effort to comfort them. Candy's willingness and desire to touch others, especially those she loves, is perhaps most obvious in her decision to prepare Elizabeth's body for the funeral by shampooing and setting her hair and applying her make-up in order to make sure Elizabeth looks "like a lady [even] in death" (123). After the funeral as the family sorts through Elizabeth's belongings and lays claim to various household articles, Candy once again consoles her siblings. Candy continues to soothe her family after the shocking discovery of the remains of Jewell Rife and the news of Fay's death, when all the family members feel overwhelmed with their own pain. Offering comfort to Clinus, the retarded son of Nettie's late husband, with whom none of the family except Arthur has any contact or concern, Candy takes his arm and leads him into the house, then later drives him home. Dorothy Hill views Candy as the "mythic ennoblement of what society would see as sweet, transitory, and pleasurable, the very way in which women are so often labeled, marginalized, and trivialized" (99). With her name and profession, Candy runs the risk of being so labeled, but Smith's treatment of her as the novel's goddess figure infused with the necessary "sweetness" for self-knowledge and sacred sexual union lifts her above such categorizing.

Candy embraces life on its own terms and demonstrates her ingenuousness throughout the novel, embodying the humility that allows her to openly accept herself and others. Like so many female characters in *Fair and Tender Ladies* (Geneva, Ethel, Violet), Candy "calls a spade a spade" (116) and sees her own problems in life as a result of consistently doing what she wanted to do. She occupies herself with making people, particularly her clients and family members, look beautiful in their own eyes. Candy possesses an almost magical touch with everyone with whom she comes into contact. Hill perceptively calls Candy the "reincarnation of Dory, but with the resources to survive" (99). Dory's presence has such a magical effect on her entire family, but Dory, once deserted by Richard, becomes untouchable. The damage his disappearance does to her proves irreparable, and she remains lost in her own angst until her suicide, silenced and unable to express her grief. Candy has also suffered, but she finds words and responses to articulate her pain, seen when she sobs loudly at Elizabeth's funeral, all the while leaning against her grown son Tony for support. Candy, unafraid to rely on those she loves, possesses the tools for survival, transcending her hardships to become the center of the family. At the end of the novel, as preparations are being made for Karen (Myrtle and Don's pregnant daughter) and Karl's wedding, Candy exists at the center of the activity, styling everyone's hair. Her generosity of spirit shows when she allows Lydia, her employee at the beauty shop, to leave early instead of thinking of herself and how much time she will need to get herself ready for the wedding.

Smith links Candy to wildness as opposed to domesticity, further emphasizing the writer's insistence on the necessity of some degree of abandonment for a protagonist's receptivity to the presence of the feminine divine and the attendant opportunity for integration. At the beginning of the novel, Sybill tells the hypnotist that Candy was "[t]oo busy dating the boys" and eventually "[r]an away and got married" (37), indicating Candy's liminal position in the family. In most cultures, sex and sensuality are associated with wildness, lack of control, and even evil, explaining Sybill's community-validated opinion of her sister. Sybill says Candy takes after their aunt Nettie, not after their mother, recalling Elizabeth's disdain for Nettie's behavior as a teenager since she dated men and acted freely on her own impulses. Candy herself admits she and her adoptive mother were "natural strangers" (123), and no statement could more clearly describe their relationship. The words resonate with irony since Candy is the biological daughter of Jewell and Fay, not Elizabeth, but Candy does not acquire this knowledge during the course of the novel.

Candy not only comforts her sisters, brother, aunts, and customers; her twenty-year affair with Don Dotson, Myrtle's husband, marked by generosity and acceptance, foreshadows the union of future divine couples in Smith. In this relationship, Smith transgresses boundaries and disturbs society's prescribed code of acceptable behavior since Candy and Don ostensibly betray their sister and wife respectively. Deeply committed to their relationship, Candy and Don harbor mutual respect and share a generosity of spirit. Here Smith subverts the usual moral code to imply a completely new set of ethics and values by neither judging nor condemning Candy and Don. In fact, Smith compassionately depicts the two as the novel's divine couple and ties them to sacredness. A healer, a giver, and associated with haloes, water, and circles, Don, like Candy, is linked to divinity. Comfortable with touching others, Don reaches out to those who are hurting in an effort to ease their pain. Smith, in depicting Don and Candy's similar caring touch, gravitates toward an image of an androgynous divinity that would heal the split between male and female, spirit and nature, and mind and body that plagues humankind and envisions what Ruether calls "a new model of reciprocity in which we actualize ourselves by the same processes that we support the autonomy and actualization of others" (*New Woman* 57–58). Complete on her own, unlike earlier females in Smith who insisted on the presence of a man, or men, to feel any sense of wholeness, Candy enjoys her occasional passionate unity with Don. Don explains that Candy is "the wild card in his deck"; with her he can relax and "let down his hair" (119). And hair is Candy's specialty as she styles each person's in a way that allows him/her to feel beautiful. Symbolically, hair represents the soul since it grows out of the head, the place of consciousness, and Candy certainly lifts and handles each soul with gentle care, offering her generous gift of touch to all.

Possessing an understanding of human beings as interdependent beings, Candy accepts life's paradoxes and complexities and consistently maintains a sense of equilibrium. After the death of Elizabeth, which affects her siblings in a variety of ways,* Candy reflects on life's mysteries, deciding, "If you're not crazy sooner, you'll be later." She thinks no simple explanation exists for why children who were "wild" grow up to be "brain surgeons," admitting that her own son Tony presents a case in point. Refusing to take credit for the successes

---

Myrtle almost denies the loss, Arthur feels bothered by the inconvenience of the death and funeral, and Sybill is enraged by her mother's death.

of her children, Candy says she's "seen it all." She concludes her reverie with profound simplicity, observing that "Life is long and wild and there is usually a point where it makes you crazy. That's natural" (113). Candy's deep understanding of life gives her the strength her brother and sisters lack. One of the novel's few characters who commands control of language, Candy speaks or holds silence accordingly. She, like her aunt Nettie, uses her voice sparingly, but nevertheless possesses a deep knowledge about life that she chooses not to share even with Don. The sexual attraction between the two, however, is obvious; after Elizabeth dies, when Don comes up to Candy's apartment, Candy thinks she wouldn't mind making love right then but knows it wouldn't be right. She explains her desires: "There's a link between somebody dying and this [sex]" (120), these thoughts again linking her to the goddess who represented the complete life cycle with its equal components of birth, sexuality, death, and regeneration.

Nettie functions as another goddess figure in the novel, and like Candy she possesses deep knowledge about life's mysteries and human nature. Candy and Nettie are the only characters totally unafraid to defy social convention and claim their own identities, the only ones who remain unchanged throughout the novel. Close to the end of the book in the section Nettie narrates, we learn the reason for her estrangement from her sister Elizabeth. Nettie, now an old woman, having lived a full life, complete with its equal measure of pain and joy, remains a generous, accepting, and strong female character, unlike Elizabeth, who lived a life of pretense. Both Nettie and Candy have taken control of their lives and their narratives, having emerged from troubled pasts to find a new sexual equilibrium in which they are no longer objects. Similar to Granny Younger of *Oral History*, Nettie establishes her integrity as narrator by defining herself as a woman "that has left one man and buried two" (213), having earned wisdom "through heterosexual love and struggle but strengthened through celibacy" (Kearns 185).

Similar to Candy and other Smith characters who align themselves with wildness, Nettie openly admits to her early sexual promiscuity and Elizabeth's growing bitterness toward her "tomboy" sister who enjoyed riding horses, dancing, and fishing "as freely as if she were a Boy" (184–85). Nettie, another female who defies women's prescribed roles, searches for the validation that the feminine divine offers. Smith relates Nettie to such freeing activities as dancing (an important ingredient in goddess-worship rituals) and riding horses (a mark of dawning sexuality). This type of woman works herself "into the gaps between culture and nature like a kind of glue that binds together apparently disparate realms" (Hall 162). Like *Oral History*'s Sally, Nettie relates a part of her life during which she "took up with a lot of men" (Smith 226), saying she says she feels neither pride nor remorse about her behavior since it seemed to help her some in dealing with the loss of a child.

Diametrically opposed to the strong, forceful Nettie, her sister Fay has suffered at the hands of a male-dominated culture. In her depiction of Fay, the victimized character in the novel who represents all the harm and destruction done to the sacred, sexual female, Smith traces the damage suffered by a female who is rejected and/or misunderstood by society. By family members and circumstance, Fay is denied the right to not only a sane mind and a life of her own, but also her role as mother in even acknowledging her own child. With Fay, Smith continues to explore female victims. Like Crystal Spangler, the physical abuse suffered by Fay leads to her complete passivity. Fay appears to be a mentally unstable recluse who lives on television and magazines until close to the end of the novel when Nettie explains the source of her presumed insanity. In her journal, Elizabeth described the teenager Fay as a "sweet presence" with a tendency to "wander about" (184), like other damaged sexual females in Smith. With thick, yellow hair that eventually turns completely white, and her love of flowers (family members give her flowers throughout the novel), Fay is aligned with divinity and female sexuality.* Additionally, her name, obviously, links her to the mysterious Morgan LeFay of Arthurian legend.† Appropriately then, Smith connects the Fay of *Family Linen* with goddess mythology and in particular, with the element of water, a consistent representation of female sexuality, rebirth, and the feminine divine.

The sensual, sexual, maternal goddess figure, Fay becomes, as best expressed by Katherine Kearns, "the ultimate receptacle for all kinds of sexual, intellectual, and spiritual trash" (194). Nettie's description of the scene she witnesses during which Jewell rapes Fay illustrates the ultimate violation that Fay endures. As Fay stands at the kitchen sink washing dishes and singing, "with her yellow hair falling in curls down her back" (Smith 231), Jewell suddenly slams his fist down onto the table and calls to her. Nettie notices that a terrible expression replaces the blank look on Fay's face, and suddenly she appears completely changed, with wet, red lips, shining eyes, and pink cheeks, her whole face taking on "a *waiting* look." With a "loose, sweet smile," Fay sings in a "high and thin" voice, indecipherable, jumbled words. As Fay is sexually violated, Nettie says she looked like "the end of the world," as Smith evokes the death of innocence for Fay, who suffers permanent damage. Fay's garbled speech can be interpreted as a regression from the cultural order represented by the male-dominated patriarchy. Fay's unrecognizable words make a sound "strained like the wind through a barb-wire fence," a striking metaphorical rendition of the damage done the goddess (represented by the wind) by the barbs of patriarchal religion as Christianity robbed the female

---

*Although traditional flower iconography associates roses, red roses in particular, with female sexuality, Smith's work includes other flowers in representing female sexuality.

†In her Book of Goddesses and Heroines, Patricia Monaghan explains that "Mor" meant "sea" in many Celtic languages, and "Morgan" was a sea goddess whose name has been broadened in Brittany to denote any one of many sea sprites, the most famous of whom was named "Le Fay" (241).

deity of her many powers. Additionally, the sexual violation and silencing of Fay call to mind the myth of the nightingale, so popular among English poets, in which Philomela is raped by her sister Procne's husband Tereus. After the violation, Tereus cuts out Philomela's tongue to prevent her from revealing his conduct. As the myth goes, Philomela weaves her sad story into a tapestry that she sends to her sister. In revenge, Procne kills her son by Tereus, Itys, and serves up the child as food to his father. The Olympian gods then transform all three characters into birds. Tereus becomes the hoopoe (listed in the Old Testament as an "unclean bird"), Procne becomes the swallow and Philomela the nightingale—a bird that twitters but does not vocalize a full song.* Smith's diction during the rape of Fay—"Her mouth was open with singing sounds still coming out of it, but garbled" (233)—powerfully reflects this well-known myth of male violence and the silencing of the female.

After the rape, Fay's voice can no longer be heard or understood as she is silenced, robbed of a will of her own, just as the voice of the feminine divine remains muted with male imagery and symbols. Nettie describes Fay sitting on the countertop, pantyless, with her legs spread apart, and Jewell, with his pants around his ankles, "fucking her," without holding her or kissing her at all (233). Deprived of love, Fay is denied the source of sensuous pleasure—the cuddling, kissing, and holding. Fay's face remains indelible in Nettie's mind, how it changed from "that waiting, knowing look into something terrible where wanting and hating went back and forth ... faster and faster, ending up as something awful which you've not got the words to say." Even Nettie, equipped with the power of language, is silenced by the horror she witnesses. As Nettie continues to watch, spellbound with shock, another look comes over Fay's face that seems to say, "*I know what I'm up to. I know.*" Nettie interprets the look as the epitome of pain, "pain so pure it was like a real thing twisting and yelling in the air between her and me"; then the look vanishes, and Fay regains the same "sweet blank expression" she had had before and has had ever since (233–34). A more graphic picture of male violation and female submission could not be drawn. This paradoxical description of the rape, with Fay's "sweet, awful smile" and her look of simultaneous "wanting and hating," emphasizes Fay's helplessness and victimization. However, unlike Crystal, who realizes that her retarded uncle Devere is unaware of what he is doing when he rapes her, Fay possesses a look that suggests her complete knowledge of and consent to this violent assault. Fay willingly sacrifices herself to Jewell despite the tremendous agony, personified as a writhing, wriggling, hissing snake.

Fay has been killed by the damage done her by society; symbolically, the

---

*In the variant versions of the myth, Tereus, when he tires of his wife Procne, plucks out her tongue by the roots to ensure her silence, and pretending she is dead, marries her sister Philomela. Procne then weaves her story into a tapestry that informs Philomela of the horrible truth. In this version, Procne is transformed into the nightingale and Philomela into the swallow.

goddess she represents has also been killed by patriarchal religion. Irigaray argues that all of western culture revolves around the idea of "the murder of the mother" and goes on to accuse the "man-god-father" of "kill[ing] the mother in order to take power" ("Women-Mothers" 47). This tragedy describes precisely the fate of Fay. After the discovery of Fay's pregnancy and the sisters' seclusion in Lynchburg, Nettie describes Fay as becoming sweeter and quieter, with a "smile spread out all over her face" (244), often sitting on the porch swing with her hands on her stomach to feel the movement of the baby, patiently awaiting the birth of her child. With the birth of Candy, Nettie observes that "having a baby came natural to her, like having a cold, and didn't hurt her the way it does most" (250), again aligning Fay with nature and natural processes. But Fay is disallowed any role in the child's life, one of society's ways of punishing those who are damaged. First stripped of her sexuality by Jewell, next robbed of her right to be mother to her child, Fay becomes quieter, sadder, more confused, eventually sinking into permanent passivity and ostensible insanity. Irigaray's comments shed further light on Fay's predicament in her description of hysteria as "the contradiction between [women's] desire to live and the conditions that are forced upon us." Women, she adds, "have no decision-making power over those conditions" and often the only "path that remains open to us is madness" (48). Fay, without power, voice, or will, finally sinks into what society labels "insanity."

A sensual creature connected to other divine females, Elizabeth's youngest daughter Lacy also struggles with the disastrous conditions forced upon women. However, she, like Candy and Nettie, confronts her pain and eventually moves toward resolution. Although in sharing Elizabeth's love of language she considers herself her mother's daughter more than the others, she resents her mother's abandoning her to Sybill's care. This longing for a mother, representative of her yearning for the presence of the feminine divine, causes Lacy's continuous angst. Considering herself "so good" while Candy was so "*bad*" (130), Lacy has searched for authenticity first in Booker Creek in relation to her mother, then in her affair with and marriage to Jack, who she says "rescued" her, then "made her." Now that he has deserted her, Lacy observes, "*It's worse to be abandoned if you were first rescued. Then you have nothing left except a void. Empty space*" (70). Like other Smith protagonists, Lacy feels that she has never grown up, having defined herself through others for so long that she has no clue to her true identity without those outside influences. A lover of language, Lacy decides after discovering and reading her mother's journal that language does offer some level of comfort and begins to understand why her mother left the Methodist church of her youth and became an Episcopalian because of the "sheer poetry" of the services (128).

Similar to other Smith protagonists, Lacy has searched for comfort in patriarchal religion. At her mother's funeral, Lacy wonders when she abandoned her belief in traditional Christianity. Remembering the "fearful intensity, with a total disregard for the facts," Lacy admits that she transferred all her faith and trust "straight from God straight to her professors straight to Jack" (129). Lacy's sentiments look forward to Rose Annie Bailey and Katie Cocker of *The Devil's Dream*, who both explain that their passion for religion shifted to sexual passion when they reached a certain age. These young women long for the presence of the divine feminine to validate them when an abstract patriarchal God seems unattainable and unapproachable.

Smith associates Lacy, like earlier sexual females, with fire and blood, elements consistently linked to passion and sacred sexuality. She enjoys the feeling of the hot vinyl of the car seat burning her legs, reminiscent of Crystal's enjoyment of the hot concrete burning her body as she sunbathes with Agnes. One of Lacy's strongest memories from her teen years is of Red McClanahan fondling her breasts. Even now, after all these years, Lacy can almost feel Red's hands touching her body. Unlike her sisters Sybill and Myrtle, Lacy remains sensual and "touchable." After her mother's funeral, as she thinks of Jack's arrival in Booker Creek, Lacy leans against the hot stone wall of the church and burns her arm and shoulder, "but she's all right" (134); in fact, she maintains control until she thinks of Jack and the old fiery passion and pain of loss resurface. Feeling "open, bloody, exposed—like a wound," Lacy has the sensation that the body at the bottom of the well belongs to her, and this terrifies her (132). Nevertheless, she faces her fear and tries to emerge from her personal hell. As Nor Hall has observed, healing must come from the wound itself (68), and Lacy finds that her emotional pain cannot be remedied by her mother, Jack, or God, but must be cured by an integration of the disparate parts of her self. Her impression that it is her own body at the bottom of the well, even though the thought frightens her, intimates Lacy's imminent rebirth since images of falling and descent hint at a woman's beginning the search for the missing part of her life. The discovery of the family secret at the end of the novel seems to offer hope for Lacy as she observes this "odd gaggle" of family members "on the brink of the past" on a beautiful June day (255). She suddenly feels like writing her dissertation and completing her Ph.D. whereas before she was trapped and paralyzed by her pain.

The wedding at the end of the novel, occurring over a month after the discovery of Jewell Rife's body and Fay's death, in marked contrast to the wedding at the conclusion of *Something in the Wind* earlier, offers hope and healing reconciliation for the family members. With the entire family present, the wedding functions to highlight the positive directions in which all the major characters are pointed. Although like earlier females in Smith, most of the female characters are damaged, for the first time the writer moves beyond the damage to suggest the possibility of healing. Memory and reconnection with the past have proven psychologically therapeutic as redemption is offered for the family in the present. Looking back has allowed the family members to imagine a more sanguine future. Karen's wedding dress, fashioned from one of

Elizabeth's old lace tablecloths, serves as a symbol for the integration of the family's past with their present. The focus at the wedding is the newly installed swimming pool that "gives off a soft blue mysterious glow right in the middle of the reception." Flowers surround the pool, and floating arrangements of red roses adorn the blue, clear water as "a kind of pearly luminescence hang[s] in the air" (267-68). The fresh red dirt, unearthed by the excavation that produced the remains of Jewell, is only visible in patches that the newly planted grass has not yet covered.

Smith carefully presents the setting of Karen's wedding as permeated with images that have been consistently linked with female sexuality and the feminine divine. The flowers (particularly roses), the water, the sense of mystery, and the emphasis on the color red all work neatly together to create a tapestry of harmony and hope for the family members, especially the females, who have become more self-directed and self-confident for the most part. With her migraines gone now, Sybill, who has been so unwilling or unable to express her deepest feelings, even secretly cries a little at the wedding, a positive sign of her budding ability to show emotion. Myrtle also seems headed in a positive direction, having rededicated herself to her husband Don and even begun a new career in real estate. Lacy has begun work on her dissertation and is seeing Jack, her ex-husband, once a week, and Arthur has stopped drinking, entered into a promising relationship with a nurse, and taken a steady job. Even "ironic" Theresa, Myrtle and Don's daughter, has fallen in love and sports a new outlook on life. As the family gathers around the new swimming pool at the exact site where the family patriarch's bones have just been discovered, new beginnings are intimated, with water's consistent association with the goddess, rebirth, and regeneration. The novel ends with a sense of a new beginning in a section focused on Lacy, the youngest daughter, and her sudden remembrance of a former boyfriend "outlined against the blue water " with his face "a shining blur in the rushing wind" (272). Smith's diction in this last line of the novel recalls the power of the seductive wind and not only its consistent association with expressed female sexuality and the feminine divine, but also, as Rosalind Reilly points out, its connection with the "preverbal ... power which arouses the imagination" (81), for Lacy's imagination has surely been awakened in her reconnection with her self. Harriette Buchanan argues that the novel ends with the image of Elizabeth as "idealistic matriarch of the family still firmly in place" (342), but the more important implication of the last section of the novel is that Elizabeth's children and future generations of female characters will now better be able to successfully integrate their sexuality with their other roles, something Elizabeth never achieved, in effect moving closer to the space occupied by both Nettie and Candy, that of the sexual, maternal, regenerative feminine divine.

Chapter V

"I WALKED IN MY BODY LIKE A QUEEN"

The Honey-Imbued Goddess in *Fair and Tender Ladies*

In *The Meaning of Aphrodite*, Paul Friedrich calls for the split between sexuality and maternity to be healed "by the religion" or by the "system of ideas" that "connects our concrete lives with the awesome powers beyond our control" (191). In her seventh novel, *Fair and Tender Ladies* (1988), Lee Smith effectively heals the schism with her creation of the sacred-sexual-maternal figure, Ivy Rowe. Repudiating the cultural taboos against sexually active adult females (particularly mothers), Ivy serves as a reunification of the multitudinous qualities of the feminine divine who discovers and accepts the sacredness within herself and her own experience. In *Fair and Tender Ladies*, Smith offers several alternatives for women's lives, enlarging her vision of the possibilities for females and emphasizing the importance of women's connections. In this novel Smith's lifelong search for the intersection of spirituality and sexuality, the union of mind and body, a mythology that recognizes and honors the female, culminates in her superb creation of the character, Ivy Rowe Fox.

Smith found her source for the novel when at a flea market she purchased for seventy-five cents a packet of letters written by one woman to her sister over a period of many years. With these letters as the creative spark at a time in her own life when she felt like she was "falling apart" due to family illnesses and pressures (Byrd 95), Smith created Ivy as a kind of personal role model, "a woman who could go through a heroic journey on her own turf and on her own terms" (107). Smith's breakthrough gives a strong voice to her protagonist in this epistolary novel that consists solely of letters written by Ivy over a sixty-two-year period to family and friends, many of whom never receive or respond to them. In fact, several letters are never even mailed since Ivy often writes to family members (her older sister Silvaney, for example) who have died.

With letters dating from 1912 to 1974, the novel depicts over a half century of change and growth in the remote Virginia areas of Sugar Fork near Home Creek on Blue Star Mountain; Majestic, the closest town; and Diamond, the nearby mining community. Ivy's letters, with her phonetic spellings and colloquial speech, interweave allusions to such writers and works as Byron, Charlotte Brontë, Shakespeare, William Cullen Bryant, Margaret Mitchell, Flaubert, and the Bible, and give an unromanticized version of life in the Appalachian region. Through her letter-writing, Ivy develops not only as a woman, but also as a writer whose strong authorial voice gives meaning to her own life. Ironically, the women survivors in the novel—Ivy, Beulah, Ethel, Granny Rowe, Geneva, Molly, Violet, and Joli—are certainly not "fair and tender ladies" in the traditional sense commonly associated with beauty, fragility, and passivity. They are female characters who are empowered through unconventional means, women who struggle, like Smith's earlier female characters, with such issues as sexuality, violence, religion, marriage, and motherhood. Some find the inner strength to live life on their own terms, choosing to remain single or childless or otherwise openly pursuing their aspirations, even against the grain of society. Smith endows these women with mythological beauty and strength as the author moves closer to a personal mythology that encompasses divine feminine spirituality.

In *The Feminine Face of God*, Sherry Ruth Anderson and Patricia Hopkins insist on the necessity of this yearning or longing in order to "connect with what is sacred" (72), since patriarchal traditions have alienated women from any understanding of the female deity (128). Unlike *Oral History*'s Dory, whose longing and sense of emptiness eventually lead to suicide, Ivy, a survivor, finds strength in her sense of yearning and desire for more, often dreaming of escape from her difficult life and even briefly leaving her family. But she always returns to her responsibilities, accepting what she calls her "lot" (236). As Ivy expresses her desires for something beyond the mountain, beyond life as she knows it, in a letter to Mrs. Brown, her school teacher, after her father's death, "I was all full up with wanting, wanting something so bad, I culd not of said what it was" (37). What Ivy longs for is a belief system—a mythology—that validates her life and her experiences as a woman. Ivy will continue to search for answers, guidance, and escape from social barriers throughout her life. When her mother moves the family to Majestic to live in Geneva Hunt's boardinghouse, amidst the booming lumber business, Ivy watches the boys riding rafts made of logs down the river to Kentucky and yearns for the freedom inherent in masculine privilege. Aware of the gender restraints, she considers disguising herself as a boy to be allowed to go on the trip. However, the idea of the prototypical male journey on a river raft proves unsuitable for Ivy, as does going to Boston with Miss Torrington, traveling to Memphis with Franklin Ransom, and even moving to West Virginia with Curtis Bostick. Each time, although Ivy is tempted to escape and make the trip, she chooses to remain in the mountains where she was born.

Just as Kathryn Rabuzzi finds the traditional quest of the hero unsatisfactory for women to achieve selfhood because of its strictly linear nature, Smith admitted in a personal interview that Ivy's journey is not the traditional linear male heroic journey but rather a circular one as Ivy eventually returns to her mountain home (Byrd 105–106). Rabuzzi postulates that, for a woman, this circular expedition allows for the integration of body and spirit in moments of "mystic communion." Arguing that "the irresistible appeal of the body mystery of the mother" is its sexuality, Rabuzzi asserts that the sexual aspect of a woman's "interiority" prompts her "call to the way of the mother in the first place" (77–79). Rabuzzi's path clearly parallels Ivy Rowe's journey throughout the novel as she successfully bridges the gap between sexuality and motherhood by achieving integration and wholeness. Ivy's body and spirit merge in "mystic communion" with Honey Breeding when they travel to the top of Blue Star Mountain.

In the first section of the novel, Smith introduces all of Ivy's major conflicts. The novel's five sections are grouped both geographically and chronologically, with the first batch of letters, when Ivy is twelve to seventeen, written from Sugar Fork, as are the last two groups. In her first letter to a Dutch pen pal who never responds, Ivy writes that "Hanneke" is such a pretty name, that when she says it, "it tastes sweet ... like honey" or the way Ivy imagines "the fotched-on candy from Mrs. Browns book about France, candy wich mimicks roses" (3). Immediately, Smith introduces two important motifs (roses and honey) that consistently relate to female sexuality and divinity. Roses and their sexual associations have appeared throughout Smith's novels, but "honey" is a new term Smith chooses to describe the sweetness, both sexual and spiritual, for which Ivy yearns until she actually encounters the man who offers her sweet sacred sexual union, Honey Breeding. In this first letter, Ivy also expresses her strongest desires: "I want to be a writer, it is what I love the bestest in this world," thus establishing early on Ivy's ambitions and love for written expression. Even at the young age of twelve, Ivy strikingly reveals the conflict she already senses between passion and motherhood in her interest in love and desire "to be in love one day and write poems about it," but she does not "want to have a lot of babys thogh and get tittys as big as the moon" (6–7). Her sentiments are reminiscent of *Dogbushes'* Susan Tobey who at age nine also dreads growing those "big blobby things" (41), as she calls breasts.

Ivy attributes her mother Maude's "hanted" look to having too many children (she has nine, including two pairs of twins) and working too hard. The happiness Maude had felt when she left her family to marry John Arthur Rowe has long since vanished, leaving for Ivy only the memory of the oft-repeated mythical, romantic story of that night many years earlier when John Arthur had swept Maude off her feet and carried her away with him on horseback up to Sugar Fork. Now Ivy witnesses and reports her mother's disturbing behavior, such as the time Maude bursts into tears as she watches her four daughters drying their hair by the fire and says the girls are all so pretty that they would "be better off dead" (7). Another day Ivy follows her mother up Pilgrim Knob and watches her stand on the cliff and stare into the distance, letting the wind blow her hair all around her face. Maude seems removed from the day-to-day activities at home, much like Dory after Richard's desertion. Driven to tears by the "soft and sweet" kiss of the motherly neighbor Edith Fox, Ivy regrets that her own mother seems "hard as a rocky-clift, and her eyes burns out in her head" (19). Ivy is able to understand her mother's behavior in terms of the pain and suffering of repeated childbearing and the struggle and hardship involved in their life of farming. It is no wonder Ivy needs to remember the story/myth of her parents' early romance in order to retain any kind of optimism for her own life. Although Ivy clings to the glamorous version of her parents' meeting and elopement, Smith suggests the destructiveness of this romanticized relationship that eventually hardens and "burns-out" Maude.

In Ivy's description of Maude and her impression of Sugar Fork, Smith introduces several important images from earlier works and continues to explore female sexuality in its connection to nature and divinity. Recounting the story of Maude and John Arthur's elopement in her letter to Hanneke, Ivy writes that when her parents stopped for a break on their long journey, Maude looked into a pool of water and almost didn't recognize her own image since she looked so wild in the "pine knots yaller ligt." With her passion reflected by the water and her face "burning as hot as fire," Maude splashed water onto it and tasted the cool water of Home Creek, "the sweetest of any she ever had" (4). Once she and John Arthur arrived at Sugar Fork, one of the first things she noticed by the porch was the "rosybush," covered with pink flowers (a mark of female sexuality); then as she looked up at the sky, she said she saw a hawk "gliding circles around and around," making three loops (5). First, a connection between wildness and fire recalls Smith's earlier protagonists who struggled between wildness and domesticity, or nature and culture. Second, Maude stopped at a pool of water and splashed her face, linking her to Red Emmy and the circular pool of water in which she was discovered bathing. Water, and in this instance the "sweetness" of it, will continue to suggest female sexuality and also rebirth. The "pale yaller ligt" of the moon brings to mind the golden color that was significant in *Oral History* and directly linked to the feminine divine. And finally, the circular motion of the hawk and the number three are suggestive of the presence of divinity here at Sugar Fork. As Gimbutas notes, in goddess mythology, circular movement represents concentrated divine energy and the number three relates to the goddess's triple source of life energy that is necessary for the renewal of life (*Language*, 322, 97). At the end of the novel, the circling hawk will be one of the final images Ivy records in her last letter to Silvaney, a representation of completion, symbolizing the cessation of Ivy's journey and the divine integration achieved in her life.

In *Fair and Tender Ladies*, as in previous novels, Smith employs images of caves, in their representation of the womb, and therefore rebirth and regeneration. Several pivotal events occur for Ivy in caves or cave-like settings. When Ivy is forty and the mother of five children (Granny Younger tells us that Red Emmy is about forty when Almarine meets her), she follows Honey Breeding up Blue Star Mountain to its highest point and stays with him in a cave, "living on love" (228), experiencing rebirth and the reclamation of her divine sexuality. Discovering the lost meaning of female sexuality, Ivy tells Honey across the camp fire, "I know what I'm doing" (226). She will take that knowledge with her when she finally emerges from the cave to descend the mountain once she realizes the time has come to move on. The first time Ivy, as a young teenager, kisses Oakley, she is higher than she's ever been on Blue Star Mountain, exploring the mouth of a cave. Several years later, Oakley's emergence from the coal mine at Diamond, which Ivy describes as looking "like a big old cave" (131), serves as a turning point for Ivy. After a deadly mine explosion, Ivy experiences what she describes as a spiritual awakening when Oakley emerges from the "mess of red light and darkness and movement and noise" at the "huge black mouth of the mine." As Oakley approaches out of the "ring of fire," Ivy realizes the significance of this moment. There, in this setting rife with religious connotations (the number three, the circle of fire, and the womb-like cave), Ivy feels as if "the mouth of the mine had opened up and let him go, like he had been spared, or like he had just been born" (168). Birth images such as this one form an integral part of the novel, functioning here to tie Ivy to Oakley much as she is connected to the land and to the earth's natural cycles. Many years later, after Oakley's death, Ivy will return to the cave and remember Oakley's first kiss as she comes to terms with her loss by experiencing symbolic rebirth.

Ivy's need for connections manifests in not only her affinity with the land and nature, but also her close relationships with several women. Luce Irigaray addresses the urgent need for women to speak out about relationships between women in order to be "consecrated" in their identity and their "female genealogy," arguing that love for "women-sisters" is necessary if we are to break from the control of the "phallic cult" ("Bodily" 44–46). Thus, to come to terms with her own spirituality and sacred sexuality, Ivy must experience the mystic communion among women. In *Fair and Tender Ladies*, Smith depicts several symbiotic relationships between women. In fact, for Ivy, it is primarily through connections with other women, and writing about her life, that she makes sense of anything that happens to her. Irigaray warns that if a woman is unable or unwilling to express her relation to other women, she may become "hysterical," what Irigarary sees as a culturally-induced symptom of repression ("Questions" 138). Perhaps it is Ivy's preponderant connection with her brain-damaged older sister Silvaney that most anchors her in the world of the mentally stable, whereas Silvaney's inability to communicate effectively dooms her to a life of alienation and eventual institutionalization. In her first letter to Hanneke, Ivy, in telling about her family, writes, "I love Silvaney the bestest, you see. Silvaney is so pretty, she is the sweetest, all silverhaired like she was fotched up on the moon" (8-9).

Ivy perceives Silvaney as the other side of herself, a side necessary for Ivy's ability to function fully, and in continuing to write to her absent, then dead, sister, Ivy preserves that divine, wild fiery part of her own spirit. In her depiction of the symbiotic relationship between these sisters, Smith expands women's relationships beyond the man-woman combinations that in earlier novels are required to make female characters feel complete. In her first letter to Hanneke, Ivy says that even though Silvaney is five years older and much bigger than she, "it is like we are the same sometimes it is like we are one" (9).* Katherine Kearns argues that Silvaney represents madness, and in sending her away to the asylum, Smith "splits the madness off from Ivy," Silvaney being the "sacrificial figure who remains necessary for the female artist to survive" (190). However, despite Silvaney's physical removal from Ivy, Smith never "splits off" Silvaney since Ivy retains her sister's "wildness" within her own personality and keeps her sister alive in her imagination and in her letters even while sensing the absence of "a chunk" of her "hart" (Smith 64). Ivy addresses Silvaney in her letters as "my love and my hart" (112),† salient reminders of the inseparability of one from the other. Ivy writes her most private thoughts to Silvaney, almost talking to herself, in an effort to "write herself into being," to validate herself and her experiences. Ivy says, "I can talk to you for you do not understand, I can write you this letter too and tell you all the deepest things, the things in my hart.... And it is like you are part of me Silvaney, in some way. So I can tell you things I would not tell another sole" (94). Until Ivy learns from her brother Victor that Silvaney died in the flu epidemic of 1918, she plans to take her sister back to the mountain one day, for, as she explains in a letter to Victor, "I have felt like I was split off from a part of myself all these years, and now it is like that part of me has died, since I know she will never come" (173-74). At the end of the novel when Ivy is ill and hospitalized, Maudy (Ivy's youngest daughter) and Marlene (Ivy's daughter-in-law) discover in the cedar chest bundles of letters Ivy has written to Silvaney over the years since Silvaney's death. When Ivy's oldest daughter Joli asks about the letters, Ivy explains that she knows Silvaney died, but that "it didn't *matter*. Silvaney, you see, was a part of me, my other side, my other half, my heart" (304). Silvaney's physical presence has not been necessary for Ivy

---

The emphasis Ivy places on her symbolic relationship with Silvaney suggests the necessity of merging mind and body, spirituality and sexuality, in order to achieve integration and wholeness. In Rebirth of the Goddess, *Carol Christ discusses at length these dualisms on which patriarchal religion operates (99).*

†*Throughout the novel, the changing in Ivy's spelling of the word "heart" is indicative of her growth as a writer. Her letters progressively become more literate as time passes.*

to keep her sister alive; Ivy has nurtured the most divine part of herself in preserving Silvaney in her imagination.

Ivy considers Silvaney her heart and will later see Honey Breeding as her soul, her own sense of self interwoven with and dependent upon these two liminal beings. When she is finally able to integrate the ethereal essences of both Silvaney and Honey with her own identity, Ivy will achieve wholeness. Paula Gallant Eckard insightfully labels Silvaney "the goddess or anima" and Honey Breeding "the animus" (171). Although she views both Silvaney and Honey as necessary parts of her being that she must possess in order to survive, Ivy perceives both as chimerical, not part of reality. Once Silvaney has been taken away to the asylum, Ivy writes to her, "Oh Silvaney! sometimes I think I made you up to suit me!" (99). Smith emphasizes Silvaney's mysterious nature by having Ivy describe her sister's movements as "gliding" across a creek as the full moon is large and low on the night of Babe's (Silvaney's twin brother) murder (60). And once Silvaney is taken away, Ivy writes to her sister Beulah, "I keep thinking I see Silvaney but it is never her, it is only ligt in the trees, and so often I think I hear her talking but no one is ther, it is only the wind" (69), suggestive of divine feminine presence.

Silvaney, a damaged character considered a "lunatic" by society, symbolizes society's destruction of the feminine divine. Smith depicts Silvaney as not only a creature of nature, consistently associated with wildness like other of Smith's sexual female characters, but also an evocation of the feminine divine in her consistent association with the wind and the moon. Barbara Walker labels the moon "the eternal Great Mother" and explains that the root word for "moon" and "mind" was the Indo-European *manas*, *mana*, or *men*, which represented the great mother goddess's "wise blood" in women, governed by the moon. The derivatives of these words—*mania*, which originally meant ecstatic revelation, and *lunacy*, which initially denoted possession of the spirit of the moon ("moon-touched"), or selection by the goddess—provide clear evidence of patriarchal thinkers' belittlement of the feminine divine since both words now mean mental instability (*Women's* 669–70). Wandering the mountains aimlessly, Silvaney eludes domestication or containment. Ivy's mother explains Silvaney's mental problems as the result of her having "brain fever" that "burned out a part of her brain" when she was a baby (9), and Smith continually links Silvaney to fire that, in Smith's fiction, consistently suggests both the passion and potential danger of female sexuality.

Irigaray views hysteria as the unheard voice of a woman who is only able to speak through somatic symptoms ("Women-Mothers" 52). Applying Irigaray's observation to Silvaney suggests that Silvaney's "brain fever" merely reflects her aphasia in a society that rejects her. Silvaney is considered abnormal since she behaves "like a wild animal" with "a ligt in her eye." Ivy says "her whole face is lit up from inside, like they is a fire in her head shining throgh," and worries that the "fire is going to burn her up" (56). Just as Maude looked "wild" as she stared at her reflection in the water and is described by Ivy as possessing eyes that "burn out of her head" (19), Silvaney reflects these same qualities of intensity, passion, and potential for destruction. Silvaney wanders the mountain, much like Ivy always longs to do and eventually does do after Oakley's death. In this novel, Smith again associates wildness with wandering, reminiscent of Dory's aimless wandering after Richard's departure. Ivy seems to be the only one who understands her sister (they are one in spirit), writing to Mrs. Brown after Silvaney has been taken to the asylum, "Silvaney is different from all, she needs to wander the woods, and she needs some woods to wander" (63–64). Ivy senses that Silvaney's containment in the Elizabeth Masters Home in Roanoke, Virginia, will destroy Silvaney. In a letter to her dead father, Ivy connects Silvaney's blue eyes to lakes with "flames, flames" right under the surface; then Ivy asks her father, "Were you ther when she walked in the fire?" (56–57). This vague reference to Silvaney's walking in fire, coupled with the earlier mention of her gliding across water, links Silvaney to Biblical references of Christ's walking on water and appearing in flames. In *Divine Women*, Irigaray examines women's relation to the elements—water, earth, fire, and air—which she says "constitute the origin" of the human body, "the flesh of our passions," and determine our feelings in all areas of our lives (qtd. in Whitford 8). Smith strikingly aligns Silvaney with all four elements in the imagery used to describe her, effectively elevating this mysterious female to a deific level and thus enlarging the possibilities for sacredness in women's lives.

Ivy and Silvaney's relationship forms the most important of the many connections between women, but there are several other striking pairings of female characters that emphasize Smith's insistence on the necessity of bonding and mystic communion among females. Ivy says about the magical Cline sisters, "you cant tell Gaynelle from Virgie, its not worth your truble to try" since they look exactly alike. In an early letter to Hanneke, Ivy describes their visit on Christmas during which the Cline sisters, who "have not been apart for a minute," tell several stories that capture permanently Ivy's imagination. The central mystery surrounding the Cline sisters remains until their disappearance and presumed deaths in that no one knows their ages or method of survival up on Hell Mountain since they don't farm or raise any animals. They only grow beans and flowers, but people take food to them in order to hear their nurturing stories. Legendary figures who seem holy in their close association with nature and their soft voices that seem to speak "a nother language almost, like bells in the snow," the Clines enter the Rowes' home "laghing like silver bells," bend down to John Arthur on his sick pallet in front of the fireplace, and touch him, with their hands "fluttering like butterflys." These mysterious women and the stories they tell captivate both Silvaney and Ivy. In fact, Ivy decides the Cline sisters "live on storys" and "do not need much food" (24–25), thus acknowledging storytelling as a form of nurturing, a consistent idea throughout Smith's works.

Irigaray postulates that women's need for speech, for language, is just as vital for sustenance as their requirement for food ("Women-Mothers" 51–52). Focusing on the deprivation of women's "autonomous ideality," Irigaray discusses the traditional way women shared and exchanged energies through providing food, a job that was considered a "woman's lot." Since this creation (the providing of food) had "no words to speak its name in the enactment of the gesture," women were left without language to share their innermost selves with others ("Limits" 107). In providing Ivy and other characters with nourishing stories, Smith offers the language to enable women to reconnect. Ivy admits that the only way she could keep from running out into the snow (committing suicide) was to hear a story. Language not only provides nourishment for Ivy, but also serves as her salvation. Ivy lives on stories, similar to the Cline sisters, both hearing and telling stories, real and fictional, throughout her long life, and stories save her life each time she is on the brink of despair. In an interview with Susan Ketchin, Smith expressed the importance of language and writing as "sort of a saving thing" for her, as "almost a religion of its own" (51). Ivy tells Honey Breeding, "I am starved for stories" (218), and on two occasions when Ivy feels desperate to relate the stories of her life to her dead sister, she writes to Silvaney, "I am dying to write" (185, 305). Lucinda MacKethan points out that Gaynelle and Virgie Cline, as they tell their stories together in one blended voice, are similarly connected and serve as doubles for Silvaney and Ivy in their symbiotic relationship (107–108). As the Cline sisters depart, Ivy and Silvaney stand outside in the snow and watch them "moving faster and faster" until "it seemed they were flying" (30), an image that illuminates the mystical nature of these chimerical characters.

Always cognizant of the vital essence of language, Ivy passes on the nourishing stories of the mysteriously divine Cline women to her daughter Joli. Once she and Oakley move back to Sugar Fork, she takes Joli on a ritualistic journey up to Hell Mountain where the sisters lived. Ivy knows that Gaynelle and Virgie couldn't possibly still be alive, but she needs to bring the old stories to life for her daughter. Only a pile of stones that was the chimney remains from the old house, but "the white roses running wild" that the Cline sisters had planted still flourish there. Once Ivy and Joli sit down to eat their peaches and rest, "bees buzzed everywhere among the roses" (192). This image, with Ivy occupied in the vital act of storytelling at the old Cline place, connects the roses of female sexuality with bees that produce honey, which will eventually bring the sweetness of sexual satisfaction with the entrance of the bee keeper, Honey Breeding. Ivy meets Honey for the first time down in the springhouse that has "wild white roses" (204), like those of the Clines', growing all down the steps. In taking her daughter to such a specifically feminine hallowed place, Ivy symbolically reintroduces Joli to what Irigaray calls the "values of desire, pain, joy, the body," that are not "discourses of mastery" but rather tools for liberation ("Women-Mothers" 51). Ivy urges Joli to accept her sacred, sexual self, thus freeing her daughter to be a "living, loving woman," beyond the constraints of patriarchal culture (47–48).

Rabuzzi insists that only in a setting where women love one another can they come to know and accept the goddess. Arguing that contemporary society discourages close ties among female friends and relatives, Rabuzzi asserts, "Instead of mirroring ourselves positively, other women ... more often reflect what is least desirable in ourselves. As a result, what we uncover in each other is anything but the fullness of the Goddess" (188). Smith, challenging conventional thought in her fiction, explores several pairings of women that demonstrate just the opposite idea. Granny (Garnett) and Tenessee Rowe, Ivy's great-aunts, two more old maiden ladies who, like the Clines, depend on each other for nurturance, strongly influence Ivy and provide additional portraitures of women's lives. Whereas Granny Rowe consistently displays a formidable strength and independence, Tenessee, another weak, mentally unstable female character like Silvaney, does not fit into society. Dorothy Hill calls Tenessee a "sort of Aphrodite-gone-to-seed" (113), a female who suffers permanent damage by society's enforced code for proper sexual behavior. In a letter to Mrs. Brown, Ivy explains the possible source of Tenessee's instability: "I have heerd tell that one time something nasty happend to Tenessee." One can only imagine what that something might be, but Ivy's choice of the word "nasty" suggests its connection to men and sex. Ivy also relates another time when a drummer came through Majestic and "fell plum in love" with Tenessee then took her away with him to Huntington, West Virginia, but brought her back in three months with no explanation. Now Tenessee dresses up in tacky clothes but thinks she's beautiful. Recalling the image of Fay in *Family Linen*, Tenessee's "hair was so blond and fine [also like Silvaney's] at one time but now it is nearly white only she dont know it, she dont know she has gotten old." Granny cares for her sister and watches her closely because if left alone, "she will go up and show herself to men" (38); "she cant keep her hands off the men" (15). This promiscuous behavior is the result of the damage done to Tenessee when she was young and beautiful, a sexual creature exploited by society.

Granny's concern for and mystic communion with her sister directly parallels Ivy's feelings for Silvaney. Like Silvaney, Tenessee often wanders the mountain despite her sister's concern. In fact, years after Granny's death and Tenessee's mysterious disappearance, Ivy, sensing Tenessee's ethereal quality, writes to Silvaney, "I don't think she's [Tenessee] dead. I think she's still wandering somewhere," but without Granny, Tenessee fails to survive in the physical world. Her spiritual nature is implicit in Ivy's description when, after Granny's death, Tenessee appears at the door in the middle of the night during a thunderstorm, "standing still in the rainy door with the lightning branching out behind her head." The obvious halo image recalls that of Dory and other sacred, sexual female characters who are destroyed by or sacrificed to patriarchy. Ivy writes to Silvaney that Tenessee is "gone, gone for sure," comparing her to Uncle Revel, "him that suffered such a love as to spin him loose for ever in the world" (190), directly connecting the pain of these two characters with their experiences in love. So Ivy has seen the despair caused by great love and loss and the despondency caused by the lack of such love. The companionship between Granny and her sister had sustained Tenessee, just as Granny has comforted and healed other family members through the years.

In *Fair and Tender Ladies*, Smith attributes mythic qualities to female characters who are empowered by their own differences. Unlike *Oral History*, in which Granny Younger tells the reader that she had experienced passion when she was young, Ivy makes no mention of a sex life for Granny Rowe, also the mountain counselor and healer. Granny Rowe's looming presence, however, directly relates to sexuality and the natural cycles of life. The name "Garnett," of course, denotes a transparent deep red mineral sometimes used as a gem, and Smith consistently links Granny to the color red, to blood, and to the moon. Ivy writes to Geneva that Granny Rowe just appeared suddenly one night, puffing on her pipe, shining red in the dark, close to Ivy's due date for the birth of her first child. As Granny announces the full moon, Ivy observes, "And sure enough, right as she spoke, the moon came up over the top of the mountain as big as I have ever seen it in my life" (135). Ivy's water then immediately breaks and her labor pains begin. Eckard suggests that Granny's arrival "evokes the image of Artemis, Greek goddess of the hunt and childbirth" and according to Adrienne Rich the goddess representative of "women's mysteries" (166). Gerda Lerner acknowledges the particularly feminine experience of "mystic contemplation, visions and communication with the supernatural" as manifested in signs as "peculiarly private forms of the miraculous" (71–72). Granny Rowe, in her mysterious powers of prophecy and healing, links Ivy to the numinous world. Seemingly an integral part of the natural birth process, Granny delivers Joli, "dripping blood and gore," and "cut the cord with a kitchen knife and bound her with the strippy cloths" (Smith 140).

Unlike Granny Younger who condemns a sexually active adult female, labeling Red Emmy a witch and describing Pricey Jane's passion as unusual for a wife, Granny Rowe accepts Ivy's sexuality as natural and never passes judgment on her nineteen-year-old unwed niece when she becomes pregnant and gives birth. Just as Granny Rowe remains to help when Silvaney has to be caught and prevented from harming herself, Granny provides Ivy with support in every crisis. Granny Rowe's innate understanding and acceptance of life's complexities powerfully tie her to the feminine divine. When Ivy, thirty-seven years old and the mother of five children, sinks into what she calls "a great soft darkness" (186) where she feels frozen, "locked in time" (188), a depression so deep that she fears she'll never be able to climb out, Granny again appears mysteriously just at the right time. Issuing instructions to Ivy on how to purify the blood, Granny establishes her connection to the life force of blood. Ivy remembers this powerful aegis long after Granny's death. Ivy can never fully accept the wise old woman's absence since vestiges of her presence remain as Ivy often catches "a glimpse of her long skirt swishing just around the bend ahead" (191), or imagines she smells Granny's pipe-smoke in the air. For all the years of her life, Ivy feels Granny's eternal presence, the voice of wisdom and encouragement whispering words into her ear, almost a mythological foremother or avatar for the feminine divine.

Ivy's need for and insistence upon bonds with women persist throughout her life as she searches for the divinity that will offer her comfort and guidance. Her sisters Beulah and Ethel are strong, determined women who live their lives the way they want, and even though Ivy loses touch when Beulah doesn't respond to her letters, Ivy always misses and longs for her connection with Beulah. With her depiction of the strong, independent Ethel, Smith transgresses societal boundaries in allowing Ethel to marry Stoney Branham after his sickly wife commits suicide. Ivy's acceptance of and deep concern for her sister are reflected in her words of support to Ethel after the marriage. She proffers wise advice reminiscent of the words of *Family Linen*'s Candy, telling her sister, "if you want Stoney Branham then I am glad you married him, even if he is 25 years older than you." Ivy says she harbors no interest in the opinions of others; she cares that Ethel is happy and advises her, "Just hold up your head and dont listen to what all they say." Furthermore, Ivy accepts and refuses to judge her sister, regardless of whether or not she was involved with Stoney before his wife's death. Then, with a touch of typically artistic Smith humor, Ivy admits, "anybody honest would own he must of *needed* a woman for years, whether he had one or not, since his own wife was just laying up there in the bed crying and eating prunes." Ivy ends her letter by reassuring Ethel that "people will forget it soon enough" (137). And of course, they do, and Ethel and Stoney have a long and happy marriage. Ivy and Ethel remain close throughout the years of their lives, never trying to tell each other how to live those lives. In fact, when Honey Breeding leaves Ivy in Majestic, Ethel and their brother Victor drive Ivy back up to Sugar Fork. When Victor, the voice of male-dominated society, scolds Ivy, "Sister! ... You hadn't ought to've done it! ... You ought to've stayed at home!," Ethel "turn[s] on him in a fury" and snaps, "You crazy old man!" Taking Ivy gently by the arm, Ethel says, "Come on honey" (229). Ethel seems to know Ivy's heart, even up to near the end of the novel when Ivy spends time in the hospital and Ethel sends to her sister white roses, a reminder of the nurturing, ethereal Cline sisters.

In addition to female family members, the love and support of other salient female friendships heavily influence Ivy's life, elucidating Smith's belief in the necessity of such bonds for recognition of the divinity in feminine experience. Ivy encounters several potent females at different points in her life and remains close and connected to each for many years. Ivy meets Molly Bainbridge, the niece of her teacher Mrs. Brown, when both girls are fourteen years old and Mrs. Brown invites Ivy to come for a visit during her niece's stay. Although their lives take quite disparate paths, the friendship formed between Ivy and Molly in their young years remains active as they maintain a correspondence through letters for a few years then eventually lose touch. As girls, they share their ideas about love, children, and careers. At sixty-one years old, now a widow and devoted mother and grandmother, shocked and delighted Ivy receives a letter from Molly, who is working for the state and asking Ivy for help with the settlement school in Majestic, which Molly plans to take over. Ivy writes to Molly, "In a way it seems like no time atall since we jumped rope together and mined for gold. In another way it seems like more than years. It seems like lifetimes and lifetimes ago" (285). But some things never change, such as Ivy's connection to these important, strong women in her life. She agrees to help Molly and does for a while but stops once the school succeeds and Molly has become an important, famous figure. Extremely proud of Molly, Ivy, however, confesses, "But this is not for me. I have got things to think on, and letters to write" (295), realizing that she finds her greatest pleasure in writing rather than pursuing an active career.

With another of Ivy's female friends, Geneva Hunt, a former schoolmate of Ivy's mother and the proprietress of the boardinghouse in Majestic, Smith offers yet another alternative for females as the writer continues to explore the expanding possibilities for women's lives. Ivy meets Geneva when her family moves to Majestic after the death of Ivy's little brother Danny, and because of the generosity, acceptance, and love of this "soft" woman (81), Ivy, her mother, and her two little brothers find a new home that provides a supportive environment. Associated with nature and sexuality, Geneva first appears emerging from the boardinghouse, where "buttercups was blooming early" like "she was blowed by the wind" (79), an image reminiscent of other divine, sexual females who have been associated with flowers and described as appearing in a gust of wind, most notably *Oral History*'s Dory. Even though Geneva has been married three times and announces that she is finished with men, Ivy's intuition about Geneva's sexual appetite proves correct when Ivy spots one of the male boarders "sneaking outen Genevas room, carrying his shoes!" (88), then later notices that Sam Russell Sage, a famous preacher holding a revival in town, has become "Genevas sweetie" (94). This affair between a sexually accommodating boardinghouse proprietress and a preacher strongly echoes the situation with *Oral History*'s Justine Poole and Aldous Rife.

With her portrayal of Geneva as openly sexual, nurturant, and deeply caring, Smith again transgresses boundaries by depicting these qualities as coexistent, desirable, and even admirable. Serving as a mentor for Ivy, Geneva offers many words of wisdom through the years of their friendship, early on telling the seventeen-year-old, when Ivy is feeling confused about God, her own sexuality, and her future, that sometimes "a girl has just got to let down her hair!" (94). Not only is Geneva sexually accommodating with her guests, she also loves to cook and prepares and serves elaborate meals to patrons and townspeople alike as Smith connects the two ideas of nurturing with food and nurturing with human sexual contact, suggesting that both appetites must be satisfied in order to achieve integration and wholeness. Right after Ivy returns to Sugar Fork from her interlude with Honey Breeding and sinks into grief and depression, seventy-year-old Geneva, similar to Granny Rowe in her innate sense of timing, visits Ivy to reassure her that what Ivy has done will soon be forgiven and forgotten. When Ivy worries about being such a "scandal," Geneva offers Ivy the same advice Ivy had given her younger sister Ethel years earlier, then openly admits, winking at Ivy, "I used to be a scandal myself ... Now I'm an institution." Geneva accepts her sexuality as part of her selfhood and encourages Ivy to do the same, but Ivy, uncomfortable doing so, writes to Silvaney that she greatly admires Geneva's way of life, but that she herself lacks the "gumption and pluck," and also she has "got to think about things too much finally." Ivy continues, "You know I have always got to write my letters, and think about what's happened and what I've done" (236–37). Ivy's words in describing Geneva's lifestyle, "riding hell for leather" (245), echo Granny Younger's interpretation of Red Emmy's sexual aggressiveness with Almarine, but in this novel, Smith presents Geneva in a much gentler way than she did Red Emmy. The sexually expressive Geneva survives and flourishes in a society that accepts and needs her; as she admits, she's become "an institution."

In her growing awareness of the feminine divine in its centrality for women's lives, Smith continues to expand women's roles. When Ivy is living with Beulah and Curtis in Diamond, she befriends and remains permanently connected to another strong woman, Violet Gayheart, a neighbor. Ivy finds a soul mate in Violet and enjoys spending time with her and her young, mentally retarded daughter Martha. Smith makes a bold statement about the necessity of women's connections when Ivy describes a scene of playfulness during which she and Violet spread a quilt on the ground and enjoy watching the children while Rush, Violet's husband, plays the fiddle. Ivy explains, "Then Violet took a dive and started tickling me, and we rolled over and over on the quilt laughing" (155), an image of two grown women bonding both physically and emotionally. Patricia Yaeger calls attention to the "seriously playful, emancipatory strategies" that women often employ to challenge and perhaps even change the status quo. Yaeger questions why we are so uncomfortable with the concept of play for women, suggesting society's discomfort with female delight, freedom, and pleasure (19–20). In this scene with Ivy and Violet, Smith "playfully" transgresses boundaries in her depiction of two adult women interacting in physical playfulness. The play in which the two engage early on in their friendship serves to bind them in a friendship that lasts for the remainder of their lives. When an explosion at the mine kills Rush, Ivy takes Violet's daughter to raise. Accepting and loving Martha as her own, Ivy feels no disappointment whatsoever in the girl's inadequacies and neither judges nor condemns Violet for leaving her daughter.

Smith's depiction of such a wide variety of female characters demonstrates her enlarged vision for the possibilities in women's lives. Motherhood remains a complex central issue in Smith's works as the author journeys toward her own spiritual integration where women may flourish and discover the feminine divine in their everyday lives, whether or not they choose to give birth biologically. Irigaray's argument that psychoanalysis colludes with a life-threatening symbolic order in which the maternal feminine is primarily a sacrificial object, "forgotten, repressed, denied, confused" ("Limits" 107) proves helpful when examining Smith's female characters and their ideas about motherhood. Irigaray urges women not to submit to a "desubjectivized social role" that disallows the coexistence of sexuality and maternity ("Bodily" 43). Violet Gayheart falls into this dichotomized way of thinking in believing she must "sacrifice" her own aspirations in order to mother her retarded daughter. In the scope of this novel, only Ivy attains divine integration of her sexual nature with her role as mother. Many of the strong women to whom Ivy is closely connected remain unmarried or childless as Smith provides Ivy with a wide variety of role models, depicting each female character with unqualified acceptance for her uniqueness. Marriage and motherhood, for several of these women, seem to be associated with depression, nervous disorders, and incapacitation. Of Ivy's three sisters, only Beulah both marries and has children, but, although she remains surrounded by family and friends, she leads an unfulfilled and miserable life, essentially dying of loneliness. Ethel marries twice and experiences two extremely successful marriages, living a long and satisfying life but choosing not to become a mother. Nursing Lois Branham during years of a nervous condition and depression and practically raising the Branham children herself must have conduced to Ethel's decision not to have children. Additionally, Molly, the young teenager who shared so many of Ivy's dreams of marriage and motherhood, neither marries nor becomes a mother. The mental condition and extended hospitalization of her own mother undoubtedly contributed to this choice. Just as Ivy, at a young age, relates her mother's "hanted" look to having so many children and watches her mother's gradual descent from depression to mere existence, these women share a reluctance to sacrifice themselves the way other important females in their lives have.

The tenet of traditional patriarchal religion that stresses the sacrifice and selflessness of mothers presents, for Ivy, one of the disturbing discrepancies between what she knows in her heart and what the mountain churches teach. Like her mother, Ivy fails to find any comfort or strength in conventional religion. Lee Smith voiced the same personal conflict in an interview with Susan Ketchin: "Ivy is like me; she is unable to find a religion that suits her—an organized religion" (51). In her article "The Protean Ivy in Lee Smith's

Fair and Tender Ladies," Tanya Long Bennett posits that Ivy "wavers between regard and disgust for the conventional Christian God" and later mentions "Ivy's wavering confidence in this [Christian] system of salvation" and the "contradictory perspectives exhibited by Ivy in regard to Christianity." Although Bennett also acknowledges Ivy's experiencing "a sort of spiritual life connected to nature" (72–73), she overlooks Ivy's discovery and acceptance of the feminine divine. At no time during the course of the novel does Ivy display any belief in traditional patriarchal Christianity. It is precisely this void that leads her to the reclamation of the divine within her self, and as Bennett accurately notes, "what Ivy does is more complex than simply rejecting patriarchal Christian myths and embracing those of the powerful goddess" (79). Ivy's spiritual perspective encompasses the divinity of nature and women's bodies as part of nature, and also the sacredness of their experiences in all forms, as conveyed by Smith's comment that "the sacred is to be found in the everyday" (Per). Further evidence of Ivy's negative feelings regarding Christianity lies in her perception of the novel's self-proclaimed "Christians," the hypocritical Sam Russell Sage and Ivy's brother Garnie, also Dreama Fox, who suffers from repression.

Ivy's moral struggles begin early in the novel. When Ivy continues to write to Hanneke, whom she calls "the Ice Queen," even though her Dutch pen-pal never writes back, Ivy feels angry and alone. She writes of God: "He is not good or bad ether one. I think it is that He does not care" (16). Ivy never sends this letter, but she continues to search for something in which to have faith, something to provide her with the hope that cannot be found in the patriarchal "anti-woman" mountain church to which she is exposed (Ketchin 54). She writes to Mrs. Brown that she cannot pray, so she knows she is evil, but she doesn't feel evil. After John Arthur's death, Ivy writes again to her teacher, who has consistently suggested that Ivy pray about her hardships, "no I do not pray, nor do I think much of God. It is not rigt what he sends on people" (31). Theologian and literary critic Carol Christ explains her own realization that something was "wrong with the traditional image of God" that insisted on the dominance of a male father and totally obliterated a female mother. Realizing she would never be "in his image," Christ struck out on a search for a female deity. Not unlike Ivy, Christ became "increasingly alienated from God" and found herself unable to attend church or pray to this patriarchal God (2). Ivy's search likewise eventually leads her to an awareness of feminine divinity. Like her daughter in her religious skepticism, Maude also rejects the patriarchal God; after her young son Danny's death, when Garnie begins praying over Danny's body, she orders him, "Cut it out, Garnie Rowe! I dont know what Jesus ever had to do with usuns anyway" (72).

Ivy shares her mother's sentiments, never experiencing anything she considers spiritual until she attends one of Sam Russell Sage's prayer meetings in Majestic with Miss Gertrude Torrington, a missionary. Ivy calls the sermon "scarry," with Mr. Sage describing death as a hungry animal "licking his chops" right outside the tent and people "crying and then yelling out." Ivy writes to Beulah, "I could feel the firey hand of God clutching me in the stomach," but Miss Torrington's "sick spell" prevents Ivy from professing her faith. Only when Ivy and Miss Torrington get away from the tent does Ivy feel "the firey hand" let go (90–91), so Ivy hopes she will not die soon since she hasn't been saved yet. Reminiscent of Crystal Spangler's physical discomfort, Ivy's stomach pain signals her emerging sexuality. Irigarary discusses women's somatic pain as a manifestation of their need for identity ("Women-Mothers" 52), their hunger for an image of the ideal, a divine female against which to measure themselves ("Limits" 111). Smith consistently links spirituality and sexuality in her insistence on the need for feminine divinity. Both Miss Torrington's "sick spell" and Ivy's stomach pain suggest the absence of an awareness of the feminine divine in their lives.

Further association between religion and sexuality occurs when Ivy discovers Lonnie Rash, a young boarder at Geneva's who works in the lumber business. Ivy says that Lonnie stares at her all the time "like he is touching me under my cloths," and that when he is in the same room with her, she feels "that firey hand again and cant hardly breth." Both patriarchal religion and her relationship with Lonnie prove suffocating for Ivy. Again, as she has done in previous novels, Smith associates sexual passion with religious passion, the "firey hand" indicating both. Linking her sensation with Jane Eyre's experience of feeling "a firey hand in her vitals" when Mister Rochester kisses her, Ivy says she knows such a feeling is a warning from God that "you are bad" (94–95). God prevents Jane from running away with Rochester, but Ivy says she does not have God to turn to since she remains unsaved.

Ivy continues to rebel against ownership and any person or belief system that attempts to possess her. Although Miss Torrington tells Ivy that God has sent her to Majestic to "save" Ivy, that Ivy has been given to her "by God as a sacred responsibility," Ivy sees Miss Torrington as "the Ice Queen." In competition with Lonnie Rash for Ivy's time and attention, Miss Torrington tells Ivy, "I feel it is a *sin*, Ivy, a great sin, if we do not use our tallents that God has given us, if we do not live up to our potenshal," asking Ivy to go to Boston with her to be properly educated. At the thought of such an opportunity, Ivy feels something like an electrical shock as she listens to Miss Torrington's words and "feel[s] her breth soft as a whisper on my neck" (97–99). Because Miss Torrington, a missionary, ostensibly offers Ivy the correct path to fulfill her "potenshal" and perhaps even serves as Ivy's "salvation," and since Ivy, a bright and eager student, feels starved for information and craves a formal education, she agrees to go to Boston. Even at this young age, Ivy perceives the path to freedom and fulfillment as one based on education and betterment of herself, unlike many earlier Smith protagonists who, trapped within patriarchy, focus only on men.

Smith suggests that Ivy's rejection of and inability to understand Miss Torrington's display of love directly result from the girl's age and inexperience. Irigaray argues that for women to discover and reclaim their sexual identity and desires, they must also embrace their "auto-eroticism," their "narcissism," their "heterosexuality," and their "homosexuality" since women, having first identified with another woman's body (the mother), "always stand in an archaic and primal relationship with what is known as homosexuality" ("Bodily" 44). It will take many years for Ivy to comprehend and accept the idea of same-sex sexual relationships. She is catapulted into a state of total confusion about love, religion, and everything in which she has ever believed when, during a private drawing lesson, both she and Miss Torrington become excited and Miss Torrington, while looking over Ivy's shoulder at her drawing, kisses Ivy on the neck. Rebecca Smith notes that "this threat of lesbianism [is] rare in Smith's work" and that "Smith intimates homosexuality here simply to negotiate with the conventional romance plot for a woman's life" (109). Perhaps, however, Smith presents Miss Torrington and her love for Ivy as another picture of a female with a life very different from Ivy's, as Smith's literary and spiritual vision expands. Immediately after the incident, Ivy writes to Silvaney that she felt paralyzed. Ivy says, "I could not breth, I could not think what to do" (102). Again, as she has felt with Lonnie and at church, Ivy feels choked, robbed of breath. This experience marks and changes the course of Ivy's life, and in Ivy's last letter to Silvaney, as Ivy approaches death and describes the shifting images in her mind, she writes that she sees "Miss Torrington so severe her kiss like fire on the back of my neck yet first born of all my kisses all my life" (307). As a nineteen-year-old girl, Ivy lacks the capability to accept or understand this demonstration of physical affection from another woman, but as years pass and Miss Torrington continues to correspond with Ivy, faithfully sending packages every Christmas to Ivy and her children, Ivy comes to understand what Miss Torrington had written to her in a letter not long after her departure from Majestic: "there are kinds and kinds of love and that sometimes we confuse them being only mortal as we are" (111). Only after Ivy's affair with Honey Breeding and her recognition of the divinity of female flesh does she intuit the many types of love to which Miss Torrington referred.

Ivy's calling Miss Torrington's kiss the "first born" of all her kisses and comparing the kiss to fire reiterate that Miss Torrington ignites Ivy's passion for knowledge and that her kiss impels Ivy to have sex with Lonnie Rash, perhaps to validate her heterosexuality. Admitting the thrill of Lonnie's hands on her body and the attractiveness of his muscled arms, Ivy feels equally disturbed that Lonnie cannot read or write and has no desire to learn. Ivy writes to Silvaney that she has "let him put his tonge way down in my mouth and the firey hand grabbed me then for good," once more associating physical passion with religious passion. Ivy yearns for the sensation of the "firey hand," writing to Silvaney, "I know this is bad but it feels so good" (95–96). Like

Carol Christ, and even Smith herself, Ivy cannot condone a religious system that upholds the "classical dualisms of spirit and nature, mind and body, rational and irrational, [and] male and female" (xiv). Ivy associates physical passion with guilt, but she is a sexual, sensual young woman and chooses to explore her sexuality anyway. As Ivy describes to Silvaney her first sexual experience with Lonnie, she makes no mention of a "firey hand," suggesting the absence of intensity and passion in this purely physical union. The pain Ivy feels during sexual intercourse for the first time is indicative of the anguish she must endure as a result of her decision to have sex with Lonnie, for immediately after their intercourse, Ivy, overcome with sadness, writes to Silvaney of her overwhelming sense of loss. Ivy has lost much more than her virginity since she will soon discover her pregnancy and inability to go to Boston to follow her dream of acquiring a proper education.

In her depiction of Ivy's relationship with Franklin Ransom, the spoiled son of the Peabody Coal Company's superintendent, Smith explores carnal pleasure, portraying this affair as sometimes violent, a sexual relationship reminiscent of the association between violence and sex that earlier female characters such as Brooke, Monica, and Crystal sensed and even desired. René Girard asserts that "sex is more involved in human violence than are thunder and earthquakes" and that "'naked' or 'pure' sexuality is directly connected to violence" and serves as the "final veil shielding violence from sight" (118). Ivy's attraction to Franklin may be explained in light of Girard's argument since she craves the purely physical aspect of their relationship and his explosive nature fascinates her. Ivy writes to Silvaney that Franklin can tell the story of his brother's death "in such a way as to make you cry, and make you want to take your dress off" (158). Unlike Lonnie, Franklin provides the nourishment of stories since he possesses the power of language. However, when Franklin calls Ivy his "baby" (161) and violently jerks up her skirt and pulls down her panties, Ivy rejects his gestures of ownership. Despite Franklin's destructive behavior and the real threat of physical harm, Ivy continues to see Franklin, though she admits that she "knew Franklin had something wrong with him" the first time she was with him (159). As Girard explains, violence and desire are often linked, and sometimes the presence of violence awakens desire (148); thus, Ivy is drawn to Franklin and to the violence and danger he represents. Later, in Ivy's affair with Honey Breeding, Smith negates the violence and offers a gentle version of sacred sexual union.

Rabuzzi discusses how patriarchal ideology pushes sexual union as "a desirable goal for salvation" and notes that if a woman desires to be saved from herself, "sexual ecstasy may work" (105). Ivy has indeed searched for salvation, with no success, in her sexual relationships. She decides to marry Oakley Fox because he seems to offer her an opportunity to redeem herself for her past behavior, a chance for salvation, much as Miss Torrington had done earlier. Ivy seems to perpetually quest for some type of atonement outside herself. But

Ivy must find salvation within herself, in her psyche, not in a relationship with another person. Oakley's feelings for Ivy have always involved a sense of ownership, however, hinting at an incipient conflict and forming a parallel to her relationship with Franklin. Even after their marriage, he tells her, "You are a sassy woman but you are mine" (186). Nevertheless, Ivy, connecting this natural man (appropriately named "Oakley") to her father, responds to Oakley's closeness to nature. Writing to Silvaney about her marriage to Oakley, Ivy explains, "And when Oakley kisses me, it seems like I can hear Daddy saying, Slow down, slow down now, Ivy. This is the taste of spring" (169). As in other novels, nature functions as the location for sacredness, and Ivy's attraction to Oakley reflects her sense of organic divinity.

The "firey hand of God" no longer clutches Ivy's stomach at church or in the bedroom with her husband as Ivy gradually realizes that neither Oakley nor God will "save" her. In an interview with Nancy Parrish, Smith admitted her lack of faith in the male-imaged God: "I *wish* I could believe in religion as Oakley Fox did, but I really can't" (399), and neither can Ivy. After giving birth to five more children and a miscarriage, all over a period of nine years, a feeling of resignation gradually replaces Ivy's old passion. Whereas Oakley continues to derive pleasure from working with the land despite the deterioration of his health, Ivy writes in a letter to Silvaney, "when his work is done of an evening then it is done, for he don't have to mend the clothes or can the corn or feed the baby" (193). Here Ivy perfectly articulates the gap between the roles of husband/father and wife/mother; the work never subsides for the female while the male at least can rest at the end of his workday. Ivy begins to fear that the same trap that caught her parents now seeks to envelop her and Oakley, for work and children are wearing her down, and her image of Oakley has become one of a man constantly working, with his back bent and his face always turned away from her.

In goddess mythology, the motif of descent is essential in a woman's search for self; Ivy's feelings of falling into a dark hole represent the intensity of her need to discover her self apart from her children and her husband. At age thirty-seven and the mother of five children, Ivy suffers metaphorical death as she sinks into what Irigaray explains as a "depressive collapse," the physical expression of years of inaudible pain ("Women-Mothers" 48). For six years, Ivy writes nothing. Ivy's silence (the absence of her letters) is like a loss of self for her since writing always validated her experiences and her life (Kearns 189). Irigaray poignantly explains this condition as the tragedy of aphasia and the lack of "a relationship of/with desire, corporeal relations, [and] love relations" ("Women-Mothers" 51). During this period of not expressing her feelings through letters, Ivy falls into what she calls "a great soft darkness, a blackness so deep and so soft that you can fall in there and get comfortable and never know you are falling in at all" (186). She wonders if this is what happened to her mother, who was never able to climb out. Ivy writes to Silvaney of her exhaustion, explaining that when her baby Maudy nurses, "it is like she is sucking my life right out of me." Even though she eats, Ivy can't gain any weight, describing herself as "nothing but skin and bones," a "dried-up husk ... leeched out by hard work and babies," a "locust—like a box turtle shell!" Ivy expresses this loss of self perfectly when she says she feels "bits and pieces of me have rolled off and been lost along the way," like she exists in a state of temporary paralysis, as if she's been "flung down into darkness, frozen there" (187–88). Ivy exemplifies Irigaray's description of the problem of the woman-mother torn to pieces, fragmented, "splitting apart," as "volume without contours" unable to articulate her feelings and therefore silent ("Volume" 53–54). Admitting that she never dreams anymore, never goes anywhere, and can't take an interest in reading anymore, Ivy says all she wants to do when she's not working is rest, "lean back and shut my eyes and fall straight as a plum down into that darkness" (188). Even this deep depression doesn't send Ivy to Oakley's God for comfort; always the lover of nature, she says she would rather sit on the porch, think and look out at the world than attend church. But unlike Crystal who sinks into permanent passivity, Ivy will eventually regain movement through starting to write her letters again and coming to know her inner sacred self.

In this novel, once more Smith juxtaposes wildness with domesticity, strongly suggesting the necessity of some degree of wildness in order to fully experience one's sacred sexuality. Ivy's feelings of "wildness" finally resurface after many years of submergence in her subconscious while she played out the role of the domestic wife. Early in the novel, Uncle Revel's comment that Ivy takes after her mother, serves as foreshadowing for Ivy's later years. He warns Maude about Ivy, "shel be truble all rigt, shel be wild as a buck like you" (22), re-emphasizing Maude's spirited nature before her decline. Even the wallpaper in Ivy's room at Geneva Hunt's boardinghouse in Majestic hints at Smith's interest in the conflict between society's attempts to confine women to domestic roles and women's desire to "escape." In a letter to Silvaney, Ivy describes the wallpaper as having "silver-gray squares with pink ribands running between, and in each square, they is a lady" arrayed in an elegant pink dress (80). Women beautifully dressed in the feminine color pink are carefully placed in boxes, suggesting their containment and the restraint placed on them. Ivy succeeds in escaping the box in not only her refusal to marry Lonnie Rash, Joli's father, but also her affair with Franklin Ransom, and most importantly her affair with Honey Breeding. Ironically, it is in this bedroom at the boardinghouse that Ivy, as a teenager, loses her virginity to Lonnie, and once she discovers she's pregnant, she lies on her bed and stares "up at the ladies marching hand in hand along my walls," describing the ladies as "marching" as if they are joined together, the force of society attempting to imprison her. Ivy imagines the baby inside her "beating ... its little fists against my stomach, trying to escape" (114) then feels as if the baby is herself, attempting to break free.

Ivy associates her feelings of wildness with Silvaney and senses a deeper connection to her lost sister since she believes she now understands for the first time how Silvaney must have felt all those years ago. She writes that she is "on fire" and can "feel it running through my veins and out my fingers" (201). Nor Hall notes that blood was traditionally believed to contain the soul, and the blood's coursing through the veins was called spiritual movement. With Ivy's consciousness of the fire-like blood pumping through her body, she expresses her ripeness for sacred experience, her readiness for "blessing." (The word "blessing" is a derivative of the Old English *bloedsen*, which means "bleeding.") As Hall states, "first the blood has to flow to make new life possible" (169–70), and Ivy will soon experience rebirth in her encounter with Honey Breeding. With her next comments, Ivy gives reasons for her unconventional behavior that help to explain the conflict she is experiencing between expressing her sexuality and performing the duties motherhood demands. Insisting that Oakley is her "life," she says she loves her husband, along with the farm and her children, but she adds, "there is something about a man that is <u>too good</u> which will drive you crazy." Ivy says Oakley's "goodness" makes her "want to run or scream or roll down the hill." Next, Ivy metaphorically describes exactly what will happen since Ivy will soon run away with Honey Breeding, leaving her husband and family, "never checking for rocks" or thinking of "where we might land" or what she stands to lose (201–202). Irigaray argues that paralysis of sexual expression manifests itself in desires to "scream" and engage in destructive behavior ("Women-Mothers" 52). Ivy's wish to dance on the mountaintop in the thunderstorm in a ritualistic dance of ecstasy powerfully connects her to goddess mythology. Anne Baring and Jules Cashford explain one interpretation of the dance as "the soul's wandering," in which obstacles represent the sacrifices one must make in order to reach the center, where one achieves transformation and rebirth (136–37). Ivy's imagined "roll[ing] down the hill" and over rocks in her path suggests her progress toward integration and regeneration although the sacrifices she makes are great but necessary for her receptivity to and encounter with the feminine divine.

Ivy's journey to self-knowledge and acceptance of the feminine divine is filled with passion in three areas: learning and the representation of feeling through language, experiencing motherhood, and openly expressing her sexuality. These are the activities that cause her the most confusion because of the encoded message from society that the three complexes cannot coexist in one woman. Knowing she will not find the sexual passion for which she longs, perhaps even subconsciously at this point, in her own bedroom with Oakley, Ivy betrays her need for language and physical touch in her thoughts that her husband "never talks nor pets me any, just does it and goes to sleep, while I lay there in the darkness immaginning god knows what, immaginning stars." Honey Breeding will bring Ivy's imagination to life since he not only talks to her, but also fashions a crown for her out of star flowers after they make love on a carpet of star flowers, directly recalling her "imagining stars" while in bed with her husband. Ivy accepts Oakley's inability to conceive of her tempestuousness, so she decides to remain silent about "how I want to scream all the time or when I look out at the mountains I want to reach out and rip them all away leaving only the flat hard sudden sky" (203–204). Ivy's resentment toward a world that has silenced her and denied her sexuality increases as she reaches middle age. Oakley can only see and accept the domesticity within his wife, having clearly separated the wildness and sexuality of Ivy from the nurturing wife and mother; thus, Ivy feels pulled in two directions at once all the time.

Hélène Cixous connects all female drives to "a desire to live self from within, a desire for the swollen belly, for language, for blood" (261). Ivy's pregnancy seems to satisfy her female drives, and Ivy's pride in her pregnant body symbolizes her self-love and her need to openly express both her sexuality and her feelings, or the divine within her, through writing. Ivy's first pregnancy and parturition illuminate her acceptance of her body and its natural processes. Noticing that boys seem embarrassed by her pregnancy and don't look at her the same, Ivy reacts by standing "real straight and stick[ing] my belly out" (130). With no sign of embarrassment or shame, Ivy clearly possesses the necessary tools to achieve divine integration. Ivy's memories of Joli's birth, during which "the blood smell was not so bad" (140), strikingly contrast the ideas of *Dogbushes*' Susan who feels repulsed by the idea of menstruation, and Crystal who experiences nausea in class when the teacher discusses the circulation of the blood. With salient connections to nature and the natural processes of menstruation, pregnancy, and childbirth, Smith allows Ivy to comfortably slide into the roles of birthing and mothering. Rebecca Smith perceptively notes that Ivy's description of the birth process "affirms it as a positive rite of passage for women, one valuing women's mystery and one whose details have been slighted in canonical literature" (110). Without acceptance of the sight, taste, touch, and smell of the life-sustaining substance—blood—a woman can never truly achieve self-knowledge or integration. In a letter to Silvaney, Ivy describes the blood smell as "sweet some way, it was not like anything else in the world, and now it will always be mixed up in my mind somehow with the moonlight and my baby." Here Smith associates blood with motherhood, tying together these often dichotomized ideas. Giving birth and holding her baby represent the most religious experiences Ivy has ever had, and Smith's diction clarifies this with descriptive details that connect stars, heaven, moonlight, and cathedrals. The movement of the moonlight, which comes "across the quilt star by star"—identified as "the Heavenly star pattern"—marks this divine experience for Ivy as she holds Joli. When the moonlight hits the star closest to Ivy, "it seemed to glow out like the cathedral windows" (140–41). The presence of the feminine divine, represented by the moonlight, permeates this symbolic setting.

Ivy's description of the blood smell as "sweet" links her birthing experience to the "sweetness of honey" for which she has yearned for so long. Mythologically honey symbolizes birth and resurrection since it was one of the few natural preservatives of the ancients. Honey was regarded as the goddess's sacred essence, and falling into a jar of honey became a metaphor for death and rebirth (Walker, *Women's* 407).* Ivy undergoes death of her old self and rebirth of her new sacred, sexual self as she experiences union with Honey Breeding. Ivy's behavior with Honey arises from an "awful longing pure and simple ... out of love," and she writes to Silvaney that she doesn't care what anyone says or thinks; she "had to do it, I had to have him" (222). Lévi-Strauss observes that women are like honey in that both are "natural and unnatural, 'raw' and 'cooked'—something that does not fit on either side of the constructed division between nature and culture" (Yaeger 27). In the South American tale of the "honey-mad woman," the woman eats tremendous amounts of honey, feeding on it "wildly and to excess" because honey, in its ambiguity, marks the place where "woman herself is asked to reside" (35). In defying social order by abandoning her family to follow Honey Breeding, Ivy denies the "systematic control of women's minds and bodies" and "act[s] out her hunger" (27), despite the risks and sacrifices. As Rebecca Smith notes, here Smith uses the honey-mad woman myth as an emancipator strategy for Ivy (115). The motif of honey appears while Ivy is living in Diamond with Beulah and Curtis. Ivy writes to Silvaney of her feelings of loneliness even though there are five people in a four-room house living "like bees in a honey comb" (133), but the sweetness of honey is missing. Then, when Ivy dates Franklin, he begs her to wear his mother's "rose-colored sheath dress" out to the "Busy Bee roadhouse" (160), but she refuses, feeling it would be wrong to wear someone else's clothes without her permission. Ivy is not yet able to recognize her sexuality (represented by the rose-colored dress) in relation to sweetness. When difficulty on the farm and life with Oakley overwhelm her, Ivy says she misses the stir-offs since she loves the taste of the "hot yellow foam" of the molasses, what Granny called "the long sweetening" (194).

The motif of sweetness and honey, as related to the feminine divine, culminates in Smith's depiction of Ivy's encounter and subsequent affair with Honey Breeding. When Honey first arrives at the Foxes' home at Sugar Fork, he finds Ivy down in the springhouse where "[h]oneysuckle vines have grown up all over the bushes along the path, and wild white roses all down the steps" (204). The setting, with wild roses and honeysuckle, is ideal for the awakening of Ivy's sexuality. Later, when Ivy and Honey reach the top of Blue Star Mountain, after they have made love, Honey tells Ivy, "You are the sweetest

---

**According to Walker, in Asia Minor from 3500 to 1750* B.C. *the dead were embalmed in honey and placed in burial vases called* pithos, *which represented "the womb of the Goddess," in preparation for their experience of rebirth (*Women's *407).*

thing I ever saw"; Ivy asks, "Sweeter than honey?" (222). Ivy and Honey's encounter has been one of sweet, sacred, sexual gratification. Honey satisfies Ivy's hunger for "sweetness," and when he tells her it is time to go, she refuses, saying, "I have not had my fill of you yet" (225). Ivy's expression of insatiable hunger reflects her need for the restorative "bee-balm" that Honey provides for her.* In snubbing the system that attempts to confine and control her, in "consuming" honey in great quantities, Ivy becomes "an archetype of sexual as well as gustatory defiance" (Yaeger 35). Union with Honey represents, in Yaeger's dialectic, an "act of pure bodily joy, of visionary excess, of consummate play between desire and fulfillment of desire," the site of both liberation and regeneration (7), as Ivy is restored to life. When Ivy and Honey finally descend the mountain, with a "sour and sweet" taste in her mouth, Ivy recalls Honey's voice telling her, "But the best of all is the sourwood honey, pale yellow and sweet and light" (229). The "honey-mad" woman comes down the mountain, having discovered her sexual, aggressive, appetitive, joyous, divine self. Eckard labels Ivy's time with Honey Breeding as "another heedless affair," similar to Ivy's purely sexual relationship with Franklin Ransom (159). The importance Smith places on this stage of Ivy's development surely disallows any comparison with the Franklin Ransom segment.

Mythology explains the symbolic significance of honey as portent of "honeyed speech," a promise of nourishing words, and Ivy receives such nourishment in her union with Honey. After Ivy's lengthy silence, expressing her deepest thoughts and feelings in letters written only to Silvaney, Honey's presence exhumes Ivy's love for language and stories. As the two walk up the mountain together, Ivy, mad for the honey of speech, finds herself talking nonstop to "a perfect stranger" about her parents, her childhood and everything dearest to her heart. She even surprises herself, writing to Silvaney, "My own voice sounded funny in my ears. It sounded rusty. I felt like I hadn't used it in such a long time" (215). Oakley has never been a talker, and through the years, Ivy has learned to remain silent. Ivy tells Honey she is "starved for stories" (213), so Honey assuages her hunger by making up stories to tell her. Together, Ivy and Honey find words to express their sexuality, much like *Oral History*'s Sally and Roy. Ivy says, "all the poems I ever knew came rushing back over my body like the wind" (224). It has been twenty-two years since she has felt this way. The depth of Ivy's emotions is measured by her desire to share the language she loves with Honey, and Smith's depiction of the poems as rushing over her body "like the wind" evokes nature and feminine divinity and further expresses Ivy's sexuality.

The name "Honey Breeding" clearly suggests the union of male and

---

*In The Myth of the Goddess, *Anne Baring and Jules Cashford discuss the ancient Minoan ritual in which honey was gathered from hives in caves and woods, then fermented into mead and "drunk as an intoxicating liquor" during "ecstatic rites" (119).*

female ("breeding") and the sweetness ("honey") of such a union, and Ivy's relationship with this man represents what psychologists call the wedding of the two sides of our basic bisexuality that struggle for reconciliation in all of us. For many centuries, the image of the goddess embodied male as well as female attributes, and many of the composite androgynous figures convey a sense of continual regeneration (Baring and Cashford 74). In Ivy's union with Honey, both male and female are given divine qualities as Smith seeks to reunite the masculine and feminine in what Irigaray calls "an alliance between the divine and the mortal," where a sacred sexual encounter is a "celebration, ... not a disguised or polemic form of the master-slave relationship" ("Sexual" 174). Ivy and Honey's reciprocal relationship is based on equality. Ivy acknowledges the communion she feels with Honey the second time he visits, before she actually goes away with him, "It's like he *is* me, some way, or I am him" (210), and in fact, the two will eventually become one in sexual union just as Richard and Dory are described as being "truly one" (155). In a letter to Silvaney, Ivy compares her size and strength to Honey's and describes Honey's legs and rear as stark white, just like her own. As she and Honey lie tangled up together "till you couldn't tell who was who," Ivy says, "I think he *is* me and I am him, and it will be so forever and ever" (222). Smith stresses the necessity of Ivy's union with Honey in the reclamation of that part of herself for which she has quested so long. Baring and Cashford call this missing element her "lost counterpart," retrievable only in "the restoration of the image of the goddess" through her connection with Honey and her "return to the divine world" (628). Ivy writes to Silvaney that after sex, she perceives she has restored a part of herself that she "had lost without even knowing it was gone." She says, "Honey had given me back my very soul" (224). In Smith's portrayal of Ivy and Honey, the writer offers the prototype for a new concept of relationships between people that is not competitive or hierarchical but mutually nourishing and sacred.

Honey's close association with nature further connects him to the feminine divine and sacred sexuality. Described as "a woods creature fetched up somehow from the forest" (205), Honey is strongly linked to Silvaney in his mysterious origins and in the necessity of his existence for Ivy to feel fully alive. As Honey approaches the orchard, a place Ivy describes as "a sea of pale pink flowers," he whistles "like a bird." Ivy, "in a fever" (206–207) after he leaves, thinks she must be going through menopause, but this feeling of fiery wildness and passion will continue until she goes away with Honey and together they climb to the highest point of Blue Star Mountain to an area "covered with little white flowers like stars" (217). As Ivy "topple[s]" (222) Honey, she takes on the role of the aggressor in a playful scene reminiscent of the earlier one with Ivy and Violet Gayheart. Ivy writes to Silvaney, "it felt natural to me to be here, to have come up this mountain with this man" (228). Honey seems to be almost a part of nature as he plays with the star flowers. On first meeting him, Ivy describes Honey as "skinny, wirey, with pale thick curly gold hair on his head and thick gold eyebrows that nearabout grow together, and hair all over him like spun gold on his folded forearms" (205), then later notes that he has "golden elf-hair curling in his ears" and "[e]ven his back [i]s almost covered with little bitty golden hairs." In this description two points demand mention in addition to the repetition of the color gold (a color Smith consistently uses to signal feminine divinity): the supernatural connotation of the word "elf," and Honey's connection to nature in resembling a bee himself. Ivy even recognizes Honey's similarity to his own bees, going "from woman to woman like a bee goes from flower to flower," but she realizes that he is "the last thing left to happen" to her (224–25). Honey deposits sweetness into each flower even as he takes nectar for himself. Gimbutas affirms that the bee was a symbol of regeneration and an epiphany of the goddess, a representation of the feminine potency of nature (*Language* 322). Furthermore, Honey resides in the woods, where sacred honey was gathered in ancient Minoan rituals. Ivy's memory of her last moments with Honey consists of his whistling and bees buzzing in the weeds and clover by the side of the road, the humming of bees traditionally understood to be "the 'voice' of the goddess" (Baring and Cashford 119). Honey is all mixed up in Ivy's mind with nature, sexuality, and divinity. Rebecca Smith notes an important aspect of Honey Breeding's character as his physical resemblance to Aphrodite and argues that Honey's "likeness to a goddess confirms that Ivy's interlude with him is a 'moment of sacred sex'" (117).

With her portraiture of Honey Breeding, Smith offers her most obvious and significant personification of the dichotomized male, whose character seems to disallow such categorizing because of Smith's depiction of him as a divinity (Hill 112). From his first appearance in the novel, Honey is powerfully aligned with sacredness as he symbolically offers to Ivy the chance for rebirth. The springhouse, a "little house right down in the creek," where Honey and Ivy meet is one of Ivy's favorite places where she feels like she's in "another world," not unlike the pool of water where Almarine discovers Red Emmy, a sacred spot of feminine divinity. At first glance, Ivy views Honey "outlined against the sun" with "the sun a blaze behind his head ... sho[oting] out in rays" (204–205), forming a golden halo. Ivy can hardly see him for the dazzling brightness of the light, and after their affair, Ivy will always remember "those moments with Honey as flashes of light" (239). Baring and Cashford trace the image of light as associated with both the goddess and god, "the androgyny of the primal source," to as far back as Sumeria and connect it with "divine unity" (629). Later, when Ivy and Honey lie in the grass on the top of the mountain, Honey spreads Ivy's hair out around her head, creating a halo for her too. And just as time seems to stand still with Red Emmy and Almarine, Ivy feels suspended in time, like she's "walking through a dream" (207) and doesn't care how much time lapses, while she's with Honey. As noted by Nor Hall, bees, like elves, move between worlds of dream and waking reality as if there were no boundaries, thus their liminal nature (232).

Further evidence of Honey's divinity appears on his next visit when Ivy and Honey climb the mountain together and he tells her that he is the third of three sons (linking himself to the number three) and that he's from "*[n]oplace particular*" (217). His nebulous origin echoes that of Red Emmy. Honey cannot tolerate confinement in a city or town; he has "to have mountains, and roam" (227), a free spirit incapable of containment, much like Silvaney. The sacred mountains, which perhaps more than any other natural objects represent the feminine divine, are Honey's natural habitat. Honey tells Ivy, "this ain't real" (221), acknowledging the dreamlike quality of their union. Honey's liminal presence allows Ivy to discover the sanctity within herself and to accept the existence of divinity in her feminine experience. Ivy describes the days after meeting Honey as seeming to happen "under water," and she feels like she's "swimming through them" (207), again associating her experience with water and rebirth.

Smith enacts a healing reversal in this depiction of a divine male whose presence supplies Ivy with the necessary insight to enable her to recognize the sacredness within herself. In a setting rife with goddess imagery, Ivy sits on a big warm rock beside a mysterious pool of water she has never seen (the goddess's power in water and stone). As Honey plays with her long red hair, she thinks, "the funny thing is, it was like I had known him. For ever, for always, years and years and years" (209). As they reunite the masculine and feminine divine principles, what Jung called the androgynous elements *animus* and *anima*, what the Taoist tradition calls the yang and yin (Hall 31), this divine couple represents sacred transformation. Ivy recognizes the timeless sanctity in Honey and automatically connects with him, a face she can see and touch, unlike the face of the God Ivy "couldn't see" (198) that Oakley senses when he looks out from the mountain. The patriarchal God is intangible for Ivy; she must discover a female image of God in order to experience rebirth. Honey provides the divine presence for which Ivy has yearned all of her life. In her letter to Silvaney when she tells about her first sensations of being "on fire," Ivy refers to Honey twice as "Him," with a capital "H" (201). Although Ivy's spelling and grammar are erratic in her early letters, she doesn't often capitalize common nouns or pronouns, especially in letters written during her middle adult years, so one strongly suspects Smith purposefully links Honey to Christ in his offering Ivy "salvation" of self.

In regaining her soul, Ivy has become a queen, the sexual, maternal goddess needed to heal the split between sexuality and motherhood. As Ivy stands naked at the edge of the cliff at the top of the mountain, Honey tells her, "you look like a Queen" (221). He creates for her "a double starflower crown" and places it on her head, saying, "Now stand up and walk, you will be a Queen" (225). Honey forces Ivy to realize that she is the queen she has longed to be ever since she wrote her first letters to Hanneke in which she said her Dutch pen-pal looked like a little queen. In naming Ivy "queen," Honey compares her to the queen bee, whom all the others serve during their brief lives since she is an epiphany of the goddess herself. Furthermore, Honey, as an image of the miraculous interconnectedness of life, parallels the "busy bee," following its impulse to pollinate the flowers and gather their nectar to be transformed into honey. In elevating Ivy to the level of a queen, a goddess, Smith imagines a mythology that permits female embodiment of the divine. Ivy admits, "I believe it was the first time I had ever been naked in the sunshine in my life," and she enjoys the sun "burn[ing] into" her sensual, sexual body (221–22). Eckard notes that Ivy's letters "foreground the female body" and serve as "a way to write out of the body" (156, 170). Similar to both Red Emmy and Dory who associate no shame with their bodies and freely expose their breasts to Almarine and Richard, respectively, Ivy stands nude on the mountain in broad daylight, boldly affirming her divine nature. As Carol Christ notes, the feminine divine "can only be understood if we question the assumptions that divinity is transcendent of the body [and] nature" (78–79). However, unlike Red Emmy and Dory whose stories are told by Granny Younger and Sally, respectively, Ivy relates her own experiences in her own voice. Ivy, finally able to accept her own female body, recognizes her physical beauty and inner sacredness. She has arrived at the summit of Blue Star Mountain, a spot she imagines Silvaney has frequented, and has reached her highest point sexually and spiritually. Ivy writes to Silvaney that, given the choice, she would have stayed with Honey until she "starved to death and died..., living on love." With profound insight, Ivy explains what she perceives as the difference between the "lover" and the "beloved," admitting that with Honey, she was the lover and she was "glad" she got to be there with him, "however long it lasted" and "whatever it cost you—which is always plenty, I reckon." This honest admission of unselfish love, totally lacking in remorse, perhaps serves as Smith's strongest indictment against those who would judge Ivy harshly for her transgression. On their last day together when Ivy and Honey sit on "a warm gray rock with little shiny pieces of mica in it," Ivy is glad to be who she is, and as she picks at the rock, she thinks, "Fools gold" (228), remembering the days of her girlhood when she and Molly mined for gold in the creek, believing at that young age she would someday find that great love that would be permanent. Now she realizes the rarity and transience of great love, just like gold, but she feels grateful for the time she has had with Honey.

Gradually, Ivy becomes more attuned to her own sacredness separate from Honey Breeding. It is only after Ivy's interlude with Honey that she is at all able to love herself, her husband, and her children completely.* With Lonnie,

---

*In his article "All in the Family," Tom Rash argues that Honey Breeding represents "something dangerous, electric, forbidden" and that once Ivy achieves "the ideal, she now finds her life as wife and mother to be more satisfactory" (134). "The ideal" for Ivy is the discovery and open expression of her sacred sexuality that Honey, in his divine configuration, awakens within her. With past lovers such as Lonnie and Franklin, Ivy discovered nothing within herself, but rather

Ivy had discovered her libido, and with Franklin, she had dallied with the violent and destructive aspect of sexuality. With Oakley, she had buried her ebullience. Finally, with Honey, she integrates all of these as he feeds her hunger for language, sweetness, wildness, and divinity. She writes to Silvaney, "At least I am alive now, since I ran off with Honey Breeding." A couple of years after the affair and Ivy's return to her family, she notes that now Oakley pays attention to her, that his face no longer turns away. Ivy notes that Oakley is always "circling around" her, a movement linked to divinity like the hawk that circled while she made love with Honey on the mountain top and the hawk that Maude saw circling the sky the first day she came to Sugar Fork. Ivy writes to Silvaney about one Sunday morning when her entire family is eating breakfast and "for a minute ... I felt like church"; then she explains, "I mean I think I felt the way you are supposed to feel in church, which I never do." Smith's description of this scene teems with religious and sexual connotations. As Ivy experiences her own divinity, the back door to the orchard stands open and sunlight streams into the kitchen, illuminating Maudy's red hair and warming the tablecloth "which is all flowers, red and white roses entwined in circles that repeat and repeat and repeat" (240). The sun-drenched rose-covered tablecloth, with its circular pattern counters the square, imprisoning design of the wallpaper in Ivy's room at the boardinghouse, offering a healing, sacred, sexual image for Ivy. Five years after her affair with Honey, in a long letter to Silvaney, Ivy reflects on the experience and its significance in her life and even in her marriage, explaining that her affair with Honey "helped not hurt, with me and Oakley." She admits her awakened sexual desire for her husband who seems somehow "new" for her, then reflects on the time she was "lost in darkness" and couldn't even "immagine the sun, or see a ray of sunshine any place." Although she couldn't see Oakley before, she says, "now Oakley stands before me full in flesh," and "I can not explain it. I am yearning towards him always." The brightness of the light of Honey Breeding has allowed Ivy to see and accept Oakley in his totality since Ivy has now discovered the divine within herself. Now she "yearns" toward him, rather than the stars toward which she longed earlier. These far-away mysterious celestial bodies have been made a reality for her as she has experienced sacred, sexual union in her affair with Honey and now has integrated divine wisdom into her life with her husband and children. She writes to Silvaney that her relationship with Oakley "is better than before," expressing ease at sharing this intimate information with her sister, whom she calls "my soul, and my soul is as wild as ever!" (262).

Smith illustrates the painful absence of the feminine divine from traditional religion in Ivy's struggle with spirituality and the idea of salvation. A

looked to the male partner for meaning and fulfillment. With Honey, she finds completion within herself. If Ivy's life as wife and mother is "more satisfactory" after her affair with Honey, it is because she is brought back to life, or reborn, as a result of her union with Honey whereas before, she was spiritually and sexually dead, resigned to that "great soft darkness."

couple of years after her affair with Honey when she begins to go to church with Oakley occasionally, she notices that no one even looks at her during the invitational anymore. She decides that people either think she's already saved or are just accustomed to her "sinful" nature. Then, after the experience with her brother Garnie, who has joined with the famous pastor Sam Russell Sage and become a preacher himself, Ivy decides, "I will not go to any Heaven that has got a place in it for Garnie Rowe," writing to Silvaney about the day she "was not saved" (245). Garnie shouts at Ivy, calling her "a whore and an abomination," and chastises her for her sin of pride that is "an abomination to the Lord." Ivy admits to Silvaney that what Garnie is saying has some truth in it: "I *have* been proud Silvaney, in my body and my mind, I am proud still, and if this is sin then I must claim it as my own" (251–52). As Hélène Cixous insists a woman must do, Ivy refuses to "censor the body," that would in effect "censor breath and speech at the same time." Instead, she writes, an act that provides "access to her native strength" and "give[s] her back her goods, her pleasures, her organs, her immense bodily territories which have been kept under seal" (250). This letter to Silvaney about Garnie's visit, Ivy signs, "Your loving, proud, and hellbent sister" (254); the three adjectives perfectly describe Ivy's feelings about herself since she is clearly overflowing with love and proud of who she is, even if pride *is* a sin, but the last descriptor, "hellbent," is questionable and seems to serve as a humorous touch on Ivy's part, due to her total lack of faith in Garnie's patriarchal God. At this point Ivy has apparently determined that salvation through this deity is not a viable option for her.

The divinity Ivy has discovered within herself that has caused her to "feel like church" and experience pride in both her mind and her body is the only form of religion to which she adheres. The cruel and punitive patriarchal God whom Garnie advocates offers no model for embodiment of the sacred in female flesh. Even in Garnie's "sermon" to Ivy, he consistently uses the masculine pronoun to represent Ivy, quoting from the Bible, "Can a man take fire in his bosom, and his clothes not be burned? Whoso commiteth adultery with a woman lacketh understanding. He that doeth it destroyeth his own soul." Ivy, disturbed by the gendered pronouns, asks, "What about the woman? ... For that is all about a man," which infuriates Garnie (253). It is only when Ivy reaches her early seventies and becomes ill and weak that she picks up the little white Bible that Garnie had left and begins to read from it. Writing to Silvaney, Ivy says she doesn't like Proverbs, the book from which Garnie quoted so much, since it is "mean-spirited," and the "Song of Solomon is dirty [and] ... reminds me of Honey Breeding who I have not thought about in years, and how it was with him" (293). Ivy says she doesn't know if Honey is still alive or where he is but admits she hasn't forgotten him. This is the first time Ivy has thought of her experience with Honey as "dirty" or immoral, and it is noteworthy that this occurs only when she reads from the predominant male-based text.

Ivy's newfound divinity allows for the expression of her sacred sexuality, and through writing—creating—Ivy makes sense of this aspect of her life. Most psychological theories about artistic creation and women assume that mothers don't write; they are written. Smith's depiction of Ivy certainly counters the age-old either/or theory that mothers don't create works of art because all of their energies and interests find expression in their children. The necessity of writing and language for Ivy stands unquestioned since for Smith, Ivy incorporates the language of the feminine divine. In Ivy's first letter to Hanneke, she says she wants to become a writer and write about passionate love, and although she doesn't make a career of writing professionally, Ivy constantly writes in order to extract meaning from her life. Smith herself admitted that she is more interested in the process of writing than in the final product itself, and the creative process of writing *Fair and Tender Ladies* enabled her to better understand what was happening at that time in her own life (Byrd 95). Similarly, Ivy writes in order to remember and understand. After years of watching her father suffer and then die, then the death of her little brother Danny, when she and her family are leaving for Majestic, Ivy writes to her dead father, "I dont want nothing else to hapen to me, ever. I do not even want to be in love any more, nor write of love, as it is scarry" (72). At age seventeen, Ivy has already experienced so much pain and loss that she feels her dreams are squashed. Nevertheless, she continues to hear, for decades to come, her father playing the guitar, his voice, his laughter, and the stories he told, and these memories and writing about them are among the forces that sustain her.

With the creation of Ivy Rowe, Smith offers a sexual, maternal, and creative female who breaks all boundaries that would attempt to define or contain her. In his study of mythology, religion, and literature, Paul Friedrich discovered that the disjunction between sexuality and motherhood serves as a barrier against the image of a creative, artistic woman (190). Expressing herself through writing is as necessary for Ivy as breathing, measuring the validity of each experience by her ability to retell it, mostly in letters to Silvaney. With the discovery of Ivy's first pregnancy, she believed she had to choose between becoming a mother and pursuing an education and career; therefore, at her mother's insistence, she resigned herself to a domestic, uneducated life and believed she was forfeiting her dream of becoming a writer. However, in pursuing her artistic talent through writing letters, without realizing it, Ivy actually experiences firsthand the inspiration for her art. After the birth of Joli, Ivy writes to Silvaney every detail about the experience that she can remember, in order not to forget it, "to hold onto what is passing," saying she wants to slow down the passage of time and squeeze as much as possible from every moment. As she holds her firstborn in her arms, Ivy says, "And all the poems I ever knew raced through my head" (139–40), the same words she had said when Lonnie left, then again when she spent time with Honey. This expression of emotion through the most beautiful language she can think of continues to represent Ivy's deepest feelings throughout the novel. As Katherine Kearns notes, at these significant moments, "maternal joy surges with poetic ecstasy" and sexuality (191). Once Ivy and Oakley have married and moved to Sugar Fork, Ivy writes to Violet about the importance of letters in helping her make meaning of her life. And in a letter to her sister Beulah, Ivy tries to explain that marrying Franklin Ransom was not right for her, nor was becoming a teacher as Mrs. Brown and Miss Torrington would have had her do; instead, Ivy says she will "just write my letters" (176). After five children, when Ivy sinks into depression, she stops reading *and* writing since children and work completely consume her time.

Ivy must give voice to what she most cares about; she must put into words what she has experienced. When Ivy finally writes again, she pens to Silvaney, "I am dying to write" (185), then begins to recall all the significant events that have occurred in the past several years, feeling the necessity of remembering and writing. When Ivy returns from her interlude with Honey Breeding and learns of LuIda's death, she writes to Silvaney, telling about the entire experience. Then, at the end of the letter, she says, "I will not be writing any more letters for a while though, as my heart is too heavy, too full. But somehow I had to write this letter to you Silvaney, to set it all down" (231). Now that this part of her life is recorded and will be remembered, even though it will always bring pain, Ivy knows she can move on.

Ivy's need to remember, and to write, stems from a sense of her exclusion from the Christian tradition; eventually, this feeling leads her to a sense of the feminine divine. This "re-membering" gives Ivy a new relation to her body, to female sexuality, and to divinity. Ivy writes to Joli about an experience she has during Martha's wedding when she says aloud without thinking, "Shakespeare." As memories and her love of language and literature overwhelm her, Ivy explains, "I have been so many people. And yet I think the most important thing is Don't forget. Don't ever forget" even though "remembering brings pain" (257). Ivy, at only forty-four, realizes the fullness and complexity of her own life and knows that her daughter has moved past her and her mountain home and will never be able to turn back. But she reminds Joli to never forget that the past provides the key to a person's identity and self-knowledge. When Oakley dies, Ivy writes to Joli, "somehow it d[oes] not seem real to me, not even then [after he is buried]. It does now, for I am writing you this letter" (265). For Ivy, writing about an event in her life makes it real to her; reality exists in her art.

Ivy's final thoughts, described in a natural setting with "crocuses poking through gold and purple, purple and gold [,] the colors of royalty and church" and "forsythia blooming under the snow" where Ivy remembers making snow angels, a "heavenly host of angels" in the yard with Silvaney (306–307), are steeped in the colors and images of divinity. Ivy's willingness to free herself from the physical world is reflected in her burning the many letters to Silvaney that have been discovered by Maudy and Marlene. Ivy releases all the emotions, the pains, the burdens, even the joys, just as she had released the fireflies from the jar that imprisoned them so many years ago. She writes to Joli, "The letters didn't mean anything. Not to the dead girl Silvaney, of course—<u>nor to me</u>. Nor had they ever. It was the <u>writing</u> of them, that signified." The creative process, the making of meaning in her life through writing, is what makes Ivy's struggles and triumphs real. In her last letter of the novel, written, as one would expect, to Silvaney, seventy-four-year-old Ivy records her last jumbled thoughts in a stream-of-consciousness style, beginning with the words, "I have been thinking, thinking, and now I am dying to write I am dying to" (305). One might also add that Ivy is not only "dying to write," but also "writing to die" since she is able to die only as she makes real her last thoughts and feelings by recording them. In Smith's vivid imagery, the color red has deepened to purple, a true mark of the royalty to which Ivy has been elevated, now a queen, an incarnation of the feminine divine. The reader is reminded of Ivy's mother's brooch, returned to Ivy by Curtis Bostick after Beulah's death, described as a "little spray of violets with tiny purple stones, held together by the pretty golden bow" (277), a combination of the two colors that serve to signal the presence of the feminine divine. Appropriately, Ivy retains possession of the brooch when she dies.

Ivy's thoughts move in a natural sequence as she thinks of important people and events in her life, then associates other images with these, forming a kind of ribbon that explains the essence of her life. As a hawk circles in the beautiful blue sky, creating the symbol of the concentrated divine energy of the goddess, Ivy is reminded of her father who always told her to slow down, "[t]his is the taste of spring," and she admits, "I never have slowed down." Thoughts of spring bring back Oakley's presence and the memory of how he loved the spring, as Ivy now closes her eyes and envisions him coming out of the coal mine (the cave serving as symbol of rebirth) the day she decided to share her life with him. Then images of other men for whom she cared begin to flood her mind as she sees Lonnie Rash the day he left to go to war, and Ivy thinks, "<u>there is a time for war</u>." Next she sees Franklin Ransom the night they danced, filled with ecstasy, and thinks, "<u>there is a time to dance</u>." Then the Cline sisters come to mind, the night Ivy and Silvaney watched them as they seemed to dance when they flew across the sparkling, moon-drenched snow, early images of the goddess in the novel. The memory of the moonlight takes Ivy to the night of Joli's birth; she thinks, "<u>and there is a time to be born</u>" and remembers how the moonlight, the mark of the feminine divine, moved across the quilt and how Joli's skin was "as pale and perfect as Mrs. Browns camio." Now Ivy's childhood dreams come to life as she writes, "I used to think I would be a writer. I thought then I would write of love (Ha!) but how little we know, we spend our years as a tale that is told I have spent my years so. I never became a writer atall. Instead I have loved, and loved, and loved. I am fair wore out with it" (307). Ivy *has* been a writer all her life, and she *has* loved and also written of love in all its different forms. Thus the memory of Miss Torrington's fiery kiss on the back of Ivy's neck fills Ivy's mind next as she remembers the many kinds of love Miss Torrington talked of.

Smith's depiction of Ivy seems to usher in a new era awaiting realization, a woman uniting within herself the previously warring alternatives of separate male or female consciousness. On her deathbed, Ivy reflects on the purpose of her life and reasserts her inner divinity. She ponders having remained on this sacred mountain, one time going "as high as you can go" up the mountain with Honey Breeding, whose "hair shone golden in the morning light," the image of sweet divinity. Thoughts of how she and Honey lived in a womblike cave and ate rabbits and squirrels bring to mind a reflection of her sensitive grandson David who "will not hunt." Ivy's memory then recalls the bear story the Cline sisters always told of Whitebear Whittington who "lives yet up on Hell Mountain" and is "wild, wild," running through the night "with his eyes on fire," a representation of both Ivy and Silvaney, and how he sleeps during the day "as peaceful as a lullaby" (307). Ivy's favorite tale shared with her by the mystical Cline sisters powerfully connects to goddess mythology as bears were considered the most sacred of all creatures and represented mankind's deep awe for the powers of nature (Gimbutas, *Language* 113). A lullaby comforts Ivy as she submits to the powers of nature and slips off into her eternal sleep, imagining "Wyncken Blynken and Nod" sailing away. But before Ivy's spirit peacefully "sails away" from her body, she writes, "there is a time for every purpose under heaven" as the hawk in the bright blue sky flies around in circles, permanently linking Ivy with divinity. Ivy's last thoughts are of "the old bell ringing" like she used to ring it "to call them home," as she has just "called home" all the memories of her rich life. The last line of the letter, which is left unpunctuated and unsigned, emphasizes Ivy's divine nature: "oh I was young then, and I walked in my body like a Queen" (308). Now that she will be leaving her physical body, she has certainly achieved goddess stature, divine in her own right, successfully healing the split between sexuality and motherhood and powerfully aligning herself with the feminine divine.

In an interview with Susan Ketchin, Smith commented, "... Ivy is like me; she is unable to find a religion that suits her—an organized religion. She makes up her own." Ivy dies without finding God in a traditional sense, and Lee Smith acknowledges, "And I might too" (51). Ivy does, however, discover redemption in her recognition and acceptance of the feminine divine, in her self and in the world around her. Smith's depiction of Ivy offers a fresh option for female characters, perhaps the ultimate option in that, given her limitations and choices, internal conflicts and struggles, Ivy discovers and honors the sacredness of her own body and mind and, through the creative art of letter-writing, makes sense of her life and provides much-needed inspiration for other women and also for other writers.

Chapter VI

"FIGURES A-DANCING ... IN THE FLAMES"

Toward Healing the Wound in *The Devil's Dream*

In *Restoring the Goddess: Equal Rites for Modern Women*, Barbara G. Walker opines that the "dominant element of cruelty in patriarchal fundamentalism ... alienates women and sends them in search of a more humane creed." Furthermore, Walker suggests that women often search for years in many places and in many ways, seeking a spiritual path that "frankly affirms and honors femaleness per se" (30).* In *The Devil's Dream* (1992), female characters continue to search for something to believe in, often mistaking bodily sensations for spiritual salvation. Like earlier Smith protagonists, they also suffer at the hands of "patriarchal fundamentalism." In this novel, Smith offers more fully realized male characters, unlike *Fair and Tender Ladies*, which Smith acknowledges is a woman's story. These male characters, like their female counterparts, struggle to survive in a world that cannot understand or accept them, caught in the trap previously occupied mostly by female characters. The ending of *The Devil's Dream*, like that of *Family Linen* published seven years earlier, offers hope of integration for the damaged characters in the beginnings of healing the wound of mind-body separation. Both novels end in conciliatory family reunions that include members of at least three generations, suggesting continuity and connections among families and intimating future harmony bereft of the haunting "figures a-dancing in the flames" (*The Devil's Dream* 54) of the past.

The Devil's Dream, written four years after *Fair and Tender Ladies*, shares

---

**Walker believes that no equality between men and women is possible until the goddess is as widely "accepted, cited, invoked, and revered as the god." She stresses that neither sex can exist without the other; for this reason, Walker asserts, the ancients resisted establishing an exclusively "god-oriented sect" for a long time and even retained vestiges of goddess worship in patriarchal Europe all the way up to present day (*Restoring 30*).*

with earlier Smith novels an examination of the dichotomy between sexuality and motherhood, but this sprawling history of country music also provocatively expresses the conflicts inherent between sexuality and religion as Smith draws upon qualities of the feminine divine in her depictions of female characters. Smith's continued interest in damaged characters, both male and female, permeates the novel, and most often these characters suffer from social constraints. Like *Family Linen*, however, the ending of *The Devil's Dream* offers affirmation in the multi-generational reunion of the Bailey family. Less immediate in plot than the earlier novel, *The Devil's Dream* chronicles about one hundred fifty years of the Bailey family history, has the tremendous scope of both *Oral History* and *Fair and Tender Ladies*, and shares the same structure as *Oral History* (the novel begins and ends in the present, with the middle related in flashbacks by various narrators). In addition, the impetus for the action in both *The Devil's Dream* and *Oral History* is a family curse. This eighth novel by Smith demonstrates her growth in character development and treatment of time. With more than twice as many narrators and major characters as *Family Linen*, the novel runs the risk of confusion and loss of focus, but Smith creates a masterpiece, inventing a vividly complex world of family ties in which music serves as the magnetic center. Each of approximately fifteen principal characters, almost equally divided between males and females, tells his/her own story. Not easily grouped or categorized, these characters are highly individualized and sharply memorable.

The Devil's Dream begins in the present with the gathering of the entire family at the Opryland Hotel in an italicized section narrated by an omniscient narrator but manages gracefully to leap backward to the year 1834 when Moses Bailey marries Kate Malone. Smith explained in an interview with Claudia Loewenstein that the original story in the novel of Kate's prohibition from playing fiddle music and her eventual descent into madness was one actually related to her that she later found in a book. Because of this unusual blend of fact and fiction, the story is both mythic and factual (494). Although the Bailey family of the novel is loosely modeled on the famous musical Carter family, when interviewed by Nancy Parrish, Smith said, "I think I have a better chance of being *true* if I call it *fiction*." Smith's love for country music, especially the early music that sounds so much like stories, prompted her to write the novel, which is intended to resemble an album with each narration a song by a different character (396), or "singer." In an interview with Edwin Arnold, Smith said that the entire history of country music, like the whole history of Appalachia, has been one of exploitation (247), so she dedicates *The Devil's Dream* to "*all the real country artists, living and dead*" whose music she has "*loved for so long.*" Paying homage to a place and people who have contributed much to the American music scene, Smith traces the roots and variations of country music from the primitive Baptist hymns and fiddle-playing, to the gospel songs, to the rockabilly movement, to the contemporary country music of today, in her first novel with music as the major subtext. She takes her title from a traditional Appalachian fiddle tune and uses as the novel's center the female character Katie Cocker, the famous progeny of the musical Bailey family. Referring to both traditional songs and invented ones whose titles various personal friends contributed, Smith has produced a novel rife with humor, and the author obviously has fun with the subject. However, she is extremely serious about the music she honors.

In allowing Katie Cocker to sing her own song, like Ivy Rowe's writing her own story, Smith demonstrates her now fully developed ability to depict fully developed female characters that exist outside society's prescribed code and achieve total integration. In an interview with Dannye Powell, Smith explained that she views singing as a pleasurable release similar to and even related to sex. According to Smith, the problem with singing in the early churches was that this "release" happened in *church*, thus producing a split between expressed sexuality and religion (410). This split that informs much of Smith's fiction, finds provocative expression in *The Devil's Dream*. As in earlier novels, Smith attributes mythic qualities to strong female characters, aligning them with nature and divinity. Images and ideas associated with the feminine divine such as the elements of wind and fire, red and gold colors, and the qualities of sweetness and powerful longing, fill this story of one family's struggle to achieve a balance between their music and their personal lives. Smith's female characters have been getting wiser and wiser with each progressive novel, and the writer admits it has taken a long time for her to be able to even envision the possibility of survival for a fully integrated female. In her interview with Smith, Powell notes that at the beginning of *The Devil's Dream*, it is a sin for a woman to be creative, and at the end, it is a sin for a woman not be creative. Smith explains that country music history as a whole serves as a "perfect literal metaphor" for this progress of women since in the beginning there were no women stars, and now there are as many women as men, and the women are just as important (411–12). Harvard literature professor Susan Rubin Suleiman notes the absence of contemporary novelists who have "explored, in fully rendered fictional forms, the violence and guilt as well as the violent energy that attend the artistic creations of mothers" (377); in this novel, Smith embarks on just such an exploration as she examines the conflicts surrounding women who choose to create both biologically and artistically.

From the beginning of the novel, the Bailey family's passion exists in three realms in particular: religion, music, and sexual love. Having strong religious faith and being musically gifted, they each suffer from the repression, violence, and uncontrollable passion that seem to haunt their existence, and for music or for sexual love, they often denounce their religion. Smith says that in country music families, religion, repression, violence, and sexual passion are "like vines climbing up the same fence" since one of the functions of the early churches was to repress and at the same time to release (Powell 410).

René Girard explains that in a religious system where "all sexual activity, sexual allusions, and erotic stimulants are forbidden," violence is a natural result, and ironically, "what motivates prohibition is the fear of violence" (220–21). Smith further explains that country music families led such difficult lives that the church had to provide them an outlet for their emotions; thus, speaking in tongues served as a release, much like singing. But when music began to spill over from the church, a split occurred between the Saturday night music and the Sunday morning music, the all-too-familiar split that still exists today in the division between the sacred and the profane (Powell 410). The Bailey family always feels the discord between these two huge polarities: how to be famous and successful and remain a devout Christian—the conflict between honky-tonk life and church and home life. Perhaps Rose Annie Bailey best expresses this antinomy when she deserts her husband and children to join her destructive childhood sweetheart in a singing career. Katie Cocker also must choose between music and religion/family in order to become successful in her music career. Rose Annie explains that although she was baptized at age twelve, after she and Johnny Rainette became sexually involved, she "lost [her] religion," describing Johnny as "st[anding] between" her and God. She says, "I made a god out of Johnny ... and I've been cut off from the other one ever since" (143). Rose Annie, like other Smith characters, feels excluded by masculine language for God and cannot accept a God who denies female sexuality.

Each member of the Bailey family has an ambiguous relationship with music that is a mixture of anger, tragedy, and satisfaction. As Fred Chappell points out, the characters' deep understanding of the "Dionysian nature" of music causes them to sometimes wonder if it should be shared with the rest of the world since it reveals so much of their souls that it could be harmful (941). After the first recording session in Bristol, Lucie, R.C. Bailey's wife, cries softly from a "sudden terrible sense of loss" at having "given up something precious by singing these songs" to strangers (124). Music *is* the Bailey family's religion, in a sense, just as Smith acknowledges writing as a religion for Ivy Rowe, and for herself. Katie makes this observation about the connection between music and religion when she describes the Ryman Auditorium, where the Grand Ole Opry was originally performed, as being "like a *church*" with pews, a balcony, and stained glass. In her portrayal of the "worshipful" audience as they approach the footlights of the stage to photograph their favorite singers, Katie offers a metaphorical representation of "people going up for Communion in a big Catholic church" (273). Similar to the myth of Zeus's nourishment on honey to ensure his capacity for "honeyed speech," the fans come forward to be "fed" on the salvific songs being sung in a type of religious ritual. In the solemn sense of reverence of the Opry, however, there exists also a certain wildness in the air like "fireworks" that makes Katie feel just like a child, completely "star-struck!" (273). What a moving and appropriate description since the Nashville music scene does require a certain surrender of the soul, reminiscent of Moses Bailey's belief that fiddle music was evidence of having sold one's soul to the devil.

Kate Malone, a young, energetic, and musical girl, serves as the novel's first embodiment of the goddess and introduces the conflict among motherhood, sexuality, religion, and music that haunts the Bailey family when in 1834 she marries the glum and rigidly religious Moses Bailey. As Chappell notes, the "division between the bright, gay, lyric side of life and the profoundly dark, discordant side" goes on for over a century through four generations of Baileys. From this sometimes comic, sometimes agonizing conflict, comes the power of genuine music, whether it occurs on the porch of a mountain home or over a microphone to be broadcast to millions of people (940). We hear the story of Kate and Moses from Ira Keen, a narrator not unlike *Oral History*'s Granny Younger in his ability to stretch out the story and tell it the way he wants. Smith emphasizes Kate's divine nature from the beginning of the tale, mentioning her pure gold hair and the fact that she gives birth to three babies, one girl and two boys. Kate believes Moses will provide "salvation" for her (15), and like Ivy, who initially searches for salvation in others, Kate is unable to recognize her own innate divinity. Ira's diction in describing the sound of the fiddle-playing epitomizes the spirit of music for the entire Bailey family in its simultaneous "sweetness" and "awfulness." This antinomy reflects Smith's consistent interest in the coexistence of opposites, as when *Family Linen*'s Lacy describes her miserable longing for a mother as "pain so bitter it was sweet almost" (69) and Ivy descends the mountain with Honey with a "sour and sweet" (229) taste in her mouth. Ira recounts his first visit to the cabin many years earlier, when he meets the sacred, sexual Kate, an image he never forgets. The "red and yeller leaves" are "a-blowing crazy" in the wind, and Kate, with her hair "all gold and merry-wild" and her lips "full and pouty and cherry red," sits on the porch rocking a doll and singing (21). Smith immediately links Kate to divinity in her direct association with the wind and the colors red and yellow, and additionally emphasizes Kate's sexual nature with the description of her "cherry red" lips.* Kate is also aligned with wildness, in the reference to her "merry-wild" hair, like many earlier goddess figures in Smith. And like other female characters such as Ivy Rowe, Kate begins to "los[e] her bloom" (23–24) in her early twenties, from the hard work of maintaining a household and caring for three children.

Smith associates Kate with the feminine divine even more blatantly on Ira's second visit to the young woman when he discovers her standing outside at a cookfire stirring a pot of apple butter, her cheeks red from the heat of the fire and her hair blowing around her face. Ira describes the "cold wind ... a-blowing through" the trees as he notices the "feel of the forest ... all around" and the closeness to the Baileys' cabin of Lone Bald Mountain, where the

---

*Since Kate holds a doll in her arms, this image also suggests her maternal nature.

ravens and bears live. As Kate douses the fire with a bucket of water from the spring, she licks the end of the sassafras stirring stick then offers Ira a taste, all the while giggling and smiling, her laughter signaling her liminal nature. Ira describes the sensation of licking the apple butter as being "real hot and real sweet"; in fact, he almost burns his tongue. Listening to the cold "wind a-moaning and a-sighing," Ira watches the breeze blow Kate's golden hair all around her face (24–25), creating an indelible halo image in his mind. In this description of setting and the character Kate, Smith carefully combines all the various ideas and images previously associated with the feminine divine and female sexuality: the elements of wind, fire, and water; the color red; the idea of wildness; and the sensual sweetness necessary for sexual satisfaction. Additionally, the writer places her goddess figure close to a mountain with caves where ravens and bears live. Mountains, caves, ravens, and bears can be directly linked to the goddess of the Paleolithic Age. Considered the "Queen of Mountains" and portrayed standing on the mountaintop, the goddess, in this role, incarnates the fertility of Nature. Caves have occurred often in Smith's work and serve as natural manifestations of the sacred mother's womb, having had particular relevance for such characters as Red Emmy, Sally, and Ivy. Furthermore, ravens manifest the goddess in her role as arbiter of death and regeneration while her role as birth-giver is mysteriously linked to bears and their specific association with motherhood. Smith infuses Kate's character with poignant imagery of the feminine divine.

Circularity exists when Ira visits Kate for the last time, after both Moses' and Jeremiah's (her oldest son) deaths, and discovers her on her front porch rocking and singing, just as he had found her the first time he visited. Her hair has turned completely white, like that of other damaged females (Tenessee, Fay, and Tampa), but her voice is still as *sweet* as ever, and Ira notices once more the wind blowing and thinks he hears a whisper in the breeze. As Ira tells this story of his encounter with the feminine divine, he admits that although sixty or seventy years have passed since he saw Kate, even now when he hears the fiddle music, he envisions himself dancing with Kate (part of a traditional goddess ritual), "together as we never was in life, a-waltzing in the dark" (32). He sees her, rosy-cheeked, standing by that fire in the wind, with her hair blowing, offering him the sassafras stick. Although Ira marries and has nine children, he cannot recall the face of his now dead wife of almost fifty years, but he says he'll never forget a single detail about Kate Malone. This experience, his encounter with the feminine divine, remains frozen in his mind much like Almarine's meeting with Red Emmy, Richard's with Dory, and Ivy's with Honey.

Smith links with caves not only Kate, but also other damaged characters. After losing her husband and son, Kate, laughing hysterically, goes insane and says ravens from the cave pursue her, suggesting perhaps her longing for the death and rebirth represented by the raven and the cave. The "madwoman's laughter" serves to underscore the injury done to Kate as her children are taken from her, and she is left alone, dismissed, like Fay, Silvaney and Tenessee, as being "crazy." With no words to express her pain, Kate, like Fay, becomes Irigaray's powerless "murdered mother." Kate's younger son Ezekiel, another broken character and heir to his mother's beautiful blonde hair and love of music, suffers from early separation from his mother but decides "not to tell anybody about the voices in his head, or that other sound he always heard, like wind through a cave" (34). Smith's diction implies that what Zeke hears is his mother's voice, evincing the presence of the feminine divine. Smith likewise ties to caves Rose Annie Bailey, Zeke's granddaughter. Creating an imaginary double whom she expects to see behind every tree, "in every cave on the mountain, down at the springhouse" (139), Rose Annie psychologically splits herself in two. The voice Rose Annie imagines as the little blonde girl's voice is actually her own voice, and she explains that over time, she came to love the little girl as much as she feared her. The apparitional girl, associated with caves, mountains, and the water of the springhouse, represents Rose Annie's suppressed sacred sexuality and her contradictory feelings toward the open expression of this part of herself.

Unlike Rose Annie, who eventually succumbs to her fears and doubts, Katie Cocker, Rose Annie's cousin, escapes the terrors of her cave-like entrapment to initiate her sacred spiritual journey. Describing her life with her mother and grandmother Mama Tampa as one filled with darkness, Katie decides to leave home for fear she will go insane or die there. Terrified of being absorbed into the lives of these women, Katie, the strongest character in the novel and the one whose life serves as Smith's focal point, determines to discover her identity apart from her family. In striking out on her own, Katie represents those women who try to control the quality of their lives despite their culturally prescribed passivity. Katie compares leaving home to coming "out of a cave and into the world" (216) as she experiences rebirth when she emerges from the symbolic maternal womb. Facing harsh reality alone, Katie becomes a wanderer in search of reconciliation for her many internal conflicts regarding her sexuality, her music, and her religion.

The wandering motif, often linked in earlier Smith novels with the idea of wildness and restlessness, plays a crucial role in this novel in signaling a character's innate need to search and explore outside the confines of home and family in order to find healing. Longing for something just beyond one's reach often accompanies the wildness and wandering as a character quests for a "lost" counterpart. The journey most often necessitates the abandonment of a religion that exalts a masculine God image and encourages women to lead limited, subordinated lives. The first Bailey characters illustrate these premises in Moses' inability to settle down, his "traipsing the woods alone" (22), then his eventual refusal to come out of the forest at all, and in Kate's despair after playing the fiddle at her parents' home, then returning to her own home where "her whole heart was filled with longing" (27) to play and sing the music she so loves. Both characters yearn for something unattainable: Moses wants to receive the call to preach; Kate longs for a voice, to be permitted to play the music so much a part of her, and for Moses to accept and allow it. Their son Zeke remains to try to resolve their conflict, but he eventually marries Nonnie, a "wildcat from Hell" (57) who "swing[s] on grapevines and play[s] with snakes," all the while singing and even "wander[ing] off singing" (53). Nonnie's illegitimate son R.C. inherits his mother's wildness and after his mother's desertion of her family to join the medicine show, R.C. leaves the mountain in a wild fury, battling his personal demons as he plunges to the depths of degradation and base sexuality. Although R.C. returns home after several years, having heard his mother's voice instructing him to do so, he never escapes the damage and accompanying wildness that characterize his entire family. Even after he marries and settles down, he still finds himself out of control and full of unexplainable energy with which he infuses his music. An omniscient narrator informs the reader, "It is always R.C.'s blessing—and curse—to understand a little too much about everything" (123). In the section of the novel narrated by R.C.'s sister Lizzie, Smith emphasizes the young girl's "wild, wild ... longing" (94) in her depiction of another broken female, "miserable and motherless" (91) from age ten. Like Nonnie's sister Zinnia and Ora Mae, Lizzie escapes her real feelings by working her "little fingers to the bone" at home, never acknowledging her own needs, including her own sexuality. Lizzie explains that she has dedicated her existence to "erasing some of the *harm* done by those who run loose about the world doing whatever pleases them," calling these people "messy and heedless, prisoners of their passion, unmindful of all others save themselves." Like Sybill, Lizzie likes for things to be ordered and neat, the opposite of her mother who had seemed always to be "falling apart" somehow with her wildness and sexuality (94–95).

Smith's characterization of Katie Cocker, the novel's most fully developed goddess figure, intimates wildness as opposed to domesticity as she yearns for something more than what her life offers, a system of belief that empowers women. She explains her feelings as a young woman: "I was wild to leave home, I was wild to get me a husband—I guess I was wild in general" (209). So when her Aunt Virgie asks her to leave and become a music star, Katie doesn't hesitate since she loves music more than anything else. Katie compares her life at home with her mother and grandmother to an animal's being held captive in a cage: "I felt like ... several girls in the same body, all of a sudden swept up by the wildest desire for something I couldn't even name" (214). Similar to earlier Smith protagonists, the sensation Katie feels of almost bursting suggests her latent sexuality. An embodiment of Irigaray's "volume without contours," Katie feels fragmented, trapped without a voice ("Volume" 52) as she struggles to escape the forces that attempt to enclose and contain her. In the scene before she leaves home, Katie looks around her room and observes the faded wallpaper with its "repeated pattern of little lattice squares and curlicues and violets" seemingly holding her back from attaining the "something" for which she yearns (215). Reminiscent of Ivy when she stares at the entrapping wallpaper at Geneva's boardinghouse and feels confined, Katie also will break out from behind the "squares" and bars and pursue happiness and fulfillment outside society's prescribed boundary.

In this novel, Smith's continued interest in the idea of sweetness provides insight into the author's desire to redeem this quality that has so often been trivialized* and further develops in her work the mythological significance of honey, sacred essence of the feminine divine. As the first narrator tells the story of Kate Malone and Moses Bailey, he explains that the tale will "grow in yer mind like a honeysuckle vine" (17); thus, Smith introduces the story of the first members of the Bailey family. Sweetness accompanies pure sexuality, a property linked to the goddess in her many forms, and bees and honeycombs are symbols of regeneration. In ancient art depicting the goddess, the bee is seen emerging from the bucranium (skull of the bull) as a representation of new life. Smith consistently links sweetness, honey, and bees with ideas of rebirth and regeneration through open recognition and acceptance of one's sacred sexuality. Damaged characters are described as possessing a certain "sweetness ... that would make you weep" (92). To this group belong Ira's brother Dummy who spends all his time rocking in a chair and whistling like a bird; Durwood who drinks himself to death; Nonnie who discovers time for herself, time she describes as "golden and slow and sweet as the thick honey that came from Ezekiel's hives" (64); Lizzie who is completely desexed but long remembers the smell of the "wild perfume of the honeysuckle" from Grassy Branch (90); Rose Annie who longs for the days of the stir-offs when she would dip the cane stick down into the pan to "get some sweetening," then lick the sweet, hot molasses right off the stalk like her great-grandmother Kate Malone (147); and Katie Cocker who describes her favorite times while growing up on Grassy Branch as sitting out on the porch and singing with the family, feeling "drunk ... on the sweet-sweet smell of the honeysuckle vine" (211). This image of Katie recalls the "honey-mad woman," feeding on sensual pleasures and transgressing borders in a blissful way. As Katie leaves home to become a star, she notices "[b]ees buzzing around" and "a little soft breeze ... blowing" (215–16), key elements signaling the presence of the feminine divine and portending the wisdom in Katie's departure.

Only Katie's third and final husband, Ralph Handy, will restore sweetness to Katie's life. On their first date, Ralph saturates his biscuits with sorghum molasses, reminding Katie of her home and family, so she shares

---

*The idea of sweetness has been trivialized in popular expressions such as "sweetie pie" and "honey," for example, and sweetness has been consistently viewed as a particularly feminine quality, diminutive and patronizing. According to Dorothy Hill, Smith explodes expectations by using such "sweet" female names as Dory, Ivy, Candy, Sandy, Lacy, etc. (99).

with him her memories of the molasses stir-offs, telling Ralph "how good that hot molasses tasted when you dipped it up out of the stirring trough on a little piece of cane" (287). This experience with Ralph serves as the impetus for Katie to return home and complete her cyclical journey. A genuinely good man, Ralph stirs Katie's memory, providing the necessary sweetness to enable Katie to come to terms with her sexuality and her music. For integration, women must discover the meanings of the relationships they enjoy with nature, their bodies, their children's bodies, another woman, or a man. With Ralph, a man closely aligned with nature himself, Katie shares such a divine union.

As in previous novels, Smith again uses the natural phenomenon of the wind to signal the presence of the goddess and to suggest healing for damaged characters. Like Kate Malone in her strong association with the wind and its mysterious power, other important characters are linked to this sacred force. Ironically, when Moses unexpectedly returns to his cabin in Cold Spring Holler and hears the fiddle music emanating from his home, he mistakes the sound for the "Devil's laughter on the wind" (29). Smith emphasizes Moses' blindness to the sacredness of his wife in his inability to accept music as a vital and necessary part of Kate. The religious experience of Moses and Kate's son Zeke occurs on a stormy night with "rushing winds and flashes of lightning" while Zeke travels homeward after a night of drinking and partying. Zeke experiences a sensation like his "head had split and parted and poured Ezekiel himself out in the world like a pail of water, like there was nothing left of him at all." He feels the lightning race through his body, "electrifying him" as God speaks to him and gives him a "gift song," after which the wind picks up again and rain "wash[es] down over him like a benediction" (42–43). In his association with the wind and water, Zeke is powerfully linked to the feminine divine and given hope for healing. Likewise, Smith connects Zeke's wife Nonnie to the wind as the presence of the wind marks each important event in her life. When she discovers the bag of money in the chimney, "the fire leap[s] up" and the "March wind wail[s] outside" (67), signaling the feminine divine and the emergence of Nonnie's latent sexuality. Then at her baptism, Nonnie feels weak and alone as the world with "all its bright trappings streamed past her like the wind." For the first time, Nonnie feels "lifted out of the moment of her life and thrust toward something beyond herself" (69). The power of the feminine divine propels Nonnie to escape conformity and instead act on instinct. At the medicine show, the musical voice of Dr. Sharpe captivates her as the "torches bl[o]w wildly" and the wind steadily rises, eventually tearing the bunting loose. Nonnie finds herself walking toward the stage and asking to sing. Some unknown force then guides her to sing the cuckoo song, the song she had sung many years ago when her father so often placed her on the store countertop. Smith once more mentions the strength of the wind as Harry Sharpe turns and kisses Nonnie with a mouth that tastes "fiery as the pit of Hell itself" (75–76).

In the description of Nonnie's encounter with Harry, in addition to the presence of the wind, a few points merit mention. First, the song that Nonnie sings that will be passed down to future generations of Bailey women demands analysis. "The Cuckoo Song" celebrates the coming of spring with the song of the bird, but the cuckoo is also linked to the goddess. Gimbutas says "a cuckoo's call is the Goddess's call" (*Language* 311) and the cuckoo, in its cyclical appearance and legendary transformation into a hawk* in autumn and winter, is connected to the goddess as overseer of the cycles of time, life and death, spring and winter, and happiness and unhappiness (195). The prominence Smith attributes to this song throughout the novel suggests that it carries more weight than simply a girlhood tune remembered and passed down for generations. The strong association between the cuckoo and the feminine divine further emphasizes the sacred presence within many of Smith's female characters. Nonnie has not felt the fiery passion she experiences with Harry Sharpe since her brief affair that produced her oldest son R.C. Her heightened libido causes her to desert her family and leave town with the medicine show, only to die soon after in a hotel fire, a victim of her own destructive passion that was never integrated with the other aspects of her nature.

Smith also uses the wind in expressing the divine sexuality of both Rose Annie Bailey and Katie Cocker. Until Rose Annie leaves with Johnny, she cannot escape memories of her youth, always accompanied by a gentle breeze. She longs for the days of the molasses stir-offs that have come to represent all the good times growing up, similar to Ivy Rowe's reminiscences of the years before her severe depression. At each stir-off, the wind makes its presence known as the family members taste the sweet, hot molasses. After years of separation from Johnny, Rose Annie suddenly hears Johnny's song on the radio while "red and gold leaves [are] blowing ever whichaway" (155). She calls the radio station to find out how to reach Johnny, and the wind, blowing symbolically colored leaves, reawakens her long submerged sexuality.

Wind functions as an important mark of the feminine divine also as Katie Cocker leaves home to pursue a singing career, finally listening to her inner voice. She rolls down the window in Virgie's car and "let[s] the wind blow [her] hair" (222) as she experiences her own empowerment. When she later meets Ralph Handy, she suddenly notices every detail about the weather, especially the wind "coming up out of the east" (284) as Ralph stirs in Katie her latent sexuality. After recovering from a nervous breakdown, Katie goes forward in church to have healing hands laid on her. She describes her experience as releasing her pain into the wind where it "shatter[ed] and bl[e]w away, nothing but dust in the wind." Katie then postulates that God entered her body through her mouth, "like a long cool drink of water" (298). Considering the

---

Smith utilizes the image of the hawk circling as a sacred sign in several works, most notably Fair and Tender Ladies *and* On Agate Hill.

imagery associated with Katie's divine experience, it seems extremely likely that Katie encounters the presence and power of the feminine divine. However, in her limited understanding, she attributes her inexplicable, mystical feeling to the force of the culturally approved version of a male God. Katie's sensation of rebirth is strongly linked to the feminine divine in its salient association with wind and water. Only after Ralph's death and Katie's descent into hopelessness is she able to define herself as a fully integrated woman, not reliant on anyone else's perception of her.

Smith's continued interest in language or the absence thereof surfaces in this novel in several of the major characters as they struggle in their individual spiritual journeys. Often the writer's damaged characters are given few or no words to express their pain, reminiscent of Dory who stops talking once Richard deserts her, and both Fay and Silvaney who are deprived of any kind of voice in being labeled "crazy." In offering more fully realized male characters in this novel, Smith more often depicts less appealing men in terms of their frailties rather than what they have done wrong. Zeke and R.C. Bailey are both presented as damaged characters who find the conventional language of the mind inadequate to express the poignant sensuality of their pain. Although Zeke rarely speaks, he loves to sing, and since he's misunderstood by most people, he chooses not to tell anyone about the voices he hears in his head. After many years of marriage, his wife Nonnie describes him as "an old man with nothing to say" (71), and soon after she deserts him and the children, he suffers a stroke that completely robs him of the ability to speak. The death of Zeke's speech, or his "asymbolia," is symptomatic of depression, not only caused by Nonnie's abandonment, but by what Rozsika Parker calls the severance of the maternal bond (163) since his own mother also vanished during his formative years. Zeke's oldest son R.C., who inherits his father's love for music and possesses a deep, gentle voice, is described as a "man of extremes" (92) who either doesn't talk at all or talks too much. After his wife Lucie's death, R.C. loses his "heart" for music and refuses to even discuss the days when they recorded music together. Eventually he commits suicide, with thoughts of his long-dead mother tormenting him. R.C.'s literal death, along with his asymbolia, like that of his father, is linked to the loss of women he loved. Hank Smith, Katie's first husband, another broken character, "never ha[s] hardly a thing to say." Since he still cares for his selfish and hypochondriac mother and has no desire to become a father, he talks even less after the birth of Annie May. Other damaged male characters, like Franklin Ransom of *Fair and Tender Ladies*, are described as charmers who use the language to attract women and satisfy their own desperate needs. Katie explains that Wayne Ricketts "had such a way with words" that he could convince her of almost anything, adding, "Sex is a factor here…. So is talking. A big talker who is great at sex can have his way in this world" (253–54), acknowledging the power of language to make connections with others.

VI. "Figures a-dancing ... in the flames" 153

Just as Smith's interest in language consistently appears in her novels, images of fire repeatedly mark the presence of sacred sexuality and link to the feminine divine in her representation of both sexuality and motherhood. Kate Malone's son Zeke inherits his mother's divinity, and Smith continues to explore new territory in her depiction of this sacred, sexual male character that is much more developed than Honey Breeding but is equally associated with divinity. Described as having whitish blonde hair that "glows fiery pale, like bright angel hair" (38) and a face as fair and blank as the full moon, Zeke spends much of his time staring into fires with his head cocked to the side as if he is listening for something. Zeke's posture is reminiscent of Dory's, after Richard's desertion, as she appears to hear something no one else can detect. Smith often depicts damaged characters in such an attitude of listening to sounds of which others are unaware. At Zeke's baptism, Smith describes him as appearing "as pretty as an angel" as he walks into the river, "blinded by the morning sun off the water" (44), further establishing his divinity. While staying with Dot Kincaid, Zeke sits by the fire and sings with her after supper, and after dislodging a stump, he burns it in a "great wildfire" (37), watching all night as his heart beats faster and faster with intense passion. On the night that he receives his "gift song," Zeke sees "three tall pine trees burning with green fire against the dark mountain" just as God speaks to him (43). With this setting, while Zeke hears the voice of the patriarchal God, Smith interweaves three elements previously associated with the feminine divine: the number three, the fire, and the mountain. Although the number three is also linked to traditional Christianity in the Trinity, it was originally associated with birth and the life-giving functions of the goddess.

Another sexual female, Zeke's wife Nonnie is likewise associated with fire; in fact, on the night of her birth and her mother's death, her sister Zinnia reports waking up to find a fire burning in the fireplace and says that those days after Nonnie's birth seem like a "blaze of light" (51). Similar to Zeke and his great granddaughter Rose Annie much later, Nonnie often stares into fires, arguing that she sees figures dancing in the flames, reminiscent of Elizabeth of *Family Linen* who sees dancing men in her fireplace, an image symbolic of the injury done to these characters that constantly burns within them. Nonnie, an openly passionate goddess figure, suppresses her sexuality to conform to the role of wife and mother after being damaged by a love affair. However, the fire within Nonnie flares up again when, sitting within a "circle of fire," she discovers the treasure that makes possible her dreams. In the "flickering firelight" of the medicine show, Nonnie feels a sensation stealing over her, a feeling from long ago, a "quivering mixture of excitement and longing and dread," and as she is swept up by her passion, she says the feelings inside her "opened up, flared" (75). Three years later Nonnie dies alone in a hotel fire; she wakes up with the sheets on fire, envisioning the "wide blank gaze of Ezekiel's blue-blue eyes." Her last words, ostensibly spoken to Zeke's image, are "Oh God ... Oh God" (79), an open acknowledgment of the divinity within Zeke. Ironically, Zeke recognized his wife's sacredness long ago, the first time she stands naked and pregnant before him and he gasps, "God Almighty" (66). Zeke's words recall Richard's similar expression when he touches Dory's breast. Unable to survive in her world, Nonnie, like Dory, another sacred, sexual, maternal female, is sacrificed, a victim of her own passion.

Just as Zeke inherits his mother's love of music and link to divinity, R.C., Nonnie's oldest son, carries the burning passion of his mother with him throughout his life. Whereas Zeke receives his "gift song" from the patriarchal God, R.C. hears the voice of his divine mother Nonnie telling him to return home after many years of reckless living. Lizzie describes her brother R.C. as having the "curliest, prettiest fair hair" and "dark eyes [that] burned out in his face" (91–92), adding, "[s]ometimes he's a ball of fire, other times he's as distant as the moon" (119), a man with a powerful passion for music and for the woman he loves. When Lizzie warns Lucie about marrying R.C., she tells her, "You are fooling with fire," but Lucie just laughs as the wind picks up and she and R.C. go out to the barn and begin petting. The desexed Lizzie watches out the window, rendered immobile by "hot and terrible" feelings she can't explain. When R.C. and Lucie come back inside the house, Lizzie notices that they both look "flushed, intoxicated, as if they'd contracted a fever" (98–99). Nor Hall notes the significance in archetypal initiation of intoxication that, "like inspiration, can enlarge a person enough for the goddess to enter" (179). During many years of a happy marriage, R.C. and Lucie freely express with one another their sacred sexuality in another of Smith's divine unions.

Years after R.C. and Lucie's marriage, when Lizzie comes home and finds R.C.'s family gathered around the fire, Lizzie exemplifies what Margaret Whitford calls Irigaray's "guardian of the body" (26), a woman who finds the female body, sexuality, pregnancy, and birth appalling. Carol Christ argues that "women's location in female bodies must shape the way we experience the world" and that to remain silent about parturition and motherhood is to deny the reality of women's extremely physical presence (92). Lizzie suffers from just such denial. Viewing Lucie with her flushed face and long red hair, "huge and beautiful in her second pregnancy," Lizzie realizes Lucie and her family are happy. However, R.C.'s touching his wife's breast makes Lizzie uncomfortable, as does their son's "little penis" and "Lucie's big belly, full of another baby." Lizzie fears that "just beyond the warm circle of firelight, the darkness, full of danger and desire..., wait[s] malevolently, patiently, for them all" (105). Smith's description of this family bathed in firelight, rife with links to the feminine divine, in its harmonious portrayal of a sacred, sexual, maternal female character peaceful and content with her husband and child, certainly suggests the fallacy in Lizzie's observation. Ironically, Lizzie dies as a young woman of what the omniscient narrator calls "romantic fever" (119), suggesting that her

VI. "Figures a-dancing ... in the flames"

inability to express passion, the repression of her sexuality, impels her to a premature death.

R.C. and Lucie's only daughter, Rose Annie, also harbors a fiery passion that ties her to both her parents and eventually serves to destroy her. Times spent with Johnny Rainette are consistently conveyed in language relating to fire and burning. Rose Annie says she feels like she is "on fire all over" when she is with Johnny, similar to the way Ivy describes her sensations in the presence of Honey. In later years, Rose Annie analyzes her problem as having "had it all" when she was young. She says it "ruined" her for men, "or for *life*," feeling so much when she was with Johnny. She confesses, "I was more alive at fourteen, at fifteen, than anybody has got a right to be ever, and I haven't got over it yet. I can't get over it." Rose Annie never recovers from what she calls "peak[ing] out" at such a young age; she spends her entire life trying to recapture that feeling of vibrancy that Johnny gave her. Her sentiments of being completely alive with Johnny are reminiscent of Ivy Rowe's when she writes to Silvaney that Honey Breeding has brought her back to life again. Ivy, however, is able to move on with her life, integrating both parts of her being to become whole without the physical presence of Honey, whereas Rose Annie never accomplishes full integration, with or without Johnny. Years after Johnny's disappearance and her marriage to Buddy, Rose Annie feels "alive" again only when she sees the necklace of "scarlet haws" that Johnny made for her. Many of Rose Annie's memories with Johnny involve singing around the fire with the family; she explains, "we were on fire in those years" (141–42), during which they kept their sexual relationship hidden. Rose Annie describes their love-making during one of the big molasses stir-offs when they could look "back at the circle of light and fire" and see "the black figures moving to and fro in the orange firelight" as people danced and sang (147), a scene reminiscent of her grandmother Nonnie's description of the imaginary figures she sees in the fire. Both images evoke the spirit of popular goddess rituals in all early cultures where dance was a way of communicating with the feminine divine. Both Rose Annie and Nonnie suffer due to the strength of their passion. Rose Annie's last words to the police officer there to arrest her for the murder of Johnny reveal her obsession with the long-dead passion between her and Johnny as she once again mentions "the figures dancing ... in the fiery light" (204). Rose Annie never escapes the flames that engulf her; she spends the remainder of her life in prison for murder.

Smith employs fire imagery at each crucial moment in Katie Cocker's life. During her first narration, Katie explains that she "felt hot and tingly all over" (212) when she sang alone for the first time in her high school talent show to win the title Miss Holly Springs, connecting the passion she feels for music with the sexual passion she is soon to experience. When she marries Hank Smith, they spend their wedding night in front of the parlor fire at the boardinghouse as the young couple enjoys the fullness of their mutual sexuality. Then, at age twenty-three, when she strikes out on her own in Shreveport only to meet and join Wayne Ricketts, she describes the sensation of being around Wayne as "having a heatstroke" (249). Once she encounters Ralph Handy, he brings back all her memories of Grassy Branch, with the music and the "great fire and full moon" (287), the molasses stir-offs that have become indelible in her mind, much as they have in Rose Annie's. Her most painful memory of losing Ralph in the "awful burst of flame" that engulfs their tour bus is replayed over and over again. She explains, "I have been seeing it ever since, it burns forever in my heart" (291). At the scene of the accident, the sight paralyzes Katie, much like Crystal Spangler when she discovers her dead father. And like Ivy Rowe, after LuIda's death, Katie wishes it were her own death instead of that of her loved one. Fire again touches Katie when Billy Jack Reems kisses her hands after the church service, leaving a place that "burned like fire" and stayed red for three days (298). Not only the image of fire, but also the number three links Katie's experience with the feminine divine.

In the last section of the novel when the family is reunited at the Opryland Hotel, Smith centers the conversation and action around an enormous fireplace, "its blazing fire tended by elves" (304), as each female character reconnects to her past by gazing into the flames. In choosing elves, ethereal, liminal creatures, to tend the fire that holds all the painful memories of the past for the characters, Smith suggests the possibility of healing the wounds of those who may find strength and reassurance in the feminine divine. Furthermore, Barbara Walker mentions the association of elves to the herb rosemary, "known as the Elfin Plant" and "named after the Goddess herself" (*Women's* 280). Now at the family gathering, Rose Annie, having always loved fires, stares into the blazes, as her grandfather Zeke had done, remembering the night she spent in the field with Johnny and how they looked back at the fire with all the dancing people. Katie sees only one thing in any fire—the burning bus—just as the courtesy bus arrives to take everyone to the recording session. Turning to Mama Tampa, Katie asks, "*doesn't this remind you of how you all used to tell stories around the fire of a night in the wintertime?*" The novel comes full circle as Mama Tampa begins telling the story of "*the fiddling woman and the preacherman*" who married and had three children (309–10), referring to the first musical Bailey family. The colors red and gold (or yellow), most commonly associated with fire and with the sun, sex, and war goddesses, play a crucial role in the novel. Gimbutas identifies the color red as representing life and the color gold or yellow as connoting death (*Language* 323–24); thus, the combination of these two colors powerfully suggests the feminine divine in her representation of the complete life cycle. Smith's descriptions of all the key female characters and a few of the male characters emphasize these two colors much more than any others.

Yellows and reds are again highlighted when Nonnie first arrives to marry

Zeke. Smith describes the couple standing among "bleeding hearts" and "yellow butterflies," Nonnie's face "red and swollen from crying" and her brown eyes with "yellow sunbursts in them" (62–63). The red/yellow combination emphasizes the divinity within both characters and suggests the possibility for their sacred union. In the first few months of their marriage, Zeke leaves gifts at the foot of Nonnie's bed as offerings to this sacred female. On the first night the couple makes love, Nonnie awakens to the sound of a screech owl saying her name. The description of the scene that follows is permeated with divine imagery. Moonlight streams in the window, making "a silver path across the cabin floor, right across Ezekiel, who look[s] like an angel sleeping there." Nonnie stands up, takes off her nightgown, and steps into the silvering moonlight. Looking down at her pregnant body, she observes her large breasts and protruding navel, suddenly feeling powerful, "like she [i]s bursting right out of her skin" (65), the sexual maternal goddess figure unashamed of her naked body. She stands in the moonlight admiring herself and breathing hard, and even her black hair looks silver in the moonlight as she goes to Zeke. The owl is a prophetic bird, a death messenger, the goddess as "Death Wielder, but [with] regenerative qualities" (Gimbutas, *Language* 324). Here Nonnie clearly represents the goddess in her dual roles as life-giver (she is pregnant) and life-taker. Ironically, she will later lose her life due to her inability to integrate her sexual passion with her roles as wife and mother. Perhaps the owl that calls her name is indeed prophetic of Nonnie's dreary fate. But for many years, Nonnie thinks of her time with Zeke as "golden" (64) since he pampers her so, giving her ample opportunity to daydream and think of herself; she even orders rose-colored silk fabric and fashions a beautiful, but impractical, dress for herself that expresses the intensity of her sexuality.

The colors red and gold appear again in Nonnie and Zeke's children, then in descriptions of their grandchildren, consistently signaling the presence of the feminine divine. Two of Zeke and Nonnie's children possess their father's yellow hair—R.C. and Lizzie—and both of these characters are seriously damaged by their mother's desertion. Smith's description of R.C. combines the two colors of fire: his wife Lucie says sometimes he's "a ball of fire," and other times, he's "distant as the moon" (119), illustrating the antinomy of R.C. Lizzie observes her brother's blonde hair and eyes that "burn out in his face" (91), similar to Ivy's description of both her mother and Silvaney's eyes. R.C.'s wife, called Lucie Queen, possesses the long, thick, red hair of the archetypal red-headed goddess, reminiscent of Red Emmy and equally sexual. Lucie and R.C.'s only daughter, Rose Annie, suffers from the early death of her mother, much as R.C. has, and she inherits her father's "light, light hair" (137). Her husband Buddy calls Rose Annie his "little old china doll" (131) and gives her gifts, reminiscent of Zeke's offerings to Nonnie.

Rose Annie describes several childhood experiences with Johnny Rainette in terms of reds and golds also. One day when they are swimming, Johnny jumps in to rescue her when her brother Clarence ducks her; she says the memory of this moment when she and Johnny "burst up into the sunlight" is more real to her as an adult than any other experience she's had. Indelible in her mind are the images of the "gold sunshine," a cousin's red swimsuit, and "the water running down Johnny's chest" (137). As Johnny pulls Rose Annie up from under the water, she experiences symbolic rebirth as she emerges from the maternal womb. Another time, Rose Annie and Johnny journey into the mountains looking for sang that has "turned yellow" (139) and Johnny saves her from attacking wild hogs when she slips "on the wet leaves" (141). For Rose Annie, Johnny is consistently associated with the warmth and security of the mother's womb to which she yearns to return until she finally leaves her husband and children to join Johnny on the road.

Smith also emphasizes these same two colors with Katie Cocker, marking each important stage of Katie's life with red and gold images. Another granddaughter of Zeke and Nonnie, Katie is a natural blonde, first introduced as possessing *"thick yellow hair"* and a *"wide, full mouth"* (12) painted with red lipstick. In each of Katie's progressive attempts to define herself through men, Smith reminds the reader of Katie's innate divinity with descriptions rife with mentions of red and gold. As she sits with Wayne Ricketts in his mobile home, Katie notices "in the last red rays of the sun" the "real gold" color of her daughter Annie May's hair and the red color of the lake next to the trailer park (250-51). Katie's relationship with Wayne, however, offers no sacred union, failing miserably when both Katie and Wayne become victims of drug and alcohol abuse. Then, when in California Katie makes the decision to leave Tom Barksdale and return home, she walks out of the recording studio and into "the bright hot sun," noticing a "hedge full of big red flowers" (280). This experience signals a big change for Katie; she becomes reacquainted with Ralph Handy, the steel guitar player from Katie and Wayne's band. On their first date, they have breakfast at a place ironically called "the Loveless Cafe"; here in a setting drenched with sunlight, Katie and Ralph eat biscuits and "red-eye gravy" at a table with a "red-and-white-checkered tablecloth" (285-86). Katie's feeling of recognition with Ralph, not unlike that of earlier divine couples in Smith, occurs when she curls her foot around Ralph's "like I'd been doing it all my life" (287). Smith further emphasizes the divine quality of Katie and Ralph's relationship by recreating a pivotal scene that occurred early in the novel between Nonnie and Zeke. On the tour bus one evening, Katie notices the moonlight shining through the blinds, illuminating "Ralph's dear face" (289), reminiscent of Zeke's angelic face as Nonnie observed it in the moonlight. Like Nonnie, Katie attributes her sentimentality to her pregnancy and to the moonlight. At the end of the novel when Katie has finally begun to heal from the devastating loss of Ralph, Smith marks the beginning of Katie's new life on her own, unconnected to any man, with a description of the spotlights on the singing fountain in the Opryland Hotel *"shining red and ... gold*

... on the dancing jets of water" (305). The imagery of this scene powerfully evokes the feminine divine as Smith concludes the story.

The culminating moment in the novel comes when Katie stops defining herself through men and learns to accept the sacredness within herself. Important to note is that after her first nervous breakdown when she feels like giving up, a woman's voice urges her to get up and make something of herself: "*You've got some more singing to do.*" Katie describes the voice, "It was a voice I had not heard before, yet it was as familiar to me as my own. Maybe it *was* my own, in some crazy way which is past understanding" (261). Unlike Crystal Spangler who hears a man's voice in her mystical experience at camp, Katie hears a female voice providing the necessary encouragement to propel Katie forward on her life's path, suggestive of the sacredness of her feminine experience. Although Smith admits Katie's journey is "sort of quintessentially American in a lot of ways" since she goes from the farm to the city, from "the rural obscure life to the big time" (Byrd 115), her pilgrimage is more like Ivy Rowe's, circular and cyclical, encompassing her gradual movement toward self-knowledge. Katie's journey embodies the female experience with its "biological rhythm" akin to "the rhythm of nature," what Kristeva observes, can be "a source of resplendent visions and unnameable jouissance" ("Women's" 352). However, Katie pays a price for ridding herself of patriarchal shackles and achieving autonomy. Similar to Candy who chooses not to be a "lady" like her mother, realizing how difficult it is to be a "good woman" (120), Katie says, "the last thing on earth I ever wanted to be was a good woman" (219). Instead, she breaks all boundaries to become a fully integrated sacred, sexual, maternal female, another character Smith says "got ahold of me the same way Ivy Rowe did" (Parrish 396). In the last scene of the novel, with the entire Bailey family gathered at the Opryland Hotel, Alice's thoughts poignantly reveal the generations-old conflict within the Bailey family: "fergit babies, fergit all that breathing and groping and rolling around in the dark, ain't no man alive that can hold a candle to God" (307). In her pronounced separation of religion from children (maternity) and sexuality, Alice gives voice to the patriarchal restraints against which Katie has fought most all her life.

As Katie's life and the Bailey family saga come "full circle ... [l]ike an album" (301), Smith reminds the reader of the powerful presence of the feminine divine in her careful delineation of Mama Tampa with her "fuzzy white hair like a halo" (160), smiling and waving to everyone as she passes through the lobby in a wheelchair, acting "exactly like a beauty queen" with a big red bow adorning her hat. The sexual, maternal, matriarchal goddess figure, even at almost one hundred years old, accepts her place of prominence at the family reunion next to the Conservatory full of "blooming flowers" and "little waterfalls and babbling brooks and grottoes and brilliant birds" (304), as she tells the story of Kate Malone and Moses Bailey that began the novel. Smith ends her novel with an image combining flowers, waterfalls, brooks, and small caves, elements strongly linked to the goddess. As Kristeva argues, "The time may have come, in fact, to celebrate the *multiplicity* of female perspectives and preoccupations" ("Women's" 353), and in the healing reunion of the Bailey family that ends the novel, Smith offers reconciliation and hope for the reclamation of the divine nature of females and recognition of the sacredness of the feminine experience.

Chapter VII

"SWIMMING FREE ... IN AND OUT OF UNDERSEA CAVERNS"

Reconciliation with the Feminine Divine in *Saving Grace*

In *The Myth of the Goddess*, Anne Baring and Jules Cashford explain how the diminishing influence of the goddess has affected Western culture in its total absence of any "feminine dimension in the collective image of the divine," thus obliterating "contemporary experience of the archetypal feminine as a sacred entity" (660). To restore hope for women's spiritual struggle, Kathryn Rabuzzi urges women to "undo the patriarchal structures we were taught to believe in" and embrace "a realm of our own instead." According to Rabuzzi, the only path to accomplish this goal lies in finding a way "to meet the mother goddess who represents this realm" so women may recognize and accept her and thus find "atonement" (171). In her 1995 novel *Saving Grace*, Lee Smith charts the journey of Florida Grace Shepherd as she seeks the religious significance in her life. Grace, like her creator, searches for a spirituality she can embrace, a divine power that neither patronizes nor silences women. In a personal interview, Smith said she had been "skirting around the issues" of salvation for a long time and that writing this novel was a reconciliation of her deep spiritual conflict with patriarchal Christianity (Byrd 96–97). In *Saving Grace*, both Lee Smith and her protagonist achieve reconciliation with their inner sacredness by rediscovering and reclaiming the divinity in feminine experience.

Smith's previous novels have explored to varying degrees the intersection of the sacred and the sexual in the lives of Southern women. In fact, most Smith protagonists spend their lives attempting to resolve religious ambivalences. In a 1994 interview with Susan Ketchin, Smith cited Richard Burlage as a type of autobiographical character; in the novel, Richard says he travels to the mountains to "become less 'Episcopalian,' to loosen up. To listen" (53). But even though he comes face to face with the divine in his relationship with Dory, he ignores what he has heard and experienced in the mountains and leaves without having acknowledged the power of the feminine divine so linked with the mountains and nature. Ivy Rowe, however, another autobiographical character, succeeds in getting in touch with the feminine divine via her brief affair with Honey Breeding. Through her communion with the divine in this male counterpart, she embraces her sexuality to rediscover the sacred spirit within herself. In *Saving Grace*, Grace Shepherd goes a step further, in discovering self-redemption at the end of the novel. Neither her father, nor Travis Word, nor Randy Newhouse can lead her to salvation; she must find it on her own, within her own sacred, sexual body and spirit.

In writing *Saving Grace*, Smith not only saves a character from the destructive clutches of self-doubt and victimization, but she also rescues and restores to its rightful place in goddess theogony the original meaning of the word *grace*. In a 1993 interview with Claudia Loewenstein, Smith said that through her writing, she keeps searching for the kind of intense religious feeling that she associated with God that she had as a child (497). That level of vehemence, that "sense of being outside yourself" (Byrd 100), according to Smith, can only be achieved in three ways, as she explained in an interview with Susan Ketchin: "There's getting saved, sex, and writing." So for Smith, writing *is* salvation, "a way to get in touch with th[e] intensity" (51) of both religious conversion and sex. In "saving Grace," Smith also saves herself as she feverishly writes to restore divinity to the female and feminine experience.

Christians took the pagan concept of grace (the Latin term *caritas*) and worked to divest it of sexual meanings, leaving us with the term *charity*, which implies relinquishing worldly goods. The cognate *charisma* meant "Mother-given grace." Reinterpreted by patriarchal Christian theology, the "graciousness" that once connoted liberality and warm physical affection came to suggest only liberality and selflessness, qualities traditionally associated with motherhood. This meant total denial of self and sublimation to the male deity. In *Saving Grace*, Smith rescues grace from the sole context of patriarchal religion and restores to it a feminine complexity and depth that reflects the original connotation of the word: "a combination of beauty, kindness, mother-love, tenderness, sensual delight, compassion and care" (Walker, *Women's* 350–51). No scene more poignantly depicts the reclamation of "grace" in its original meaning than the one when fourteen-year-old Grace climbs to the top of Chimney Rock, stands proudly in the wind, naked to the waist, then with a sharp white rock carefully carves her name in large capital letters across the flattest spot, going over each letter repeatedly "so they would last" (59). It will be difficult for this feeling of self-possession to last for Grace. To retain the grace implicit in her name, she must reclaim her name two other times in the novel. When Randy Newhouse calls her "Missy," she immediately tells him, "My name is not 'Missy'" and informs him that it is "Grace" (223). At end of the novel as she leaves Scrabble Creek for good, she thinks, "Travis called me Missy but my name is Florida Grace" (272–73). Now, without a doubt, she knows her true identity, having discovered genuine selfhood through the power of the feminine divine.

Grace must also reclaim the "mother tongue" of the feminine divine before she can achieve salvation. Grace's sense of alienation from her father's God is largely due to the patriarchal "father tongue" of her culture and her family's Holiness religion in particular. One of the aspects of her father, Virgil Shepherd, she most loves is his ability to use language, his "beautiful deep voice which made everything true" (29). When the children are young, the family sleeps outside on pallets during the hot summers and Virgil tells stories from the Bible in his pretty "singing voice" (127). Fully aware of the power and influence of his voice, Virgil uses his gift not only to win souls to the Lord, but also to coax women to his bed. Grace describes his sonorous voice as "one of his greatest blessings from the Lord" and explains that her father had the power to make a person want to do whatever he said because he "made you feel good" (17). Even after her mother's suicide and her father's incarceration, while being well taken care of by Ruth and Carlton Duty, Grace voluntarily leaves with her father when he comes for her and her sister Billie Jean. Grace resolves, "It was his voice that did it.... I *had* to go to him then, I *had* to go with him" (116). Grace uses similar words to describe her magnetic attraction to and sexual relationship with Lamar, her half-brother who is likewise a storyteller and "the kind of boy that you have to do whatever he wants" (70), reminiscent of Ivy's description of Franklin Ransom's effect on her. Realizing that "the Holiness girl or woman does not have a voice ... she can't decide things" (99), Grace feels powerless to speak in a language reserved for males. Grace's fears of being permanently "silenced" are clear in her concern that if she looks too deeply into Lamar's eyes, she "might fall into them and be forever lost" (100), anguish that recalls Ivy's feeling of being in a deep dark hole unable to crawl out. Both women feel they are risking annihilation by not being allowed to use their voices. Grace describes love-making with her husband Travis in terms of being silenced also. She says, "he *did it to me*. For he did not like me to move much, or say anything, while he was doing it" (197). Assuming that both language and sexuality are solely the birthrights of men, she complies for years.

Patriarchal traditions have alienated women from their deepest understanding of God as Mother. Women in search of validation need to recognize the historical imbalance and restore the holiness of female embodiment and the sacredness of the feminine divine. Perhaps this unfulfilled need is why Grace never hears an answer to her prayers or feels the presence of the Father God to whom she continues to pray. Dorothy Hill insightfully observes that in Smith, "finding such a [female] language is tantamount to finding the self" (2). Thus Grace must rediscover the "mother tongue" and accept its power before she can be saved. Although Grace calls her mother a "real saint in this world" (53), the growing girl is not yet able to connect the power in her mother's sweet, soft words with the feminine divine. Grace only associates mystery and authority with her father's male-centered religion. Virgil not only possesses a voice that Grace understands to be an instrument of God, but also looks to Grace like "the God of the Old Testament" (28), with his white hair standing out around his face. In Hebrew mythology Yahweh-Elohim creates the world with his *word*, not from his body, hence the idea that all things originate from the male-owned domain of language. The Greek word *logos*, meaning *word*, refers to the theory of creation whereby the deity could create anything by the power of words: "when the name was spoken, the thing materialized" (Walker, *Women's* 545). Grace's suspicion that words spoken by her father seem to "ma[k]e everything true" (29) certainly suggests her misconception over not only her father's powers, but also the sovereignty of the patriarchal God. Walker explains that one reason why men were particularly enthusiastic about the "Logos doctrine" was that it relegated to male gods the power of creation that was "formerly the exclusive prerogative of the birth-giving Goddess."* And although male gods popularized the doctrine, Walker argues that the ability to create, destroy, and re-create by "Word-power" originally resided with the goddess, who "created languages, alphabets, and the secret mantras known as Words of Power" (*Women's* 545–46). The words that ultimately empower Grace come not from God, or her father, or her preacher-husband Travis Word, whom she marries in a subconscious effort to possess the "Word," the language of divine male power. These words come from her mother, whose "wavery voice" hangs in the "hot still air like the butterflies over the flowers" (28) as she appears to her daughter in a dream and whispers, "*Come to me, Gracie*" (269), inviting Grace to end her search for affirmation outside herself and accept the sacredness within.

Not only did patriarchal religion rob the female deity of her original powers of creation through language, but it also withdrew her ability to breathe forth life. In ancient times, people believed that the mother gave her child both its name and soul, along with its first nourishment, "as she breathed a Word that would henceforth define and personify the child." In fact, the biblical Yahweh claimed to give life by the power of his breath or "wind" (Walker, *Women's* 546–47). Smith says that for her, writing has the same intensity as religion, and that giving over to it is like being caught up in a "whirlwind" of inspiration (Ketchin 50). Inspiration is defined as inhalation, breathing, or the power of moving the intellect or emotions. As Smith breathes life into her stories and characters, she eliminates the subordination and devaluation of

---

*Walker explains how "Hermes-the-Logos" became "Hermes-the-Creator," appropriating "magic feminine powers" from living in "androgynous union with Mother Aphrodite" (*Women's* 545).

women and allows their inner sacredness to emerge in settings filled with wind and breath imagery that strongly connects to the earliest goddess religions. In the subordination and eventual elimination of female deities in cosmogenesis, representations of breath and wind were erased from feminine association. Of particular interest are the earliest creation stories in which the primal Mother, or "Mother of the Gods" as well as of the cosmos, parthenogenetically produces successive generations of gods and goddesses who represent first Heaven and earth, then sea and air, then various aspects of the agricultural and urban domains (Ruether, *Womanguides* 38). Over a period of centuries of patriarchal revision, the original maternal goddess gradually lost her power, and wind, air, and breath, like language, were relegated to the Hebrew Yahweh.

In Smith's imagery, these primal forces related to the air we breathe are restored to a feminine domain. The presence of the feminine divine as marked by the wind, the source of inspiration, accompanies every crucial moment in Grace's life, as it has done for several of Smith's characters. As she struggles to come to know a God she can neither understand nor accept, she repeatedly feels ignored and rejected, but she fails to recognize the presence of the feminine divine represented by the wind. In the significant symbolic ritual mentioned above, Grace describes Chimney Rock as essentially "two huge boulders perched on top of ... [a] cliff," where there are "miles and miles of nothing but sky and mountains" and "the wind ... always bl[ows]." Sacred mountains and hills were revered up until the twentieth century, and the goddess was celebrated on mountain summits crowned with large stones since stones were believed to possess the goddess's magical healing powers. Grace's first unconscious celebration of her inner sacredness occurs in just such a location. Standing in a "windy place of flat table rocks" bathed in sunshine, Grace takes deep breaths of cold air that make "my blood race all through my body," the blood's coursing suggesting spiritual movement that makes new life possible. Then Grace removes her jacket and shirt and takes her hair down, hair symbolizing the soul, and "let[s] the wind blow my hair all around" (56–58). The naked goddess with her blonde hair forming a halo presents a potent image not unlike the one of Ivy Rowe standing nude on the mountaintop with Honey Breeding.

In this symbolic setting, Grace feels empowered and seems receptive to the presence of feminine divine. As she stands on a rock, Grace looks up to see "three hawks swooping great circles," a divine image reminiscent of three crucial scenes in *Fair and Tender Ladies* strategically placed at the beginning, middle, and end of the novel. In a setting drenched with goddess imagery, Grace feels like she has grown and is now larger than life. No longer worried about what her friend Marie might be doing today, Grace knows she can "do anything" with the "wind fe[eling] great on my chest and my back" (58). The full power of the feminine divine resides within the young Grace as she carves her name on the top of Chimney Rock before descending to the reality of her difficult and painful life. As she climbs over the table rocks on her way down the mountain, Grace desires "any sign of God or Jesus." But she reports, "I didn't see a thing but the bright cold day, and I didn't feel a thing but the hard rough rocks beneath my hands and the wind and the sun on my face" (60). Her senses are attuned to the signs of nature that signal the presence of the feminine divine, but the glorious revelation she expects from the patriarchal God eludes her.

The presence of the feminine divine again surrounds Grace at the church's Homecoming celebration when she allows herself to be taken over by a feeling of sacredness. The "little breeze" that begins to blow seems immediately to transform the "tone" of everyone's voices (97). As though possessing divine powers, Grace detects a connection among all humankind as the people appear "naked and new" to her; she explains, "I felt like I was seeing everybody for the first time, and yet I felt I'd known them all forever and ever too, as if they were part of me" (101). As Grace becomes caught up in the ecstatic singing, swaying and dancing, she feels "the Spirit running through me like a grass fire" (105). The frenzied dancing of the congregation in the "big circle cast by the light," accompanied by the "wind [coming] off the river and mov[ing] through the trees" (103), suggests the ecstatic mountaintop dancing, often performed near lakes or springs, of ancient goddess worship, ring dancing being particularly popular. Rituals embody the nonrational, physical side of religion, "putting us in the presence of the body and blood..., song and dance, sexuality and ecstasy" (Christ 77). During this ritual, Grace recognizes the divine quality of the wind; she thinks "all of a sudden that it was God's breath ... touching the leaves, and ... each one of us." She feels transformed, loving and accepting of each "beautiful" face around her as she finds herself "caught up and held in something beautiful and solemn and grand" (103). With the breeze caressing her face, she says the "holy wind ... blew around and touched us every one" (105).

This similarly ecstatic experience, though Grace is not alone this time, links to Grace's earlier mountaintop ritual when she emanated her inner sacredness. Grace's words of prophecy on the night of the Homecoming further illustrate the relevance of the divinely inspired wind. Although no one will tell her exactly what she said when she was "possessed of the Spirit," upon Grace's insistence, Carlton Duty finally relates to her that she "was talking about the wind ... and then about the Devil." Within Grace's subconscious, the feminine divine battles the guilt and despair threatening to overtake the young girl's soul. At the knowledge of having spoken in tongues, the primal, rhythmic, babbling discourse that Kristeva terms the semiotic, the "mother tongue," Grace feels "something sho[o]t through me, from the top of my head to my feet." However, similar to Katie Cocker, Grace can only understand religious ecstasy in terms of the Holiness religion. Frightened by the sense of power she has experienced, she divorces her subconscious from her conscious mind: "*I don't have anything to do with this, just forget it,*" she screams (107–108). Barbara Walker's comments concerning speaking in tongues add a touch of irony to Grace's experience. Walker asserts that in goddess religions, glossolalia often occurred during episodes of "religious ecstasy" and usually connoted the presence of "divine grace" or "temporary possession by the divine spirit" (*Women's* 956–57). Grace's ecstatic religious experience and "speaking in tongues" powerfully evoke the grace of the feminine divine.

Smith also provides signs of the feminine divine during Grace's relationship with and marriage to Travis Word, but again she is left unfulfilled since she looks to him and his strong faith, rather than inside herself, for salvation. While talking to Travis, Grace feels the "soft cool breeze blow on my neck," but instead of interpreting this stimulus as evidence of divine inner strength and power, she mistakes this sensation for a sign that she needs a man, a replacement for her father who has vanished with the church funds and the red-headed witch-like Carlean Combs. And what better man than another preacher, a genuine one this time? Grace fails to understand that when she approaches Travis and he "suck[s] in his breath" (167) and moves away, this behavior serves as an early indication of his inability to express the physical love that she so desperately needs, and also provides an interesting contrast to the inspirational wind that *blows* (rather than "sucks in"). In a setting rife with goddess imagery, next to a beautiful stream "rippled by the breeze" (173), Grace thinks she will "jump right out of my skin" (171), as her libido heightens. Allowing her ebullience to escape, Grace unashamedly exposes her breasts to Travis just as Red Emmy does with Almarine, Dory with Richard, Ivy with Honey, and Nonnie with Zeke. As on the mountaintop, Grace displays her acceptance of and sensual delight in her body. Although horrified, the puritanical Travis "d[oes] not close his eyes" and shouts, "Lord God Almighty!" (174), like earlier male characters acknowledging, if humorously and unconsciously, the sacredness of the female before him. And again, when he sees Grace in her wedding dress, he tells her she looks "like an angel" (177). Ironically, however, Travis cannot accept divinity in the flesh. Grace describes her feelings for Travis as "worshipp[ing] him" (179) since she considers him her savior.

Grace encounters a mystical presence that evokes the feminine divine in a poignant scene that serves to warn her of a future life of unfulfillment if she persists in her refusal to claim her inner sacredness and selfhood. After years of a marriage to Travis, the care of two young daughters, and a miscarriage, Grace has sunk to a level of despair not unlike Ivy's "dark hole." While visiting Travis Jr.'s grave, Grace decides, "for no particular reason," to go inside the Tabernacle where she receives a portentous vision of her life. She explains when she entered the church, a big gust of wind accompanied her as she saw "a shadowy girl ... moving through the Tabernacle like a ghost." First the female materialized accompanied by "her shadow husband and shadow children"; then, after appearing alone for a moment, the woman "was gone, all gone, nothing left of her but a little mist in the sanctuary" (211–12). The implication that Grace is a ghost, not even alive, directly reflects her current situation, in which Grace's inability to claim her own identity, sexuality, and inner sacredness evinces a sense of death. She lives a life of definition through others, especially her husband and her children, the epitome of Irigaray's "paralyzed and enclosed" woman ("Questions" 138), masquerading to provide herself with a protective skin by "envelop[ing]" herself "in the needs/desires/fantasies" of others (136). The powerful wind of the goddess ushers in Grace's divinely-inspired vision that serves as the impetus for a monumental change in her life.

After a marriage that demanded she live only in the spirit and deny the flesh, Grace must now reclaim her sexuality as another step toward self-redemption. At age thirty-three and after fifteen years of marriage, she allows her physical passion to take control as she is "born again" (225) through an extramarital affair with a painter and part-time rock-singer, Randy Newhouse. On the night before her first sexual encounter with Randy, Grace once more seeks spiritual guidance from the God of her father and husband. Standing in the yard "in the cold blowing wind," she asks "Jesus out loud to help me, to give me some sign not to go over there [to meet Randy], but He didn't do a thing. Nothing. The wind kept on blowing." Just as Grace had sought God and been denied on Chimney Rock, she now feels abandoned and desperate as she cries out to a God who doesn't seem to speak her language or care about her at all. And as before, the only detectable force is the wind, as Smith once again counters the totally male-based religion of convention. Perhaps Grace subconsciously acknowledges the female deity since she admits to a power beyond herself demanding she express her long-suppressed sexuality: "the fact is, I was going to do what I was going to do long before I even knew I was going to do it" (222–23).With this conundrum, Smith suggests a visceral force within Grace impelling her to follow her instincts and embrace her sacred sexuality. Just as she had substituted Travis for her father, she now replaces Travis with Randy in another effort to find salvation outside herself, this time through the physical world of sex.

Grace describes her first encounter with Randy as being "in slow motion, as if it was meant to be," phrases reminiscent of the first meetings of earlier pairs. As the "long shaggy blond hair[ed]" Randy arrives at Grace's home to begin his painting job, Grace sits on the porch in a glider, "hover[ing] on the air ... like I might just stand up and walk out into the universe" (213–14). However, rather than accepting her inner sanctity and the potential divinity in her life—rather than standing up and walking out into the universe on her own—Grace, starved for physical passion, once more mistakes the "electric shock" (219) Randy arouses in her body for the passion of salvation. Just as she had felt transformed by the ecstasy she experienced at the Homecoming,

Grace feels energized, "sizzling ... on fire" after she spends an afternoon in the dark, cave-like motel room with her new lover. Like Ivy's desire to remain in the cave forever with Honey Breeding "living on love," Grace, overcome with the passion she has craved, admits, "I would have stayed in that room forever. I would have told Travis ... any lie. I would do *anything.*" As she drives home with the windows down, "fresh air streaming in," she shouts, "Glory hallelujah!" (225). Once more, she thinks she's been saved and moves on to another stage in her growth toward self-redemption, deserting her husband and children to live with Randy.

The absence of any judgment or condemnation of Grace on Smith's part disturbs some readers and critics; the 1995 *Publishers Weekly* review of the novel calls Smith's characterization of Grace "shallow" and "less successful than usual in winning sympathy for her flawed heroine," and adds that Grace's abandonment of her children seems "implausible" (74). Readers who accept this disparaging portrait of Grace and demand that a "good mother" suppress her sexuality (if she has any) and remain with her children, choosing a life of sacrifice, perhaps fall victim to society's false scission between maternity and expressed sexuality. Smith explained that many people are trapped by their "stereotypical" expectations and are "conditioned" to see a mother's desertion in a certain way, as an "either/or" situation. "She wouldn't leave with a lover and be a good mother. She can't do both," according to the paradigm (Byrd 110). With Grace, Smith images a divine female who must, in order to achieve wholeness, experience and express both her motherhood and her sexuality.

Nancy Chodorow argues that a woman learns her female role identity from her mother through "a personal identification with her mother's general traits of character and values" (51). In leaving her children and an unsatisfying marriage, Grace breaks from the model of behavior provided by her mother and demonstrates completely different values and traits of character. Grace refuses to allow her story to end the way her mother's did—in suicide. In an interview, Smith discussed the conflicts for women regarding religion, motherhood, and sexuality, observing that today the alternatives for women are greater. Smith acknowledged the deep conflict for women that is "misunderstood and condemned because people don't have a frame of reference to put it into" (Byrd 110). Providing Grace with a choice quite different from her mother's, Smith continues expanding the possibilities for women in their spiritual journeys. When Grace is waiting for Randy to arrive to take her with him permanently, she sits in the glider on the porch just as she had done when Randy first came to the Word house. Once again, the imagery of the feminine divine surfaces as Grace "hover[s] on the air," watching a beautiful sunset over the mountain. "I felt like I was seeing everything with brand-new eyes," she says, as she "trembled on the breeze, waiting for Randy Newhouse" (230). Nevertheless, the salvation Grace anticipates will not emanate from Randy Newhouse, though the expression of her libido is necessary for Grace.

She must restore that part of herself that has been disowned, reviled, and feared in order to meet the divine completely, and sexuality is only one way to spiritual and physical satisfaction. Grace must learn to experience the power of the erotic in all areas of her life.

Smith insists on the interrelatedness of sexual passion and religious passion; one cannot exist without the other. In *When God Was a Woman*, Merlin Stone emphasizes the sacredness of sex in ancient religions found in many areas of the Near and Middle East. Sex was considered "holy and precious," and "the Goddess was revered as the patron deity of sexual love." Stone explains how modern religions defile sexual acts, especially those outside of marriage, which they label "naughty, dirty, even sinful" (154–55). In traditional Christianity, a person is asked to renounce the physical world that is full of temptation and sin, in favor of the spiritual world that promises salvation (Ketchin 48). Thus, the sensual is effectively separated from the spiritual, the body from the mind.*

Travis Word, a victim of just such a dichotomized way of thinking, has effectively severed his mind from his body. Accepting traditional and largely unquestioned ideas about God as a disembodied mind or spirit, totally transcendent of the world, Travis views the human body as a symbol of imperfection, corruption, and base physicality. Ruether notes, "the hierarchy of spirit over body is expressed in the dominion of males over females" (*New Woman* 189), and Rita Gross concurs that men are traditionally believed to be spiritually superior to women, who are grounded in the physical body (*Feminism* 106). The Bible verse John 1:1 states not only that "the Word [was] with God," but also, "the Word was made flesh and dwelt among us." So the Word must first become flesh in order to become spirit, and "sexual fulfillment is one stage of a woman's journey for spiritual fulfillment" (Yow 12). Smith's careful choice of Travis Word's name, the "Word" but a man of flesh and blood, emphasizes this puritanical preacher's significance. Unable to accept the human body as a channel to receive and emit divine energy or recognize God's presence in sexual ecstasy as well as prayer, Travis is tortured by a past experience in the Navy when he says he "succumbed to the desires of the flesh" (168). Afraid he possesses an unholy sexual appetite, he deprives both himself and Grace of the sexual fulfillment necessary for the survival of their marriage by completely divorcing the sexual from the sacred.

Due to Travis's inability to integrate the spiritual and the corporeal, his life is tortured and unfulfilled and eventually ends in violent suicide, as Grace has foreseen. After sexual relations on their wedding night, Grace says, "it was like a great dam had given way in his soul. He could not get enough, nor do enough." After their love-making, Travis drops to his knees and urges Grace

---

*This dichotomy between mind and body, the spiritual and the sensual, is also true of traditional Western philosophical traditions, not just religion.

to "come to Jesus" as he quotes from the book of Romans about "our sinful passions working in our members to bear fruit for death." Next, he attempts to purify them for the sexual act they have committed, explaining, "the mind that is set on the flesh is hostile to God; it does not submit to God's law, indeed it cannot; and those who are in the flesh cannot please God" (188). Christian ethicist Beverly Harrison expresses the fallacy of a belief system like Travis': "All knowledge is rooted in our sensuality," and "feeling is the basic bodily ingredient that mediates our connectedness to the world." Harrison goes on to argue that all power of any kind is "rooted in feeling," and to reject that truth negates the existence of God and ensures our own destruction because one must *sense* in order to *feel* (218). Grace cannot believe in or accept Travis' God, who denies the bodily passion she enjoys. Although Travis is, like Jesus, the "Word" made flesh, he rejects the physical and sexual dimension of his existence, ultimately driving Grace to an adulterous affair, which she calls "the worst sin a woman can commit" (222). And because she is so starved for physical passion, she admits to having little difficulty making the decision to be unfaithful. "[M]emorizing" Randy's body (224), she immerses herself in the ecstasy of expressed sexuality. Grace, like other of Smith's female characters, cannot differentiate between sexual passion and religious fervor. Her sexual relationship with Randy Newhouse takes her out of her self much like her mountaintop experience and the Homecoming ritual. As Smith comments at the end of the novel, religious ecstasy—and, one might add, sacred sexuality—seem to be "when we are most truly 'out of ourselves' and experience the Spirit directly" (Notes).

Like earlier goddess figures who share similar ecstatic experiences, Grace is closely aligned with nature and wildness as opposed to culture and domesticity. The goddess as an incarnation of the mysterious powers of nature and her dominion over its forces helps to explain the significance of nature in Smith's work. In goddess worship, every part of nature is suffused with deity. In her influential essay "Is Female to Male as Nature Is to Culture?" anthropologist Sherry Ortner argues that the devaluation of women is directly linked to women's being identified with nature. Every culture, according to Ortner, asserts itself to be superior to nature, and men are associated with culture or the triumph over nature (71–73). Smith's writing seeks to subvert this preconception as she portrays women's links to nature as liberating and empowering forces. Ortner's contention assumes that domesticity has necessarily accompanied women's link with nature and therefore remains the realm of the female (77). In her portrayal of sacred females, Smith consistently associates wildness, not domesticity, with nature, and instead, culture relates more to domesticity.

The connection between a woman's reproductive system and a domestic role is not a necessary one, but rather one that culture has imposed and most have accepted, as Grace does initially. Grace says that parturition comes "natural" for her and that the days of young motherhood are like "paradise" and seem to "stretch out full and golden, and last forever" (193). Like Nonnie of *The Devil's Dream*, however, Grace soon becomes "idle and restless" (190) with her domestic existence. She explains, "sometimes, something would happen to make me come up gasping for air" (195). Perhaps the breath for which she gasps is the acceptance and validation represented by the feminine divine. When Travis sinks into a deep depression after Grace's miscarriage, Grace wants "to run around and act up and smash things." She says, "I scared myself" (200). As Hélène Cixous argues, when the repressed female finally emerges, "it's an explosive, *utterly* destructive, staggering return, with a force never yet unleashed and equal to the most forbidding of suppressions" (256). Having remained silent and quelled her sexuality for so many years after deciding it was useless to try to tempt Travis, Grace says that finally "my true nature came out" (197). Her sexuality, or what she describes as wildness, demands expression.

Grace's alignment with wildness occurs early in the novel. Grace describes herself as a "daredevil" (82), taking unnecessary risks in her sexual relationship with Lamar. Like both Ivy and Nettie, Grace associates maleness with freedom and power and therefore envies Lamar's apparent liberation. She wonders why she is so filled with energy, curiosity, and sensuality while her sister Billie Jean never desires to "run down the hill or up the mountain or *anywhere* out in the world at all, like me." A wild, free spirit attuned to nature, Grace possesses sharp senses and a vivid imagination. As a young teenager standing among a grove of dogwood trees, she explains, "then I *was* the blossoms, all blossom—me, Gracie. I drew in great sweet breaths." With her skin rubbing against the fabric of her blouse, she feels she has "grown new nerves" as she rushes out to her secret, private spot, the tobacco barn, where she "stand[s] in the sweet dusky stillness" (77–79), her sensuality intensified. Strong physical sensations repeatedly make Grace feel alive, "real again" (96). A hot car seat burning the back of her legs, "scratchy seat covers" biting into her back (106), and ridges on a chenille bedspread pressing into her body, all anchor Grace in the physical world, reminding her that salvation must come through acknowledgment and acceptance of both the sensual/sexual and the spiritual, complexes that are implicit in the feminine divine. In consoling Grace about her angst, the wise old surrogate mother Ruth Duty, assuming that most of Grace's life choices have been mistakes, tells Grace, "You ain't bad, honey. You have just got too much nature, that's all" (261), meaning too much libido. Ironically, however, it is only through Grace's reclamation of her sexuality, her inner sacredness and connection to nature, that she achieves salvation in the end, or rather saves herself.

As in earlier novels, Smith's use of water and cave imagery throughout the novel suggests the presence of the maternal, sexual goddess and the mysterious life-creating moisture of her womb from which all life emerges. The only home that Grace ever really calls her own is the one near Scrabble Creek, and almost half the novel is devoted to the seven years her family lived here, a period Grace calls the happiest time of her life. Their meager four-room house sits beside Scrabble Creek, which runs down a steep mountain "in a line of little waterfalls," each with its own pool at the bottom (12). When Grace makes her ritualistic journey past the streams to the top of the mountain and carves her name on Chimney Rock, she describes a difficult passage through "a laurel slick where it was dark and steep, almost a tunnel," and when she comes out on the other side, she comments, "but it was all worth it" (57). Goddess mythology suggests that the act of crawling through a dark, cave-like area represents a process of renewal, initiation, strengthening; furthermore, the foliage of the laurel tree is traditionally an emblem of victory or distinction. It is after Grace passes through this tunnel-like area that she reaches the summit of the mountain and stands with arms folded and feet apart, looking out over the scenery pretending she owns "mountain after mountain" (58), a goddess in her own right. This empowering experience for Grace occurs on a mountain bathed in sacred, life-giving water. Never feeling "like a sinner girl" (84), Grace shares with Lamar the special places that evoke the feminine divine, taking him to the caves up on the mountain and to the limestone spring, but she never takes him to the very top, to Chimney Rock where her name is carved. Carol Christ notes that in our culture, caves often elicit fear since they are places of mystery. She adds that in patriarchal cultures, the darkness of the womb, or the cave, symbolizes "women's irrationality, ignorance, and deceitfulness" and suggests death more than regeneration. Christ asserts, "to reclaim the darkness is thus to reclaim the female body" (96–97). In taking Lamar to the mountain cave and springs, Grace attempts to initiate him into the world of divine feminine experience where female sexuality is sacred and natural, but the highest spot on Chimney Rock remains her own. In the biggest pool formed by Scrabble Creek, Lamar coaxes Grace into the water with him although Holiness girls are not allowed to swim. However, as a young girl with little parental supervision, she had experienced a "great thrill" when she went "all the way down under the cold rushing stream" (12). While floating on her back in the pool with Lamar, Grace senses a tremendous feeling of freedom from the constraints of a patriarchal God who denies sensual pleasure; she explains, "I felt ... as if I didn't even have a body ... like Lamar and me were both boys together." Grace's thinking reflects the tenet of patriarchal religion that associates male with spirit and female with body. Being female no longer restricts Grace as she lies suspended on the water, mentally abandoning her physical body temporarily. Infused with the concentrated life-power of the feminine divine, represented by the water, Grace delights in the essence of her sacredness as her hair drifts out around her head "like the rays of the sun" (84), forming a bright halo.

Water again offers sustenance and the will to survive when, locked in a small cave-like room in Carlean Combs' trailer thinking she might be insane, Grace imagines herself as a fish peacefully swimming around in an aquarium. Then, listening to the sound of raindrops hitting the metal roof, she says, "I ... let go of everything until I was swimming free, beyond the aquarium, in and out of undersea caverns through shafts of light" (148). Grace's imagination takes her to a sense of feminine sacredness, "in and out of ... caverns," places Carol Christ calls centers of "deep nonverbal communication" with the goddess (51). When Grace is released from her physical entrapment (her father unlocks the door and vanishes with Carlean), she rushes "out into the dark, wet woods," breathing in deep gulps of "cool sweet" air (149). This gesture reinforces both Grace's connection with nature and her wildness. Ironically, when Travis Word arrives at the trailer, concerned for Grace's welfare, she considers herself "saved" by him. But Smith's imagery suggests something quite different. With Travis there, Grace notices "the air had gotten too thick for me to walk through, like I was walking underwater," not swimming freely, as before. Travis' suffocating presence is further indicated by Grace's comment that she tried to say something, but with Travis, "I couldn't talk right either" (155). Travis, a man of God's "Word," robs her of language, the "mother tongue," and she is temporarily cut off from any sense of the feminine divine.

Smith consistently associates Grace's mother, a goddess figure sacrificed to patriarchal religion, with water and nature imagery. The "happy sound of Scrabble Creek" (12) always reminds Grace of her mother's voice, which she describes as sounding like "running water" (3). Similar to earlier divine females, Fannie is linked to flowers (particularly roses) and honeysuckle, and butterflies "flutter around her" (7); her voice hangs in the air "like butterflies" (28). The butterfly as symbolic of transformation and rebirth is a matter of tautology, but interesting to note is that the butterfly continues to represent the soul in many lands. In fact, in Greek the word for butterfly and soul were the same— *psyche*. Over eight thousand years ago, the caterpillar and the butterfly suggested the existence of two aspects to a single life-form—one born from the other—thus representing "the regeneration of life from an outworn form and, analogously, the survival of the soul after the death of the body" (Baring and Cashford 73). This information offers further insight into Grace's relationship to her mother when viewed metaphorically. It is only through Grace's long dead mother (specifically her voice which is directly compared to butterflies) that Grace experiences the transformation necessary for self-redemption. Grace is literally "born out of" her mother, obviously, but in her reclamation of her inner sacredness at her mother's urging, Grace abandons the "outworn form" of traditional Christianity and ensures new life for herself. Reminiscent of other sexual females in Smith, described as being "as fragile as a moth" and possessing "fluttering hands" (93), Fannie Flowers, as her name suggests, is lovely "in spirit as well as flesh" (3). However, Fannie lacks the volition and/or ability to integrate the two and claim a selfhood of her own. Grace tells us,

"Daddy was all her life" (94). Even after her mother's suicide when Grace leaves her beloved home, she can still "hear the musical waters of Scrabble Creek," like her mother's "soft good-night kiss on my cheek" (118). Throughout her life, Grace continues to feel her mother's presence in nature, often represented by a "stream of air" (183) or the sweet smell of flowers.

Not until the end of the novel when Grace, now over forty, completes her journey and returns to Scrabble Creek is she ready to listen to her mother's voice. For many years, Grace has put her mother "in another place" in her mind (97), much as Susan Tobey does. Grace had disclaimed her inherited "gift of discernment" (15) when she arrived home to find her mother's dead body hanging in the barn, and again when the "March wind" left her "shaky and breathless" (211) just before she met Randy Newhouse. Nor Hall calls the gift of discernment a distinguishing characteristic of the archetypal image of the "medial feminine," In an earlier novel, with her depiction of Crystal Spangler, Smith had dallied with this archetype, but in the full development of Grace Shepherd, the author further explores the "embodiment of specific powers of transformation that have been called magical, spiritual, and psychic" (161). This female possesses the ability to foresee change and discern life's mysteries. Extremely threatened by the archetype of the medial feminine, many cultures condemn or simply deny it since it attributes to women strength far beyond the conventions of mere femininity. By bestowing this particularly feminine gift upon Grace, Smith adds further mythic dimensions to her protagonist and emphasizes her liminal nature. Only when Grace reaches her lowest point "both spiritually and physically" and the "cold wind hit me in the face like a fist" (245) does the feminine divine again manifest in order to "save" Grace. Traveling back toward her childhood home, Grace allows "the sharp clear air [to] fill my lungs," feeling "suddenly, completely *alive* in a new way" (253). Back at the old homeplace at Scrabble Creek, she drinks the sweet water from the creek and focuses on "the fruits of the spirit" (268). In ancient initiation rituals, the initiate must drink from the stream of "forgetfulness" in order to leave the past behind, then from the stream of "memory" in order to remember and integrate his/her experience into everyday life. In drinking from the creek, Grace accomplishes both tasks as she patiently awaits rebirth and the redemption offered through reconnection with both her biological mother and her spiritual mother. Grace has "liv[ed] a lie with Travis," worshipping him for what she perceived as his sainthood, and "worshipp[ed] flesh and the things of the world with Randy Newhouse" (266).

Now Grace must find the divine within herself, not through the physical or spiritual touch of another. At the urging of her mother's whispers, Grace proudly walks nude across the floor of the old homeplace, the naked goddess unifying flesh and spirit as she listens to what Hélène Cixous calls the "equivoice," the "mother" who "launches your force" that is "no more describable than god, the soul, or the Other" (252), allowing Grace to reconnect to the feminine divine. Grace thinks, "Among true believers we find the Word" (269), but now she knows the Word was first made flesh, and a sexual woman must find that fulfillment before she finds redemption. When Grace feels the Spirit enter her body, she describes it as a "blow to the top of my head ... run[ning] all over my body like lightning." Driven by a divine force, she reaches into the stove to pick up hot coals, just as her mother had done many years before, describing the sensation as "a joy which spreads all through my body" (271). Alone, "unsaved" in the traditional Christian sense, Grace has reclaimed the feminine divine in an ecstatic experience and found within herself a source of strength. Smith discussed her feelings of terror at "that sort of giving over" involved in ecstatic religious experience, comparing rebirth to "annihilation" and the loss of identity. With Grace, Smith said what she was really doing was "acting out." Writing the book was "a way to go with Grace on this particular journey without having to do it myself" (Byrd 97). But Grace is not annihilated, nor does she lose her self in reconnecting with the divine. The last halo-like image of her with her hair brushed "all out like a cloud around my head" (270) leaving the old homeplace with a declaration of her name, her "grace," certainly creates an alternate ending for the story of her mother's life. Before her departure, Grace takes final possession of her story and her life with the affirmation, "this is the story of light[,] Mama, this is the story of snow" (272), letting her mother know that *her* journey to salvation is now complete.

The journey on which Grace and earlier female protagonists (such as Katie Cocker, Ivy Rowe, and *Oral History*'s Sally) embark is not the "prototypical male heroic journey" that Smith says is "unsatisfactory for women" (Byrd 105), but rather a circular one. In a personal interview, Smith said that she knew when she first began writing the novel that Grace's "journey to salvation" would have to be a "circle," would have to end where it began (96), and the setting Smith creates is permeated with imagery of the feminine divine, at Scrabble Creek on the mountainside with running streams of water. The symbolic system of the feminine divine represents not linear, but cyclical—mythical—time; perhaps this is why Smith says she finds it impossible to write about women's lives "in a linear way with some prize to be plucked at the end" (114). Thus Grace ends her narrative as Ivy and Katie before her concluded theirs, at "home," where she began her journey. She has completed the circle and achieved integration and self-acceptance. In her influential essay, "Women's Time," Julia Kristeva labels linear temporality "masculine" and "obsessional," noting that "female subjectivity" offers a measurement of time that is cyclical and "essentially retains *repetition* and *eternity*," having "so little to do with linear time that the very term 'temporality' seems inappropriate" (352–54). Gracie's circular journey follows Rabuzzi's prescription for transformation in allowing this woman's body and spirit "to become one" in a moment of "mystic communion" (77) with the goddess. Surely the epigraph for *Saving Grace*, taken from T.S. Eliot's "Little Gidding," a paean to traditional Christian salvation, subverts male-dominated religion and serves as a challenge to all women to "not cease from exploration" until we "arrive where we started/And know the place for the first time." Perhaps, as Carol Christ suggests, with increasing knowledge and acceptance of ancient goddess religions and cultures, "we [may] begin to understand that we do not have to live as we do today: in cultures that worship one male God, where the domination and control of women, the earth, and other people are taken for granted" (69). As Grace comes full circle, she stands as Smith's full embodiment of the feminine divine.

Chapter VIII

"PRAYING STRAIGHT INTO THE WIND"

The Sacred Circular Journey in *The Last Girls*

In *Women and Spirituality*, theologian Carol Ochs posits that the journey metaphor employed to describe traditional spirituality falls painfully short in expressing women's spiritual experience. Suggesting an alternative metaphor, Ochs offers the term "walk" to represent a woman's spiritual life since the goal of a walk "lies in the way of living and relating, doing and being," rather than progressing along a specified route toward a predetermined destination (113). Ochs goes on to explain that the walk differs from the journey much as cyclical time contrasts with linear time (113–14). Although in her tenth novel, *The Last Girls* (2002), Lee Smith takes a group of four women down the Mississippi River on an ostensible linear journey, the book teems with stories of women's circular paths. The trip may best be viewed as a walk, in terms of these middle-aged women's lives of "doing and being."

Smith populates the novel, her first after the spiritual reconciliation achieved in *Saving Grace*, with strong female characters who, like their predecessors in Smith's earlier works, exhibit qualities that link them to the feminine divine. Smith commented after the completion of *Saving Grace*, "I don't think really that I'll be setting many more things in the mountains, or at least not in the mountains and back in time" (Byrd 103).* In her fiction, Smith has already journeyed back to the mountains and explored their link to the feminine divine, fully integrating sexuality, maternity, creativity, and spirituality within one female. Like Ivy Rowe, Smith's female characters in *The Last Girls* "go through a heroic journey on [their] own turf and on [their] own terms" (107). Initially planning to write a nonfiction book about going down the Mississippi River on a raft, Smith abandoned the idea when she realized "the jour-

---

*With the writing of On Agate Hill, Smith changed her mind, but only after ten years.

ney doesn't even work as a plot anymore in my writing." She explained that women's lives, in their circularity, differ greatly from those of men. Discarding the whole journey motif in describing women's experiences, Smith admitted, "the notion of the journey doesn't conform.... It's very American.... It's very male..., the heroic quest. But I just don't think it works for women" (105–106). Women need another type model to follow, one that draws on the feminine divine in her circularity and relation to cyclical time. In the novel, gracefully shifting from present to past, Smith explores the various paths by which women journey, or "walk," through life. The tales of the women's pasts are tangled and complex, rife with accounts of their college days in the 1960s prefeminist South, along with more recent stories of love affairs, marriages and divorces, infidelities, health crises, career choices, and even hidden desires. The plot is challenging and non-linear, an honest portrayal of the way girls grow into women and struggle with their own validation.

Smith originally planned for the book to serve as a follow-up and re-examination of her 1966 personal experience during which she and fifteen other female students at Hollins College in Virginia, after reading *Adventures of Huckleberry Finn* in class, decided to take a raft trip. They sailed down the Mississippi River from Paducah, Kentucky, to New Orleans, on a raft they built themselves. Although Smith had considered interviewing the original women who made the trip to find out how their life journeys had unfolded, she decided against it, realizing that she would be forced to write a "sanitized" version. Making the decision to avoid revealing the painful details of this group of women's lives over the last thirty plus years and refusing to adhere to a linear journey, Smith landed on a brilliant idea: she fictionalized the trip. The novel would explore the reunion of four of the raft's passengers thirty-five years later.

Having sold over a hundred thousand copies, *The Last Girls* has been received with great enthusiasm by the popular reading public and literary critics alike. Modest about the attention, Smith attributes much of the book's success to effective marketing. Since the book was marketed as a "feel good" novel that would fit into the popular women's fiction mold, some readers were upset and felt cheated that the ending of the novel fails to provide complete resolution. Just as in her earlier work (*Family Linen*) she had been experimenting with the conventions of the mystery novel, in *The Last Girls*, Smith toys with the conventions of the romance novel. However, in a romance novel, everything is supposed to work out and be resolved at the end. For this reason, Smith has a problem with genre fiction with its insistence on endings that make readers feel good. She says she is "totally unable to give" this to her readers, that life is full of uncertainties and pain and when we reach a particular point in life, "all the things that you think of as the certainties suddenly come into question in a way that you never thought they would" (qtd. in Tebbetts 56).

What Lee Smith has boldly accomplished in this novel falls nothing short of a complete revision and rewriting of the myth of the American hero's journey. While the real-life experience of the raft trip, inspired by the reading of *Huckleberry Finn*, served as the genesis for Smith's imaginative journey, the "last girls" of the novel also receive encouragement from their college English teacher. Harriet explains how Mr. Gaines enlightened them: "Huck—their inspiration—was an American Odysseus off on an archetypal journey, the oldest plot of all. According to the archetype, the traveler learns something about himself along the way" (21). Thus, a group of female students, both historically and fictionally, embarked on the hero's quest—a journey to knowledge of self. Ironically, however, this first raft trip proved its value only as the first step in these young women's lives. Reflecting on the initial journey, Harriet decides that they didn't learn much. The ostensibly linear river journey, however, impelled the classmates on their many and diverse journeys—circular life journeys—that return over and over again to moments and memories, gathering meaning with each new circle and over time changing tenor with new perspectives.

Feminist critics have long pointed out that *Huckleberry Finn* fails miserably in accurately representing the classic American hero's journey. Using the same river made famous by Twain's masterpiece, Smith subverts the prototypical male heroic journey. On the Acknowledgements page of *The Last Girls*, Smith explains, "the idea of river journey as metaphor for the course of women's lives has intrigued me for years." With this raw material, Smith effectively "lights out for new territory," offering a new mythology that recognizes and honors the female in her sacred circularity. Smith has replaced the young male American hero with four (actually five) middle-aged American women and endowed them with the supreme knowledge that there exist "no beginning and no end" to the "real story" (363). The classmates had embarked on that first raft trip thirty-five years ago expecting "to be taken care of. Nobody had yet suggested to them that they might have to make a living or that somebody wouldn't marry them and look after them the rest of their lives" (18). Now, the "last girls," all in their fifties, know or at least suspect, as Smith acknowledged, that "each person in there is telling herself a different story" (qtd. in Tebbetts 51). Smith's vision allows complete ambiguity about Baby's death. Was it suicide or an accident? We never know for sure, and it really doesn't matter. Smith sees women's lives as oftentimes "discontinuous," held together by "threads that r[u]n through a whole life which [are] often almost symbolic" (qtd. in Byrd 113–14). Chronology and accuracy of events mean nothing.

The depth, current, length and width of the Mississippi River reinforces the complexity of the last thirty-five years for these college suitemates, and Smith organizes the novel like a travel log-book, with date, mile marker, location, and hour given in each entry. At the beginning of the book, we find a newspaper article titled "It's Girls A-Go-Go Down the Mississippi," with the account of the original raft trip, dated June 10, 1965. Then the story opens on

May 7, 1999, in Memphis, Tennessee, at the Peabody Hotel, with the first segment from the point of view of Harriet Holding, the principal voice in the novel, former roommate of Baby Ballou and Baby's closest friend in college. An unmarried schoolteacher from Staunton, Virginia, Harriet possesses intelligence and innocence, but she is also introverted and self-sacrificing to the point of silently blaming herself for her unhappiness and perhaps even for that of her closest college friends. Other members of the cast include Catherine Hurt, Courtney Ralston, and Anna Todd. Catherine, happily married to her third husband Russell, is a lawn sculpture artist, described as beautiful, sexual, and maternal. Courtney, a North Carolina socialite, fills the role of the proper, but brittle, Southern belle; however, she needs another man besides her husband to feel complete. Anna has become a successful and wealthy romance novelist. A once poor West Virginia girl, the mysterious, flamboyant Anna has fled her roots. With shifting viewpoints among the four women (and even that of Catherine's husband), Smith moves smoothly back and forth from the present to the past when the girls attended Mary Scott College together, then even further back, as the author delves into their individual childhoods, then to the more recent past of their adult lives.

In his interview with Lee Smith at the end of the book, Silas House calls Harriet's friendship with Baby "the emotional anchor" of the novel, and Smith explains Harriet's total withdrawal from life as a result of the trauma she experienced at college. Smith goes on to discuss the threat she felt during the writing process that each of her four major characters would take over the novel, "grabbing the wheel whenever it was her turn to tell her story, steering the whole steamboat down some dark bayou of her own!" (393–94). What Smith has beautifully and masterfully accomplished with this multi-narrational work is explore the disparate journeys of four women as each has led her own spiritual search for wholeness. We see in the stories of the most pivotal moments in the lives of Harriet, Courtney, Anna, and Catherine imagery and diction preciously associated with the feminine divine in Smith's fiction. Whereas Baby, with her ethereal nature, presents the most obvious link to divinity, Smith also powerfully connects the others to a female deity. The words of these four strong women reverberate with the positive female voice of *Oral History*'s Sally Wade, who narrates the last section of the earlier novel. In "The Power of Language," Corinne Dale argues that Sally subverts traditional linguistic patterns in her narrative. Rejecting the beginning-middle-end story structure and the necessity to make her tale(s) coherent, Sally offers "overlapping and conflicting testimonies" (33–34). If, as Paula Gallant Eckard suggests, Sally serves as Granny Younger's "modern-day counterpart" (152), then Harriet, Catherine, Courtney, and Anna of *The Last Girls* exemplify the postmodern-day equivalents of Sally Wade. Just as Sally relates the events of her life and the lives of her family members, these college suitemates, in sharing their stories, re-create female experience devoid of conventional structures.

Beloved Margaret Burns Ballou (Baby) is the enigmatic divine presence of the novel, as Smith steps back to allow Baby's four suitemates to tell her story. With no voice given to her except through her existing poetry, Baby remains as equivocal to the reader as she has been always to her college friends. Although missing from the present riverboat cruise, the wild and promiscuous yet fragile heiress serves as the impetus for the current journey, just as she was the instigator of the 1965 river trip. After Baby's recent death in a car accident that could possibly be suicide, Baby's husband has contacted her college friends and asked them to reunite on a steamboat cruise and scatter Baby's ashes. So the purpose of this river journey, honoring the dead, is quite the opposite of the motive for the first one, which was celebrating life and youth. Baby becomes the powerful "absent presence" around which the entire novel revolves. Smith said Baby "literally never grew any older" in her college classmates' minds; thus, they have difficulty seeing her as any different than she was at Mary Scott (qtd. in Tebbetts 50). Baby fits the archetype of the hetaira—the sexual and artistically gifted free spirit whose "response to everything" is *"Yes"* (15).

From the beginning of the novel, when Baby is first introduced (from Harriet's point of view), her presence evokes the feminine divine, "float[ing] across the room" (117) with "cheekbones like wings" (4) and "hair spread out" around her face like a halo (131). On the first day of school, freshman year, as Harriet entered her dormitory, she saw Baby on the front steps "among the blooming roses" locked in a passionate kiss with a boy (114). Then Baby, compared to a "hurricane" (116), entered the dorm room with a "line of dried blood" running down her face, a cut from "a thorn in the roses" (117). Baby's early association with roses, passion, and blood portends her intensity and potential danger. The cut on Baby's cheek foreshadows the "short diagonal red slash" (171) Baby made on her forearm when later she attempted suicide and was discovered by Harriet in a bathtub of red water. The damage Baby had suffered remains a mystery to her suitemates, and to the reader, for her story is never fully revealed, even at the end of the novel. Describing Baby, who required no sleep, as "another order of being," Harriet admits that "the gold dust on the butterfly's wings" touched everyone around her (118–19). Smith's linking Baby with the image of the butterfly proves important symbolically not only because of the butterfly's obvious affinity with the feminine divine, but also, in light of Russell's (Catherine's husband) later observation that "'the butterfly effect,'"* based on the "interconnectedness of the atmosphere," seems true to him. The actions and behavior of Baby, as butterfly, affect all those who loved her for the rest of their lives, and even after her death, as the present cruise clearly indicates. In Russell's cynicism, he decides that the "butterfly effect" makes

---

*Russell explains that *"the butterfly effect"* is the theory that one small occurrence in the weather at any given time can later cause a major disturbance at a different location.

greater sense than "believing in some big God guy up in the sky" (231). Thus, Smith gently and playfully substitutes the idea of the feminine divine for belief in the patriarchal male figure.

Baby's poems, read by Harriet at intervals throughout the cruise, best illuminate the complexity, internal conflict, and pain within this Southern girl. Harriet articulates the dichotomy inside Baby, accurately observing "two Babys"—the moody, irrepressible girl at college and the proper Southern "lady-in-waiting" (165). The reality is that Baby was both—a complex mixture—as her poetry reveals. In an interview, Smith revealed her concern during the writing process that Baby doesn't speak for herself in the novel, even though Baby is "the catalyst for the whole plot." Smith explained that one day when she was "worrying about this," poems started pouring into her head "from somewhere"; she could barely keep up with writing them down. Smith soon realized these were Baby's early poems that the girl had written on the raft and stuffed into her blue-jean pockets. Calling this experience "a revelation," Smith includes in the novel a fraction of the poems "Baby" left (House 395). The subjects of the poems reveal deep conflict and anguish for Baby, mostly in regard to three interrelated subjects: memories of her mother, her mother's painful life, and the death of her mother; her brother Richard's tortured life, Baby's closeness to him and emptiness after his premature death; and the duality of her own nature and the conflict between her heart's desires and her family and Southern society's expectations of her. Some of the poems manifest mature insight as Baby's brilliance is obvious to everyone in her life. Harriet explains that during the intense period of Jeff and Baby's relationship, "poems kept pouring out" of Baby. Herself struggling with the creative process, Harriet describes Baby's writing as "automatic," and after observing Baby "star[ing] into space, listening," she says she asked Baby what she heard. Baby answered, "Not the poem ... but the *voice* of the poem" (175). The implication is that Baby heard the voice of the feminine divine, a voice and a presence that allow for the complexity and depth of feminine experience. One of Baby's poems resonates with the connection between sexuality and religion, a link upon which Smith has consistently insisted. A poem titled "Vespers" depicts a drunken female speaker having sex with a boy behind a cathedral in the shadow of a giant statue of "Christ or somebody," "a huge whoever/I lie in his arms/on the soft damp holy grass." Another, the last poem in the novel, titled "The Undead," connects death to sex with the parenthetical closing couplet "(After every funeral/I fuck somebody)" (351–52). The juxtaposition of these two ideas elicits not only the feminine divine in the evocation of the complexity of life, but also other Smith characters such as Candy, Ivy, Katie Cocker, and Grace observed this crucial connection.

Harriet's voice opens the novel, setting the scene for the current riverboat cruise and also providing the first of many flashbacks to the 1960s at Mary Scott. Harriet's journey to acceptance of herself and reconciliation with her past is marked by several scenes in the present during which her memory is jarred by an image linked with the feminine divine. The repressed thirty-year veteran of community college teaching, Harriet admits that she avoids remembering her college days and busies herself "taking care of everybody." However, lately she has discovered her mind wandering and has even awakened "with her body on fire" (6). Smith marks this crucial time in Harriet's life with the fire imagery of sacred feminine sexuality. At the beginning of the novel, in her hotel room, Harriet suddenly experiences shortness of breath, and as she stares into the mirror, "the light flares up behind her" and her heart begins "beating through her body like blood," preparing her (and the reader) for her first flashback. Psychically transported back to the days of college, Harriet considers the first raft trip, explaining how the whole idea originated and giving details about the excursion. After a short nap, Harriet returns to the present, feeling energized, her body "tingling all over" (21). In this first sojourn to the past and Harriet's concomitant feelings, Smith foreshadows what the future holds for this shy, introverted woman filled with sadness and longing but unable to actively participate in life. Harriet's next mystical experience occurs when, at dinner with Courtney on the night before sailing, she encounters a strange, sick feeling in her stomach while thinking of her childhood. Smith has consistently linked women's somatic symptoms, particularly stomach pain, with unexpressed sexuality. Triggered by this sensation, Harriet's memories of her mother and her home come flooding back. In her portrayal of Alice Holding, Smith revisits the image of the maternal, sexual goddess. Described as exotic, "too sweet," mysterious, always laughing, with blonde curls that sometimes look "wild" and a "full red bottom lip" (33, 96), Alice, with her small sewing shop and lounge area, provided a haven for both men and women as she lovingly bolstered each customer. Harriet recalls the centrality of conversation in the shop, describing stories as "float[ing] back and forth through the magic air." Reminiscent of the Cline sisters with their blended voices, Harriet says the voices wove "in and out of themselves, until it was almost impossible to distinguish one from another" (29).

Memories of her mother and her mother's long-time married lover usher in Harriet's recollection of her first mystical experience as a twelve-year-old. On a "blowing spring day" with a full "March wind," Dabney Carr brought with him his son Jefferson, who was the same age as Harriet. Smith's diction signals the presence of the feminine divine with her emphasis on the wind before, during, and after Harriet met Jeff. Empowered by a sense of the divine, Harriet says she ran "like the wind" as she and Jeff chased one another, then laughing uncontrollably, they fell down in the pine needles where she says, "she couldn't breathe." As the two sailed "up into the gray cloudy sky" on the park swings, Harriet thought, "Yes. I will die now, in a kind of rapture at the very top of the arc" (34–36). Harriet has measured all her experiences against this one, and from this point forward in the novel, almost all of her flashbacks, accompanied by the presence of the wind, relate in some way to Jeff Carr. On the second day of the cruise, as she sits out on her balcony, with thoughts of Baby, Harriet "feels more alive" than she has in years; "her nerves are like wires in the wind" (148). Again, she slides into a flashback, this time when Jeff re-entered her world after several years. On a day when the air seemed "iridescent," Jeff mysteriously materialized on the Mary Scott campus, spinning Harriet "around and around" until everything blurred. Harriet says she "felt like a girl in a kaleidoscope" (151). Previously, Harriet had described the intensity, excitement, and confusion of living with Baby as "being caught inside a kaleidoscope" (123), thus portending the imminent bond between Baby and Jeff.

With her depiction of the interconnection among Harriet, Baby, and Jeff, Smith again crosses boundaries as she further explores the possibilities for relationships among people. In contrast to Smith's earlier divine couples that are described as possessing the same body size and type, as "completing" one other, the writer experiments with "divine othering" in her portrayal of Harriet and Baby, both with nail-bitten fingers, as "exactly the same height" and "exactly the same weight" (1). When, after the death of Harriet's sister, Baby "wrapped around [her] like a vine," Harriet describes Baby, with her hair spreading out over Harriet's shoulders, as "totally familiar somehow, and totally comforting." Then, emphasizing the bond between these young girls, Smith writes, "They breathed in and out as one" (130–31). In *The Feminine Face of God*, Anderson and Hopkins describe the spiritual life of females as the search for wholeness, and "a life of the spirit implies relationship in its very essence" (16). Although the friendship with Baby proves detrimental to Harriet in some ways, this memory of the two girls curled up together and breathing as one remains with Harriet for over thirty years. In Harriet's recollection, she associates this incident with images suggestive of the feminine divine: the slow breathing of Baby, the "blowing" wind, three chimes from the tower clock, and the snowflakes "whirl[ing] around and around, dancing" (Smith 132).

Hints of an unusual "divine union" of three exist in Harriet's perception of the inextricability of herself from Baby and Jeff's relationship. Viewing herself as "necessary" to Baby and Jeff's union, Harriet felt she "completed them" (163). When Baby and Jeff left a party together soon after Harriet had introduced them, Harriet thought, "how wonderful it was for the people she loved the most in the world to know each other" (154). With no sense of jealousy or rejection, Harriet felt like "part of it—it was like being in love herself"; she decided that Baby and Jeff's love for her was enough. Smith describes another mystical experience for Harriet when, with a "high blue sky arching" over them, the three journeyed halfway up Morrow Mountain and swam in a lake "like a bowl of black water surrounded by rocks." In this symbolic setting, with her "heart thudding, hot all over," her "blood running through every vein in her body," and "her whole body pulsing in the heat," Harriet masturbated, gasping "in delight or dismay." This lake, with its emblematic black water, fails to provide the rebirth and regeneration most often associated with water in Smith's fiction. Harriet's memory of this event ends with the important confession that "the sweet part was already gone" (176–77). Harriet must experience the sacred part of herself outside her relationship with Baby and Jeff, and this will not happen for many years.

Pete Jones, the steamboat's Riverlorian, proffers an opportunity for Harriet to feel alive again, to get in touch with her most sacred self. Smith implies Pete's salience in his early association with the wind and Harriet's feeling, when around Pete, of breathlessness. Additionally, when the two have lunch together, Smith further develops the character of this "Mark Twain"–looking man with details of his past and his association with such wholesome, vibrant activities as gardening, reading, and dancing, all previously linked to the feminine divine in Smith's fiction. Soon after her time with Pete, Harriet begins behaving "in an otherworldly sort of way," staring off into space in what Courtney perceives as "the mooniest possible way" (257–58). Pete Jones impels Harriet to her next inner expedition to her past, as the steamboat docks at Natchez and Harriet notices the rocks and "haloed" neon signs (216) and remembers her sojourn there over thirty years ago. The preponderant imagery used in the description of the Natchez episode evokes the feminine divine: the mention of the local women who, delivering food to the girls, "appeared like apparitions," and "vanished as quickly as they had come, like good fairies" (218); the description of the moonlit setting on the beach with the girls' "cozy circle in the firelight" (220); the detailed account of Harriet's overnight stay in the old farmhouse with mysterious, earthy Noah, who reminds Harriet of Jeff. Harriet recalls, as if she were "sleepwalking," Noah's hand "like fire on the small of her back," as Noah led her to a mattress on the floor. When Harriet encountered the enigmatic LaGrande, noticed the pond's shimmer "like a lady's oval hand mirror in the moonlight," and heard the strange sound of what she identified as a "woman's cry," her experience powerfully manifests the feminine divine. Noah convinced her that the noises emanated from the "squealing and thrashing around" of owls. His comforting words to Harriet, "Listen to the owls. Go to sleep" (223–24), assuaged her anguish as he stroked her hair. Barbara Walker notes the owl's sacredness in its association with the "Triple Goddess of the Moon." Christian legend transformed the significance of the owl to suggest disobedience, and medieval iconography labeled the owl "night hag," or witch (*Women's* 754). Viewed symbolically, the scream of the owls that Harriet interpreted as a woman's cry evince vestiges of the feminine divine. Although Harriet was initially frightened by the sound, Noah's reassurance of the soothing and sleep-inducing quality of the owls' presence reminds the reader of this young man's salvific potential in Harriet's spiritual journey. As Harriet returns mentally to the present, she muses, perhaps that night with Noah and the woods was a dream, "time out of mind." Then she wonders why it feels "more real" to her at this moment than "her own real life" (226). The juxtaposition of Harriet's psychic sojourn to the past, in which she dismissed the opportunity for sacred sexual union and the recognition of the divine in her own experience, and her present situation with Pete, another chance for healing, demonstrates the link between these two pivotal events in Harriet's life.

Harriet begins to get in touch with her sensual, sexual self during the swamp tour and her trip to the Myrtles estate. As the tour bus penetrates a "large leafy glade beneath enormous live oaks," Harriet feels they are entering "a different world" (261). The setting evokes the image of the cave, where Harriet's senses awaken and from which she emerges reborn and regenerated. Although most of the other passengers cringe at the sight of the live baby alligator the guide has brought on board, Harriet voluntarily "strokes its back" (263), surprising even herself. Then, as Sandy, one of the guides, dances around the deck of the tour boat, Harriet feels her heart begin to race and senses some "mysterious yet inevitable selection process" going on when Sandy requests a female partner. By inexplicable will, Harriet rises and moves over toward Sandy where the two begin dancing "cheek to cheek" with Sandy breathing hotly into her ear. The movement of the dance swings Harriet "around in a circle" as she abandons herself and allows her body to respond to the music and her senses (264–65). Two days later, she undergoes a similar transformation when she tours the Myrtles estate, described as decorated with a "bee motif" where "real bees buzz in and out of the open windows" and butterflies dart about the garden. Surrounded by two insects powerfully linked to the feminine divine in their association with rebirth and regeneration, Harriet wanders alone to the second landing off the grand hall where she feels "a cool breeze" that "lifts the hair off the back of her neck" and "touches her skin in a way which is both intimate and familiar." Paralyzed, Harriet senses a presence with her, and sunlight from the windows grows so bright that "it's like an explosion." Unable to breathe, Harriet looks up where she perceives "a kind of shimmering brilliance, a white radiance" that quickly disappears, allowing Harriet to catch her breath. Although the Myrtles hostess, upset that Harriet has ventured off-limits in the house, explains that the house is haunted, Harriet and the reader recognize the import of this mystical experience that forces Harriet "to stand outside that door," to confront the painful past (293–94).

Just as earlier images of the wind marked Harriet's psychic return to her college days, so does her encounter with the chimerical presence in the Myrtles mansion. Harriet remembers learning of Baby's break-up with Jeff and seeing out the window what she thought was "something moving beneath the water" (297). Here, her instinct, her inner sense of knowing, informed her of the magnitude of this life-changing moment. The description of Harriet's journey to visit Jeff and her time there with him is permeated with imagery associated with the feminine divine. This summer day would be fixed "forever in her mind." With the Blue Ridge Mountains a beautiful blue on the horizon and the "noon sun spread out thick and golden as butter over everything," Harriet senses the divine nature of this experience, the sky reminding her of "a cathedral." At the top of the garden with "old stone walls" outside the house Jeff and some friends had rented for the summer, Harriet sat on "the big warm rock," amid buzzing bees and nodding sunflowers. After briefly dozing off, she woke, feeling suddenly energetic, with her "pulse pounding" in the "crystal air." She thought, "I'm going to remember this ... for the rest of my life" (300–302). Similar to the swamp tour's resemblance to sinking into a cave for Harriet in the present of the novel, her descent into Jeff's basement room also evokes a womblike image. Here with Jeff, the sound of a "droning bee," the feel of a "hot little wind" coming through the open window, and the smell of honeysuckle infused Harriet, and she felt erotic "explosions and sparks" for the first time. She knew she would always have this moment, frozen in time. Likening their passion to "a storm" and "the pouring rain," Smith portrays Harriet and Jeff's lovemaking as natural and revitalizing. Harriet sensed the same thrill she felt at Gypsy Park, swinging with Jeff "higher and higher," then "out into the sweet open air" and "flying through it up and up and up into the endless sky" (304). For Harriet, unable to accept her own inner sacredness and the sanctity of day-to-day feminine experience, this temporary connection with Jeff blocked from her view the possibility of any other means of achieving integration and a sense of completeness. With the news of Jeff's accidental death, the hopefulness Harriet felt after emerging from the cave quickly dissolved into despair. Blaming herself for his death, she sank into invisibility and illness, envisioning Jeff "blaz[ing] up suddenly out of the blackness, outlined in flames," pushing her away (310). Harriet has remained in this spot, untouched by nature or another human, for over thirty years. Anytime anything or anyone has gotten too close, a victim of the mind-body split, Harriet says her "mind flew right straight up in the air and perched in a tree like a bird" (7). This is the door Harriet must enter, the image she must face and integrate in order to achieve wholeness, and on the last day of the cruise she proves her readiness to experience life again. As the steamboat passes River Road, Harriet thinks back to the college raft trip when they passed the same way, recalling the fire the girls made, the moon's ascent and the brightness of the night. During a silent moment among the group of suitemates, Harriet, in her brief comment, "Angel passing," acknowledges, if unconsciously, the presence of the feminine divine and links this instant to her memory of Baby "pirouet[ting] the length of the verandah," with "her hair swinging out on the turns" (323). This positive image suggests healing and reconciliation for Harriet.

Smith admitted that of her four female protagonists in the novel, she identifies the least with Courtney Ralston; however, Smith is extremely sympathetic to Courtney since the author hears so much of her own mother's voice in this character, "the voice of duty and tradition and conformity" (qtd. in House 394–95). Courtney has truly internalized the code for appropriate "Southern behavior," and although in her eight-year affair with Gene Minor, she ventures outside the high stone and wrought-iron wall that borders her ancestral home and protects her heart, in the end she opts for the same choice as Monica Neighbors. In fact, Courtney perfectly reflects Monica in her fifties, married to Manley but still missing the passion and excitement of Buck Fire. Much of Courtney's point of view is rendered in her explication of her photo albums, a fitting metaphor for Courtney's life of keeping an accurate record of the events, complete with husband, children, civic duties and social responsibilities, rather than truly participating in and deeply experiencing life. During the riverboat cruise, one of Courtney's main concerns is taking photographs, even planning titles for each picture she captures.

With the portraiture of Gene Minor, Smith challenges stereotypes as she vividly creates another male character linked to the divine. Associated with flowers (roses in particular), sweetness, mystery, fireworks, and "white twinkling lights," Gene, a florist by profession, seems to hover "everywhere and nowhere" (46). Gene exists on a plane with nature and possesses an affinity for growing things. When at his house, Courtney uses the herbs from his garden for cooking as she feels the "spring sunlight" coming through the open door. Courtney tells us that Gene is legally blind and wears thick glasses but that she doesn't care, explaining, "when he took his glasses off and made love to her, his eyes were round and blue and unfocused as baby-doll eyes." Confessing "she could see herself" in Gene's eyes and that with Gene, "[t]ime stood still," Courtney explains the effect Gene has on her, exciting her and soothing her, "both at the same time." With thoughts of Gene, Courtney remembers the air rushing into the open window of her car and taking a deep breath, "the wind fe[eling] good in her hair" (49–51). Although at the beach house Courtney was surprised to find her husband Hawk* and at that exact moment became aware of his mental lapses (he asked for their dog that had been dead for fifteen years), Courtney's thoughts continued to bounce back and forth from husband to lover. She recalls laughing with Gene like she hadn't laughed in years and describes time spent with him as existing "outside of time and space, like their relationship." Courtney felt Gene wasn't "anybody real, anybody that people knew" (54), as if his reputation or the record (as in photo album) of his life is what makes a person "real." In the present, on the riverboat before she heads to the Captain's Champagne Reception, Courtney pauses before going out to the deck and notices "the warm breeze" stirring her hair and "frizzing [it] around her face" (101).

*With the name of Courtney's husband, Smith implies the most popular mythological connotation that links hawks with death (Gimbutas, Language 195). In light of this symbolism, Courtney's description of Hawk as "[a] man accustomed to killing things" (48) reiterates his destructive effect on her.

With the mention of the wind and this haloed image of Courtney, Smith, with consistent imagery, implies the divinity in feminine experience, jogging Courtney's memory as her mind slips back to thoughts of Gene. The recollection of what Gene did to her "sweeps over her like the hot breezy Arkansas air." One evening Gene had confessed to her he was "enchanted" by her "loopy curls" that sprang up naturally "all over her head" when she didn't use a curling iron. As he playfully announced he was a "licensed phrenologist," he massaged her head and rubbed one particular spot on her scalp, identifying it as her "lump of Venus." Then he commented that this area was "extremely well situated and highly developed" (102). With this brief mention of the Roman goddess of love and sexuality, Smith subtly alerts the reader to the possibility for Courtney's integration. An early indication of this potential, Courtney had previously thought of herself as a "butterfly" when around Gene Minor. Gene provides the link for Courtney to become reacquainted with her girl self, her self before Hawk and the drowning of her individual identity. The first time Courtney and Gene had connected twenty years after high school graduation, Gene reminded her of an incident at Spring Lake during their junior year when he had gotten an accidental glimpse of her breast when her swimsuit top fell down as she was diving into the water. He described Courtney's surprising reaction of acceptance and complete lack of embarrassment as "so cool"; he called this memory "the sweetest moment." With Courtney's response, "'But I thought you were gay,'" as she was "hardly breathing" (59–60), Smith challenges the system that applies labels to people based on some preconceived notion of expected appearance and behavior. The complexity and depth of Gene's character, along with his association with divinity, powerfully suggests the salvific quality of this relationship for Courtney.

Courtney also experiences a mystical encounter much like that of Harriet. Again, Smith marks this occurrence in the present of the novel with the characteristic presence of a cool "little breeze" that almost sighs, in a beautiful cemetery with "[w]hite stones rising into consciousness like ideas, like memories, like ghosts." Having missed the bus for the group tours, Courtney strikes out on her own photography excursion, thinking, "[s]he's not going after anything sexual, no weird Georgia O'Keeffe stuff." For Courtney, "[t]ime has stopped dead" and the trees seem to be "leaning toward each other, telling old, old secrets" (283–84). Still adhering to her plan to capture and record the significant moments, Courtney perfunctorily labels a pair of photographs (an actual rose alongside a marble rose) "'Life and Death,' a study in contrasts." Immediately she psychically links this picture to Gene Minor and his ultimatum. Aware now that she holds the power to make the choice between life (the living rose—Gene) and death (the marble rose—Hawk), she feels her heart rate increase, so she searches for a water fountain. Finding the symbolically red door (the entryway to her sexuality, her feminine spirit), Courtney steps inside the "stone vestibule" and notes the "[d]amp and holy and utterly familiar" smell inside. After drinking from the fountain (water representing the possibility for rebirth and regeneration), she enters the sanctuary, bathed in "soft muted light" rising from the shiny pews "curving in toward each other in a timeless embrace." In this safe and familiar setting where she feels enfolded and protected, she kneels to pray as a "shaft of light falls on Courtney's folding hands" (285–86).

With gentle humor, Smith prods the commonly held belief in the esotericism of mystical experience. When Courtney's wedding ring flashes in the light, she asks, "Oh God. What is this, some kind of sign?" Then she dismisses the prophetic incident and decides that "signs don't come to women like her, they come to tacky fat women in revival tents with scraggly hair and flip-flops." Additionally, we soon learn that Courtney has never desired any kind of "actual religious experience"; her lifelong involvement with her church has reflected her sense of moral obligation and civic duty. She admits that during her legion communions, her mind has always wandered to other, more pressing issues—"the little things of life that are holy." This insight, delivered by Courtney, most closely corresponds to Smith's spiritual vision that manifests the sacredness of women's day-to-day activities that reflect the presence of the feminine divine. With her wedding ring shining "like a headlight in the shadows," Courtney embraces the complexity of her life and suddenly "everything becomes very clear." Courtney hears the voice of Gertrude Marshall, who was banished from Courtney's Episcopalian church for seeing visions and speaking in tongues, saying with her characteristic "little lisp," "'The Peath of the Lord be alwayth with you.'" With typical Smith humor, the author supplies a female voice, however distorted, to direct Courtney to her duty, presenting the confused Courtney with yet another conundrum. When she opts not to photograph the next scene since "she's in it," hope exists for Courtney's integration; then, "suddenly she sees herself in the frame anyway." The message is double-edged and ambiguous. Her realization that "she's in" the photograph implies Courtney has chosen to participate in life rather than photograph it. However, with her last thought of being inside the frame, we fear that she once again sees her life in frozen moments. At least in the last frame, she captures her own "insignifican[ce]" (286–87).

Anna Todd, like Harriet and Courtney, houses in her heart secrets and past tragedies that define the woman she is in the present, and just as the riverboat cruise impels the other suitemates back into their memories to find healing and integration, Anna's flashbacks function the same way. Arguably the character having suffered the greatest amount of personal pain, Anna long ago found a survival mechanism that has not only allowed for her subsistence, but also made her a wealthy and famous woman. A bestselling romance novelist, Anna has published thirty-four novels and been translated into fourteen languages. Anna pours her supreme sensory perception and sensitivity to all stimuli into her writing. Hiding her eyes behind dark shades and smoking "nasty, black cigar[s]," Anna buries her self under her image; her wake leaves a "kind of shimmering in the air" (80).

Through her flashbacks, we learn that Anna has experienced her share of brushes with the feminine divine throughout her life. Her earliest memories involve her mother, a damaged goddess figure who, like many mothers in Smith's fiction, died at a young age, worn down by the demands of her life as wife of a freelance evangelist and mother of four children, Anna (her actual name was Annie Stokes) and three blonde little boys whom Anna calls "angels." Anna remembers her mother as beautiful but frail, with "red-gold hair that fell to her waist." After her mother's death and her father's remarriage, thirteen-year-old Anna escaped her confinement, where her father forbade her "to dance, to take gym classes, or to try out for cheerleader," nor could she "wear jeans or sleeveless blouses or drink Coca-Colas." However, Anna says she loved her handsome, "sweet" daddy who had a voice "like God" (136–37). Although Anna's childhood experience with evangelical religion did not seem to damage her like other characters in Smith, Anna found greater acceptance, nurturance, and imaginative space in the home of an "old missionary health nurse," Miss Todd (from whom Anna took her assumed name). This elderly unmarried woman ignites the literary spark in Anna, as the gentle woman provides for Anna a classical education and encourages her creativity and love for literature. Smith's brief portrait of Miss Todd reminds the reader of Miss Torrington and her genuine love for Ivy, as Anna recalls that Miss Todd enjoyed tying back Anna's hair "with a black velvet ribbon and kiss[ing] her on the mouth," an exchange that Anna viewed as reasonable and "fair" (138).

Anna next grazes the presence of the feminine divine when, in abject loneliness and disillusionment, she made a fresh start. Her husband had left her, she was pregnant, and she had sunk to a state of total despair. With the story of this chapter of Anna's life, Smith acknowledges the age-old plot whereby a young woman sacrifices everything for her husband, supporting and encouraging him as his work eclipses her own and her sense of self-worth dwindles. Anna, already pregnant, had married Kenneth Trethaway, a moody, brilliant Ph.D. student, out of genuine love, but after her miscarriage, the marriage deteriorated as Kenneth escaped into his work and drugs. Called "the Madonna" by Kenneth and his friends, Anna took care of everything and everyone. Pregnant again and with no fellowship money, having spent that on household needs, Anna found herself working at a menial job and doing all the chores at home too, while Kenneth and his buddies were "smoking dope and listening to jazz and talking about literature" (142). Although Anna never would have chosen to leave this arrangement, her abandonment by Kenneth and thoughts of her baby impelled her to a new life. On Piggott's Island, Georgia, Anna moved into the Flamingo, a boardinghouse run by two old sisters who evoke the image of the Cline sisters in their ethereality and nurturance.

The flashback that takes the reader, and Anna, to this memory is ushered in by the presence of the moon, mentioned four times as Anna, Courtney, and Harriet end their day on the riverboat deck. Under the full "moon's yellow light" (267), Anna's mind carries her back to her sunrise arrival on the island as "she stretch[ed] her arms out to the wind" (269), symbolically embracing her own sacredness through the feminine divine.

The stillbirth of Anna's daughter sent Anna plummeting and she spent the next year in and out of a mental hospital, but once she began working again, this time as a housecleaner, Smith situates her in a prime position to encounter a touch of divinity in the form of Lou Angelli, her angel, "the love of [her] life" (268). When Anna first met Lou, he looked to her "like a bear" and she "recognized him"; "she felt she *did* know him from someplace." Lou, her "divine other," possessed the look of familiarity characteristic of many of Smith's protagonists' lovers. Anna recognized that she and Lou were "two of a kind" (273–74), and their life together flourished and fulfilled Anna in every way. Besides the obvious connotation of "angel" with Lou's name, Smith's choice of a bear in describing Lou's likeness powerfully evokes the image of the feminine divine. According to Gimbutas, the holiness of the image of the bear is universal in the northern hemisphere. Vestiges of worship of the "mother bear," linked with the primeval mother, exist all over Old European culture. One form of the bear goddess, the "Bear Madonna," is depicted as a woman wearing a bear mask and holding a cub, the representation of sacred motherhood (*Language* 116). Recalling Anna's nickname given to her by Kenneth and his friends, in combination with Lou's resemblance to a bear, deepen the significance of Anna's symbiotic relationship with this sacred man. Additionally, Ivy's favorite story of the Cline sisters was the tale of Whitebear Whittington, the mystical representation of both Ivy and Silvaney in their divine nature. In the present of the novel, when Anna, on the swamp tour bus, hears the tour guide mention, among several other protected creatures, the bear, she spontaneously writes in her notebook, "'BEAR!'" (261). Though Smith chooses not to disclose exactly what Anna feels at this time, the reader surmises that Anna recalls Lou and the sacredness of their relationship. Although Lou died many years ago, his love and acceptance had allowed Anna to re-enter life. Mythology adds another layer to the meaning of Lou's death since in many Old European cultures, the sacred bear was sacrificed annually to ensure the renewal of life in spring. With the loss of Lou, Anna receives an opportunity for another new life, born out of her whole and integrated existence with Lou. Anna and Lou had formed their own strange little menagerie of family at their home in Key West, having taken in their decorator, Anna's personal assistant, their financial manager, the one living sister from the Flamingo and her personal nurse, and "one of Lou's daughters with her illegitimate child" (278). With this assorted collection of people all living together, Smith redefines family to include all those important and necessary people in our lives, along with those to whom we are tied by blood, creating a paradigm for a divinely inspired world of tolerance, forgiveness, and acceptance.

Catherine Wilson Hurt is the woman most closely aligned with the feminine sacredness of the earth and nature. One of the first morsels of information we learn about Catherine, "head thrown back and laughing, down to earth and natural," comes from her husband Russell when he explains to the group how they met. Immediately linked to images of the feminine divine, Catherine, a sculptor—"a very well known artist" according to Russell—specializes in the creation of garden sculptures of women. Russell describes one of them as "placed half in and half out of a stream," making a "little waterfall," what he interprets as "some kind of mythological animal or something." When Catherine corrects him about the figure, telling him that she "just made it up," her link to the imagination and nature is suggested. Lying in her stateroom, Catherine looks over at the mirror that Russell has placed strategically so the two of them can view themselves making love, "which turns them both on." Then, watching her reflection, Catherine "lifts one heavy breast to her mouth and licks the nipple, sucks it just for a minute to get that little twang—like a single note plucked on a banjo—between her legs." Comfortable with her sexuality, Catherine thinks of herself as a "middle-aged wild woman." Her next thoughts travel to her maternal role, and she confesses her love for her children and grandchildren, the portion of her life spent with all their "many comings and goings and friends and dogs and muddy shoes and sweatshirts flung down in the hall, the phone always ringing, the TV on, the school lunch menu taped to the refrigerator, brownies to bake for the bake sale" (199). Enumerating the tasks of motherhood, Smith beautifully captures the spirit of this role for so many women. Catherine, her life full to overflowing, embraces the entirety of life. She is the earth mother, in touch with both her sexuality and her maternal instincts. However, in her section of the novel, Catherine reveals that she always has been "easily overtaken: by her husbands, by her children, by her images and ideas, by life itself" (188). In fact, at the end of the novel, Catherine realizes that she has been surrounded by other people her entire life, beginning with her menses, then "cramps boys dates birth babies, *the works*" (337).

Catherine's most poignant memory and her most magical and mystical experience occurred in her childhood with her beloved brother Wesley in time spent at their grandparents' farm at China Hill. While Catherine sits in her stateroom on board the *Belle of Natchez* and looks out the window at the river and the beautiful tri-colored horizon, her mind rushes back to those summers she and Wesley, "like children in a fairy-tale book," spent in their river house watching the rain as it hit the river water, splattering and swirling in the gusts of wind along the banks lined in willows. In this symbolic setting, Catherine and Wesley hid a wooden chest filled with art supplies and their "treasures gleaned from the river itself." Catherine remembers feeling that "she would never love anybody else as much as she did Wesley, ever" (190–91). In the present, Catherine thinks of Russell and their first meeting when he purchased "three of her concrete women," then moved in with her three weeks later. With these sacred threes as a backdrop, Smith transports Catherine back to the past with Catherine's thoughts that her entire life "seems distant to her..., not nearly as real as the days when she used to wander the woods and fields with Wesley." Alone in her stateroom, Catherine closes her eyes and "smells the honeysuckle" and hears the sounds of "the foggy woods" (198). Describing Wesley's movements as circular, "run[ning] around in little circles" (201), Smith re-emphasizes the divine nature of this beloved brother who, although long dead, remains alive and sacred in Catherine's mind.

Another strong example of the presence of divinity in Catherine's everyday life occurs in her meeting with and marriage to Dr. Steve Rosenthal, which Catherine describes as mystical, like something "she had simply made ... up." His immediate association with blood, in the mention of his "nice white coat ... all bloody" and Catherine's reaction of "reach[ing] out and touch[ing] his bloody collar," aligns him with feminine experience and its link to blood. Also, Catherine had taken her son Will to the emergency room with a cut on his forehead "bleeding like crazy," and Dr. Rosenthal, although in psychiatry, displayed comfort and ease around blood, suggesting his closeness to nature and natural processes. Catherine admits at that time in her life, "Will was the best thing that had ever happened to [her] so far." However, another miracle happened for Catherine when Steve Rosenthal appeared at her door a few days later, dripping wet in the middle of a rainstorm when Catherine was nursing Will. She instinctively grabbed his collar and pulled him inside where they "started laughing and couldn't stop" (194–96). The stage was set for Catherine's exposure to and acceptance of the feminine divine in her union with this man.

In the present of the novel, Catherine's discovery of a lump in her breast impels her on a journey to self-knowledge. Catherine begins to feel disconnected from life and everyone around her. As she and Harriet tour Vicksburg, stopping at the highest point of a bluff to gaze down at the river, "a wind comes up" and Catherine feels "nervous, exposed," like she's "in the sky itself." Just as throughout the novel the presence of the wind has triggered flashbacks for the other protagonists, for Catherine, her feelings of transcendence are accompanied by images associated with the feminine divine. Feeling detached from her breast, she imagines "it rolling down the hill" and "losing her whole body bit by bit, as if pieces are falling off and tumbling down the bluff to disappear into the river forever" (203). Reminiscent of Ivy Rowe's period of deep depression during which she felt she had lost her self in fragments, this image of Catherine suggests her feeling of losing each section, or facet, of her carefully constructed being, having admitted earlier in the novel that "[s]he was a kind of a creation of herself" (189). The artificially constructed self, even if bound by the strongest mortar, crumbles at the inevitability and reality of illness, aging, and death. Catherine must reconnect to her sacred self, the part of her inundated with divinity, aside from the physical body. When she and Harriet exit the courthouse tour and step "into the windy, changeable day," Catherine feels relieved at having left a place that connotes "some kind of judgment." At this point Catherine feels she cannot share her disturbing news with anyone, including Russell, for it seems to her "that she has given her body nearly away already, to her children and her husbands, and now she wants to hold on to what she can" (204–205).

On the last day of the cruise, Catherine undergoes another mystical experience that reconnects her to her inner sacredness and to her husband. As she slowly approaches Russell, Catherine, with her "wild hair," feels like she is moving "underwater or like she's a girl in a dream." When Catherine tells Russell about the lump, she feels that "the dam crumbles, the water rushes through" as she shares her worry and pain with the man she loves, "her old buddy, her old flame, her old man." After they make love, Catherine watches "the sun make its fiery trail across the water straight to their window"; she imagines "walking across the water into the trees" on the other side of the river where she smells flowers and honeysuckle (337–38). A potent image of the feminine divine, Catherine has surely achieved integration.

With the last scene of the novel, Smith offers hope and healing for all four protagonists as they join together to sprinkle the ashes of Baby into the Mississippi River. After Harriet reads Charlie Mahan's letter to the group, they all are forced to face the truth about life—"there are no grown-ups" and "it's always the storyteller's story." Charlie's account of Baby's (Maggie, as he calls her) adult life differs greatly from the one the four suitemates had imagined. Smith mixes the sacred with the profane in her description of Baby's ashes, which look and feel nothing like anyone anticipated; instead, they are "not all like powder, but some of them grainy, like kitty litter." With the sprinkling of Baby's ashes off the deck of the boat and into the waters of the Mississippi River, Smith supplies, at the end of the novel, imagery of the feminine divine. With "an arch of lights above them" and the wind blowing softly, Courtney, with no other vocabulary for understanding the divine, offers up the Lord's Prayer; then, the puff of Baby's ashes "floats back like smoke on the wind" (363–65). Anna's comment, "Oh my God! She's coming back," aside from the obvious humor, suggests more than the indestructibility and endurance of Baby's essence. As the ashes settle on the bodies and clothing of the assembled group, the implication is that divinity resides with and inside each of these women. Courtney at least has awakened to her own passion, in her relationship with Gene Minor. The last image of Courtney combines the ideas of life (Gene's "wild garden") and death (the cemetery next to Courtney's home) as Courtney feels "this terrible sense of desolation sweeping over her." As she "closes her eyes and sways in the wind," she reassures herself that she is doing "the *right thing*." Anna allows herself to remember Lou's death and the ritual of sprinkling his ashes into the ocean, recalling the magical moment when the sun "spread out at the bottom and swelled up bigger and bigger until its rosy light filled the entire sky." Openly sobbing, Anna thinks back over her life and her choices, finally determining, "What's done is done; whatever *should* be, *is*. Touch, see, smell, hear, taste, feel. *Be here now*" (366–67). Anna seems to follow her own dictum as she fully "feels" the last moments with this group of women on board the steamboat. During the last scene, Catherine and Russell are dancing as Catherine basks in the closeness of the man she loves while celebrating with her college suitemates. With the last portion of the novel from Harriet's point of view, Smith ends with the image of Harriet leaning over the rail "like a figurehead, facing into the breeze," realizing the senselessness and extravagance of the decades-long torture she has been inflicting upon herself. As she "shoot[s] up higher many feet above the Sun Deck" (recalling her earlier mind-body separation), Harriet psychically merges the city's "twinkling lights" with the constellations the "last girls" composed back in creative writing class. However, a new one—Jeff's constellation—joins the group: "Jeff blazing out in the night," beckoning to her (369–70). Pete's calling Harriet's name jolts her back to the present and to the deck of the riverboat, effectively rejoining her mind with her body and reminding her of her opportunity to re-enter life.

The narrative of the novel ends with the music of Creedence Clearwater Revival's "Bad Moon Rising" and the image of the girls "running up that hill" back at Mary Scott College (371), as the circularity of their journey is re-emphasized. At the conclusion of the book, Smith provides an update on the rest of the girls who went on the original raft trip. In the brief accounts of their lives, we see once more the complexity, the mystical moments, the pain and the joy of these disparate women who all have experienced at least a glimpse, or a touch, of divinity in their everyday lives. Lee Smith said that the Mississippi River, in its "vast, brooding, mysterious majesty," exemplifies our need and "our eternal push" to advance "deeper and deeper" into the "unknown" (qtd. in House 391). As we travel down this grand, historic river with this group of women, we journey deeper and deeper into each of their lives, circling back to the present as they continue their voyage. Catherine's astute observation about life—that "it's all about holding back and letting go," about "[p]ulling apart and getting back together," about "keeping and giving" (337–38)—echoes the words of Carol Ochs in *Women and Spirituality*. Ochs notes that in our spiritual "walks," we sometimes "draw closer and sometimes draw back in what amounts to a cosmic dance," approaching and moving away, opening up and withdrawing (114). The circularity of the sacred spiritual journey for women teems with profundity, complexity, and contradiction. During the prayer at the end of the novel, Smith alerts us, "They're [the women] praying straight into the wind" (365), a salient reminder of the presence of the divine in each of the lives of these "last girls."

Chapter IX

"PART OF THE EARTH AND THE SKY, THE LIVING AND THE DEAD"

The Divine Cycle of Life in *On Agate Hill*

Part of our female selves has been lost in our culture's blindness to and denial of the feminine divine. In *Women Who Run with the Wolves: Myths and Stories of the Wild Woman Archetype*, Clarissa Pinkola Estés offers hope for the retrieval of a feminine spirituality through tapping into the primordial language of myths. Estés calls the realm where goddess mythology exists an "inexplicable psychic land," "the locus betwixt the worlds," equating it with Jung's collective unconscious. In order to reconnect with her true self, a woman must revisit this place where "visitations, miracles, imaginations, inspirations, and healings of all natures occur." Then she may return "wholly washed or dipped in a revivifying and informing water." For females, this experience "impresses upon our flesh the odor of the sacred" (27). Fairytales are stories that exist in this world between worlds, in the space where imagination rules, where validation and power exist for females.

In her most recent novel, *On Agate Hill*, published in 2006, Smith taps into the world of fairies, opening up a "fairy religion," as she provides an alternative to patriarchal religion for the novel's protagonist, Molly Petree. Throughout the novel, as a counterpoint to the negative references to patriarchal religion and its deadening effects on Molly, Smith gently places suggestions for an alternative religion—one that celebrates women and embraces an understanding of the divinity in people and in nature. In a recent interview, Smith explained that a young woman struggling to get in touch with her self and searching for something that speaks to her, something that accepts and validates her, is drawn to a sense of the feminine divine—the sacredness of the female body and female experience. Describing her own spirituality as rooted in ideas that encompass the feminine divine, Smith admitted, "My idea

IX. "Part of the earth and the sky, the living and the dead" 199

of divinity is a more feminine divinity ... one completely outside the box." One means for conveying this "untraditional kind of spiritual search" (Per) for Smith is with the inclusion of a fairy land, what Estés calls an "inexplicable psychic land, according to Barbara Walker a "land of women" where fairies exist. Walker points out that pagan gods and goddesses and all who worshipped them were categorized "fairies" and discusses the "fairy religion" that was practiced secretly through most of the Christian era, especially by women, "whose Goddess the patriarchal church kept trying to take away" (*Women's* 298–99). Simone de Beauvoir's twentieth-century insight that young girls often experience moments of mystical communion in nature rather than in society holds true with Molly. Throughout the novel, Smith explores the feminine divine in the spiritual journey and natural, sacred experiences of Molly.

The action of *On Agate Hill* covers about fifty-five years, from the first diary entry Molly makes at the age of thirteen to the day of Molly's death at age sixty-eight. However, reminiscent of *Oral History*'s opening, Smith sets the novel in the present day, in the year 2006, and begins the story, in an italicized section, with a letter from Tuscany Miller to the Director of the Documentary Studies Program at Carolina State University. Having dropped out of graduate school, Tuscany now seeks readmission and includes with her letter a recently discovered box of paraphernalia that she says has changed her life. Tuscany then delineates the contents of this *"box of old stuff"* (1): a girl's diary from the 1870s, various letters, poems, songs, a Bible, newspaper clippings, court records, and other oddities such as marbles, rocks, dolls, and even assorted bones. Tuscany explains that she has arranged the materials in the most logical order to tell the story of Molly Petree. From here Smith moves to the diary of Molly and the record of this poor orphaned girl's life on a run-down plantation from 1872 to 1873. In this first major section of the book, dubbed "Agate Hill" for the name of the plantation, not only do we learn about Molly's family and her past, but also, Smith introduces all the major themes of the novel. This section ends with Molly's departure to Gatewood Academy in Hopewell, Virginia. Throughout the novel, Smith intermittently shifts back to the present as Tuscany inserts what she calls "Notes," along with additional letters of explication to Dr. Ferrell, pertinent documents and other relevant information. The second major section of the novel, called "Paradise Lost," covers the next five years of Molly's life (until age nineteen), but we only hear from Molly's first person point-of-view in correspondence to her childhood friend Mary White. The rest of the story of Molly's life during these years is pieced together through letters and journal entries of other characters and with official information on the Academy. From Gatewood, Molly leaves to teach at a tiny rural school "Up on Bobcat," and in this section of the novel, we follow Molly's life journey until the year 1883 when she leaves to marry Jacky Jarvis. Agnes Rutherford, a teacher from Gatewood and dear friend who accompanies Molly on her trip and teaches with her at Bobcat School, provides most of the details of Molly's life during these five years. In what she calls "Final Impressions," dated June 8, 1912, Agnes records events that occurred over thirty years ago. The fourth major section of the novel, "Plain View," consists of evidence given at the coroner's inquest of Jacky's death in Wilkes County, North Carolina, on November 18, 1907. Through his testimony, John Howard Willetts, known as BJ, provides all the pertinent information about Molly and Jacky's twenty-four-year marriage, the births and deaths of their children, and the fatal night of Jacky's death. Between the last two sections of the novel, Smith inserts a traditional ballad, "Molly and the Traveling Man," as Tuscany has discovered this puzzle piece among the others. The last section of the novel, "Another Country," consists primarily of Molly's diary entries, written twenty years after Jacky's death from Agate Hill, where she has come to live in 1907 and has remained until her death in 1927. The novel ends with a letter from Tuscany to Dr. Ferrell, in which Tuscany, in addition to updating the reader on the condition of the current Agate Hill Bed and Breakfast, unveils the last details of Molly's story.

In her writing, Smith has consistently depicted orthodox Christianity as oppressive and unfulfilling for women. Smith has acknowledged that increasingly as she has gotten older, she has moved away from the "real organized patriarchal kinds of religions toward a more organic spirituality" (Per). In *On Agate Hill*, any mention of traditional Christianity is shadowed by negative feelings and connotations as once again, as in previous novels, characters fail to find any acceptance or reassurance in what they've been taught is God. As a girl of thirteen, Molly refers to Mister Gwyn, the local minister, as an "old sourpuss Presbyterian" and adds that "he has got a poker up his ass" (11) because of his self-absorption and rigidity. When he advises Uncle Junius, after Aunt Fannie's death, to turn back to God, Molly's uncle tells Mister Gwyn that he has no desire to associate with, much less worship, any "God who has done what he has done" (22). Molly's sentiments essentially parallel those of Junius. Another of Molly's supposed role models, Aunt Cecelia, forces her granddaughter Mary White and Molly to read aloud the catechism and the Ten Commandments, harping, "Hell looms wide for such frivolous girls as yourselves" (46). However, one realizes Cecilia's extreme superficiality with her response to Molly and Mary White's discovery of a dead black man hanging from a tree in the forest, obviously a victim of the Ku Klux Klan. When the girls report this crime to Aunt Cecilia, she tells them it's none of their business and to forget about the experience. Furthermore, Cecelia, both elitist and racist, forbids her granddaughter from associating with Washington, the young Negro boy who lives on the plantation and is Molly's dearest childhood friend at Agate Hill until Mary White arrives.

At Gatewood, an all-girl charity Christian school, Molly's experience with orthodox Christianity proves much more destructive with Smith's portrayal of Mariah Snow, Headmistress, and her husband and Headmaster, the

Rev. Cincinnatus Snow. Between the Agate Hill section and this second part of the novel, Smith inserts a copy of an "Infant Catechism" under "Notes from Tuscany." This brief piece seems perfectly fitting since it expounds the Christian belief that "good children" go to heaven when they die and "bad children" go to hell, that everyone, including God, loves "good children," and only "The Devil" loves "bad children" (123). Both Mariah and Dr. Snow teach Bible Studies, and one of the stated purposes of the school includes offering particular instruction for the "souls" of the students. Instructed in "exquisite neatness, decorum, and silence," the girls receive rewards or punishments based on their "perfect" or "imperfect" behavior (142). In Mariah's numerous journal entries, ominously titled "For No One's Eyes," she reveals her bitterness and resentment for her husband and her life, admitting early on that for no apparent reason, she dislikes Molly, recognizing Molly's "dormant spirit" and ability to "do anything. Anything" (152). Although she quotes bible verses to suit her purposes, Mariah struggles with contradictory impulses of aggression and passivity, and God's word offers no comfort or guidance for her. With Smith's depiction of Mariah Snow, the author discloses the tortured life of a woman trapped in a role that society condones. Her severe depression and descent into insanity and eventual institutionalization reflect the hopeless fate for a woman in her situation. Whereas the reader dislikes Mariah (due to her hatred and mistreatment of Molly), Smith disallows judgment of this unfortunate victim of the "system" that demands that she submit to her abusive, pedophiliac husband in all ways, performing sexual acts and bearing child after child to suit his fancy. Meanwhile, Dr. Snow, all in the name of imparting "Christian" morals to his students, conducts private counseling sessions with the girls during which Molly says, "we have to talk to him individually about the state of our souls, and then we have to kiss him," writing to Mary White, "it is awful" (170). But after graduation when he starts to fondle Molly's breast and tells her he needs her to "perform a few additional duties" (207), his reign of terror comes to an abrupt halt as Molly not only kicks him and runs away, but also, she and Agnes illuminate to his wife his behavior with Molly. Although Mariah refuses to accept the truth and remains at Gatewood, behind the "gate," trapped from the natural "woods" of her female self, Agnes and Molly escape this suffocating environment to enter into the feminine world of nature and explore their true selves.

Throughout her early life, Molly experiences an attempt by others to vanquish the fairies (or imagination) from her life, and Smith juxtaposes the fairy world with the world of traditional Christianity. One of the most memorable admonitions she receives comes from Aunt Mitty, her grandmother's mysterious lifelong mate. When Molly and Mary White take custard to the two old women, Aunt Mitty, aware of Molly's rebellious nature, advises Molly, "turn to God my dear, for He is watching you every moment, always and everywhere. Forget all the make-believe. Read your Bible." Molly quickly tells Aunt

Mitty that she's already read the Bible, but she prefers poetry, or the realm of the imagination. Deciding she doesn't want to go to heaven anyway (in fact, she "doesn't give a damn about Heaven"), Molly thinks "I want to live so hard and love so much I will use myself all the way up like a candle," concluding, "this is the point of it all, not Heaven" (78). The juxtaposition of traditional religion and Molly's "fairy religion" occurs again with Smith's placement of the "Infant Catechism" immediately before two famous fairytales: Eugene Field's "Wynken, Blynken, and Nod" and William Allingham's poem "The Fairies." Both pieces celebrate the world of the imagination, the spiritual realm of fairies. Two opposite kinds of spirituality are here contrasted: Christianity with its message of "be good or go to Hell," and the fairytales' message of the sacredness of life and the divinity present in many magical moments of our everyday lives. After a short time at Gatewood, a rigid, puritanical setting, Molly finds her only comfort in books, in particular "a collection of Fairy Tales" (150). Feeling guilty for her secret devotion to what for her has become a "fairy religion," she grabs the book and hides it in the folds of her skirt, a fitting metaphor for a female's tendency to conceal from the judgment of others the true nature of her self. Smith explained that when she was young, she felt a tremendous amount of guilt for her inability to find fulfillment inside the walls of the church where there existed a white male God always watching and judging us. Her most sacred moments occurred out in nature or with other human beings (Per).

Smith introduces Molly's fairytale world early in the novel when Molly writes the first entry in her diary. Describing the house and land at Agate Hill, Molly reveals her secret, cave-like cubbyhole in the middle of the house, "invisible and unknown to all" (12) where she sits in her "fairy tale chair" and reads or writes by using "fairy tale lights" (19), actually finger bowls filled with sweet gum balls floating in lard. However, when Mary White arrives from Alabama, Molly's fairy world comes to life. Immediately associating Mary with a "princess in a fairy tale book" (42), Molly welcomes her frail, imaginative counterpart into her coveted hidden cubbyhole where Mary, speaking "fairy language" (59), instructs Molly on the ways of the fairies. Molly writes in her diary about the girls' discovery of a "fairy ring" out by the river in a secret place, hidden from view by large draping branches, where the two girls sit, talk, and read together. Although the girls miss the appearance of the ring of fairies the first time they hope to see it, Mary White concludes that they must return to the sacred spot in the "light of the moon" in order to see the supernatural beings (44). On the girls' third try, "the air was suddenly filled with fairies like a swarm of bees," their wings beating so fast that it brightens up the night, and their voices laughing and singing (59). Barbara Walker identifies fairy mounds or rings as "entrances to the pagan paradise" (*Women's* 298), and while it is unlikely that Smith here invokes strict paganism, she certainly suggests an alternative spirituality apart from traditional Christianity. Molly and

Mary White flourish in this fairy world, which, by all definitions, would refer to a realm of spirituality in great conflict with traditional patriarchal religion. In *The Living Goddesses*, in a section devoted to "women's collective power," Gimbutas explains that "groups of fairies who dance in circles ... or around stone rings" create enormous energy. Gimbutas continues, "These goddesses appear alone or with large groups of assistants, and they exercise supernatural power in control of nature: the moon, the sun, eclipses, storms, hail" (119–20). One of the requirements for a "fairy sighting," according to Mary White's "fairy rules," is the occurrence of a storm on that night. Interestingly, Molly has written in her diary, long before Mary White's arrival, "Myself I love a thunderstorm better than anything" (13). The climax of Molly and Mary White's mystical experiences occurs the night of their third attempt to spot the fairies. The girls recognize and identify Titania, "the queen of the fairies," as she lands on a rock just inches away from them. Molly describes Titania as wearing a flower crown and having long red hair, her wings rapidly beating, "giving off light like a firefly" (59). Walker labels Titania as the ancient fertility-mother goddess, predating the Olympian gods. According to Walker, one of the strongest attractions of the fairy religion was its permissive view of sexuality, a stark contrast to the "harsh anti-sexual attitudes of orthodoxy" (*Women's* 300). It is not surprising that Molly, feeling like a "bad girl" (117), especially when her own sexuality begins to emerge, feels drawn to a spirituality that condones her corporeal pleasures.

Following a poignant brush with her fairy world, Molly returns to her life and her spiritual search. About two months after Mary White's departure, Molly writes about her near-death experience when, because the well had frozen over, she went to the spring in the forest to break the ice and get water. Exhausted, weighed down by the heavy buckets and depressed over Mary's absence, Uncle Junius's marriage to Selena, and the deaths of Mama Marie and Aunt Mitty, Molly decides to lie down and rest in the snow, "underneath that big pine tree" that she imagines singing her a lullaby. Having fallen asleep in the freezing cold, Molly wakes to see a fairy sitting on a branch right above her head. This time, however, it's not Titania, the goddess fairy, who appears; Molly describes this fairy as male, with a dark, sharp face and red cap. Pointing his gloved finger at Molly, he chirps, "Wake up Molly Petree.... Go home," then disappears in a "silvery blur" into the tree (105). This scene calls to mind the one in *Fair and Tender Ladies* during which Ivy experiences a similar sense of hopelessness and desire to remain in the snow, never to awaken from her frozen state. Ivy has also gone to the spring to get water and carries heavy buckets when she slips and falls in the snow. Rather than drifting to sleep though, Ivy lies there crying until she feels her tears freezing on her face, her only wish to remain there with the air so "pure and sweet." The wind blows across the snow and Ivy's face and awakens her from her paralysis; then, her mother calls her three times before Ivy arises to go home. Ivy says, "I wuld of layed there forever if I culd of," and in her letter to her Dutch pen pal, she asks, "Do you think this is evil?" (23–24). In both situations, a spiritual force urges the young girl to return to life. Odd that the fairy that rescues Molly appears as a male since traditionally, fairies are depicted as female. Smith's openness to the embracing androgyny of the feminine divine manifests itself here in the sole mention in the novel of a fairy's gender being masculine.

The male fairy's appearance on the day before the mysterious arrival of another liminal figure—Simon Black—serves an oracular function also. With Mary White's departure from Agate Hill, Molly temporarily loses her refuge in the fairy world. Although Nicky Eck has awakened her sensual body by fondling her breasts, conflicted Molly writes in her diary that she hates Nicky Eck. Immediately after this declaration, she explains that she took Blanche and Godfrey down to the river, but that she didn't tell them anything about the Willow House or the fairy ring; in fact, she says, the fairy ring "is gone from the woods now," along with "anything else that me and Mary White used to do" (117). At the end of section one, Molly prepares to leave Agate Hill after being rescued from Nicky Eck's molestations by her enigmatic benefactor, Mr. Black. Molly writes in her diary, "I do not care that the fairy ring is gone from the woods now.... I do not care about anything" (122). Although Molly fails to recognize it until the end of the novel, Simon, depicted consistently throughout the novel as otherworldly, even as a "saint" (329), provides Molly with the guidance, support, and acceptance that her fairy religion has offered her. Furthermore, Simon's true connection to Molly is through the feminine spirit of Alice, Molly's mother.

Both Simon Black and Mary White serve as the "divine other" for Molly. Only when Mary White leaves does Simon Black appear, and, at some point in the novel, both characters are described as being integral parts of Molly's being. Smith's interest in the necessity of connection to others for females and in the need to experience "other lives" has remained central in her novels. In a recent interview, the writer explained that oftentimes the protagonist's spiritual search is linked to union with another person who may "seem like the other half" (Per). Both Mary White and Simon Black are crucial in that most sacred spot—Molly's "cave" or cubbyhole: Mary White in Molly's girlhood, and Simon Black when Molly returns to her cubbyhole in 1907 and sits in her "fairy tale chair" (332) to read and look through her box of phenomena that represents her true self. With Mary White, Molly is most in touch with her spiritual self. Molly says, "it is like I am thinking aloud when I talk to her" (75). Similar to Silvaney, Ivy Rowe's divine "other half," Mary White, with her halo image created by hair "stand[ing] out around her head" (43), exists in Molly's literal reality for only a short while, but she remains in Molly's heart and mind her entire life. Just as Ivy continues to write to Silvaney even after Silvaney's institutionalization and death, Molly persists in writing Mary White years after she stops receiving a response from the sick girl. Molly still sees Mary White dancing along the path to the woods, as "light as a fairy in her red coat" and observes with wonder that "sometimes she seemed not even to touch the ground" (74). Mary White's ethereal presence (represented by the red coat) recalls that of Granny Rowe. Ivy sees Granny's skirt swishing through the woods long after the old woman's death. Although an older Molly acknowledges that Mary White has gone "into the world of light" (332), she continues to imagine Mary White's red coat out in front of her, leading the way. At the end of the book and Molly's life, Molly sees Mary White's red coat "at the edge of the trees," beckoning Molly to "climb the hill in the moonlight" with her (357), as Molly feels drawn to the world of light where Mary White exists.

Smith provides a subtle link between Mary White and Simon Black in Simon's unexpected visit to Bobcat Mountain where Molly lives and teaches at the country school. When Simon arrives, Molly is "walking in the woods" (241) in the dazzling sunlight, wearing a "red scarf [that is] flying out behind her." Agnes describes having "the oddest sensation" and feels her heart in her throat immediately before she discovers Molly and Simon talking at the gate. With the second mention of Molly's red scarf amidst the dull surroundings, Smith powerfully reminds us of Mary White, Molly's "other half" that Molly has said she is "living for" and wants to "know everything [about], and be a part of" (192). Now, however, Simon Black is added to the couple's symbolic significance in Smith's description of Molly with Simon, as "their [Simon and Molly] breaths ... made clouds in the air, eventually drifting together as one" (241). The instant Agnes leaves the door where she has been watching Molly and Simon's exchange, having early on noted the "mythical qualities" (139) of Simon, Agnes expresses her strange "sense of devastating loss as well as relief." She writes, "I felt *saved* from something" (242). Agnes and Molly both have been "saved" from the confines of the world of traditional patriarchal religion; Simon Black functions as an avatar of the feminine divine.

Just as Mary White, with her arrival at Agate Hill, "saves" Molly from her dull, deadening world, Simon Black rescues Molly over and over again and offers a salvific presence throughout the novel. When Simon Black first visits Agate Hill to request guardianship of Molly, Smith emphasizes his healing nature. Before magically producing a vial from his pocket, he informs Selena that he has "taken the liberty" of delivering Uncle Junius's medication because of Dr. Lambeth's (the regular physician) illness. Molly, "a deep thrill" passing through her (106–107), is captivated by Simon's presence that seems "to fill the room" (109). Simon's function as savior is most notable when Simon removes Molly from Agate Hill and delivers her to Gatewood Academy, a place he believes to be safe and nurturing. Ironically, however, he unknowingly delivers her into the hands of hypocrisy, cruelty, and abuse.

The second section of the novel, appropriately named "Paradise Lost," not only describes Molly's five years of confinement and education at Gatewood, but also reveals another vantage point from which to view the character of Simon Black. Although initially Mariah Snow suspects Simon and writes with great sarcasm in her journal that he "can do no wrong in the eyes of Dr. Snow" (147), she grudgingly acknowledges Black's generous nature when Simon, with his sizable regular monetary contributions to the school, literally saves the school from financial ruin and closure. However, Simon's curative presence has a distorted effect on Mariah. She writes in her journal, "When I have closed my eyes to Pray these past two nights, I have seen—unaccountably—His face. I mean Simon Black's face" (152). In a tortured state, Mariah says she prays to God for deliverance from her "troublesome thoughts and dreams" (161), but her prayers go unanswered and her fantasies about Simon escalate as her hatred for Molly and her bitterness toward her husband increase. After commencement when Simon Black has returned after a four-year absence, Mariah writes in her journal that what she must do has come to her in a dream. Regarding Simon, she scribes three sentences, each in a separate paragraph: "I see Him now." "I know Him." "I simply cannot resist Him." Then a few lines down, she admits, "I am ready to go with Him" (200). In her anguish, she has made a god out of Simon Black and anticipates being rescued, or saved, by him. She writes, "I have a Fire running through my veins like a precursor of Hell itself." In deciding to give her soul over to Simon Black, Mariah believes she is "succumb[ing] to sin" and she will "lose Eden," but she admits, "'With thee to go is to stay ... in Paradise' ... For Gatewood is not Paradise, but rather Hell for me" (201). Quite predictably, Mariah's plans are dashed, but what emerges as noteworthy is not only that this woman automatically senses Simon Black's unusual powers, but also, that this early in the novel, Smith hints at the complexity in Simon's character.

Only later in the novel does Molly realize the salutary power of Simon Black, but, through her epistolary relationship with Mary White, she holds on to her memories of her fairytale world. While at Gatewood, Molly drifts away from the land of her imagination, and in her letters to Mary White she betrays a longing for this mystical connection. Molly has been silent for two years since her last diary entry dated July 2, 1873, when she said she didn't care about anything anymore. Only when she receives a letter from Mary White does she open up again—not in her diary this time, but in a letter written back to Mary. Mary White, now hospitalized with advanced scoliosis, reminds Molly of how they "ran through the woods like the wind" (165) when they were girls at Agate Hill, recalling to Molly's mind the freedom and exuberance of her spiritual self. In Molly's long letter back to Mary White, she reconnects to their fairytale land when she writes out the first verse of "Wynken, Blynken, and Nod" for her long lost friend. A year later, in the brief next letter from Mary White, the ailing girl provides the encouragement Molly needs to endure and survive her disappointments and losses. Mary jogs Molly's memories of a time when the girls "wandered the woods at Agate Hill" and walked barefoot in the cold river. She recalls that "the thunder rolled and the lightning came down like a fork and hit the sycamore tree on the hill," splitting the tree in two, and the girls "rolled over and over in the wet grass laughing." Then, they "ran through the woods ... and drank from the spring" and "the fairies came." With Mary's penultimate words to Molly, "Get up from there and live for me" (182), Smith links Mary White to the male fairy of section one, instructing Molly to move on with her life.

From here on out in the novel, Molly's letters to Mary White go unanswered, but they serve an important purpose for Molly; as she acknowledges in the novel's first section, when Molly communicates with Mary White, it's like talking to herself, the spiritual part of herself that Mary fosters. With the disappearance of Mary White, Smith brings to the forefront of Molly's life another important female companion. Molly writes to Mary White that after commencement, she will remain at Gatewood as a teacher and stay with Agnes in her "little stone fairy house" (192). Comparing her small living quarters to her cubbyhole back at Agate Hill, Molly thinks once again she will enjoy the nurturing world of her fairy religion. At this time everything in Molly's life suggests that she will progress on her spiritual journey to full knowledge of self. Describing the school "transformed into a brilliant fairyland" for commencement, with the flowers and lights (195), Molly writes to Mary White that the school looked like a "fairy tale school" with all the enchantment of a dream. However, because of Dr. Snow's inappropriate advances, Molly's fairytale world loses its beauty. Molly writes her last letter to Mary White for four years, recounting the reason that she and Agnes left Gatewood suddenly and unexpectedly. She describes her feelings after the funeral of Harry, one of the Snows' children, as "still want[ing] to run and scream when it storms" and asks Mary White to "remember how you and I used to dance around on Indian Rock when it thundered." Molly explains that when Dr. Snow approached her suddenly and touched her breasts that she felt trapped "under a spell," and for a moment Molly is drawn to his office, which she says is "almost a twin of the fairy house" she shares with Agnes. However, Molly quickly realizes that her feelings of intoxication and abandonment from the thunderstorm and the "thick sweet scent of roses" conflict with the suffocating presence of cold, hard Dr. Snow. The spell is broken with her twice repeated words, "'No Sir.'" Molly explains to Mary White, "I felt suddenly like I was flying, full of power" (206–207), as she kicks Dr. Snow twice. The sign Molly sees in the sky is a rainbow, a symbol of hope and reassurance that her journey will continue. Molly and Mary White had witnessed a rainbow in their Willow House, and their interpretation of the rainbow directly links it to their world of fairies. Molly writes in her diary that the fairies "flew away so fast on their gossamer wings leaving only a rainbow" (44). According to Barbara Walker, rainbows are equated with several mystical signs "usually connected with Goddess worship but sometimes taken over by male deities"

(*Dictionary* 349–50).* Molly's mention of the rainbow here, at this crucial turning point in her young life, suggests her recognition and acceptance of her own worth, the sacred, powerful force within her, and the rejection of what Mariah Snow has been forced to accept and endure all these years Molly has once more been rescued by the spirit of the feminine divine.

Mountains have consistently been linked to the feminine divine in Smith's works, and *On Agate Hill* is no exception. In her first diary entry, Molly invites the reader to come to Agate Hill where "the land will rise as you come up and up" (12) and describes one of her favorites spots as "the top of the hill" where Indian Rock is located (13). Almost every significantly symbolic scene occurs on a mountainside or on the top of a mountain. Smith recently explained that many of her female characters experience "a sort of union with the ineffable, with the sacred," and that oftentimes this mystical experience "has to do with the top of the mountain and nature and the cave." Emphasizing the centrality of the mountain in her works, she added, "There's a real spiritual element to it" (Per). In her journal, Agnes describes the trip from Gatewood Academy to Bobcat Mountain as a journey into "realms of gold" and says she feels "electrified watching the great blue shapes of the mountains gather around us" (220). She senses her "soul expand to meet the country" as she and Molly symbolically journey through the mountains of Ashe County, "ford[ing] creeks, pass[ing] through dense pine forests," crossing "a windy bald." In this section of the novel, considering Smith's spiritual vision, one would expect Molly to get in touch with her sacred sexuality, and this is exactly what happens among the breast-like "great rounded mountains" (230). When Molly meets Jacky Jarvis, Smith paints a symbolic scene with vibrant goddess imagery. Molly writes to Mary White about her trip with Martha Fickling to a house-raising party, calling her retelling of the evening's events "a fairy tale itself." Riding through the mountains, Molly notices "[f]reshets of water had burst out everywhere" and were "run[ning] down the mountain"; she begins "drinking the Spring" (255). Molly's union with Jacky, a vital, divine part of her self, occurs in Smith's most mythological setting, on top of a mountain.

Molly's holy experience with Jacky Jarvis directly parallels Ivy Rowe's sacred interlude with Honey Breeding. Calling Jacky "beautiful" (272), Molly understands that Jacky, like Honey, is a "back door man" (278), a wanderer, a free spirit. Like Ivy's comparison of Honey's body to that of a bee, with his coat of soft, yellow hair all over, Molly notes the "curly tangle of gold hair" covering Jacky's body (314). Similar to Ivy's sensation of fire running through her veins in its connection with both Silvaney and Honey, Molly describes

---

*Walker gives a blatant example of the sublimation of female stories to those of male deities in her account of the Biblical flood story, which derived from an earlier Babylonian myth. In the earlier version, the goddess Ishtar, angry at the god who caused the flood because of the overwhelming number of deaths, created the rainbow to block the male deity from "feeding on the offerings placed on earth's altars" (*Dictionary 350).*

having the same feeling and associates it with both Mary White and Jacky. However, unlike Ivy Rowe who stays only a short time in the cave with Honey, Molly leaves her teaching job at Bobcat School and elopes with Jacky. Molly's life with Jacky is perhaps what Ivy's life with Honey would have been, had Honey allowed her to go with him. With this novel and the longevity of Molly and Jacky's relationship, Smith takes the divine couple a step further in her depiction of the openness and acceptance of the feminine divine.

Another character imbued with mystical qualities, Jacky consistently inspires in Molly the same feelings she had with Mary White, linking him to the world of her imagination, her fairytale world. After their first meeting, Molly writes to Mary White, "I feel like running down the mountain drooping trees the way we used to at Agate Hill" (259), and Jacky will continue to fulfill the spiritual, as well as the sexual, needs of Molly. One of the first connections Molly and Jacky have is with their love for dancing, a bond she and Mary White have shared all these years. In Molly's first diary entry, she describes dancing on the mountaintop in a thunderstorm, "whirl[ing] around and around, ... like a dance I can not stop" (13). With Martha at the house-raising party, Molly admits, "I have loved to dance ever since I was at Gatewood" (256), and just as she's begun to dance to the fiddle music, Jacky enters and immediately starts dancing all around, picking his banjo. Two days later when Molly and Jacky travel up to Manbone Rock together, their playful behavior echoes earlier scenes at Agate Hill. Molly says, "together we rolled over and over down the steep hill ... laughing too hard to quit" (266). She hasn't felt this way since she and Mary White had the same experience ten years before. And just as Mary White and Molly had seen a hawk "making lazy circles in the sky" (74) when they were on their way to Mama Marie and Aunt Mitty's house, Molly and Jacky, while standing on Manbone Rock, also see hawks circling. The hawk circling, an important symbolic image introduced in *Fair and Tender Ladies*, in this novel again suggests mystical experience. Although mythology most commonly identifies the hawk as a death symbol, in the iconography of goddess mythology, rebirth and regeneration always coexist alongside death, and circles and circling motions are transmitters of power and energy. At several turning points for Molly, the circling hawk may be interpreted as a sign of the omnipresence of the feminine divine, a powerful force assuring the continuity of the life of the spirit.

Molly must learn to accept the transitory nature of physical connections and find assurance in the cycle of birth-death-regeneration represented in the feminine divine. Although she tries, she cannot hold on to and keep the people she loves. The symbolic link between Jacky and Mary White, in their mutual symbiosis with Molly, is even more pronounced when Molly describes the tallest pine tree being struck by lightning and cracking in two before crashing onto the rocks. We immediately recall Mary White's letter in which she reminds Molly of their childhood experience when a sycamore tree was struck by lightning. Both pairs have experienced a terrifying and potentially fatal event, but in both situations, the couple reacts by "laughing to beat the band" (276). On the night that Jacky asks Molly to marry him, Molly, on her way to meet him, says, "I thought I saw your little red coat just ahead of me, Mary White, flitting through the trees, showing me the way," the way to Jacky, who "emerge[s] from the tree like a forest sprite," the tree to which Mary White has led Molly (271). Mary White's little red coat becomes Jacky's little red bowtie he purchases along with a wagon and a mule when he invents the "rolling store" (297) and starts traveling around and absenting himself for long stretches of time. The red bow tie is linked to Jacky's wandering, his roaming around, and the impossibility of his staying in one place for very long. At the coroner's inquest, Molly recalls how Jacky kept his "red bow tie," along with his other ties, in a willow basket* in their bedroom (320). Just as Mary White's red coat evokes the frail girl's ephemeral essence and Molly's thoughts of her suggest movement and roaming, Jacky's red bowtie suggests the same. Molly and Mary White's lifelong connection began in the "cave" of Molly's cubbyhole; Molly and Jacky's love commences in a literal cave, where they find shelter during the storm. At the end of the novel as Molly writes her last diary entry, she says she sees Mary White's "red coat at the edge of the trees" and is going down there so the two of them can "go up to our Indian Rock" where they will "dance and yell when the storm comes closer, first the thunder then the lightning" (357). Then Molly sees at the top of the hill Manbone Rock and the cave with Jacky and the "jumping fire" inside, just before she reveals that she was the one who shot Jacky twenty years ago, in order to end his suffering. Molly's last memory of Jacky—dragging Jacky "outside just as the dance floor fell in"—is joined to her last thought of Mary White. Molly asks, "Oh, Mary White, don't you remember how we danced and danced as the storm came on, what did we know then of lightning?" (359). For now, Molly understands the lightning-like feeling of having given one's heart completely. Indian Rock, Manbone Rock, thunder and lightning, and dancing all merge in Molly's mind as she concludes her last diary entry and Smith ends the novel.

Imagery associated with the feminine divine permeates the novel as we consistently see the presence of the wind, rocks and stones, water and springs, the moon, honeysuckle and bees, caves, fire, roses and the colors yellow and red. In settings of mystical significance, often all these images are present. As Smith explores an alternative spirituality, one apart from traditional orthodox Christianity, she uses nature and natural imagery to convey a sense of sacredness and suggest divinity in feminine experience. From the beginning of the novel, as Molly is drawn to the "fairy religion," we become aware that her most worshipful moments are those in nature. In the first diary entry, we learn about

---

Smith specifically names the type of basket—willow—a link to the Willow House and the metaphorical significance of willow trees in their connection with ancient goddess figures.

IX. "Part of the earth and the sky, the living and the dead" 211

one of Molly's special spots—Indian Rock—a large flat rock that stays warm long after dark because of the direct sunlight hitting it all day. She describes lying on the rock in the bright moonlight, letting the wind blow over her face and body. Admitting that she likes rocks instead of jewelry (creature of nature that she is), Molly shares her most private thoughts, telling us how she loves to read, watch a thunderstorm, and dance in the wind on her Indian Rock, all sacred activities of the feminine divine. The Willow House, another hallowed place for Molly, sits in the middle of cool, running water in a shallow place in the river. Here, Molly says, "time stops still it seems," where she and Mary White sit on "three white rocks" and first see the fairies (44). Barbara Walker explains that willows possess a "notorious connection with ancient Goddess figures" and that in many religions, willows were placed around a central altar in a temple (*Dictionary* 474–75). Aside from the size and shape of an adult willow tree and the girls' natural attraction to this location for privacy, the symbolic association of the willow adds another dimension to the girls' chosen place of retreat. As soon as they return from their trip to Hillsborough where they saw the Tableaux Vivants, Molly and Mary White run to their Willow House, their own secret place for "fairy worship," where their imaginations and their feminine spirits flourish. Their sacred spot provides safety and sanctity for the girls after they have encountered the judgment and narrowness of the world of Aunt Cecelia's religion.

When at Gatewood, Molly manages to bring with her a part of the world of the Willow House and even participates in what resembles a goddess ritual on a mountaintop. She pens to Mary White that she plans to write her graduation composition about the Willow House with the theme, "society where none intrudes" (193). Molly's time at Gatewood has been sparse with spiritual instances. However, when a group of the younger girls take a day trip to Onaluskee Mountain for a picnic, Smith paints a scene with mythical proportions. As reported in Agnes's letter to her sister Mariah Snow, the carriages travel up the "incline of the mountain road beneath the arch of trees" to reach the overlook where the group of girls spread their picnic supplies upon "the flat gray rocks quite warm from the sun" (157). For the first time during Molly's tenure at Gatewood, she visits a setting that reminds her of Agate Hill and the sanctity of Indian Rock and the Willow House. Smith implies the innate divinity within females as the girls first make daisy chains, then adorn themselves with crowns. Walker notes that the wearing of a crown, or any prominent decoration of the head, has always accompanied some form of apotheosis (*Dictionary* 132). In addition to the wearing of crowns, one of the girls explains to the group that the word "flora" comes from the goddess Flora, then continues by telling the story of how the Greek gods, led by Jupiter,* became pow-

---

*In her explanation of Greek mythology, Eliza Valiant confuses Roman and Greek mythology. Zeus is the Greek counterpart of Jupiter.

erful and lived on Mount Olympus, "which might have looked something like *this* mountain" (159). However, Smith implies that Onaluskee Mountain totally lacks governance by a male god. Certainly the author intends for us to note the absence of any male on this outing. Smith takes the goddess symbolism a step further when some of the girls join together in a ritualistic circle dance, "prancing around the outside of the daisy circle" (159). Despite the blatant cruelty of their condemnation of Molly as "'Bad girl! Orphan!'" (160), the appropriately named Eliza Valiant quickly breaks the spell by standing up for Molly and uniting the girls in tolerance and acceptance of our unconventional heroine. Here in this goddess-imbued setting, with clouds gathering "over the brow of the mountain behind them" (158), the girls, having crowned themselves in honor of Flora and dined together on "flat gray 'table rocks' of the mountainside" (160), usher in a storm, complete with thunder and spattering raindrops on the rocks. Smith's wise humor hints that the rolling thunder suggests the male god Jupiter's anger at the power of this group of young females celebrating the pleasure-loving deity, the goddess of flowers and the spring.

The divine sense of "other" that Smith introduced in her second novel, *Something in the Wind*, with Brooke and Bentley, and has progressively developed in her subsequent novels, reaches full development and force in the depiction of the divine couple—Molly Petree and Jacky Jarvis. From their fairytale meeting, through their seven-day courtship, to their elopement by "the light of the moon" (279), Molly and Jacky's symbiotic relationship resonates with the appurtenances of the goddess. Jacky represents for Molly the religion of love, of the spirit, of nature, and of the body. Jacky's mysterious, ephemeral presence makes Molly feel suspended in time when she's with him, like the way she felt with Mary White in the Willow House. Jacky says he "never figured on getting old," his timelessness in keeping with the divinity he represents. When Jacky visits Molly for the first time on a Sunday, he uncovers his plan to "hold church" for her. When Molly says she's a "bad girl," he corrects her, "there ain't no such thing" in his church. Calling his church the "Jacky Jarvis Church of Love and Light and Redemption for All," Jacky promises to "save" Molly (260–61). Subsequently, Molly says she felt like she and Jacky had been "saved for something" when they narrowly escape the lightning-struck crashing pine tree. Then when Molly returns home after this adventure with Jacky, she learns from Chattie Badger, the woman with whom Molly currently lives, that while Molly was being "saved" by Jacky, "tens [sic] of people rush[ed] forward to be saved" in church that day (269). This parallel once again juxtaposes traditional patriarchal religion with Molly's fairytale religion, the salvation she experiences with Jacky.

Goddess imagery permeates the setting of Molly and Jacky's symbolic journey to Manbone Rock and the time they spend there during the storm. On a windy day, atop Jacky's horse Betty, Molly and Jacky travel down a "steep trail through thick mountain laurel" that Molly says was "like going down a

IX. "Part of the earth and the sky, the living and the dead" 213

tunnel," finally stopping in a "windy open field" near an "outcropping of big white boulders" at the edge of the mountain. Jacky identifies the location as "Bone Valley" and points out lone white Manbone Rock, "as big as a cabin." As hawks "dipped and wheeled" through the sky, Molly writes that she felt "exposed," like she was in "another country." For a moment, she thinks she hears "voices in the wind, singing church songs" (263–64). The wind, consistently associated with the feminine divine in Smith, speaks to Molly, but, like a number of other characters, her limited understanding of this sacred feeling prescribes that the "voices" must be coming from the traditional country church. Jacky's "church," however, resonates with the sanctity Molly felt in her Willow House and on her Indian Rock when she roamed her "beloved woods" (37) with the fairies. With the wind "blowing like crazy" (266) and the couple talking, laughing, and playing together, a "long deep roll of thunder," then a "jagged bolt of lightning" sends them racing up the hill to Manbone Rock for cover. Molly writes that she felt she was in a dream, for storms always accompanied her contact with the fairy world and the ecstatic sensation of being outside her self. What she feels now with Jacky parallels the exhilaration of her fairytale world—the world of the feminine divine. Molly and Jacky find shelter in a cave up under Manbone Rock, and Smith twice refers to the "mouth of the cave" (267) through which they enter and eventually exit after the storm subsides. Inside the symbolic womb, Jacky builds a fire and the two watch the "firelight flicker on the cave walls" while Jacky makes shadow animals across the "red rocky walls of the cave" (268). When the storm passes, the couple emerges to witness the splitting in two of the huge pine tree and realizes their good fortune. Then they journey back up the trail "through the dripping laurel"* just as the sun is "setting all red through the lacy trees" (269).

Smith insists on the centrality of language in her spiritual vision, what she calls the "feminine way of telling a story" (Per). For Smith, telling stories, talking, writing, and reading are all necessary for life and for validation of one's sacred self. Before the storm, while they sit together, Jacky says to Molly, "'Now ... start talking. I want to know all about you. I want to know everything.'" Molly describes the words escaping her mouth "in a big rush like a creek running down off a mountain." When she pauses for a break, she tells Jacky, "'Now it's your turn,'" and he gives her his whole family history (264). When Jacky leaves that day and says simply, "'I'll see you,'" Molly muses, "those words seemed to enter my body" (269). Aside from the obvious Biblical allusion in Smith's diction, Molly's recognition of the necessity and importance

---

**In addition to its association with victory (discussed in Chapter VII), the laurel also has been linked to divinity and prophecy. Additionally, in Roman mythology it was believed that the laurel was never struck by lightning (Walker,* Dictionary *466). This mythological detail sheds further significance on Smith's mentioning twice that Jacky and Molly's journey is marked with laurel trees.*

of her flesh, of the response of her body to Jacky, reflects Smith's philosophy that "the way to the mind and the heart is only through the body.... The way to the soul is through the body." Recently Smith reiterated, "for me, the body is the only way" (Per). Throughout their courtship, Molly describes Jacky as "talking a mile a minute" (270) and she relishes every word. In keeping a diary, Molly shows her love of language and verifies its necessity for her. As Smith comments in her "Note" at the end of the book, writing is "a source of nourishment and strength" and can "always help us make it through the night" (373). Molly pens in her diary, "I am remembering everything" (117), and putting it into words is a way of codifying her world, as Lee Smith says, a way "to create some order where it did not exist, to give a recognizable shape to the sadness and chaos of our lives" (374). Twenty years after Jacky's death and following forty-four years of silence, Molly writes in her diary about the events following her husband's death. She says she would not allow "the slimy pockmarked preacher or the fat old righteous preacher" to visit her in jail; she was "too busy remembering Jacky, memorizing him" (313). Then, with the story of the last twenty years Molly tells in her diary, which has been neglected for fifty-four years, Smith brings Molly back home to Agate Hill where she finds healing and fulfillment in her reunion with Simon Black, her first savior.

Though throughout the novel Molly has rejected Simon Black's offers of assistance and has even described him as "crazy" in a letter to Mary White, Smith highlights Simon's significance with Molly's words in the same letter, when Molly associates Simon with "destiny, and stars" (250). Simon, consistently depicted as "larger than life" (139), a mystical being who never sleeps, has been an omnipresent force in Molly's life although she has refused to acknowledge him. We learn in BJ's testimony at the coroner's inquest that Simon had visited Plain View a few days after Molly arrived there as Jacky's new wife. Recognizing that Simon "had a way about him. A presence," BJ says he had the feeling that Simon Black knew "everything about us." Simon Black again "saves" Molly, in fact, the entire Jarvis family, by purchasing Rag Mountain for what BJ calls "a pure fortune" (289–90). Though Simon seldom spends time there, BJ says Simon's presence on the mountain "seemed natural" and even admits, "I liked it when Mister Black was over there, I felt like he was watching over us, or something" (292). The implied divinity of Simon Black is felt by many, but none so much as Molly once she returns to Agate Hill after learning that Simon had bought the place right after her departure. Simon, by purchasing Agate Hill, had "saved" Selena, Uncle Junius's widow, and their unborn child from being turned out with no place to go.

At the end of the novel, in her concluding letter to Dr. Ferrell, Tuscany Miller describes the relationship between Simon Black and Molly Petree with the words of Martha Fickling: "Sometimes there can come an attraction between two people ... that is going to last though all hell breaks loose and longer than death" (229). Tuscany understands the complexity of this unusual, sacred kind of love. With Molly and Simon, Smith features an unusual relationship in which the partners alternate the roles of mother and child. As strange as that may sound initially, this arrangement is integral to Smith's vision of a world open to the feminine divine. Simon Black, by necessity, "mothers" the motherless Molly from afar, for while he is healthy, she rejects his nurturance every possible way. He is the divine mother, "a saint in the stain-glassed window" (329), providing salvation for her and, when possible, for those she loves. Only when Molly returns to Agate Hill and cares for the ill and dying Simon are the roles reversed as she finally is able to "mother" him. Remembering the warmth of her Indian Rock, she travels with Henry through the "fairy tale forest" that looks like a "cathedral" inside and finds Simon in Uncle Junius's old study, which she had earlier described as her uncle's "cave" (60). The womb imagery connects to Molly's experience with Jacky and once again, Molly enters the symbolic cave to later emerge more in touch with her spiritual self. Almost as if she is asking about Jesus's purpose on earth, Molly asks Henry about Simon's presence at Agate Hill, "'Why did he come, then?'" Henry's response: "'You will see.'" And she does, for when she first sees Simon, Molly thinks, "<u>I have been waiting for this</u>. It was the last thing left to happen to me" (328–29), language reminiscent of Ivy's words to Honey Breeding when he tells her of the insignificance of their affair. Simon's love for Molly's mother Alice has blended into his love for Molly, and Molly, by taking care of Simon and watching over him until his death, gives Simon the love that has eluded him most of his lonely life. Soon after her return to Agate Hill, Molly explains that she woke in the night and went to Simon's room and lay with him, explaining, "I found there an indescribable sweetness and peace, a sort of joy." She shared her fairy world with Simon, the world of poetry, reading to him words that he seemed to enjoy. However, Molly says in the end he didn't recognize her, and she admits, "I am not sure I knew who I was either." Their roles have shifted and complicated themselves through the many years of their relationship. Molly describes their lying together, "flesh to flesh, bone to bone," and when he died, she lay beside him. Molly writes, "We are like a sarcophagus, I thought, remembering the Etruscan tombs" she studied at Gatewood. Then she repeats, "Now we are the sarcophagus itself" (333–34).

Smith's diction here, with the repetition of the sarcophagus image, strongly suggests the feminine divine, the mother goddess as destroyer or death-bringer. The Greek word "sarcophagus" literally means "eater of flesh," referring to the belief that the stone used for coffins (limestone, at that time) aided in the decomposition process. Another definition of sarcophagus, not quite as literal, is "stone coffin," the coffin conceived in antiquity as another version of the symbolic womb from which the dead might rise in rebirth (Walker, *Dictionary* 129). In many societies the sarcophagi actually took on a uterine shape (160) and the goddess was painted on the inside of the lid "where the dead person could see her and respond to her kind ministrations." Consistently, throughout ancient history, the hope for rebirth and renewal was "intimately and inextricably involved with the divine Mother" (129). Since sarcophagi existed in many ancient cultures and Smith mentions specifically the "Etruscan tombs," a brief look at this ancient society and religion might prove helpful. Gimbutas discusses the striking freedom and power of Etruscan women, who were recorded to exercise in the nude, drink alcoholic beverages, dance, and dress in a manner similar to that of their male counterparts. In sharp contrast to Roman customs where women had no name of their own, Etruscan women's names reflected their legal and social status. In fact, in inscriptions, individuals are referred to by their mothers' names only. Not only is it important that Smith, i.e., Molly, at the moment of Simon's death, imagines the two of them as a sarcophagus and recalls the Etruscan tombs because of the centrality of the female and the feminine divine in both, but also, Gimbutas points out that this ancient tomb "presented the final chapter in the Old European philosophy of life and death, in which they viewed death as a joyful transition necessary for the renewal of life" (*Living* 170). Scenes on these tombs depicted the "sweetness and joy" that Molly experienced while lying with Simon—scenes with music, dancing, lovemaking, and also depictions of the tree of life (171).

Smith also develops the facet of the feminine divine that embraces the natural cycle of birth-death-regeneration with her treatment of motherhood throughout the novel. About her own spirituality, the author identifies mothering as the most sacred of all experiences of the feminine divine: "The most important role really for me, where I have felt more in touch with my self and whatever else is out there was being a mother.... There's nothing quite like being a mother" (Per). In this novel, childbirth and loss of children play an important role. Smith allows for the feminine divine to exist in her duality of life-giver and life-taker. Somehow all of this must make sense, so Molly, i.e., Smith, writes about it to someway "order" the tragedy and loss in her life. The motif of childbirth appears in the second section of the novel in the Gatewood portion with Mariah Snow's journal. Prior to Molly's arrival at the school, Mariah, now pregnant, has eight children—all boys—and we never learn their ages since they are largely absent from any of our sources of information about this chapter in Molly's life. In a period of four years, Mariah gives birth to three more babies, two of whom die before age two. The last child is born a couple of weeks after Molly and Agnes leave; we learn about this event in Mariah's last journal entry that states simply, "Gave birth" (212). Mariah's depression, her alternations between aggression and passivity, her eventual loss of touch with reality, are intricately linked to her lack of choice in sexual relations with her husband, pregnancy, childbirth, and maternal concerns.

Admitting repeatedly that she wants to "cleanse and purify" what she calls her "black soul" (146), Mariah copes with her restlessness, anxiety and guilt by taking her oft-mentioned cold baths. Molly writes to Mary White about Mrs. Snow's "shrieks" when she steps into her "icy cold bath[s]" (169). In *The Wandering Womb: A Cultural History of Outrageous Beliefs About Women*, Lana Thompson discusses what was referred to in the nineteenth and early twentieth century as the "cold-water treatment," in which women who "felt unfulfilled, or verbalized negativity toward domestic responsibilities" were diagnosed as insane and often immersed in tubs of icy water as a type of "shock therapy." Women also performed this type of self-abuse in order to "assault the body and horrify the mind until both withered from exhaustion" (133) and they could more easily submit. Although Molly identifies Mariah's bath as a daily practice for the woman, Mariah most often comments in her journal about a cold bath on the occasions when Dr. Snow has demanded sexual service. At one point confessing she cannot sleep anymore because of the "awful thoughts in her head" at which "even her old friend John Milton" would have shuttered (162), Mariah immerses her body in this "frozen hell" (Thompson 133) to curb her "Temper, Impatience, & Nervousness" (Smith 146). Forced to accept her role of subservience and submission to her husband, Mariah spirals to certain doom.

Dreading each time Dr. Snow exercises what she calls his "Conjugal Rights" (152), Mariah often "suffer[s] the attentions" of Dr. Snow (173) by "reciting the beginning of Paradise Lost" (152). Her powerlessness is made obvious when she decides to name her newborn daughter Susannah, but her husband, after a week, comes to see the child for the first time and renames her "Frances Theodosia, for his Mother," whom Mariah says, "I Hated with all my being." Worn down by pregnancy and childbirth and desperate for some type of birth control, Mariah consults her physician who helpfully advises, "'Abstinence, Mariah.'" Silenced by the male-dominated world around her, Mariah pens in her journal that she cannot tell the doctor or anyone else what "a perfect Demon" her husband is; then she writes, "Once I heard of negro girls using marbles for the purpose.... perhaps I shall give this dire remedy a try if necessary" (163–64). After this post, there are no others for three months, and as Mariah sinks into deep depression, her entries become clipped; one section is even torn out. After the death of Frances, Mariah's guilt overwhelms her, but she delivers another child only a year later. Again, Mariah remains silent for three months, until she becomes obsessed with Simon Black. Once she, out of necessity, abandons her scheme to abscond with Simon, Mariah says, "it was as though a heavy iron door had swung to with a resounding clang that will echo in my mind forever" (204). Her destruction is imminent; she will never escape her prison. The image of Mariah clawing at her bleeding face with her fingernails, "her black hair ... out all around her head like Medusa" (210) strongly suggests the image of the damaged goddess. Agnes's last letter to her sister illuminates the tragedy of Mariah's life. Agnes assures Mariah, "I shall always think of you, unspoken, secret Mother" (211). The mother goddess, the feminine divine, has remained trapped inside a patriarchal system that has forced her submission to negligence, mistreatment, and even abuse. The result of this disaster can be seen in the fate of Mariah Snow, committed to an asylum two years after the departure of Agnes and Molly.

Molly's experience with motherhood, almost the polar opposite of Mariah's except in their common loss of children in death, reflects Smith's sense of the feminine divine and the centrality of motherhood in the writer's spiritual vision. Giving birth to, and losing, seven children over a period of sixteen years, Molly endures the ultimate pain for a mother. After her first child Christabel lives to the age of two, Molly only delivers one more live baby who survives just three weeks, the five others being stillbirths. Molly's pregnancies are not the product of male domination or the result of a man's inflated ego, as in the case with Mariah and Cincinnatus Snow. Molly and Jacky's union has been one of equality and mutual love and respect. Unlike Mariah who felt fortunate to have a wet nurse for her baby Frances, Molly nurses Christabel herself. After her daughter's death, Molly tells BJ that she wants to think about her baby "every hour of every day," that the emptiness left in her heart will never be filled. She will always remember breastfeeding Christabel, "the rain drumming so loud on the roof, and the moon shining out on the snow" (296). Smith repeats this divine image of sacred motherhood later when Molly writes in her diary twenty years after returning to Agate Hill and forty years after Christabel's death. As she recounts the events after the coroner's inquest when she returns to her home at Plain View, she recalls sitting in the rocking chair, nursing Christabel. She writes, "I could still feel the steady pull of her mouth on my nipple, the sweet release in my breasts as the milk came down. There is nothing like that in the world" (321). The lucidity of Smith's depiction of this sacred female, nourishing her child with her breast milk, leaves no doubt about Molly's connection with the feminine divine. However, the antinomy of motherhood prescribes pain as well as joy for this young mother. After her memories of nursing Christabel find their way to the page, Molly writes of the "sweet shallow breath and little curled fingers and rosy feet" (321) of all her other dead children buried up on the mountain, their graves marked by stones. In their exploration of signs of the divine feminine around the world, Andrew Harvey and Anne Baring note that stones remain the densest, oldest and most enduring aspect of life on earth and have consistently through the ages represented the feminine divine (14–16). BJ has placed rocks on all the babies' graves, even the ones without a carved stone. He observes, "Just a row of rock babies up on the mountain like a stone wall," and Jacky, in his grief and frustration after several babies have died, has called the row of graves a "crop of babies" (298–99).

Molly's "stone babies," as she calls them at the end of her diary and her life (359), symbolically link to Molly's memories of her fairytale world, the world of the feminine divine. Rocks and stones have been a critical image in all of Molly's mystical experiences. The novel is inundated with rock and stone imagery: Molly's large, flat, warm Indian Rock; the three white rocks in the Willow House and the fairy ring in the circle of rocks at Agate Hill; the flat rocks that Molly and Mary White use for digging up bones; the "table rocks" the Gatewood girls use for their picnic; huge, white Manbone Rock with its womb-like cave; the stone tomb of the sarcophagus that Molly imagines as her and Simon; and finally Molly's last trip to market with Juney and Henry as "the land flows past on each side, tree and rock and fence and flower," all on Agate Hill (359). Agate—a stone frequently credited with divine attraction, a lucky stone—remains the most poignant image in Molly's life. She begins with it; she ends with it.

In a brief section called "A Conversation with the Author" at the conclusion of the book, Smith calls the appearance of Juney in the last section of the novel an unexpected "blessing" (382). A culmination of natural images of the feminine divine, Juney serves as the healing presence that sustains Molly and gives her an opportunity to experience love and joy once more. The idea of wandering, roaming, living wild and free, as opposed to being contained or limited, has consistently concerned Smith, and her writing persistently questions any belief system that would tie a person down to a prescribed code of behavior. In previous novels, divinely inspired, mystical characters have been linked to the woods, the forest, the world of nature. Prominent examples include Silvaney and Honey Breeding of *Fair and Tender Ladies*, Faye of *Family Linen*, and Dory of *Oral History*.

In this novel, Juney, an "extraordinary little personage" (329), continues this line of powerful, sacred presences. The unwanted and dwarf-like son of Selena and Uncle Junius, Juney was abandoned as a child by his mother, left in the woods and presumably raised in nature perhaps by animals. However, Smith leaves the details of Juney's past a mystery. All the divine images Smith has used in the novel, and in previous works, amalgamate in the creation of Juney, Molly's "little man" whom she says twice she "could not do without" (355, 359). When he first appears shortly after Molly's return to Agate Hill, Molly says she was unsure initially if he were a girl or a boy, a child or an adult. Smith consistently challenges our tendency to define, to categorize people; these categories often cloud our ability to understand the presence of divinity in our everyday experiences, those outside the traditional Christian church. In placing labels on people, we limit the possibilities for understanding human nature and the nature of divinity. Smith images Juney as almost totally blind, but ironically, as Molly learns, his vision encompasses all. And since his vision subsumes all of time and place, Molly says Juney sees her nursing Christabel all those years ago and he sees Simon's wife and twin sons swirling around in the lake where they drowned. Juney sees pain as well as joy and heals all things naturally.

An early indication of Molly's relationship with Juney, Smith describes

Juney's "sweet radiant face" and his smile as one of "incredible sweetness, like a small child." Just as Molly and Simon in their sacred relationship had alternately "mothered" the other, Juney and Molly do the same. Juney is the consolidation of all the children Molly has buried, both daughter and son, child and adult, as most of Molly's children would be grown by the time she meets Juney. And as Molly ages, she admits she becomes child-like herself, even sleeping in a child's bed since her body has shrunk to such a small size. Molly says when she first said her name to Juney, he "ran his hands quickly all over my face with the lightest skittering touch, like a hummingbird." As she closed her eyes, "giving myself over to it," she lost her balance and almost fell; then, she reflects, "I felt entirely refreshed when I came back to myself" (330–31). According to Erich Neumann in *The Great Mother*, the hummingbird, associated with fertility, is a symbol of "the vegetation of the beginning of the rainy season," specifically linked to the "maize tree in the west, the realm of the Great Mother" (199). Smith joins Molly and Juney with hummingbird imagery. One might recall that in Molly's first diary entry at age thirteen, Molly compares herself to "the ruby-throated hummingbird that comes again and again to Fannies rosebush but lights down never for good and all, always flying on" (7). Now, at age sixty-eight, Molly compares Juney to a hummingbird whose touch is refreshing, and Molly has not only become one with this ethereal creature, but also, "lit down for good" here at Agate Hill, the place she began her story.

Juney's mysterious "gifts" become evident almost immediately. On the first day of Molly's return to Agate Hill, Juney appears suddenly with a perfect apple pie. Molly says, "it was as if he had produced it out of thin air, by magic" (321). Along with Henry, Juney works in the garden raising a huge variety of large, healthy vegetables that the three of them take to market every week. Molly describes Juney moving across the garden on all fours "as the sun moves across the sky, pulling radishes like jewels out of the earth" (351). Along with providing food, gardening has often served as a creative outlet, for women especially. In *The Feminine Face of God*, Anderson and Hopkins add another dimension to the symbolism of the garden, suggesting its metaphorical connection to spirituality and inner sacredness (15–16). Not only is Juney's presence spiritually elevating for Molly, but also as he pulls "jewels from the earth," Juney, compared to the sun, brings out the inner sacredness of Molly and others around him. Having "lived in the woods and the place by himself for so long like an animal," Juney "always knows everything" (334, 355), Molly repeats twice. People from miles around come to either bring their babies to Juney for healing by his mysterious ways or just to converse with Juney. Molly explains Juney's reticence and notes that he just listens to people's troubles and "touches them, or touches something they have brought with them" (353). Just as Juney's presence proves salvific for Molly, it heals others too. Smith twice repeats, "Juney's illness, if it is an illness, has left him with certain gifts" (353, 355). The religion of the ancient Etruscans included, along with a group of gods and goddesses similar to the Greek deities, belief in the existence of the "divine child," associated with the image of the egg—a symbol of regeneration (Gimbutas, *Living* 169). Other than the obvious implication that eggs hold new life, because of their shape, eggs also suggested the womb (51). Along with their vegetables and flowers, the divine trio (Molly, Juney, and Henry) take their eggs to market. In the last few words of her diary, Molly writes, "Juney is the one who holds the basket of eggs" (359), a symbol of regeneration and rebirth. With Juney's "gift" in not only curing ailments, but also, incarnating sacredness and divinity, he provides for Molly a link to Simon, Mary White, Jacky, Christabel and Molly's other dead children. Molly says of Henry, Juney and herself, "We are a part of the earth and the sky, the living and the dead, and we make no distinction between them" (356). All are connected; all are part of each other and each other's stories.

In Molly's last diary entry, she says, "I am the one who tells the stories" (359); in fact, she writes that she "say[s] the world for" Juney. Like Molly, Juney loves stories, and just as Molly had shared with Simon her world of the imagination through poetry and had written love stories for Mary White, she shares her fairytale world with Juney. Molly recites poetry and sings songs for him, as well as tells him stories such as "the time Spencer caught the big fish, ... the time the ghost horse galloped around the circle, ... the time Old Bess and Virgil flew away over the snow, ... the time Mary White and me saw the fairies" (354). By retelling these stories, by bringing to life her fairy world—the realm of the feminine divine—Molly keeps alive that most sacred part of her self. With Tuscany Miller's letters framing the novel, Smith suggests the timelessness and continuity of Molly's story, Molly's life. Another powerful female figure, Tuscany, like Molly, sorts, organizes, and orders the events represented by the items in her discovered box of paraphernalia. Just as Molly's diary gives shape and form to her life, Tuscany's letters, notes, and comments throughout the novel give shape to a whole period of history. By "ordering" Molly's life, Tuscany makes sense of her own, tying together all the loose ends and creating a coherent story. Besides entertainment, Tuscany's digressions into news of her own personal life allow a portrait of a modern-day young woman whose "contrary streak" (245) very much resembles Molly's. At the end of the book, Tuscany even admits, "*Sometimes I feel like I AM Molly Petree*" (362), as storyteller and story become blended. With her depiction of Tuscany Miller, Smith offers an updated, divinely inspired, integrated version of *Oral History*'s Jennifer Bingham. Whereas Jennifer fails to recognize the significance and sacredness of the Cantrell family saga she records, Tuscany perceives the salience of the story she exhumes and memorializes. In the "Conversations" at the end of the book, Smith emphasizes "the haphazard, arbitrary nature of history," noting that what we study in school as "historical *truth*" actually depends on many variables, like "who finds it, who interprets it, how it is dessiminated and publicized..." (380). Thus, Molly's story, through Tuscany's story, through Smith's story, remains alive, fixed in our "fleeting memories" (373), not because Molly as an individual woman changed history, but because Molly Petree's journey, to use Estés's words again, "impresses upon our flesh the odor of the sacred" (27). Her journey, in its reflection of the search for the feminine divine, represents all our spiritual journeys.

CONCLUSION

Molly Petree's journey and Lee Smith's two-year journey of writing *On Agate Hill* have led both Molly and her creator to a place of healing and reconciliation. The writing of the book not only served as therapy for Smith, but also provided the writer a means to move through her tremendous grief over the tragic death of her thirty-three-year-old son Josh. Smith said Josh came back to her in a sense with her creation of the fictional character Juney, for Juney embodies "all those really dear and deep and moving qualities that Josh had" (Per). In her Note at the conclusion of the novel, Smith describes her son as "a huge whimsical man of immense kindness with a special sort of gravity and eccentric insight." In his final stages of illness, Smith said Josh was "like the bodhisattva, a person who has achieved the final apotheosis, beyond desire and self" (371). Calling him "a man like a mountain that you could rest against" (Per), Smith lucidly links her son to the most enduring symbol of the divine in her writing, the majestic mountains of North Carolina. In preserving Josh's sacred presence in this moving image, Smith truly has come to rest against this mountain.

Through her tremendous oeuvre, Lee Smith embarks on and undertakes a spiritual journey that leads her to a sense of the feminine divine in nature and in everyday experiences for women. Smith's protagonists initially search for validation in traditional patriarchal religion but find this path an unsatisfactory means to achieve integration and wholeness. Next, they often turn to sex and even the experience of giving birth and mothering children in hopes of finding personal salvation. These females, victims of a dualistic society that has split apart the various complexes of the feminine psyche, yearn to attain a sense of wholeness. Often mystical experiences reflect women's traditional attunement with nature and the natural processes associated with the cycle of female life—birth, sexuality, maternity, creativity, aging, death, and regeneration. This innate sense of the sacredness of all of life predisposes females to a highly developed consciousness of their own sensuality, sexuality, and maternal nature. To achieve integration and reconciliation, a protagonist must embrace her inner sanctity, oftentimes awakened through sexual ecstasy or maternal experiences, and accept the presence of the feminine divine in her everyday life. Oftentimes a Smith protagonist, as a means of coping with the rigidity and confinement of her environment, longs for and creates a world of make-believe, a fairytale world, in which she experiences abandonment and exhilaration and feels accepted and treasured. A female arrives in this world of the imagination, this "inexplicable psychic land" (Estés 27), through language—reading or writing, telling or listening to stories. Thus, language becomes a salvific way to order and explain the sadness and loss in her life. Stories—invented or real—whether they occur in the present of a novel or come to life through a journal or diary from the past, or a bundle of letters found in an attic or basement, or a tape recording of the voices and sounds of a "haunted house," or the songs on a record album that combine to uncover an entire history—provide the link among past, present, and future—birth, death, and rebirth, the natural cycle that exemplifies and embodies the feminine divine.

In Jung's dialectic, the artist speaks for the collective, bringing to consciousness what otherwise is hidden or one-sided in the culture. In her writing, Lee Smith fulfills the role of the artist, by Jung's definition, as she brings to consciousness the heroic, spiritual journeys of women's lives. The absence of these stories from our literature leaves a gaping hole in understanding the human condition as a female. In his 2003 article "Shadow in Mythic American Stories," Don Eulert, a professor of cultural psychology, notes that in America, the active principle is portrayed by the male in our mythology and cultural history. In Smith's new mythology, the feminine principle possesses the active spirit, as it reaches for validation in the presence of the feminine divine. Eulert acknowledges that to achieve a sense of wholeness in our culture, we must incorporate "the other, literally and symbolically." Smith's vision has defined this "other" as a divine presence linked with femininity. Oftentimes, a female character seeks and sometimes finds "divine union" with another person, but the wholeness she achieves must result from the acceptance of the sacredness within herself. Whereas Campbell's monomyth prescribes that the (male) hero find and unite with his feminine counterpart, Smith's heroines discover wholeness as individuals. If a "male principle" exists in Smith's fictional world, it is essentially one half of the androgynous ideal toward which the writer gravitates in her imaging of the feminine divine. Androgyny, frequently equated with holiness, according to Ochs (*Behind* 120), offers a vision of wholeness that presents a major step for the restoration of women to a key position in the Godhead without alienating men (129).

As we move into the fifth decade of Smith's writing, we can only anticipate that her spiritual vision will serve as a guidepost for the twenty-first century. Much more study needs to be done as Smith continues on her spiritual—and literary—journey. A recent event in Abingdon, Virginia, confirms the timeliness of Smith's writing and demonstrates our need for more stories like Smith's, fiction that images a world of complexity, confusion, reconciliation, and grace. In September of 2007, Smith's masterpiece, *Fair and Tender Ladies*, was challenged by a school board member—a minister—who launched a formal complaint and entered a motion that the novel be removed from the curriculum. His reason—the book's "crude language" and "offensive sexual comments" (qtd. in McCown A1). Fortunately, when a formal review of the book was conducted by a committee of parents, teachers, students, and one minister, the outcome confirmed the value and integrity of Smith's novel, and it has remained on the reading list. As frightening as this incident is, it serves as a poignant reminder of the opaque presence, at least in Southern society, that continues to dichotomize sexuality and religion and persists in alienating females from any sense of their inner sacredness. In Lee Smith's literary vision, the body and the spirit are inextricable and co-dependent. As Smith has stated, the only way to the spirit is through the body (Per).

In Smith's work, we find a sexual, maternal, creative, spiritual female who finds empowerment in the feminine divine. With a writing career and a spiritual vision that have spanned four decades, Lee Smith has "danced" her way through the "flames" of conventional thought. In the world of Smith's fiction, there is room for everyone—the marginalized, the damaged, the mentally and physically challenged, as well as the gifted and charmed. Contemporary writer Sue Monk Kidd observes, "Bringing forth a true, instinctual, powerful woman who is rooted in her own feminine center, who honors the sacredness of the feminine and who speaks the feminine language of her own soul is never easy" (15). Lee Smith has accomplished this task with grace and distinction. In her literary and spiritual vision, with the creation of females who find healing, acceptance, and an abundance of choices, Smith has reclaimed the feminine divine and provided hope for all our life journeys.

WORKS CITED

Allison, Dorothy. "This Is Our World." *All Out of Faith: Southern Women on Spirituality.* Ed. Wendy Reed and Jennifer Horne. Tuscaloosa: University of Alabama Press, 2006. 14–25.
Anderson, Sherry Ruth, and Patricia Hopkins. *The Feminine Face of God: The Unfolding of the Sacred in Women.* New York: Bantam, 1991.
Arnold, Edwin T. "An Interview with Lee Smith." *Appalachian Journal* 11.3 (Spring 1984): 240–54.
Baring, Anne, and Jules Cashford. *The Myth of the Goddess: Evolution of an Image.* New York: Viking, 1991.
Bennett, Tanya Long. "The Protean Ivy in Lee Smith's *Fair and Tender Ladies.*" *Southern Literary Journal* 30.2 (Spring 1998): 76–95.
Buchanan, Harriette C. "Lee Smith: The Storyteller's Voice." *Southern Women Writers.* Ed. Tonette Bond Inge. Tuscaloosa: University of Alabama Press, 1990. 324–45.
Byrd, Linda. "An Interview with Lee Smith." *Shenandoah* 47.2 (Summer 1997): 95–118.
Chappell, Fred. "Family Time." *The Southern Review* 28.4 (Autumn 1992): 937–43.
Chodorow, Nancy. "Family Structure and Feminine Personality." *Woman, Culture, and Society.* Ed. Michelle Zimbalist Rosaldo and Louise Lamphere. Stanford: Stanford University Press, 1974. 43–66.
Christ, Carol P. *Rebirth of the Goddess: Finding Meaning in Feminist Spirituality.* New York: Addison-Wesley, 1997.
Cixous, Hélène. "The Laugh of the Medusa." *New French Feminisms: An Anthology.* Ed. Elaine Marks and Isabelle de Courtivron. Amherst: University of Massachusetts Press, 1980. 245–64.
Dale, Corinne. "The Power of Language." *Southern Quarterly* 28.2 (1990): 21–34.
Eckard, Paula Gallant. *Maternal Body and Voice in Toni Morrison, Bobbie Ann Mason, and Lee Smith.* Columbia and London: University of Missouri Press, 2002.
Estés, Clarissa Pinkola. *Women Who Run with the Wolves: Myths and Stories of the Wild Woman Archetype.* New York: Ballantine, 1992.
Eulert, Don. "Shadow in Mythic American Stories." *AHP Perspective Magazine* (Oct./Nov. 2003): 6 pp. Online. Internet. 5 April 2008.
Friedrich, Paul. *The Meaning of Aphrodite.* Chicago: University of Chicago Press, 1978.
Gimbutas, Marija. *The Language of the Goddess.* San Francisco: Harper & Row, 1989.
———. *The Living Goddesses.* Los Angeles: University of California Press, 1999.
———. *The World of the Goddess.* Prod. Green Earth Foundation. Mystic Fire Video, 1990.
Girard, René. *Violence and the Sacred.* Trans. Patrick Gregory. Baltimore: Johns Hopkins University Press, 1977.

Gross, Rita M. *Feminism and Religion: An Introduction.* Boston: Beacon Press, 1996.

———. "Hindu Female Deities as a Resource for the Contemporary Rediscovery of the Goddess." *Journal of the American Academy of Religion* 46.3 (Sept. 1978): 269–91.

Hall, Nor. *The Moon and the Virgin: Reflections on the Archetypal Feminine.* New York: Harper, 1980.

Harrison, Beverly. "The Power of Anger in the Work of Love." *Weaving the Visions: New Patterns in Feminist Spirituality.* Ed. Judith Plaskow and Carol P. Christ. San Francisco: Harper and Row, 1989. 214–25.

Harvey, Andrew, and Anne Baring. *The Divine Feminine: Exploring the Feminine Face of God Around the World.* Berkeley: Conari Press, 1996.

Hill, Dorothy Combs. *Lee Smith.* New York: Twayne, 1992.

House, Silas. "A Conversation with Lee Smith." *The Last Girls.* By Lee Smith. New York: Ballantine, 2002. 387–399.

Irigaray, Luce. "The Bodily Encounter with the Mother." Whitford 34–46.

———. "The Limits of Transference." Whitford 105–17.

———. "Questions." Whitford 133–39.

———. *Sexes and Genealogies.* Trans. Gillian C. Gill. New York: Columbia University Press, 1993.

———. "Sexual Difference." Whitford 165–77.

———. "Volume without Contours." Whitford 53–67.

———. "Women-Mothers, the Silent Substratum of the Social Order." Whitford 47–52.

Johnson, Elizabeth. *She Who Is: The Mystery of God in Feminist Theological Discourse.* New York: Crossroad, 1993.

Jones, Anne Goodwyn. "The World of Lee Smith." *The Southern Quarterly* 22.1 (Fall 1983): 115–39.

Kalb, John D. "The Second 'Rape' of Crystal Spangler." *Southern Literary Journal* 21.1 (Fall 1988): 23–30.

Kearns, Katherine. "From Shadow to Substance: The Empowerment of the Artist Figure in Lee Smith's Fiction." *Writing the Woman Artist.* Ed. Suzanne W. Jones. Philadelphia: University of Pennsylvania Press, 1991. 175–95.

Ketchin, Susan. *The Christ-Haunted Landscape: Faith and Doubt in Southern Fiction.* Jackson: University Press of Mississippi, 1994.

Kidd, Sue Monk. "Awakening." *All Out of Faith: Southern Women on Spirituality.* Ed. Wendy Reed and Jennifer Horne. Tuscaloosa: University of Alabama Press, 2006. 29–44.

Kristeva, Julia. *Revolution in Poetic Language.* Trans. Margaret Waller. New York: Columbia University Press, 1984.

———. "The Semiotic and the Symbolic." Oliver, *Portable* 32–70.

———. "Stabat Mater." Oliver, *Portable* 308–31.

———. "Women's Time." Oliver, *Portable* 349–69.

Lerner, Gerda. *The Creation of Feminist Consciousness.* New York: Oxford University Press, 1993.

Lodge, Michelle. "Lee Smith." *Publishers Weekly* 228 (20 Sept. 1985): 110–11.

Loewenstein, Claudia. "Unshackling the Patriarchy: An Interview with Lee Smith." *Southwest Review* 78 (Autumn 1993): 486–505.

MacKethan, Lucinda. "Artists and Beauticians: Balance in Lee Smith's Fiction." *Southern Literary Journal* 15.1 (Fall 1982): 3–14.

Mann, A.T., and Jane Lyle. *Sacred Sexuality.* New York: Barnes & Noble, 1995.

McCown, Debra. "Review set for contested book." *Herald Courier* [Bristol] 30 Oct 2007: A1+.

Monaghan, Patricia. *The New Book of Goddesses and Heroines.* St. Paul: Llewellyn, 2000.

Motz, Lotte. *The Faces of the Goddess.* New York: Oxford University Press, 1997.

Neumann, Erich. *The Great Mother*. 1955. Trans. Ralph Manheim. Princeton: Princeton University Press, 1983.
Ochs, Carol. *Behind the Sex of God*. Boston: Beacon Press, 1977.
_____. *Women and Spirituality*. 2nd ed. New York: Rowman & Littlefield, 1997.
Oliver, Kelly, ed. *The Portable Kristeva*. New York: Columbia University Press, 1997.
Ortner, Sherry B. "Is Female to Male as Nature Is to Culture?" *Woman, Culture, and Society*. Ed. Michelle Zimbalist Rosaldo and Louise Lamphere. Stanford: Stanford University Press, 1974. 67–87.
Oswalt, Conrad. "Witches and Jesus: Lee Smith's Appalachian Religion." *Southern Literary Journal* 31.1 (Fall 1998): 98–118.
Parker, Rozsika. *Mother Love/Mother Hate: The Power of Maternal Ambivalence*. New York: HarperCollins, 1995.
Parrish, Nancy. "Interview with Lee Smith." *Appalachian Journal* 19.4 (Summer 1992): 394–401.
Powell, Dannye Romine. *Parting the Curtains: Voices of the Great Southern Writers*. New York: Anchor, 1994.
Rabuzzi, Kathryn Allen. *Motherself: A Mythic Analysis of Motherhood*. Bloomington: Indiana University Press, 1988.
Rash, Tom. "All in the Family." *South Carolina Review* 22 (Spring 1990): 131–41.
Reilly, Rosalind B. "*Oral History*: The Enchanted Circle of Narrative and Dream." *Southern Literary Journal* 23.1 (Fall 1990): 79–92.
"Review of *Saving Grace*." *Publishers Weekly* 242 (27 March 1995): 74.
Rich, Adrienne. *Of Woman Born*. 1976. New York: W.W. Norton, 1986.
Ruether, Rosemary Radford. *New Woman, New Earth: Sexist Ideologies and Human Liberation*. New York: Seabury, 1975.
_____. *Womanguides: Readings Toward a Feminist Theology*. Boston: Beacon, 1985.
Showalter, Elaine. "Feminist Criticism in the Wilderness." 1981. *Feminist Literary Theory and Criticism*. Ed. Sandra M. Gilbert and Susan Gubar. New York: W.W. Norton, 2007. 527–44.
Smith, Lee. *Black Mountain Breakdown*. New York: G.P. Putnam's Sons, 1980.
_____. *The Devil's Dream*. New York: G.P. Putnam's Sons, 1992.
_____. *Fair and Tender Ladies*. New York: G.P. Putnam's Sons, 1988.
_____. *Family Linen*. New York: G.P. Putnam's Sons, 1985.
_____. *Fancy Strut*. New York: Harper & Row, 1973.
_____. *The Last Day the Dogbushes Bloomed*. New York: Harper & Row, 1968.
_____. *The Last Girls: A Novel*. Chapel Hill: Algonquin, 2002.
_____. *On Agate Hill*. Chapel Hill: Algonquin, 2006.
_____. *Oral History*. New York: G.P. Putnam's Sons, 1983.
_____. Personal Interview. 19 May 2008.
_____. *Saving Grace*. New York: G.P. Putnam's Sons, 1995.
_____. *Something in the Wind*. New York: Harper & Row, 1971.
_____. "Southern Exposure." http://www.beca.org/fotl/leesmith/accent.html (2 Feb. 1998).
Smith, Rebecca. *Gender Dynamics in the Fiction of Lee Smith: Examining Language and Narrative Strategies*. San Francisco: International Scholars, 1997.
Stone, Merlin. *When God Was a Woman*. New York: Barnes & Noble, 1976.
Suleiman, Susan Rubin. "Writing and Motherhood." *The (M)other Tongue*. Ed. Shirley Nelson Garner. Ithaca: Cornell University Press, 1985. 352–78.
Tate, Linda. *A Southern Weave of Women*. Athens: University of Georgia Press, 1994.
Tebbetts, Terrell. "*The Last Girls, Family Linen*, and Faulkner: A Conversation with Lee Smith." *The Philological Review* 31.1 (Spring 2005): 43–65.
Thompson, Lana. *The Wandering Womb: A Cultural History of Outrageous Beliefs About*

Women. Amherst: Prometheus, 1999.
Walker, Barbara G. *Restoring the Goddess: Equal Rites for Modern Women*. Amherst: Prometheus, 2000.
———. *The Woman's Dictionary of Symbols and Sacred Objects*. San Francisco: HarperCollins, 1988.
———. *The Women's Encyclopedia of Myths and Secrets*. Edison, N.J.: Castle, 1996.
Whitford, Margaret, ed. *The Irigaray Reader*. Cambridge: Basil Blackwell, 1991.
Yaeger, Patricia. *Honey-Mad Women: Emancipatory Strategies in Women's Writing*. New York: Columbia University Press, 1988.
Yow, Dede. "Claiming the Passion: From *Black Mountain Breakdown* to *Saving Grace*." Southern Women Writers Conference. Berry College. Rome, GA. 13 April 1996.

INDEX

Novel titles are abbreviated as follows: *Black Mountain Breakdown (BMB)*; *The Devil's Dream (TDD)*; *Fair and Tender Ladies (FTL)*; *Family Linen (FL)*; *Fancy Strut (FS)*; *The Last Day the Dogbushes Bloomed (LDDB)*; *The Last Girls (TLG)*; *On Agate Hill (OAH)*; *Oral History (OH)*; *Saving Grace (SG)*; and *Something in the Wind (SIW)*.

Adventures of Huckleberry Finn 179–80
Agate Hill 199–202, 204–209, 211–12, 214–15, 218–20
Agnes McClanahan (*BMB*) 46–47, 48, 53, 55, 58–59, 104
Agnes Rutherford (*OAH*) 199–201, 205–208, 211, 216–18
Aldous Rife (*OH*) *see* Rev. Aldous Rife (*OH*)
Alice Petree (*OAH*) 204, 215
Allison, Dorothy 6, 227
Almarine Cantrell (*OH*) 62–71, 73–74, 79, 80, 83, 109–110, 119, 132, 134, 146, 167
Anderson, Sherry Ruth 107, 185, 220, 227
androgyny 7, 84, 132, 204, 224
angels/angelic 40, 52–53, 64, 89, 138, 153, 157–58, 167, 188, 192–93
Anna Todd (Annie Stokes) (*TLG*) 181, 191–93, 196–97
Annie Stokes (*TLG*) *see* Anna Todd
Aphrodite 66, 69, 106, 115, 132, 164n, 227; *see also* Venus
Arnold, Edwin T. 62, 227
Arthur (*FL*) 92, 97–98, 99n, 105
Aunt Cecilia (*OAH*) 200, 211
Aunt Fannie (*OAH*) 200, 220
Aunt Mitty (*OAH*) 201–203
Aunt Virgie (*TDD*) 148, 151
ax(es) 87, 93–94

Babe Rowe (*FTL*) 112
Baby Ballou (Margaret Burns Ballou) (*TLG*) 12, 180–86, 189, 196
Baring, Anne 24, 93, 127, 130n, 131–32, 161, 174, 218, 227, 228
the Baron (*LDDB*) 16, 19, 20
bears 9, 24, 26, 41, 140, 145–46, 193
bees 9, 50, 92, 95, 114, 129–30, 132, 134, 149, 187–88, 202, 208, 210
Bennett, Tanya Long 120–21, 227
Bentley T. Hooks (*SIW*) 15, 30–36, 44, 47–48, 51–52, 54, 59, 68, 75, 85, 212
Betty Tobey (*LDDB*) 16, 20–22, 26
Beulah Rowe Bostick (*FTL*) 107, 112, 117, 119–20, 122, 138–39
Bevo Cartwright (*FS*) 38–40, 71–72
Bible 34, 48, 71, 107, 136, 163, 170, 199, 201–202
Billie Jean Shepherd (*SG*) 163, 172
birds 16–17, 27, 48, 63, 66, 90, 102, 131, 149, 150–51, 157, 159, 188
BJ (John Howard Willetts) (*OAH*) 200, 214, 218
Black Jack Johnny (*TDD*) *see* Johnny Rainette
Black Mountain Breakdown 10, 36–37, 46, 59, 62, 228
blood 21, 30–31, 36, 52, 54–57, 65, 67, 70, 82, 89, 94, 104, 112, 116–17, 127, 128–29, 157, 165–66, 174, 182, 184–85, 193–94, 195, 217

231

Blue Star Mountain (*FTL*) 77, 108, 110, 129, 131, 134
Bob Griffin (*SIW*) *see* Houston (Bob Griffin)
Bob Pitt (*FS*) 39–41, 68, 95
Bobcat Mountain (*OAH*) 199, 205, 208–209
body-mind split *see* mind-body split
Booker Creek, Virginia (*FL*) 88, 103–104
breast-feeding/nursing 54, 70, 84–85, 126, 195, 218–19
breasts 21, 27–28, 43, 54, 65, 67, 70, 73, 78, 84–85, 104, 108, 134, 154, 157, 190, 194–95, 201, 204, 207–208, 218
breath/breathing 23, 29, 51, 50n, 75, 122–23, 136, 164–65, 167, 172, 174, 184, 187, 189–90, 201, 205, 207, 218
Brooke Kincaid (*SIW*) 9–10, 15, 26–36, 37–38, 41, 44–45, 47, 50–52, 54, 59, 65, 68, 75, 85, 95–96, 124, 212
Buchanan, Harriette C. 105, 227
Buck Fire (*FS*) 42–46, 48, 51, 65, 75, 85, 96, 189
butterflies 93, 157, 164, 174, 182–83, 187, 190
Byrd, Linda 8, 43, 53, 68, 106, 108, 137, 159, 161–62, 169, 176, 178, 180, 227

Candy (*FL*) 11, 93, 96–100, 103, 105, 117, 149n, 159, 183
Cadean Combs (*SG*) 167, 174
Carlton Duty (*SG*) 163, 166
Carolyn Kincaid (*SIW*) 15, 26–29, 31, 33, 49
Carter Kincaid (*SIW*) 27, 31, 36
Cashford, Jules 24, 93, 127, 130n, 131, 132, 161, 174, 227
catechism 200, 202
Catherine Wilson Hurt (*TLG*) 181–82, 194–97
caves 9, 22–23, 32–34, 50, 52, 65–67, 77–78, 110, 139–40, 130n, 146–47, 159–60, 161, 169, 172–74, 187–88, 202, 204, 208–10, 213, 215, 219
Chappell, Fred 144, 145, 227
Chimney Rock (*SG*) 162, 165–66, 168, 173
Chodorow, Nancy 169, 227
Christ *see* Jesus Christ
Christ, Carol P. 121, 123–24, 134, 111n, 154, 166, 173, 174, 177, 227
Christabel (*OAH*) 218, 219, 221
Christianity 5–9, 15, 37, 39, 69, 74, 78n, 89, 101, 120–21, 138, 144, 153–54, 161–62, 170–71, 174–77, 186, 199–203, 210, 219
Cincinnatus Snow (*OAH*) *see* Rev. Cincinnatus Snow (*OAH*)
circles/circularity 8n, 9, 12, 24–25, 35, 64–65, 65n, 99, 109–10, 135, 139–40, 146, 151n, 153–55, 159, 165–66, 176–77, 179–80, 186–87, 195, 197, 202–203, 209, 212, 219, 221, 229
Cixous, Hélène 73, 128, 136, 172, 175–76, 227
Cline sisters (Gaynelle and Virgie) (*FTL*) 113–15, 117, 139–40, 184, 192–93
Courtney Ralston (*TLG*) 181, 184, 186, 188–93, 189n, 196–97, 293
creeks *see* water/streams/pools/springs/creeks
Crystal Spangler (*BMB*) 10, 37, 46–60, 56n, 62, 65, 66, 72, 74, 75, 80, 82, 84–85, 86, 95, 96, 101, 102, 104, 122, 124, 126, 128, 156, 159, 175, 228
culture, as opposed to nature *see* nature vs. culture
Curtis Bostick (*FTL*) 107, 119, 129, 139

Dale, Corinne 83, 181, 227
dance 16, 90, 100, 127, 139, 141, 146, 153, 155–56, 158, 166, 185–87, 192, 197, 203, 205, 207, 209–12, 216, 225
Danny Rowe (*FTL*) 118, 121, 137
death/dying 9, 19, 24–25, 28, 29, 50, 53–54, 56–57, 56n, 66–67, 70–71, 77–78, 81–82, 83, 88–89, 93, 97–98, 99–100, 99n, 101, 104, 107, 110, 111, 113–14, 115, 117, 118, 121, 123–25, 128–29, 134, 137, 138–40, 146–47, 149–50, 152–53, 154, 156–57, 168, 170–71, 173–74, 180, 182–85, 188, 189n, 190–193, 195–97, 198–200, 203–205, 208n, 209, 214–18, 223–24
De Beauvoir, Simone 26, 199
The Devil's Dream 11, 48, 80, 104, 141–43, 172, 229
Diamond (*FTL*) 107, 110, 119, 129
Diana (*SIW*) 28–29, 33
diary 12, 199–200, 202–204, 206, 207–11, 214, 218–19, 220–22, 224
dichotomy 6–7, 11, 15, 21, 25–26, 31, 36, 39, 41–42, 49, 82, 85, 86, 95–97, 141, 170n, 183
Dr. Diamond (*FL*) 94–95
dogs 24–25, 189, 194
domesticity *see* wildness vs. domesticity
Don Dotson (*FL*) 96, 98–100, 105

Dory Cantrell Wade (*DB*) 10, 61–85, 87–89, 91, 98, 107, 109, 113, 115, 118, 131, 134, 146, 149n, 152–54, 162, 167, 219
Dry Fork (*BMB*) 48–49, 50, 56, 62

Eckard, Paula Gallant 8, 63, 68, 81–82, 112, 116, 130, 134, 181, 227
Edward Bing (*FL*) 94–95
Elizabeth Bird Hess (*FL*) 87–93, 96–101, 103–105, 153
Elsie Mae (*LDDB*) 17–18, 20, 24
elves 132, 156
Estés, Clarissa Pinkola 198, 199, 331–22, 224, 227
Estruscan society/tombs 215–16, 220–21
Ethel Rowe (*FTL*) 98, 107, 117, 119, 120
Eugene (*LDDB*) 18, 20–23, 24, 29, 68
Eulert, Don 224, 227
Ezekiel "Zeke" (*TDD*) 80, 147, 148, 149–50, 152–54, 156–58, 167

Fair and Tender Ladies 10–11, 39, 43, 48, 70, 88, 94, 97–98, 106–107, 110, 116, 121, 137, 141, 151n, 152, 165, 203, 209, 219, 225, 228
fairies/fairytale/make-believe 12, 16, 18, 20, 35, 186, 194–95, 198–99, 201–209, 210–13, 215, 218–19, 221, 224
Family Linen 10–11, 86–88, 101, 115, 117, 141–42, 145, 153, 179, 229
Fancy Strut 10, 36–38, 45, 59, 62, 71, 81, 95, 229
Fay (*FL*) 88, 90–91, 96, 97–99, 100–104, 101n, 115, 146, 152, 219
fire/flame/blaze/burn 5, 38–39, 40, 43, 45, 46, 48–49, 51, 54, 59, 65, 71–72, 74–75, 81, 88–91, 104, 109–13, 121–25, 127, 131–34, 136, 138–40, 141, 143, 144–46, 150–57, 166, 168, 172, 182, 183–84, 186, 188–89, 196–97, 206, 208–210, 213
Flamingo (*TLG*) 192–93
flowers 9, 16–17, 22, 25, 33, 44, 48, 69, 90, 92, 93–95, 97, 101, 101n, 105, 109, 113, 118, 127–28, 131–32, 135, 158–160, 164, 174–75, 189, 196, 203, 207, 212, 219, 221
Frances Pitt (*FS*) 42, 62
Franklin Ransom (*FTL*) 107, 124–25, 126, 129–30, 134n, 135, 138, 139, 152, 163
Freud 76, 84
Friedrich, Paul 69, 82, 84, 106, 137, 227

Gamie Rowe (*FTL*) 121, 135–37
Gary Vance (*FL*) 95–96

Gatewood Academy (*OAH*) 199–202, 205–10, 211, 215–16, 219
Gaynelle Cline (*FTL*) *see* Cline sisters
Gene Minor (*TLG*) 189–91, 196
Geneva Hunt (*FTL*) 97, 98, 106–107, 116, 118–19, 122, 126, 149
Gertrude Torrington, Miss (*FTL*) 107, 121–24, 138, 140, 192
Gimbutas, Marija 9, 9n, 24, 64–66, 93, 109, 132, 140, 151, 156–57, 189n, 195, 203, 216, 221, 227
Girard, René 34, 46, 59, 124, 144, 227
glossolalia (speaking in tongues) 75–78, 75n, 144, 166–67, 191
God/goddess 5–11, 7n, 8n, 9n, 15, 19, 20, 23–25, 33, 35, 39, 54–55, 57–58, 61–71, 73–82, 85, 87, 89–94, 96, 98, 100–105, 101n, 107, 111–12, 115–16, 118, 120–22, 124–28, 129n, 130n, 131–34, 136, 139–40, 141n, 144–57, 159–60, 161–68, 170–74, 175–77, 183–86, 190–93, 196, 198–203, 206–208, 208n, 209–12, 210n, 215, 217–18, 221
gold/golden 43, 56, 56n, 62–63, 69, 74–75, 118, 131–32, 134, 138–39, 143, 145, 151, 156–59, 182, 191–92, 208–209
grace 7, 78, 161–63, 166–67, 176
Grace (Florida) Shepherd (*SG*) 7, 12, 51, 161–77, 183
Grace Harrison (*FL*) 89, 91
Granny Rowe (*FTL*) 107, 115–17, 119, 129, 205
Granny Younger (*OH*) 62–63, 65–70, 80–81, 83, 100, 110, 134, 145, 181
Grant Spangler (*BMB*) 48, 50, 50n, 82
Grassy Branch (*TDD*) 149, 156
Gross, Rita M. 6, 7, 84, 170, 228

Hall, Nor 17, 19, 32, 38, 50, 55–57, 68, 73, 75, 77, 78, 94, 100, 104, 127, 132, 154, 175, 228
haloes 11, 43, 64, 74–75, 79–80, 89, 94, 100, 115, 132–33, 146, 159, 165, 173, 176, 182, 186, 189–90, 204
Hannecke (*FTL*) 108–109, 111, 113, 121, 133, 137, 203–204
Harriet Holding (*TLG*) 179–88, 190, 191, 193, 195–97
Harrison, Beverly 171, 228
Harvey, Andrew 218, 228
Hawk (*TLG*) 189–91, 189n
hawks 9, 109, 135, 139–40, 151n, 165, 189n, 209, 213
Hell Mountain (*FTL*) 113–14, 140

Henry (*OAH*) 215, 219, 220–21
Hill, Dorothy Combs 36, 38, 42, 62, 64, 66, 71, 82, 87,96, 98, 115, 132, 149n, 163, 228
honey 9, 50, 89–92, 95, 108, 109, 114, 117, 129–31, 129n, 130n, 132, 134, 144–50, 149n, 153, 155, 162, 165, 167, 172, 174, 188, 195, 210, 230
Honey Breeding (*FTL*) 11, 12, 43, 48, 91, 106, 108, 110, 112, 114, 118, 119, 123–24, 126–38, 134n–135n, 140, 145–46, 153, 155, 162, 165, 167, 208–209, 215, 219
Hoot Owl Holler (*OH*) 62, 67, 72, 73–74
Hopkins, Patricia 107, 185, 220, 228
House, Silas 181, 183, 189, 197, 228
Houston (Bob Griffin) (*SIW*) 29–32, 45

Indian Rock (*OAH*) 207–208, 210–12, 213, 215, 219
insanity/craziness/lunacy/madness 40, 41, 81, 89, 99–101, 103, 110–12, 117, 127, 129–30, 142, 145–47, 149, 152, 158–59, 174, 195, 201, 213, 214, 217
integration 6, 9–13, 15–16, 25–29, 31, 35–36, 37, 39, 41–42, 43, 44–51, 53, 54–57, 58, 59–60, 6871, 73–74, 75, 76–77, 78–79, 82–85, 90–92, 96–99, 104–105, 107–109, 111–12, 111n, 119, 120, 127–28, 134–36, 141–43, 150–52, 154–55, 157, 159, 170–71, 174–77, 178, 188, 190, 191–94, 196, 221–22, 223–24
Ira Keen (*TDD*) 145–46, 149
Irigaray, Luce 8, 89, 92, 93, 95, 103, 110, 112–15, 120, 123, 125, 126, 127, 131, 147, 148, 154, 168, 228, 230
Iron Lung (*LDDB*) 18–19, 22–23
Ivy Rowe Fox (*FTL*) 11–12, 88, 91, 92, 95, 106–40, 111n, 134n–135n, 143, 144, 145–47, 149, 149n, 151, 155, 156, 157, 159, 162, 163, 165, 167, 169, 172, 176, 178, 183, 192, 193, 195, 203–205, 208–209, 215, 227

Jacky Jarvis (*OAH*) 48, 199–200, 208–10, 212–15, 213n, 218, 221
Jefferson Carr "Jeff" (*TLG*) 183, 184–86, 187–88, 197
Jennifer Bingham (*OH*) 62, 82, 221
Jerold Kukafka (*BMB*) 55–57
Jesus Christ 17, 25, 29, 33, 35, 43–44, 57–58, 63, 77–78, 113, 121, 133, 166, 168, 170–71, 183, 215
Jewell Rife (*FL*) 90–91, 94, 96, 98, 99, 73–74

John Arthur Rowe (*FTL*) 88, 108–109, 113, 121, 176
John Howard Willetts (*OAH*) *see* BJ (John Howard Willetts)
Johnny Rainette (Black Jack Johnny) (*TDD*) 38, 144, 151, 155–56, 157–58
Johnson, Elizabeth 90, 228
Joli Fox (*FTL*) 107, 111, 114–16, 127, 128, 137–39
Jones, Anne Goodwyn 45, 70, 228
journey 5–13, 36, 37, 44, 46–47, 55, 57, 61, 85, 106, 107–109, 114, 120, 127, 147, 150, 152, 158–59, 161, 169, 170–71, 172–73, 174–77, 178–81, 183–84, 185–86, 186–88, 195–97, 199-200, 206–208, 212–13, 221–22, 223–25
Juney (*OAH*) 219–21, 223
Jung 51, 78n, 133, 198, 224
Justine Poole (*OH*) 62, 76, 97, 118

Kalb, John D. 55–56, 228
Kate Malone (*TDD*) 11, 142, 145–53, 145n, 159–60
Katie Cocker (*TDD*) 11, 103–104, 143–44, 147–59, 166, 176, 183
Kearns, Katherine 29, 97, 100, 101, 111, 125, 138, 155, 228
Kenneth Trethaway (*TLG*) 192–93
Ketchin, Susan 5, 9, 114, 120, 121, 140, 161, 162, 164, 170, 228
Kidd, Sue Monk 225, 228
Kristeva, Julia 8, 32, 40, 61, 75, 77, 81, 83, 75n, 159–60, 166, 176, 228, 229

Lacy Hess (*FL*) 86–88, 91–92, 103–105, 145, 149n
Lamar (*SG*) 169, 172, 173
language/words 6, 7, 9, 17–20, 23–26, 29–33, 35–36, 39–40, 44–45, 49–54, 57–58, 56n, 64–70, 75–79, 75n, 81, 83–85, 86, 88–90, 93, 94, 97, 98–100, 101–102, 103, 102n, 109, 111n, 112, 113–15, 117, 119, 122–23, 124, 126–28, 130–32, 134–35, 136–40, 144, 146–47, 150–54, 156–57, 162–65, 166–71, 174–76, 181–82, 186, 191–93, 197, 198, 201–202, 206–207, 211-12, 213–16, 221–22, 224–27
The Last Day the Dogbushes Bloomed 10, 15–16, 26, 38, 41, 48, 62, 64, 78, 108, 128, 229
The Last Girls 12, 178–81, 228, 229
laughter 16–17, 21, 28, 40, 66, 77, 85, 91, 119, 137, 145–47, 150, 154, 184, 189–90,

193–94, 195, 202–203, 207, 209, 213, 227
Lerner, Gerda 44–45, 76, 116, 228
letters/letter-writing 74, 80, 86, 89, 106–109, 111, 113, 117–19, 121, 123, 125–26, 128–31, 133–40, 143–44, 155, 183, 191, 193, 197, 199–200, 202–11, 213–15, 217–18, 221, 224
Levi-Strauss 89, 129
Little Arthur (*LDDB*) 18–25, 29
Little Luther Wade (*OH*) 79–80
Lizzie Bailey (*TDD*) 148–49, 154, 157
Lodge, Michelle 96, 228
Loewenstein, Claudia 28, 41, 87, 142, 162, 228
Lone Bald Mountain (*TDD*) 145
Lonnie Rash (*FTL*) 122–24, 127, 134, 134n, 137, 139
Lorene Spangler (*BMB*) 49, 50n
Lou Angelli (*TLG*) 193, 197
Lucie Queen Bailey (*TDD*) 11, 144, 152, 154–55, 157
LuIda Fox (*FTL*) 11, 138, 156
Lyle, Jane 56n, 69, 74, 78, 78n, 228, 228n

Mack Stiltner (*BMB*) 48–49, 51–55, 57, 59, 65, 72
MacKethan, Lucinda 114, 228
Majestic (*FTL*) 108, 115, 117, 118, 121–23, 126, 137
Mama Marie (*OAH*) 203, 209
Mama Tampa Rainette (*TDD*) 11, 147, 156, 159
Manbone Rock (*OAH*) 209–210, 212–13, 219
Manly Neighbors (*FS*) 10, 41–46, 49, 56, 59
Mann, A.T. 56n, 69, 74, 78, 78n, 228
Margaret Burns Ballou (*TLG*) *see* Baby Ballou
Mariah Snow (*OAH*) 200–201, 206, 208, 211, 216–18
Marlene (*FTL*) 111, 139
marriage 10–12, 16, 18, 20, 37–38, 40–42, 46, 52, 56, 59, 68, 71, 79–80, 83, 85, 88, 80–91, 95–96, 98, 102–103, 107–108, 117–18, 120, 124–26, 135, 138, 142, 145–46, 148, 152, 154–57, 164, 167–70, 179–81, 184, 189, 195, 199, 200, 203, 210
Martha Fickling (*OAH*) 97, 208–209, 214
Martha Gayheart (*FTL*) 119–120, 138
Mary Scott College (*TLG*) 181–83, 185, 197

Mary White (*OAH*) 199–212, 217, 221
maternity/motherhood 7–13, 15–22, 25–26, 28, 30, 33, 36–38, 45, 54, 61, 63, 68, 70, 84–86, 94, 97, 106–108, 120, 127–28, 133, 137, 140, 142, 145–46, 153–54, 159, 162, 169, 172, 178, 193–94, 216, 218, 223, 229
Maude Rowe (*FTL*) 88, 108–109, 112, 121, 126, 135
Maudy Fox (*FTL*) 111, 126, 135, 139
medial feminine 51, 175
menstruation/menopause 21, 33, 57, 95, 128, 131, 194
mind-body split 6–7, 9–10, 15, 19, 25, 27–29, 31, 36–37, 41–45, 49, 51, 54, 58–59, 70, 72, 74, 76, 79–81, 83, 86, 99, 106, 111n, 124, 129, 136, 140–41, 170, 170n, 188, 190, 197, 214, 217
mirrors 38, 47, 56–57, 115, 184, 186, 194
Molly Bainbridge (*FTL*) 107, 118, 120, 134
Molly Petree (*OAH*) 12, 92, 198–222, 223
Monica Neighbors (*FS*) 10, 37–38, 41–49, 51, 56n, 59–60, 65, 75, 78, 84–85, 96, 124, 189
moon 11, 17, 24–25, 90, 108–109, 111–12, 116, 139, 153–54, 156–57, 186, 193, 197, 202–203, 210, 212, 218, 228
Moses Bailey (*TDD*) 142, 145–50, 159
mother tongue 32, 75, 163, 166, 174, 229
mountains 8–10, 12, 24, 48, 58, 62, 66, 68, 71–73, 76–77, 81, 88, 107, 112, 128, 133, 146–47, 158, 161–62, 165, 176, 178, 188, 208, 212, 223
Mrs. Brown (*FTL*) 107–108, 113, 115, 118, 121, 138–39
Myrtle Dotson (*FL*) 92, 95–99, 104–105
mythology 6–8, 12, 23–24, 47, 61–62, 64, 67, 70, 85n, 87, 92, 101–102, 106–107, 109, 121, 125, 127, 129–130, 130n, 134, 137, 140, 144, 161, 164, 173, 180, 193, 198, 208n, 209, 211n, 213n, 224, 227, 230

Natchez (*TLG*) 186, 194
nature 6–9, 11–12, 16–17, 22, 24–25, 27, 39, 47–49, 52–53, 55, 58, 63–64, 71–72, 75–78, 100, 103, 109–10, 112–13, 115, 118, 121, 125–26, 128–32, 134, 140, 143, 146, 150, 159, 162, 166, 171–72, 174–75, 188–89, 194, 198–99, 201–203, 208, 210–12, 219, 223, 229
nature vs. culture 48, 55, 76–77, 100, 109, 115, 129, 171

Nettie (*FL*) 90–91, 98–103, 105, 172
Nicky Eck (*OAH*) 204
Noah (*TLG*) 186
Nonnie Bailey (*TDD*) 11, 148–58, 167, 172
novels *see Black Mountain Breakdown; The Devil's Dream; Fair and Tender Ladies; Family Linen; Fancy Strut; The Last Day the Dogbushes Bloomed; The Last Girls; On Agate Hill; Oral History; Saving Grace; Something in the Wind*

Oakley Fox (*FTL*) 110, 113–14, 124–29, 133, 135, 138–39
Ochs, Carol 178, 197, 224, 228, 229
Oliver, Kelly 83, 228
On Agate Hill 12, 70, 97, 151n, 178n, 198–200, 219
Opryland Hotel (*TDD*) 142, 156, 158–59
Ora Mae Cantrell Wade (*OH*) 62, 70–71, 79–82, 148
Oral History 7, 10–11, 60–62, 64–65, 83, 85, 87–88, 95, 97, 100, 107, 109, 116, 118, 142, 145, 199, 219, 221, 229
Oswalt, Conrad 63, 229
otherworldliness/timelessness 63, 67, 71, 78, 80, 133, 186, 191, 204, 212, 221
owls 62, 67, 72, 73, 157, 186

Parker, Rozsika 75, 84, 152, 229
Parrish, Nancy 125, 142, 159, 229
Parrot Blankenship (*OH*) 66, 80, 81
patriarchy 5–9, 15–16, 24–25, 27, 32–35, 37–38, 40, 77, 46, 48, 59, 62–63, 66–67, 71, 75–78, 8081, 85–86, 89–91, 93, 101, 103–104, 107, 111n, 112, 115–16, 120–22, 124, 133, 136, 141, 153–54, 159, 161–65, 173–74, 183, 198–200, 203, 205, 212, 218, 223, 228
Pearl Wade Bingham (*OH*) 62, 80–83
Pete Jones (*TLG*) 187, 197
pools *see* water/streams/pools/springs/creeks
Powell, Dannye Romine 143, 144, 229
pregnancy/childbirth 26, 30, 32–34, 41, 45, 68, 77, 79, 98, 103, 116, 124, 126, 128, 137, 154, 157–58, 192, 211, 217
Pricey Jane Cantrell (*OH*) 62, 68–70, 80, 82, 84, 116

the Queen (*LDDB*) 15–16, 18–21, 26–27, 78

Rabuzzi, Kathryn Allen 8–9, 64–65, 73, 76, 85, 88, 108, 115, 124, 161, 176, 229

rainbows 207–208, 208n
Ralph Handy (*TDD*) 149–52, 156, 158
Randy Newhouse (*SG*) 48, 162, 168–69, 171, 175
Ransom McClain (*FL*) 89–91
rape 18–19, 23, 25, 29, 34, 37, 46, 49–51, 55–59, 91, 101–102
Rash, Tom 134n, 229
ravens 9, 65–66, 146
R.C. Bailey (*TDD*) 11, 144, 148, 151–52, 154–55, 157
rebirth/regeneration 22–23, 30, 32, 35, 50, 52–53, 61, 66–67, 77–78, 89–90, 93, 100–101, 104–105, 109–110, 111n, 127, 129, 129n, 130–32, 133, 135n, 139, 146–47, 149, 152, 158, 173–75, 186–87, 191, 209, 215–16, 221, 224, 227
red (color) 10–11, 17, 34, 39–40, 42–43, 56–57, 64–65, 68, 72, 75, 88, 91–94, 101, 101n, 105, 110, 116, 133, 135, 139, 143, 145–46, 151, 154, 156–59, 167, 182, 184, 190, 192, 203, 205, 210, 213
Red Emmy (*OH*) 10, 62–67, 69–71, 73–75, 79–83, 109–10, 116, 119, 132–34, 146, 157, 167
Reilly, Rosalind B. 64, 65n, 71, 105, 229
religion 5–9, 11, 15, 19, 24–25, 33–34, 38, 40, 44, 63, 67–68, 75–76, 75n, 86, 89, 101, 103–104, 106–107, 111n, 114, 120, 122–23, 125, 135–37, 141–45, 147, 162–70, 170n, 173–74, 177, 183, 192, 198–200, 202–203, 205, 207, 210–12, 216, 220, 223, 225, 228–29
Rev. Aldous Rife (*OH*) 76, 118
Rev. Cincinnatus Snow *(OAH)* 201, 206–207, 217–18
Rich, Adrienne 7, 116, 229
Richard Burlage (*OH*) 10, 68–69, 71–80, 83–85, 95, 98, 109, 113, 131, 134, 152–54, 161, 167
rocks *see* stones/rocks
Roger Lee Combs (*BMB*) 49, 52, 55–57, 56n, 59, 74
Ron-the-Mouth-of-the-South (*FS*) 39, 44, 81
Rose Annie Bailey (*TDD*) 11, 80, 104, 144, 147, 149, 151–53, 155–58
roses 17–18, 23, 41, 58, 69, 71, 82, 86, 90–91, 93–94, 97, 101n, 105, 108, 114, 117, 129, 135, 157, 174, 182, 189–90, 207, 210
Roy (*OH*) 83–85, 130
royalty 16–18, 97, 138–39
Ruether, Rosemary Radford 86, 99, 165, 170, 229

Russell Hurt (*TLG*) 181–82, 182n, 194–97
Ruth Duty (*SG*) 163, 172
Ruthie Cartwright (*FS*) 39–40, 44, 81

sacred union/divine couple 30, 43, 51, 53, 65, 70, 73, 77, 85, 88–89, 96, 99, 133, 150, 154, 157–58, 185, 204, 209, 212, 224
Sally Wade (*OH*) 62, 66–67, 70, 79–80, 82–85, 100, 130, 134, 146, 176, 181
Sam Russell Sage (*FTL*) 118, 121, 136
Sandy DuBois (*FS*) 38–41, 43, 48, 68, 95, 149n
sarcophagus 215–16, 219
Saving Grace 5, 7, 12, 48, 51, 161–62, 176, 178, 229, 230
Scrabble Creek (*SG*) 13, 163, 173–76
Selena (*OAH*) 203, 205, 214, 219
sexuality/sensuality 6–13, 15–16, 19–21, 26, 29–32, 36–37, 39–41, 44–47, 49, 53–55, 59, 63, 65, 69–70, 72–74, 76–77, 81, 83–84, 93, 96–98, 100–104, 115–16, 123–24, 131, 134, 141n, 143, 146, 149, 152–53, 156, 162, 167–68, 170–73, 170n, 183, 187, 204, 223, 228–29
Shakespeare 36, 107, 138
Sharon DuBois (*FS*) 38–39, 72
Showalter, Elaine 75, 75n, 229
sibyl 66, 94
silence 15, 17–19, 23, 29–35, 44–46, 50–51, 55, 58, 61, 75–77, 79, 98, 100, 102, 125, 128, 130, 161, 163, 201, 214, 217
Silvaney Rowe (*FTL*) 39, 106, 109–16, 111n, 119, 123–25, 127–31, 133–40, 147, 152, 155, 157, 193, 204, 208, 219
Simon Black (*OAH*) 199, 204–206, 214–17, 219–21
Smith, Rebecca 61, 66, 85, 123, 128–29, 132
somatic symptoms 29, 49–50, 53–54, 92, 112, 125, 127, 184
Something in the Wind 9, 16, 26, 35, 38, 62, 104, 212, 229
Southern code 6, 9, 13, 15, 17–18, 28, 30, 37, 39, 41–42, 46, 49, 91–92, 97, 161, 181, 183, 189, 225, 227–30
speaking in tongues *see* glossolalia
Speed, Alabama (*FS*) 38, 44
split identity 7, 9–10, 15–16, 27–31, 41–42, 48–49, 76, 81, 86, 95, 99, 106, 111, 133, 140, 143–44, 150, 223
springs *see* water/streams/pools/springs/creeks

Stone, Merlin 170, 229
stones/rocks 8–9, 24, 68, 78, 104, 114, 133, 129, 165, 170, 188–90, 203, 207, 210, 215, 218–19
Stoney Branham (*FTL*) 117
stories 15–17, 50, 57–58, 62, 83, 85, 113–14, 124, 130, 134, 137, 142, 156, 163–65, 178–79, 181, 184, 198, 208n, 213, 221, 224–25
streams *see* water/streams/pools/springs/creeks
Sugar Fork (*FTL*) 107–109, 114, 117, 119, 129, 135, 138
Susan Tobey (*LDDB*) 9–10, 15–25, 26, 28–29, 31, 33, 35–38, 41, 47, 50, 59, 64–66, 68, 80, 108, 128, 175
Sybill (*FL*) 92–96, 98, 103–105, 148

Taoism 69–70, 73, 133
Tate, Linda 68, 76, 229
Tebbetts, Terrell 179, 180, 182, 229
Tennessee Rowe (*FTL*) 115–16, 146–47
Thompson, Lana 217, 229
Titania 203
transgression 6, 39, 82, 99, 117–19, 134, 149
Travis Word (*SG*) 162–64, 167–72, 174–75
Tuscany Miller (*OAH*) 199–201, 214, 221

Uncle Devere (*BMB*) 49–50, 56–58, 102
Uncle Junius (*OAH*) 200, 203, 205, 214–15, 219
Uncle Revel Rowe (*FTL*) 116, 126

Vashti (*OH*) 70–71, 80–81
Venus 69, 74, 95, 190; *see also* Aphrodite
Verner Hess (*FL*) 92, 96
Victor Rowe (*FTL*) 111, 117
violence 7, 15, 21, 23, 25, 33–35, 38, 40, 42, 44, 46, 58–59, 96, 102, 107, 124, 135, 143–44, 170, 227
Virgie Cline (*FTL*) *see* Cline sisters
Virgil Shepherd (*SG*) 163–64
Virgin Mary 61, 74
voice 8–10, 15, 17, 19, 22, 25, 31, 33–34, 44, 48, 50–51, 53–55, 58, 61–62, 66, 71, 75, 81, 85, 88, 97, 100–103, 106–107, 112–14, 117, 120, 130, 134, 137–38, 146–48, 150–54, 159, 163–64, 166, 174–75, 181–84, 188, 191–92, 202, 213, 224, 227, 229

Walker, Barbara G. 7n, 66, 69, 73, 112, 129, 129n, 141, 141n, 156, 162, 164,

164n, 167, 186, 199, 202–203, 207, 208n, 211, 213n, 215, 230
wandering motif 19, 23, 33, 46–47, 52, 57, 66, 71, 79–80, 88–89, 95, 101, 103–104, 107, 112–13, 115, 117, 127, 129, 133, 135, 143, 145–49, 151, 153, 184, 187, 191, 195, 206, 210, 219, 224
water/streams/pools/springs/creeks 9, 24–25, 63, 65, 66–67, 70, 71, 73, 77, 87–88, 93–94, 97, 99, 101, 105, 109, 112–13, 116, 132–133, 146–47, 150–53, 158–59, 166–67, 172–76, 182, 185-87, 190–91, 194, 196, 198, 203, 207–208, 210–11, 217
Wayne Ricketts (*TDD*) 48, 152, 156, 158
Wesley Wilson (*TLG*) 194–95
wildness vs. domesticity 39–40, 43, 58, 68, 70–71, 79–80, 84, 90, 98, 101, 109, 111–13, 126–28, 131, 135, 137, 144–48, 171–72, 174

Willow House (*OAH*) 204, 210n, 211–13, 219
willows 194, 210, 210n, 211
wind/breeze 17, 27, 35–36, 48, 50n, 54–55, 70, 74, 90, 101, 105, 109, 112, 119, 130, 143, 145, 146–47, 149–52, 154, 162, 164–69, 175, 178, 184–90, 193–97, 203, 208, 210–13
womb 22, 23, 33, 50, 61, 65–67, 78, 85, 110, 129n, 140, 146–47, 158, 172–73, 188, 213, 215, 219, 221

Yaeger, Patricia 40, 85, 119, 129–30, 230
yellow (color) 43, 101, 129–30, 145, 156–58, 193, 208, 210

Zinnia (*TDD*) 148, 153